EXECUTIVE CONTROL PROCESSES IN READING

PSYCHOLOGY OF READING AND READING INSTRUCTION

A series of volumes edited by **Rand Spiro**

SPIRO, BRUCE, and BREWER • *Theoretical Issues in Reading Comprehension*

SCHANK • *Reading and Understanding: Teaching from the Perspective of Artificial Intelligence*

ANDERSON, OSBORN, and TIERNEY • *Learning to Read in American Schools: Basal Readers and Content Texts*

BRITTON and BLACK • *Understanding Expository Text: A Theoretical and Practical Handbook for Analyzing Explanatory Text*

GUTHRIE • *A School Divided: An Ethnography of Bilingual Education in a Chinese Community*

HALL, NAGY, and LINN • *Spoken Words: Effects of Situation and Social Group on Oral Word Usage and Frequency*

STEINBERG • *Teaching Computers to Teach*

ORASANU • *Reading Comprehension: From Research to Practice*

BRITTON and GLYNN • *Executive Control Processes in Reading*

EXECUTIVE CONTROL PROCESSES IN READING

Edited by . . . . . .

BRUCE K. BRITTON

SHAWN M. GLYNN

University of Georgia

LEA LAWRENCE ERLBAUM ASSOCIATES, PUBLISHERS
1987 Hillsdale, New Jersey   London

Lawrence Erlbaum Associates, Inc., Publishers
365 Broadway
Hillsdale, New Jersey 07642

Library of Congress Cataloging-in-Publication Data
Executive control processes in reading.

Bibliography: p.
Includes index.
1. Reading, Psychology of.   2. Choice (Psychology)
3. Control (Psychology)   I. Britton, Bruce K.
II. Glynn, Shawn M.
BF456.R2E97   1987   153.6   86-24333
ISBN 0-89859-883-4

Printed in the United States of America
10   9   8   7   6   5   4   3   2   1

CONTENTS . . . .

LIST OF CONTRIBUTORS . . . .

A. E. Boerger · Center for the Study of Reading, 174CRC, University of Illinois, 51 Gerty Dr., Champaign, IL 61820

Bruce K. Britton · Department of Psychology, University of Georgia, Athens, GA 30602

Gary L. Conboy · Department of Psychology, Muenzinger Psychology, Building Campus Box 34J, Boulder, CO 80309

Adam Drewnowski · Human Nutrition Program, School of Public Health, University of Michigan, 1420 Washington Heights, Ann Arbor, MI 48109

Shawn M. Glynn · Department of Educational Psychology, University of Georgia, Athens, GA 30602

Arthur C. Graesser · Department of Psychology, Memphis State University, Memphis, TN 38152

Karl Haberlandt · Department of Psychology, Trinity College, Summit St., Hartford, CT 06106

James Hartley · Department of Psychology, University of Keele, Keele, Staffordshire ST5 5BG, ENGLAND

Alice F. Healy · Department of Psychology, Muenzinger Psychology Building, Campus Box 345, Boulder, CO 80309

David Koizumi · Department of Psychology, Rutgers University, Busch Campus, New Brunswick, NJ 08903

Michael E. J. Masson · Department of Psychology, University of Victoria, Victoria, British Columbia, CANADA V8W, 2Y2

Richard Mayer · Department of Psychology, University of California, Santa Barbara, CA 93106

Ala Samarapungavan · Center for the Study of Reading, 174CRC, University of Illinois, 51 Gerty Dr., Champaign, IL 61820

John G. Schmitz · Center for the Study of Reading, 174CRC, University of Illinois, 51 Gerty Dr., Champaign, IL 61820

Gary Schumacher · Psychology Department, Ohio University, Athens, OH 45701

Rand J. Spiro · Center for the Study of Reading, 174 CRC, University of Illinois, 51 Gerty Dr., Champaign, IL 61820

Robert J. Sternberg · Department of Psychology, Box 11A, Yale Station, Yale University, New Haven, CT 06520

Robert Waller · Institute of Educational Technology, Walton Hall, The Open University, Milton Keynes MK7 6AA, GREAT BRITAIN

Richard Wagner · Department of Psychology, Florida State University, Tallahassee, FL 33306–1051

Carol Walker · School of Education, The Catholic University of America, Washington, DC 20064

Patricia Wright · Medical Research Council, Applied Psychology Unit, 15 Chaucer Rd., Cambridge CB2 2EF, ENGLAND

Walter L. Vispoel · District 214, Administrative Center, 799 W. Kensington Rd., Mount Prospect, IL 60056

Frank Yekovich · School of Education, The Catholic University of America, Washington, DC 20064

INTRODUCTION. . . . .

The first thing the reader of this volume needs to know is: What *is* executive control in reading, exactly? We provide some definitions extracted from the chapters. The second thing the reader needs is some idea of the content of each chapter. We describe each chapter briefly, sometimes using extracts from it. Finally, we tell how this book came to be, and acknowledge some debts.

DEFINING EXECUTIVE CONTROL PROCESSES
IN READING

Mr. Youmans, a grizzled rustic who used to mow the Britton lawn, once described one of his customers (whom we knew to be a high-powered New York executive) in the following words: "Mr. Rosenbaum? Oh, he don't do nawthin', he just tells other folks what to do." Following Mr. Youmans, executive control processes are broadly defined here as processes that tell other processes what to do.

The authors of the chapters in this volume define executive control in reading in a variety of fascinating ways. Here are some of their definitions, which have been extracted from the chapters and freely adapted:

Executive control processes deal with how individuals plan and direct, select, and orchestrate the various cognitive structures and processes available to them for attaining some goal. (Schumacher, Ch. 5)

Executive control processes coordinate the functioning of the human cognitive system. Control functions are aspects of cognitive processes that contribute to the achievement of particular reading goals. Executive control functions exhibit *sensitivity* during reading comprehension and they also have certain *responsibilities*. Sensitivity can be seen operating by observing modulations in reading speed, gaze durations on individual words, and/or regressive fixations. Control functions also have numerous *responsibilities,* such as the coordination of the component reading processes (e.g., prioritizing word identification over lexical access), the coordination and allocation of cognitive resources (e.g., optimizing the use of the short-term memory), and the selection and use of knowledge to fill gaps in text (e.g., inserting knowledge into a composite representation of the text and subsequently using this knowledge for inferencing or reasoning). (Yekovich and Walker, Ch. 6)

We seek to examine how mature, skilled readers use information about the difficulty and importance of text, and of their comprehension tasks in allocating their reading time and effort. We distinguish three constituent parts of executive control of reading: (a) devising or accessing previously devised strategies for optimal allocation of reading time, and effort given one's reading goals and text; (b) implementing one's strategies, in a manner that does not disrupt the reading process unnecessarily; and (c) monitoring the success of one's strategy implementation, which may lead to revision or outright replacement of the strategy. (Wagner & Sternberg, Ch. 1)

"Executive control" is used loosely here to refer to those deliberate (although not necessarily articulated) choices that readers must make to read a text in a particular order or at a particular pace, to start reading and to stop, to skip or skim. (Waller, Ch. 4)

When reading a text the reader (or executive) is faced with a number of activities, all of which compete for time and resources. Different sets of activities are consequent upon the decision of whether to read for gist or for detail. In essence the crucial problem is deciding where to go next. Should one plough on remorselessly, should one skip ahead, should one ignore a particular figure for the time being, and so on. (Hartley, Ch. 3)

There are several alternative ways that executive control processes may influence inference generation. Perhaps variations in the readers' goals and conscious reading strategies determine what inferences are generated and how much processing resources are allocated to different categories of inferences. Alternatively, perhaps executive control processes merely determine the overall amount of cognitive resources allocated to inference generation, without any selective allocation to specific inference categories. As yet a third alternative, perhaps varia-

variations in executive control processes have no impact on inference generation. This would occur if inference generation is confined to a mechanism that is entirely insulated from the reader's goals and conscious reading strategies. (Graesser, Haberlandt, and Koizumi, Ch. 9)

BRIEF CHAPTER SUMMARIES

Chapter 1
Executive Control in Reading Comprehension

Richard Wagner and **Robert Sternberg** introduce a paradigm in which several different types of questions, differing substantially in difficulty, can be asked about a passage. Subjects are informed in advance about which one of the types of questions they will be getting, and then effects on their reading behavior are observed.

In Wagner and Sternberg's first experiment, *Gist* questions were the easiest type: They asked which of a list of titles would be best for a passage, or which of a list of themes best represented the topic. *Main idea* questions were more difficult, asking for specific information about some of the main ideas in the passage. *Detail* questions, even more difficult, were of the type that students routinely castigate as "picky." Finally, most difficult of all were *analysis and application* questions, which required not only knowing the information in the passage, but going beyond it in significant ways. In the second experiment, Wagner and Sternberg manipulated the difficulty of questions by using items of known difficulty from the Graduate Record Examination, and informing subjects of the level of difficulty.

The dependent measures included the time Yale undergraduates spent on reading passages that they knew would have questions at specified levels of difficulty, the accuracy of their answers to the questions, verbal reports about their strategies, and ability measures of verbal aptitude and reading skill. The results showed that even after holding constant verbal aptitude, reading skill, and reading speed, the subjects' time allocation—the measure of allocation of time resources—was significantly related to reading comprehension performance.

Chapter 2
Reading and Writing for Electronic Journals

In her chapter, **Patricia Wright** considers how the new computer-based information management technologies will influence on-the-job reading and writing processes of academics and professional researchers. She focuses on scholarly journals that can be accessed electronically through a computer-based system, and describes some field- and laboratory-based research strategies for studying how users interact with these journals.

On the basis of several studies she has conducted, Wright offers some insights into the kinds of system developments that are needed if electronic journals are to become a fully acceptable communication mode rather than just a convenient information dissemination facility. She believes that the most exciting developments for the readers and writers of electronic journals will come about when the readers themselves are able to make decisions interactively about the way the information is displayed to them.

Chapter 3
Typography and Executive
Control Processes in Reading

James Hartley's goal in this chapter is to suggest how the typographic design of text can help or hinder the cognitive processes that readers must perform. He accomplishes this by considering four topics: typography, layout, typographic cueing, and access structures. He argues that typographic details can assist with automatic bottom-up processing while layout can facilitate the reader's deliberate top-down processing.

A common problem that typographic designers face is that they have to provide one single optimum format for different readers with different reading purposes. Hartley argues that text, particularly electronic text, can be designed to encourage deeper processing by readers, but such text will require considerable typographic expertise.

Chapter 4
Typography and Reading Strategy

According to **Robert Waller,** the decisions about when to pause, rehearse, skim, or skip material in a text are all manifestations of executive control. These decisions are strongly influenced by typography, which Waller broadly defines as the visual attributes of written language. He, like Hartley, points out that typography can either enhance or diminish the comprehensibility of a text.

According to Waller, comprehensibility is dependent not only on the reader possessing an appropriate level of skill but also on a text which makes its structure clear enough for comprehension strategies to be formulated. Typography is one of a range of cueing systems that the author can use to signal the structure of ideas in a text. To support his views, Waller reviews research evidence he has collected about the effect of typography on reading. He concludes that before our concept of literacy can be extended, we need a deeper understanding of typography as an integral part of written language.

Chapter 5
Executive Control in Studying

Gary Schumacher begins his chapter by arguing that it might be very useful to view studying through the perspective of the studier, with special emphasis on executive control. According to him, an understanding of executive control could explain the inconsistencies in studying research and the powerful role that contextual factors play in studying activities.

He considers three major ways of conceptualizing executive control and studying: an information processing model, a cognitive monitoring model, and a computer simulation model. Each model emphasizes different aspects of how the studier interacts with the studying task, and each suggests a number of research questions.

Schumacher believes that there is a need for research in naturalistic settings so that the role of contextual variables important in everyday studying (e.g., time factors, text characteristics, and exam type) can be better understood. He also calls for more process-oriented research in studying.

Chapter 6
The Activation and Use
of Scripted Knowledge
in Reading about Routine Activities

Frank Yekovich and **Carol Walker** present a subtle, elegant, and detailed account of the interweaving of the two strands that create the phenomenologically rich experience of understanding a story: the reader's prior knowledge, and the bare text. The reader's prior knowledge is represented as a densely interconnected script, and the bare text activates different parts of the script to different degrees. Even those parts of the script that are never explicitly mentioned can achieve very high levels of activation through accrual of indirect activation. Yekovich and Walker's detailed predictions are tested in six experiments with on-line measures as well as memory measures.

Chapter 7
Knowledge Acquisition for Application:
Cognitive Flexibility and Transfer
in Complex Content Domains

Rand Spiro and his colleagues **Walter Vispoel** and **John Schmitz** emphasize that success in such areas as text comprehension, problem solving, and decision making depends on the activation and appropriate application of relevant prior knowledge. They address a critical issue relating to knowledge transfer: Namely, how should knowledge be acquired and organized to facilitate a wide range of future applications?

Spiro and his associates contend that in the many real-world situations when knowledge cannot be routinized, mechanized, or automatized, it must be flexibly controlled. In their chapter, they present a theory of learning and instruction and of knowledge representation and application, for the flexibility-based control that makes transfer possible. The aim of their research program is the validation of a set of principles and associated instructional practices that will permit students to better apply the knowledge they acquire in formal school settings to informal, real-life settings.

Chapter 8
Instructional Variables that Influence
Cognitive Processes During Reading

In this chapter, **Richard Mayer** summarizes a series of research studies of the effects of instructional manipulations on learners' comprehension of expository text. The three cognitive processes he views as most important for meaningful text learning are: paying attention to conceptual information, building internal connections, and building external connections. All of his instructional manipulations involve encouraging the reader to actively connect to-be-learned information to familiar experience or concrete models.

Mayer's results provide some examples of how it is possible to influence the reader's cognitive processing and the quality of what the reader learns from a text. He points out that if his research had focused merely on the question of whether instructional manipulations affect how *much* is learned, he would have found few important results, and he argues that performance tests should include many different measures, such as "far" versus "near transfer" and conceptual versus verbatim recall.

Chapter 9
How is Reading Time Influenced
by Knowledge-Based Inferences
and World Knowledge?

Readers make inferences as they read. Does it take extra time to make these inferences? **Arthur Graesser, Karl Haberlandt,** and **David Koizumi** test three hypotheses about how much time it takes to make inferences:

1. *The Strenuous Inference Generation Hypothesis* proposes that inferences are generated by mental work, so the more inferences are generated, the longer it takes. This hypothesis predicts a positive correlation between reading time and the number of inferences.

2. *The Scanty Knowledge-Base Hypothesis* predicts a negative correlation between reading time and the number of inferences. It proposes that sentences that generate few inferences are difficult to understand because they draw on a scanty knowledge base, and so take a long time to read, while sentences that generate many inferences are easy to understand because they draw on a rich knowledge base, and so take a short time to read.

3. *The Automatized Knowledge-Base Hypothesis* proposes that certain generic knowledge structures, like the one for eating at a restaurant, generate inferences automatically and so take no extra time, but nonautomatized knowledge structures require extra time for controlled processes to generate their inferences.

Chapter 10
Remembering Reading Operations
With and Without Awareness

According to **Michael Masson,** the perceptual and cognitive operations carried out during fluent reading cannot conceivably be under direct executive control throughout the entire course of their functioning. Instead, he assumes that a number of these operations carry on outside the bounds of awareness and produce results or data that eventually are used by centrally controlled processes. In this chapter, Masson considers the implications of his assumption for (a) the memory representation of specific reading episodes and (b) the role played by such memory representations when material is read on multiple occasions. He gives special consideration to a form of memory for reading episodes that appears to operate outside the domain of executive control processes.

Chapter 11
Characterizing the Processing Units of Reading:
Effects of Intra- and Interword Spaces
in a Letter Detection Task

In their chapter, **Alice Healy, Gary Conboy,** and **Adam Drewnowski** describe a letter detection experiment in which asterisks or blank spaces were inserted between characters in continuous text; participants made significantly fewer errors when the test word subtended a larger visual angle. In a second experiment, the interword space before the test word *the* was found to be more critical for unit formation than the space after *the*.

According to Healy and her colleagues, these results suggest that the size of the processing units used by readers depends on visual angle, and that the reading units for frequent function words such as *the* extend beyond the word itself, include the interword space, and are influenced more by familiarity than by linguistic function. They discuss these results in terms of the notions of the cognitive module and input system proposed by Fodor (1983).

ACKNOWLEDGEMENTS

This book was conceived when we were developing our own executive control model of reading (see Britton, Glynn, & Smith's chapter on the cognitive workbench model in *Understanding Expository Text,* edited by Britton & Black, 1985). The model is based on the notion that the reading task is made up of a large number of subprocesses, which obviously cannot operate optimally in a state of anarchy; they need some executive control. Around the same time, we heard Robert Sternberg and Richard Wagner deliver an early version of the paper that appears as a chapter here, from which we derived the title of the volume.

Those most influential in shaping Britton's early research in reading were Thomas Andre, Ellen Gagné, and Ernst Rothkopf, and his debt to them is acknowledged here.

REFERENCE

Britton, B. K., Glynn, S. M., & Smith, J. (1985). Cognitive demands of processing expository text: A cognitive workbench model. In B. Britton and J. Black (Eds.), *Understanding expository text* (pp. 227–248). Hillsdale, NJ: Lawrence Erlbaum Associates.

EXECUTIVE CONTROL IN READING COMPREHENSION 1

Richard K. Wagner
Florida State University

Robert J. Sternberg
Yale University

Provided we have written a chapter that is to some degree comprehensible (a wildly questionable assumption, we admit!), there are two obvious prerequisites to an individual's ability to comprehend it. First, the individual must have mastered the basic decoding skills that serve to attach meaning to written symbols, including letters, numbers, and words. Mastery of these decoding operations is, of course, absolutely prerequisite to reading of any kind. Second, the individual must have access to relevant "world knowledge" so as to interpret and evaluate the presented information in a meaningful way. We read, understand, and remember material that we can relate to prior knowledge much differently than we do material that bears little relation to anything we know about (Bransford & Johnson, 1972; Britton, Holdredge, Curry, & Westbrook, 1979; Dooling & Lachman, 1971; Gardner & Schumacher, 1977). Although these prerequisites may suffice for at least rudimentary comprehension, in our view there is an additional prerequisite of truly *skilled* comprehension of written material: the ability to determine how and where to apply one's reading resources in order to maximally reach one's comprehension goals in a given situation.

We view the intelligent application of one's reading resources, given the nature of one's comprehension task and one's text, as an important facet of *executive control of reading,* and of reading comprehension more generally. We distinguish three constituent parts of executive control of reading: (a) devising or accessing previously devised strategies for optimal allocation of reading time and effort, given one's reading goals and text; (b) implementing one's strategies, in a manner that does not disrupt

1

the reading process unnecessarily; and (c) monitoring the success of one's strategy implementation, which may lead to revision or outright replacement of the strategy.

We do not consider the study of the intelligent application of one's reading resources as being the only way, or even the best way, to begin to understand executive control phenomena associated with reading. One glance at the titles of the contributions to this volume makes obvious what is perhaps the most certain fact about executive control in reading: There is as yet little, if any, consensus about what executive control is, or even what it is not. We have little to say about the scope and nature of executive control phenomena in reading broadly defined. Frankly, it is grossly premature to worry much about such issues of definition. Rather, our goal is much more modest. We seek to examine a limited, yet important, aspect of executive control of reading, namely, how mature, skilled readers use information about the difficulty and importance of text, and of their comprehension tasks, in allocating their reading time and effort.

The chapter begins with a brief summary of some relevant research in the areas of flexibility in reading, allocation of reading resources, and executive control skills, that sets the stage for the work we describe. Next, we review the results of two experiments we carried out to investigate allocation of reading resources as a function of the variable difficulty of comprehension tasks and the variable importance of sections of text.

READING FLEXIBLY

Flexibility of reading in the face of variation in reading purpose and text difficulty has long been considered a hallmark of efficient reading (Gibson & Levin, 1975), even though early laboratory studies found readers to be surprisingly *inflexible* in their rate of reading in response to manipulations of passage difficulty or instructions to read in a certain way. However, readers have shown more flexibility in response to manipulations of material presented along with text (e.g., Mayer, 1980), and especially manipulations of adjunct questions (e.g., Rothkopf, 1970). Questions presented before a text facilitate the acquisition of information needed to answer them (Anderson & Biddle, 1975; Rothkopf, 1966). Questions presented after a text facilitate the acquisition of the kinds of information needed to answer them on subsequent text, but also facilitate the acquisition of incidental information (Rothkopf, 1965, 1966; Rothkopf & Bisbicos, 1967). McConkie, Rayner, and Wilson (1973) examined the effects on reading strategies of manipulating question type (i.e., factual, inferential) and payoff for correct responses within a given amount of time. Under these conditions, skilled readers adjusted their reading rate as a function of payoff condition and showed evidence of altering the type of information acquired as a function of type of question anticipated.

In sum, whereas readers seem to be surprisingly inflexible in reading in response to changes in text difficulty or to instructions about how to read, there appear to be effects of adjunct information such as questions on the nature of reading. One approach to understanding flexibility in reading is in terms of variable allocation of reading resources such as time and effort.

ALLOCATION OF READING RESOURCES

There have been two major approaches to examination of issues about the allocation of reading resources. The first approach has involved observing performance on a secondary task done concurrently with reading. The second approach has been to use a cognitive model of reading to observe allocation of reading resources more directly. We briefly consider each approach in turn.

The secondary task technique (e.g., Navon & Gopher, 1979; Ogden, Levine, & Eisen, 1979; and Wickens, 1980, for recent reviews) applied to reading has involved presenting individuals with a secondary task, such as removing one's finger from a key when a click is heard, to be performed concurrently with a reading task. Changes in performance on the secondary task are interpreted as reflecting changes in amount of cognitive resources allocated to the primary reading task: The more resources required by the reading task, the poorer performance should be on the secondary task, provided both tasks share a resource pool, and a finite amount of resources is available. For example, resources allocated to the primary reading task have been found to vary with changes in the syntactic structure of texts (Britton, Glynn, Meyer, & Penland, 1982); with changes in the meaningfulness of texts (Britton, et al., 1979); and with changes in text difficulty (Britton, Zeigler, & Westbrook, 1980).

A related approach to the study of resource allocation in reading has been to examine the allocation of reading time as a function of text characteristics and one's reading task in terms of a cognitive model of reading (e.g., Aaronson & Scarborough, 1976; Carpenter & Just, 1981; Kieras, 1981; Miller & Kintsch, 1980). For example, the Just and Carpenter (1980) model of reading was used to model eye fixation times for readers anticipating either a verification (true–false) comprehension test or a test of free recall (Carpenter & Just, 1981). Regression weights for variables representing components of the reading model were computed across test conditions for the purpose of accounting for variation in reading as a function of type of test anticipated. The major finding of interest for present purposes was that readers in the recall test condition spent more time on details and less time pausing at the end of sentences than did readers in the verification test condition. A second illustration of this approach is provided by Kieras (1981), who presented a process model to account for reading times under conditions of (a) an immediate gist recall task, (b) a topic choice task, and (c) a free-reading (no test) condition. Subjects in this experiment also read more slowly when a recall test was anticipated.

EXECUTIVE CONTROL SKILLS

There is ample evidence of flexibility in reading from manipulations of adjunct material, but how are these changes in reading actually carried out? One possible account of the means by which reading may change in response to adjunct material centers on executive or metacognitive skills. Executive or metacognitive skills have been proposed as the means by which readers monitor and control their reading (Brown, 1980). Taking a developmental approach, Brown (1978, 1980) reported that young children are deficient at, among other things, the executive skills of (a) predicting the difficulty of a task and recognizing when task difficulty has changed (e.g., Salatas & Flavell, 1976); (b) comprehension monitoring—being aware of whether one does or does not understand (e.g., Markman, 1977, 1979); (c) study-time apportionment—studying in anticipation of a future test—which includes determining what is important to remember and what is not, choosing a strategy to maximize learning, determining one's success with the chosen strategy, and determining whether a different strategy should be tried (e.g., Masur, McIntyre, & Flavell, 1973); and (d) predicting test performance—knowing when a task has been mastered. To date, most of the evidence for the importance of executive control in cognitive performance resides largely in comparisons of performance across groups differing substantially in developmental level. Whereas deficiencies in executive skills have been shown to be responsible for at least some limitations in cognitive performance that are characteristic of young children, the importance of efficient executive functioning to adult skilled performance remains largely an open question (Brown, 1980).

Our research has focused on the executive skill of resource allocation—matching reading resources (e.g., time, attention, effort) to task demands. There is not enough time to read all that one must read as exhaustively as one is able. Fortunately, much that is read can be given only cursory attention with little loss in comprehension. Our approach has involved manipulation of two kinds of adjunct material: the difficulty of adjunct questions readers were given, and the kind of adjunct information provided to readers that might be useful in allocating their reading resources.

The goal of the first experiment was to isolate and quantify one aspect of resource allocation, namely, time allocation in response to real-world reading tasks of varying difficulty, and to determine its importance for effective comprehension in mature, skilled readers. Our plan was to obtain a measure of effectiveness of time allocation, and then to determine whether effectiveness of time allocation was related to comprehension performance after holding constant individual differences in verbal ability and reading skill. College undergraduates were given fixed time intervals to read sets of four medium-length passages for the purpose of answering, for each passage, a different one of four types of questions (gist, main idea, detail, and analysis), which differed in level of difficulty. Duration and order of passage display within a time interval were under subject control. Effectiveness of reading-time allocation—the extent to which more time was spent when reading for more difficult purposes— was compared across subjects to their comprehension performance on the experimental task, and to their performance on reference measures of reading and of verbal reasoning ability. In a second experiment, passages and questions from reading comprehension sections of recent Graduate Record Examinations were presented in three conditions that differed in the amount and type of adjunct information provided, which could be used in matching reading resources to task demands.

EXPERIMENT 1

Method

Forty Yale undergraduates (29 males and 11 females) served as subjects in the experiment. All participated to fulfill an introductory psychology course requirement. All but one participated in an additional session of reference ability testing, for which they were paid $3.50.

Subjects were given 11 trials, of 150 seconds in duration, during which they were to read four passages. Subjects were informed that they would be tested on their understanding of the gist of one of the passages; on their comprehension of the main idea of a second passage; on their memory for the details of a third passage; and on their ability to analyze and apply what they read in a fourth passage. The method of passage selection— pressing one of four keys labeled "GIST," "MAIN IDEAS," "DE-

TAILS," and "ANALYSIS"—informed subjects about which type of questions they would be asked about each particular passage at the conclusion of a trial. The order of passage selection and the duration of passage display were under subject control, with the constraint that subject had 150 seconds to read the four passages.

Subjects were presented eight comprehension questions at the conclusion of a trial, two questions each for the four question types (gist, main ideas, details, and analysis). The usual questioning procedure of presenting eight comprehension questions at the conclusion of a trial was omitted for three trials (the fifth, tenth, and final trials) containing passsages that later were used in tasks that are not discussed here.

Forty-four untitled passages were used in the experiment. The passages were approximately 150 words in length and were drawn in equal numbers from novels, newspapers, introductory liberal arts textbooks, and introductory science textbooks. Minor editing of several of the passages was done to constrain variance in total number of words. An example of a passage is presented in Table 1.1.

Four types of questions were constructed for each passage. *Gist* questions asked about the gist or global theme of a passage and were written to be the easiest question type. Examples were selecting the best title or identifying the theme of a passage. *Main idea* questions, which were written to be more difficult, asked about the main ideas of a passage and were similar to questions commonly used to measure reading comprehension. *Detail* questions, written to be even more difficult, required subjects to recall specific details mentioned in a passage. *Analysis* questions, written to be the most difficult, required subjects to analyze the ideas

TABLE 1.1
Sample Passage from Experiment 1

The United Nations Human Rights Commission today condemned Israel's policies concerning the occupied Arab territories, including alleged "war crimes that are an affront to humanity."

The vote was 31 to 3, with 8 abstentions. The United States, Canada, and Australia voted against the resolution and most Western European countries abstained.

The resolution said that Israel had failed to acknowledge that one of the Red Cross conventions, or treaties, on the protection of war victims applied to the territories occupied by Israel.

Although Israel questions on legal grounds the applicability of the pact to the territories, in practice it allows the International Red Cross to visit them, meet privately with prisoners, and otherwise carry out the protective functions provided by the conventions, Red Cross sources say.

The coalition of countries that submitted the resolution also obtained the commission's recognition of the right of the Palestinian people to a "fully independent and sovereign state in Palestine."

presented in a passage or to extend the ideas to a new domain. All questions were of multiple-choice format with a correct answer and three distractor options. The order of presentation of question type was random. Examples of the four types of questions are presented in Table 1.2.

Subjects read passages for each of the four question types (gist, main idea, detail, and analysis) in every trial. Each of the four passage types (novels, newspapers, liberal arts texts, or science texts) was represented in every trial. Across subjects, every question type was paired with every passage. Paper and pencil reference ability tests consisted of the Verbal Reasoning Subtest of the Differential Aptitude Tests (Form T) and the Nelson–Denny Reading Test (Form D), which were administered during a second session.

Results and Discussion

Basic Statistics.   The observed difficulty of the four question types as measured by accuracy of question answering was consistent with the expected order of difficulty. Descriptive statistics for accuracy of question answering and for mean reading times (the next topic of discussion) as a function of question type are presented in Table 1.3.

The mean accuracies, out of a possible 16, were reliably different, $F(3,108) = 42.2, p < .001$. A Newman–Keuls follow-up indicated that the accuracies associated with the gist and main idea question types did not differ significantly. All other pairs of mean accuracies were significantly different.

Mean reading times for passages associated with the four question types calculated for each subject (after excluding reading times that were attenuated by the ending of the time interval) reflected question type difficulties and were reliably different, $F(3,108) = 5.6, p < .01$. A Newman–Keuls follow-up indicated that the mean reading times associated with the detail and analysis question types differed from the mean reading times associated with the gist and main idea question types, but that the two times within each group did not differ significantly from each other.

Approximately half the subjects selected passages on the basis of the ordering of the passage selection keys ("gist," "main idea," "detail," and "analysis"). The rest of the subjects used a variety of different passage selection strategies. However, passage selection strategy was unrelated to task performance or to performance on any of the reference ability measures.

Allocation of reading time was quantified in the following manner. Mean reading times for passages read for the two easier question types (gist and main idea) were combined, as were mean reading times for passages read for the two more difficult question types (detail and

TABLE 1.2
Sample Questions from Experiment 1

Gist Questions

---

1. Which of the following titles best fits this passage?
    a. *"Human Rights Dispute with Israel."
    b. "Red Cross Conventions Updated."
    c. "Policies of the United Nations."
    d. "The Palestinian Question."
2. The theme of the passage is:
    a. how the Red Cross functions abroad.
    b. *a U.N. Human Rights Commission against Israel.
    c. the right of the Palestinian people to self-determination.
    d. the problem of the legal rights of prisoners of war.

Main Idea Questions

---

1. The United Nations Human Rights Commission's resolution condemned Israel for failing to:
    a. *acknowledge a Red Cross convention.
    b. recognize the right of the Palestinian people to a sovereign state in Palestine.
    c. permit the Red Cross to visit prisoners.
    d. relinquish occupied territories.
2. Which of the following best characterizes the position of Israel?
    a. It questions the authority of the Human Rights Commission.
    b. *It questions the applicability of the Red Cross conventions.
    c. It refused Red Cross visits for national security reasons.
    d. It refuses to acknowledge the existence of the resolution.

Details Questions

---

1. Israel questions the applicability of the Red Cross pact on:
    a. moral grounds
    b. *legal grounds.
    c. religious grounds.
    d. political grounds.
2. Which of the following countries voted against the resolution?
    a. United States, France, and West Germany.
    b. United States, Egypt, and Saudi Arabia.
    c. United Stats, Great Britain, and Mexico.
    d. *United States, Canada, and Australia.

Analysis and Application Questions

---

1. From the information presented in the passage, it can be inferred that Israel and France have a poorer relationship than do Israel and:
    a. West Germany.
    b. *Australia.
    c. Great Britain.
    d. Egypt.
2. The nature of the second issue on which the coalition obtained the Commission's recognition suggests that the coalition countries are:
    a. more pro-Israeli than the original resolution would suggest.
    b. *consistently anti-Israeli.
    c. divided into anti- and pro-Israeli camps.
    d. moderating their position.

---

*indicates correct response.

TABLE 1.3
Descriptive Statistics for Accuracy and Latency by Question Type

Question Type	Accuracy Mean (S.D.)	Latency Mean (S.D.) (seconds)
Gist	13.3 (1.8)	37.98 (2.84)
Main idea	12.6 (2.2)	37.53 (2.76)
Details	10.5 (2.8)	39.77 (3.77)
Analysis	7.9 (2.8)	40.40 (3.91)

analysis). Reading times were combined in this manner because reading times associated with the gist and main idea question types were reliably different from reading times associated with the two more difficult question types, but not from each other; and moreover, reading times associated with the detail and analysis question types were reliably different from reading times associated with the two easier question types, but not from each other.

By combining reading times in this manner, we do not suggest that the processes underlying reading for different question types are identical, but merely that in the present experiment subjects spent about the same amounts of time when reading for the two easier question types and *also* spent about the same amounts of time when reading for the two more difficult question types. The *time allocation score* was a measure, in seconds, of how much more time was allocated on average to the two more difficult question types (detail and analysis) than to the two less difficult question types (gist and main idea).

Time allocation scores ranged from a high of 20.2 seconds to a low of −12.1 seconds. Mean time allocation score was 4.7 seconds, with a standard deviation of 7.1 seconds. Positive time allocation scores reflected greater time allocated to passages associated with the two more difficult question types (detail and analysis) than to passages associated with the two less difficult question types (gist and main idea). Negative time allocation scores reflected greater time allocated to passages read for the less difficult question types than to passages read for the more difficult question types. These results indicate that marked individual differences in effectiveness of time allocation were characteristic of a relatively homogeneous sample of mature readers.

Time Allocation and Comprehension.   Zero-order correlations among accuracies in question answering, reference ability measures of reading and reasoning abilities, and time allocation are presented in Table 1.4.

The validity of the experimental task as a measure of reading comprehension was supported by the magnitudes of the correlations between

TABLE 1.4
Simple Correlations Among Accuracies in Question Answering,
Reference Ability Measures, and Time Allocation Score

	1	2	3	4	5	6	7	8	9
1 Gist									
2 Main idea	.58*								
3 Detail	.21	.45*							
4 Anaysis	.29*	.15	.04						
5 Total	.70*	.77*	.66*	.58*					
6 Reasoning (DAT)	.47*	.73*	.48*	.45*	.78*				
7 Reading (ND Tot)	.37*	.46*	.51*	.26	.60*	.51*			
8 Rate (ND)	−.18	.08	.35*	.15	.18	.24	.22		
9 Reading time measure	−.14	−.15	−.33*	−.34*	−.39*	−.27	−.14	−.17	
10 Time allocation	.31*	.02	.32*	.18	.30*	.00	.34*	.15	−.08

*$p < .05$

reading comprehension performance on the task and total score on the Nelson–Denny Reading Test ($r = .60$, $p < .001$), and between reading comprehension performance on the task and score on the Verbal Reasoning Subtest of the Differential Aptitude Test ($r = .78$, $p < .001$). Effectiveness of time allocation was related to the reference measure of reading ability ($r = .34$, $p < .05$) but not to the reference measure of verbal aptitude ($r = .00$, $p > .05$).

Time allocation scores were predictive of comprehension performance on the reading task as measured by total number of comprehension questions answered correctly, $r = .30$, $p < .05$. The magnitude of this correlation was comparable to the split-half reliability of the time allocation score of .28. Interpreting this result requires consideration of two plausible but competing explanations. First, effective time allocation may have resulted in better reading comprehension performance or second, the observed correlation between time allocation scores and question-answering performance may have been indirect, resulting from time allocation and comprehension performance both being related to individual differences in reading ability or verbal aptitude, but not directly to each other. In other words, more able subject may have been better at both time allocation and reading comprehension, but there may have been no direct relation between time allocation and comprehension performance.

It was possible to test which explanation is more plausible. If better time allocation directly affected reading comprehension, then time allocation scores should predict comprehension performance on the task even after individual differences in reading ability and verbal aptitude are held constant. If the relation between time allocation and reading comprehension was indirect (more able subjects better at both), then holding constant individual differences in reading ability and verbal aptitude should attenuate, if not eliminate entirely, the relationship between time allocation and reading comprehension performance on the experimental task.

Total number of questions answered correctly on the task was regressed on reference ability measures and time allocation scores. Reading ability was measured by performance on the Nelson–Denny Reading Test. Verbal aptitude was measured by performance on the Verbal Reasoning Subtest of the Differential Aptitude Tests. Individual differences in reading ability and verbal aptitude were held constant by using them to predict total number of questions answered correctly, with hierarchical regression used to determine the extent to which adding time allocation to the prediction equation increased variance accounted for.

Reading ability, verbal aptitude, and time allocation together accounted for 73% of the total variance in question answering performance. This prediction model yielded a significant $F(4,24) = 16.3$, $p < .001$. Standardized parameter estimates (*Betas*) were .73 ($p < .001$), .12 ($p < .05$), $-.09$ ($p < .05$), and .30 ($p < .05$), for verbal ability, reading ability, reading rate, and time allocation, respectively.

The significant standardized parameter estimate for time allocation indicates that time allocation was related to reading comprehension performance on the task, even after holding constant reading speed, verbal aptitude, and reading ability. Substituting a computer-recorded reading time measure for Nelson–Denny Reading Rate scores (the reading time measure was more highly correlated with number of questions answered correctly on the task than was the Nelson–Denny rate measure) did not change the picture, yielding a significant standardized parameter estimate for time allocation of .25, $p < .05$. Because effectiveness of time allocation was related to comprehension even when individual differences in verbal ability and reading ability were held constant, other explanations for their relation such as preexperimental knowledge differences for the content of the passages between subjects at different levels of reading skill are implausible.

Effectiveness of time allocation accounted for approximately 10% of the total variance in comprehension performance. Although this figure is not large in absolute terms, it should be remembered that (a) this figure represents the unique contribution of reading time allocation to prediction of comprehension performance; (b) the internal consistency reliability of the time allocation scores was around the .3 level; (c) based on question answering performance, the differences in difficulty of the question types were relatively subtle, similar to that characteristic of naturalistic reading situations; and (d) subjects were neither informed of the differences in difficulty nor told to read in any special way.

The results of Experiment 1 showed that skilled readers adjusted their reading rate in response to changes in the difficulty of their comprehension tasks. One explanation for the observed individual differences in comprehension performance is that our subjects were differentially sensitive to information about the difficulty of their comprehension tasks. We sought to determine in a second experiment the consequences of making information such as the difficulty of one's comprehension task and the importance of different parts of the text explicit, in the form of adjunct information.

EXPERIMENT 2

In this experiment, passages and questions from reading comprehension sections of recent Graduate Record Examinations were presented with adjunct information that could be useful in alloating one's reading and study resources. Our interest was to determine whether the effectiveness of adjunct information depended on (a) the skill level of the reader, and (b) the kind of adjunct information provided. On the one hand, it is possible that highly skilled readers are better able to take advantage of adjunct information when reading compared to less highly skilled readers by virtue of their more flexible reading processes. On the other hand, highly skilled readers may be less likely to abandon their naturally efficient reading strategies for the purpose of adopting a new strategy that makes use of the adjunct information, whereas less highly skilled readers may be more likely to abandon their less efficient natural reading strategies and to adopt a new strategy that makes use of the adjunct information. Finally, it is possible that the usefulness of adjunct information depends on the kind of adjunct information provided as well as on the skill level of the reader.

Method

Ninety Yale undergraduates read passages from previous Graduate Record Examination Reading Comprehension subtests in one of three conditions.

In a *difficulty information condition,* subjects were given two types of explicit difficulty information. General difficulty information consisted of ratings of the average difficulty of questions associated with each passage to be read. This information was viewed as potentially useful in planning *what* to read to maximize task performance (i.e., in which order to read the passages). Specific difficulty information consisted of ratings of the difficulty of each specific question to be answered. This information was viewed as being different from the general planning information, in that it was potentially useful for determining *how* to read to maximize task performance (i.e., selecting specific task strategies such as reading twice information for which difficult questions were asked). Subjects were instructed to use the difficulty information in order to maximize their performance. They were not told how to do so, however. Examples of questions labeled according to difficulty were provided.

Both general and specific difficulty information was presented through use of the phrases "very difficult," "moderately difficult," "moderately easy," and "very easy." Difficulty level was determined by the proportions of examinees who passed the question when it was administered nationwide as part of the Graduate Record Examinations. Examples of questions as they appeared in the difficulty information condition are presented in Table 1.5.

In an *importance information condition,* subjects were informed about the relative importance of sentences in a passage by our highlighting the sentences that conveyed each passage's central meaning. An example of a highlighted passage is presented in Table 1.6. Of particular interest were

TABLE 1.5
Sample Questions from Experiment 2

(Moderately easy)

1. The institutional method of literary criticism argues that:
    (A) writing should ultimately be judged as the offspring of the social conventions and institutions of its time.
   *(B) writing should be viewed as the product of the interaction between the individual writer and the conventions and concerns of his milieu.
    (C) writing that reflects private and individualistic concerns unfortunately ignores relevant social conditions.
    (D) the credit accorded to writing belongs more properly to society than to the individual writer.
    (E) public institutions and public views form the most convenient basis by which to judge writing.

(Moderately Difficult)

2. The analogy in lines 11–14 serves to:
    (A) explain how writing changes from era to era.
    (B) suggest that the basic quality of good writing is predictable in any given age.
    (C) emphasize that the nature of a literary work is largely determined by forces outside the writer.
   *(D) illustrate the degree to which the individual skill of a writer contributes to the development of literature.
    (E) call into question the extent to which an individual writer can be given credit for what he writes.

TABLE 1.6
Sample Passage from Experiment 2

The institutional method of literary criticism gives due credit to the never-ending collaboration between writer and public. Psychology, on the other hand, treats literature too often as a record of personal idiosyncracies, too seldom as the basis of a collective consciousness. Yet it is on that basis that the greatest writers have functioned. Their originality has been an ability to "seize on the public mind"; conventions have changed and styles have developed as lesser writers caught the traditional rythm of an age. *The irreducible element of individual talent seems to play the same role in the evolution of genres that natural selection plays in the origin of species. Amid the mutations of modern individualism, we have overstressed the private aspects of writing.* If we recognize the writer's intention as a figure in a carpet, we must recognize that he is guided by his material, his training, his commission, and by his imagination to the extent that it accepts and masters those elements.

---

readers' strategies for using the adjunct importance information and the effects of importance information on comprehension performance. Subjects were instructed to use the importance information in order to maximize their performance. Again, they were not told how to do so. An example of highlighted text was provided. Subjects in a control condition received no adjunct information.

All subjects were instructed to read passages in whatever order they wished and were told that they had 35 minutes to complete the task. The questions to be answered were available to subjects while they were reading the passages. Subjects were instructed to work as rapidly as possible without losing accuracy and were told that no penalty would be imposed for incorrect responses. A digital clock was placed in a position for easy viewing. Subjects were instructed to look at the clock each time they began work on a new page and to mark the time on their answer sheet, thereby producing a record of the order of passage reading.

At the conclusion of the task, subjects provided written descriptions of their task strategy. Subjects in the two experimental conditions additionally described whether they made use of the adjunct difficulty or importance information, and if so, how. Subjects finished the 2-hour session by taking reference ability measures.

Results

Overall Performance.   Subjects in the three conditions were comparable in performance on all reference ability measures of reading and verbal ability. Means (and standard deviations) for the control, difficulty information, and importance information conditions, respectively, were 131.9 (21.4), 130.3 (21.0), and 128.7 (20.1) for Nelson–Denny Total Score; and 44.6 (4.0), 44.0 (5.6), and 45.0 (3.9) for the DAT Verbal Reasoning

Subtest. These differences were not significant, $F(2,87) < 1$. Task performance in terms of total number of questions answered correctly was 25.7 (8.3), 23.6 (8.0), and 21.6 (7.3), for the control, difficulty information, and importance information conditions. These means did not differ significantly $F(2,87) = 2.02, p > .05$.

Written reports of task strategies provided by subjects were scored for presence of explicit mention of revising strategy during task performance. These results and results to be discussed shortly of analyses conducted separately by experimental condition are presented in Table 1.7.

Twenty-eight percent of subjects reported strategy revision during task performance. This percentage remained essentially constant across experimental conditions, with percentages of 30, 30, and 23 for the control, difficulty information, and importance information conditions, respectively. Two reasons for strategy revision were given: A strategy chosen

TABLE 1.7
Task and Reference Measure Performance by Reading Strategy

Condition Strategy	% Using	Performance Measures		
		Measure	Scores	Significance
Entire Sample				
1. Strategy Revision	28	Reading Task	26.1/22.7	$t(88) = 1.86*$
		Verbal Reasoning	45.7/44.1	$t*(64) = 1.78*a$
		Reading Ability	134.8/128.7	$t(86) = 1.24$(n.s.)
Difficulty Information Condition				
2. Use General Information to Select Passages	53	Reading Task	26.3/20.6	$t(28) = 2.00*$
		Verbal Reasoning	43.8/44.1	$t(27) = -0.74$(n.s.)
		Reading Ability	136.3/123.9	$t(27) = 1.64$ $(p<.1)$
3. Use Specific Information	27	Reading Task	18.8/25.4	$t(28) = -2.12*$
		Verbal Reasoning	41.6/44.8	$t(28) = -1.39$(n.s.)
		Reading Ability	111.0/136.5	$t(27) = -3.24**$
Importance Information Condition				
4. Read Highlighted Sections Exclusively	27	Reading Task	21.8/21.6	$t(28) = 0.05$ (n.s.)
		Verbal Reasoning	46.9/44.3	$t*(28) = 2.43*$
		Reading Ability	125.0/130.1	$t(27) = -0.60$(n.s.)
5. Read Highlighted Sections More Carefully	43	Reading Task	20.7/22.4	$t(28) = -0.61$(n.s.)
		Verbal Reasoning	44.9/45.0	$t(28) = -0.04$(n.s.)
		Reading Ability	128.6/128.8	$t(27) = -0.01$(n.s.)
6. Search for Unknown Answers in Highlighted Sections	33	Reading Task	23.8/20.6	$t(28) = 1.50$(n.s.)
		Verbal Reasoning	46.1/44.4	$t(28) = 1.10$(n.s.)
		Reading Ability	139.8/123.7	$t(27) = 2.11*$

[a]The $t*$ statistic is reported whenever the variances of the two groups being compared differ significantly (Winer, 1971).
$*p < .05$
$**p < .01$

before beginning the task was not working out, or a strategy was changed, when time began to run out, for the purpose of at least trying all remaining questions. Compared to subjects who did not report revising strategy, subjects who reported strategy revision performed better on the reading task, better on the reference measure of verbal reasoning, but not reliably better on the reference measure of reading.

Adjunct Difficulty Information.   Subjects marked the time when they began work on each passage, producing a record of the order in which passages were read. This record was used to score the presence or absence of the strategy of reading passages in their order of difficulty. Scoring the presence of this strategy was straightforward because subjects either read passages in their order of difficulty or in their order of presentation in the booklet. The only complication was that some subjects switched to another strategy such as reading the shortest remaining passage when the time limit approached. In such cases, the strategy of reading passages in their order of difficulty was scored as present even if it was abandoned as the time limit approached. As reported in Table 1.7, the 53% of subjects in the difficulty condition who used this strategy performed better on the reading task, performed marginally better on the reference measure of reading ability, but were comparable to subjects who did not use this strategy in their performance on the reference measure of verbal reasoning. More able subjects, then, used general difficulty information in planning their order of passage reading to correspond with the order of passage difficulty. It was possible to determine the validity of subjects' written reports of task strategies by comparing actual strategy as determined from the record of passage order with written reports of strategy. All subjects who used the strategy of reading passages in order of their difficulty reported doing so; conversely, no subjects who did not use this strategy reported doing so.

Subjects' written reports of task strategy were scored for the presence of a strategy for using the specific difficulty information. Subjects who reported using the specific difficulty information described a strategy of matching how much effort they spent searching for and evaluating possible answers to the difficulty level of the questions. Referring to Table 1.7, the 27% of subjects reported using the specific difficulty information actually performed more *poorly* on the reading task than did subjects who did not. These subjects also performed more poorly on the reference measure of reading ability but their performance on the reference measure of verbal reasoning was comparable to those subjects who did not report using specific difficulty information. One commonly given reason for the general unhelpfulness of the specific difficulty information was that the difficulty rating of a particular question did not coincide with a subject's personally perceived difficulty. The group validity of the difficulty ratings for the present sample is supported by the high correlation ($r = .88$) between the proportion of subjects that passed an item in the present experiment, and the proportion of examinees that passed the same item when it was administered as part of the Graduate Record Examinations, which was the original source of the difficulty ratings. A second reason given for the general unhelpfulness of the specific difficulty information was that subjects disliked being told how difficult a question was and that, in some cases, knowing that a question was very difficult made them anxious.[1]

Twenty percent of subjects reported that the specific difficulty information was distracting. Subjects who reported the specific difficulty information as distracting performed better on the reading task (31.2 vs. 21.8, $p < .01$, but were comparable in performance on the reference measures of reading (140.8 vs. 127.8, $p > .05$) and verbal reasoning (46.7 vs. 43.2, $p > .05$) to those who did not.

In sum, the effects of adjunct difficulty information were a function of type of information and the skill of the reader. More able subjects were (a) more likely to use *general* difficulty information for planning order of passage selection, were (b) less likely to use *specific* difficulty information, and were (c) more likely to find the *specific* difficulty information distracting.

Adjunct Importance Information.   Three strategies for using importance information were identified. As reported in Table 1.7, 27% of subjects reported using a strategy of reading highlighted sections exclusively. These subjects performed better on the reference measure of verbal reasoning than did subjects who did not use this strategy, but performance on the reading task and on the reference measure of reading ability were comparable. A second strategy, related to the previous one, was reading the highlighted sections more carefully than the nonhighlighted sections. The 43% of subjects who reported using this strategy were comparable in performance to those who did not, for the reading task and for the reference measures of verbal reasoning and reading. A final identifiable strategy was searching for unknown answers in the highlighted portions. This was an understandable strategy because a majority of the answers were to be found in the highlighted sections and subjects were informed of this fact. Whereas the 33% of subjects who reported using this strategy performed better on the reference measure of reading than those who did not, performance on the reading task and on the

---

[1]The possibility of a relationship between difficulty information and text anxiety was pointed out by Earl Hunt.

reference measure of verbal reasoning was comparable. In sum, the strategies of exclusively reading the highlighted sections and of searching for answers in the highlighted sections were used by more able subjects, although task performance did not appear to be dependent on use of these particular strategies.

GENERAL DISCUSSION

In Experiment 1, reading time allocation was isolated and quantified, and effectiveness of reading time allocation was found to be predictive of the comprehension performance of skilled readers. Individual differences in effective time allocation were not attributable simply to differences in verbal reasoning ability or reading rate: Time allocation scores were neither related to performance on a standardized test of verbal reasoning nor to two measures of reading rate.

It is generally acknowledged that one fundamental function of an executive system is the monitoring of the success of task performance and then revising strategy for the purpose of improving ongoing performance. The result from Experiment 2 that subjects who revised their strategy during task performance obtained significantly higher average scores on the task than those who did not, provides a needed empirical confirmation of this point of view in the domain of skilled reading.

The pattern of results for the adjunct difficulty information condition in Experiment 2 supports two roles of executive control in reading: determining *what* to read and determining *how* to read it. When provided with general adjunct difficulty information, more able readers used the information in a strategy that was reflected in the order of passage selection (i.e., in determining what to read) to a greater extent than did less able readers. The finding that more able readers made better use of planning information is related to the work of Sternberg (1981) in a different cognitive domain. Verbal analogies that varied in format (i.e., the number and location of analogy terms for which answer options were presented) were given to college undergraduates in either a blocked or mixed fashion. By comparing response time latencies across blocked and mixed conditions, it was discovered that more able individuals spent relatively more time in "global planning" (i.e., generating a plan for handling a block of items), and relatively less time in "local planning" (i.e., generating a plan for handling a specific item), than did less able individuals. In terms of the present experiments, knowledge that the analogies were to be presented in blocked fashion was a source of general adjunct information that was used by more able subjects in planning task strategy.

The finding that more able readers were less likely than less able readers to abandon their presumably more efficient natural reading strategies when specific adjunct information was available, and that more able readers were more likely to find the specific difficulty information distracting, confirms a result reported by Brown (1980). In her experiments, externally imposed metacognitive strategies were not effective in improving task performance relative to strategies spontaneously adopted by individuals. The results of the present experiment suggest that more able readers are aware of the effectiveness of their natural reading strategies and therefore are less likely to abandon their natural strategies, even in the face of circumstances that encourage them to do so.

Why providing adjunct importance information had no effect on task performance is difficult to determine. An explanation that is suggested by Anderson (1980) is that, with approximately half the text highlighted and with at least some questions tapping information from nonhighlighted areas, the highlighting may not have been very informative about what to read. Perhaps the only conclusion to draw from the adjunct importance information condition in Experiment 2 is that the effects of adjunct information appear to depend heavily on the nature of the adjunct information.

The results of both experiments suggest that executive control skills such as effective allocation of reading time and efficient planning of task strategy are related to comprehension performance, even for mature skilled readers. Our immediate goal for future research is to specify the nature of this relation, a goal we are beginning to pursue by attempting the integration of an executive control mechanism and a model of performance components of reading. Other goals for future research include determining which executive processes are specific to reading and which are not, and determining more precisely sources of individual differences in executive performance. For example, in the second experiment, more able readers revised their task strategy during ongoing performance more than did less able readers. The actual source of this difference could be (a) more accurate performance monitoring, (b) availability of a wider range of well-practiced reading strategies, (c) differential ability to implement alternative strategies, or (d) some combination of the aforementioned.

The development of cognitive models of reading that better represent the intricacies of the reading of skilled readers in naturalistic situations depends on our willingness and ability to incorporate—into our already well-specified models of performance components of reading—equally well-specified executive controlling mechanisms.

ACKNOWLEDGMENTS

The work described in this chapter was supported by Contract N0001483K0013 from the Office of Naval Research and the Army Research Institute. Preparation of this chapter was supported by Contract MDA903-85-K-0305 from the Army Research Institute.

REFERENCES

Aaronson, D., & Scarborough, H. S. (1976). Performance theories for sentence coding: Some quantitative evidence. *Journal of Experimental Psychology: Human Perception and Performance, 2,* 56–70.

Anderson, R. C., & Biddle, W. B. (1975). On asking people questions about what they are reading. In G. Bower (Ed.), *Psychology of learning and motivation* (Vol. 9). New York: Academic Press.

Anderson, T. H. (1980). Study strategies and adjunct aids. In R. J. Spiro, B. C. Bruce, & W. F. Brewer (Eds), *Theoretical issues in reading comprehension.* Hillsdale, NJ: Lawrence Erlbaum Associates.

Bransford, J. D., & Johnson, M. K. (1972). Contextual prerequisites for understanding: Some investigations of comprehension and recall. *Journal of Verbal Learning and Verbal Behavior, 11,* 717–726.

Britton, B. K., Holdredge, T. S., Curry, C., & Westbrook, R. D. (1979). Use of cognitive capacity in reading identical texts with different amounts of discourse level meaning. *Journal of Experimental Psychology: Human Learning and Memory, 5,* 262–270.

Britton, B. K., Glynn, S. M., Meyer, B. J. F., & Penland, M. J. (1982). Effects of text structure on use of cognitive capacity during reading. *Journal of Educational Psychology, 74,* 51–61.

Britton, B. K., Zeigler, R., & Westbrook, R. (1980). Use of cognitive capacity in reading easy and difficult text: The allocation of attention hypothesis. *Journal of Reading Behavior, 12,* 23–30.

Brown, A. L. (1978). Knowing when, where, and how to remember: A problem of metacognition. In R. Glaser (Ed.), *Advances in instructional psychology* (Vol. 1). Hillsdale, NJ: Lawrence Erlbaum Associates.

Brown, A. L. (1980). Metacognitive development and reading. In R. Spiro, B. Bruce, & W. Brewer (Eds.), *Theoretical issues in reading comprehension.* Hillsdale, NJ: Lawrence Erlbaum Associates.

Carpenter, P. A., & Just, M. A. (1981). Cognitive processes in reading: Models based on readers' eye fixations. In A. Lesgold & C. Perfetti (Eds.), *Interactive processes in reading.* Hillsdale, NJ: Lawrence Erlbaum Associates.

Dooling, D. J., & Lachman, R. (1971). Effects of comprehension on retention of prose. *Journal of Experimental Psychology, 88,* 216–222.

Gardner, E. T., & Schumacher, G. M. (1977). Effects of contextual organization on prose retention. *Journal of Educational Psychology, 69,* 146–151.

Gibson, E. J., & Levin, H. (1975). *The psychology of reading.* Cambridge, MA: MIT Press.

Just, M. A., & Carpenter, P. A. (1980). A theory of reading: From eye fixations to comprehension. *Psychological Review, 87,* 329–354.

Kieras, D. E. (1981). Component processes in the comprehension of simple prose. *Journal of Verbal Learning and Verbal Behavior, 20,* 1–23.

Markman, E. M. (1977). Realizing that you don't understand. *Child Development, 48,* 986–992.

Markman, E. M. (1979). Realizing that you don't understand: Elementary schoolchildren's awareness of inconsistencies. *Child Development, 50,* 643–655.

Masur, E. F., McIntyre, C. W., & Flavell, J. H. (1973). Developmental changes in apportionment of study times among items in a multitrial free recall task. *Journal of Experimental Child Psychology, 15,* 237–246.

Mayer, R. E. (1980). Elaboration techniques that increase the meaningfulness of technical text: An experimental test of the learning strategy hypothesis. *Journal of Educational Psychology, 72*, 770–784.

McConkie, G. W., Rayner, K., & Wilson, S. J. (1973). Experimental manipulation of reading strategies. *Journal of Experimental Psychology: Human Learning and Memory, 6*, 335–354.

Miller, J. R., & Kintsch, W. (1980). Readability and recall of short prose passages; a theoretical analysis. *Journal of Experimental Psychology: Human Learning and Memory, 6*, 335–354.

Navon, D., & Gopher, D. (1979). On the economy of the human-processing system. *Psychological Review, 86*, 214–255.

Ogden, G. D., Levine, J. M., & Eisner, E. J. (1979). Measurement of workload by secondary tasks. *Human Factors, 21*, 529–548.

Rothkopf, E. Z. (1965). Some theoretical and experimental approaches to problems in written instruction. In J. D. Krumholtz (Ed.), *Learning and the educational process.* Chicago: Rand McNally.

Rothkopf, E. Z. (1966). Learning from written instructional materials: An exploration of the control of inspection behavior by test-like events. *American Educational Research Journal, 3*, 241–249.

Rothkopf, E. Z. (1970). The concept of mathemagenic activites. *Review of Educational Research, 40*, 325–336.

Rothkopf, E. Z., & Bisbicos, E. E. (1967). Selective facilitative effects of interspersed questions on learning from written materials. *Journal of Educational Psychology, 58*, 56–61.

Salatas, H., & Flavell, J. H. (1976). Behavioral and metamnemonic indicators of strategic behaviors under remember instructions in first grade. *Child Development, 47*, 80–89.

Sternberg, R. J. (1981). Intelligence and nonentrenchment. *Journal of Educational Psychology, 73*, 1–16.

Wickens, C. D. (1980). The structure of attentional resources. In *Attention and Performance* VIII. New York: Academic Press.

Winer, B. J. (1971). *Statistical principles in experimental design.* New York: McGraw-Hill.

READING AND WRITING FOR ELECTRONIC JOURNALS..... 2

Patricia Wright
Medical Research Council
Applied Psychology Unit

INTRODUCTION: WILL THE NEW MEDIA CHANGE READING AND WRITING ACTIVITIES?

There is a real sense in which the new technologies provide a testbed for evaluating our understanding of reading and writing processes. For example, the first draft of this chapter was written on a lap portable computer having only an 8-line screen. Consideration of such an activity seems to challenge our knowledge of the various executive control processes of writing. Do we yet have theories of reading and writing which will predict how the constraints imposed by this machine will influence either the content or style of what gets written?

The impact on cognitive processes of some of the constraints appear obvious. The smaller screen may well increase the memory load for material that has just been written. Does this affect the cohesion of the text or do authors have their writing goals so adequately nested that visual support is a minimal requirement? The adequacy of this goal structure seems unlikely if Wason is correct in suggesting that, in some important senses, authors may not know what they are intending to say until it has been written (Wason, 1970, 1980). To a casual eye, paragraph length seemed shorter for the draft text generated via the 8-line screen than it usually is with a 24-line CRT display. Without further research it is not possible to say whether such shrinkage reflects a reduction of substantive content within the paragraphs, corresponding to an attenuation of the way ideas are elaborated, or whether this is primarily a stylistic change in expression with the smaller screen promoting tighter writing.

The use of a keyboard, particularly by unskilled typists, may take more attention than the manual skills of some other authoring modes. Does this impinge on the attention that can be given to organizing and interrelating ideas? Gould has suggested that the quality of short business letters is not affected by authoring modes as different as handwriting and dictation (Gould, 1978, 1982). However, letters written with line-oriented text editors took 50% longer than handwritten letters (Gould, 1981). One possible reason for this mentioned by Gould is that the first draft of the computer text may have received more revisions by authors, although the reason for this increase in revising is not clear. There is some evidence that the characteristics of the text editor being used will change the number of revisions made while composing a first draft. Poller and Garter (1984) showed that the need to change between "text entry" and "editing" modes tends to reduce the frequency of alterations made to the text.

These questions about the impact of the new technologies on reading and writing skills suggest important differences between past and future research on reading. To date the major concern in the research literature has been with the acquisition of reading and writing skills. Relatively little is known about the executive control processes that encompass strategy selection by skillful readers and accomplished writers. To keep pace with developments in information technology there is a growing need for theories of such control processes. For example, people accustomed to writing texts with computer-based tools that offer facilities such as "searching" may well expect similar facilities to be available to them as readers (Wright & Lickorish, 1984b). Consequently, the way they interact with electronic texts may be very different from their interactions with texts on paper.

In this relatively unexplored territory concerning the way readers select their reading strategies, another important issue relates to the factors that predispose people to stop reading. In a London museum I watched a small crowd wait eagerly for a paragraph to be written by a moving cursor that went steadily along the wall. Many of the people from this group subsequently walked on in total disregard of many static, printed notices in the room. In itself this may not be surprising. Movement is well known to be attention getting, and the inability to glance ahead may have heightened people's anticipation. Yet this phenomenon of preferring the computer-generated display seems almost totally reversed when academics are faced with the option of reading lengthy texts either on CRT screens or as printouts. The paper versions are often preferred. Of course, in this comparison between the museum visitors and the academics there are differences in audience, in subject matter, in text structure, and in reading environment. The point being made is simply that some kinds of written information may be much more successfully transferred from paper to screen than are other kinds of communication.

One of the few investigations that has looked at the desirability of putting different kinds of text on CRT screens was carried out in Denmark by Nielsen (1984). He reported that in a survey of computer science students many said they would like technical documentation on-line (50% of those sampled were for this proposal, 27% against), but they did not want fiction material on-line (6% for, 88% against). There are many differences between these two kinds of text, so it is difficult to be certain what the crucial factors are or where to locate electronic journals between these extremes. Technical documents are used for reference, so the length of text being read at any one time is much shorter than for narrative fiction. Whether this is an important factor or whether differences in the structure of the texts are more critical is hard to say. This chapter explores some of the reasons why particular kinds of reading activity may be better suited to some media than others.

The focus of the present chapter is on the reading processes used by academics and professional researchers as part of their daily work. In this respect, the focus is distinct from many of the recent studies that have examined the clerical use of alternative text-editing systems (e.g., Gould & Alfaro, 1984; Neal & Darnell, 1984). Our concern is with the kinds of reading matter found in scholarly journals. Consequently, the executive processes of interest are those concerned with metacognitive processes, to use the terminology of Waern and Askwall (1981) and Waern and Rollenhagen (1983). That is to say, the emphasis is on strategy selection rather than on the microprocesses of reading (e.g., word decoding). This focus is not intended to belittle the importance of such microprocesses. Indeed, given the current state of technology, it is undoubtedly the case that decoding processes in the form of legibility problems can disrupt the reading of electronically displayed materials. Stewart (1979) listed eight display parameters, such as character size, shape, spacing, and stability, which are often less than optimal on CRT displays. Several studies have shown that texts may take longer to read on CRT screens (e.g., Muter, Latremouille, Treurniet, & Beam, 1982). Nevertheless, this chapter is primarily concerned with other influences on reading, not with legibility nor comprehension as such.

One of the important aspects of reading which emerges from the studies reported here concerns the close coupling of reading and writing processes for many academic purposes. Journal readers may often have a pen in hand and a notepad close by when reading, particularly if reading for a purpose such as scholarly refereeing. Comments about the lack of ability to write on electronic manuscripts resulted in some special purpose software being written for the United Kingdom experimental project on an electronic journal that was funded by the British Library Research and Development Department. Detailed reports of some of the work carried out within that project are now available (Pullinger, 1984a and b; Shackel, 1982; Shackel, Pullinger, Maude, & Dodd, 1983). Several of the experimental studies presented in this chapter resulted from participation in that larger scale investigation of electronic journals.

The requirement that the presentation and formatting of text should take account of readers' needs is not a requirement that can be met only at late editorial stages. It has implications for writers because a change in medium may well require changes in the organization of the material. At present, the main responsibility for the format of a published article rests with the editor. However, it is not clear that professional or semiprofessional editors will continue to function as the intermediaries that they now are for printed publications. In their place are other controlling voices. An electronic medium affords authors much more direct contact with, and feedback from, their audience. A computer-based environment also offers facilities that have no counterpart in print (e.g., computerized searching within a text). Therefore, the reading and writing strategies that have been developed for print may need to be supplemented in order to adequately handle texts in electronic media. This issue is taken up again later.

Psychological Reasons for Studying Electronic Journals

Focusing on scholarly journals which are accessed electronically through some computer-based system (for convenience, let us call these electronic journals) has several advantages for those interested in the executive control processes of reading and writing. One benefit is that this is a domain within which a variety of reading activities occur. People skim through journals in order to locate information; they browse through journals, sometimes with a very broad range of criteria for selecting what will be read; they study the text, carefully cross-checking information in different sections; and, of course, they "read" in the conventional sense of proceeding in a fairly linear fashion through portions of the text. For academic readers these different activities are all overlearned skills. This should make them readily available for exploration in the laboratory.

A second advantage is that an electronic medium tends to make some of the executive control processes within various reading strategies easier to observe. For example, limitations of screen size may require the operation of some specialized device to turn pages, where a loose-leaf typescript might only have required eye movements or slight head turning to glance across adjacent pages. For this reason computer-based presentation media may be well suited to the study of established reading and writing skills. Even if these skills are disrupted by the special characteristics of the medium, complaints from the users will help to make explicit just what functionality they sought from the system.

A third advantage is perhaps the most important reason for psychologists to be interested in the problems posed by new communications media such as electronic journals. Not only do the new technologies challenge current theories of "reading" but, because they offer a much richer choice among media (visual, auditory), they invite us to develop more broadly based theories of communication (Nickerson, 1981). In particular, the problems of electronic journals invite theorists to consider in very general terms how people process technical information. The domain of technical information includes not only prose but also formatted material such as lists and tables, not only verbal material but also numbers in graphs and charts, not only alphanumeric displays but also illustrations and diagrams. Traditionally these areas have tended to be the province of research groups who saw no communality across the domain. Yet people seem adept at generalizing information-processing strategies from one sphere to another (Schank & Hunter, 1985). Recently, attempts have been made to show that at the macrolevel many of the metacognitive processes relating to strategy selection do in fact serve very similar functions for people consulting information as diverse as numerical tables and instruction manuals (Wright, 1980b, 1981). Just how far these similarities range across different categories of information has yet to be determined. Indeed, the challenge from technology grows stronger because the options for ways of displaying information are rapidly increasing. Presentations can vary in both medium and modality and can include the use of interactive dynamic pictorial displays of film-quality information (e.g., computer-controlled optical discs, Cook, 1984). As writers become more familiar with selecting among these options, so readers may become more sophisticated in the way they manipulate the information that is made available to them. It is less certain that research on people's processes of communication and understanding are keeping pace with these developments.

One final set of reasons for a concern with electronic journals is essentially practical rather than psychological. The economics of print, at least as it is created and distributed at present, make it expensive to generate, disseminate, and store. Other media offer attractive alternatives. Computers can provide ready access to a wide range of up-to-date reports and journals, many more than most individuals or institutions can personally subscribe to. Computer-based dissemination could allow subscribers access to only those articles of interest. Both the capture and the manipulation of information in an electronic medium could be more flexible than is possible in print. For example, because many behavioral science experiments are conducted under computer control, it would be perfectly feasible for the method section in a technical paper to give the reader the opportunity to "participate" in the experiment. As the display options expand in number, so the design decisions become harder. An optimist might hope that the findings from applied research in the behavioral sciences may lessen the risks of the design of these new systems being dictated by guess, by fashion, and by the economics of the market place.

RESEARCH STRATEGIES

It may not be an idle observation that one of the difficulties of studying how people read and write in an electronic medium is that there are limitations to the major research approaches that one might adopt. Indeed, some of the major theoretical breakthroughs in HCI design (e.g., Card, Moran, & Newell, 1983) have succeeded by focusing on categories of interaction where the variabilities in cognitive factors are reduced. When interest centers on cognitive activities such as reading and writing, theories will inevitably become more complicated and their design consequences may be harder to determine. Undoubtedly it is important to frame research questions so that the answers can be stated in ways that are relatively independent of the characteristics of any specific system (Nickerson, 1984); the difficulty is in knowing how to do this. Consider four alternative research approaches:

1. conventional reading studies in a printed medium,
2. similar studies but in an electronic medium,
3. cognitive ergonomic studies that explore the behavioral consequences of design options, and
4. contrastive evaluations that seek to compare the merits of different media for specific reading purposes.

Each of these research paradigms has both strengths and weaknesses.

Conventional studies of reading printed material have enabled psychologists to explore the cognitive processes recruited by readers for various reading tasks. For example, Light and Anderson (1983) have demonstrated the relationship between readers' ability to make use of script-based knowledge and their ability to benefit from the introduction of headings into a text. However, it is possible that people's information needs may require different support in different media, even though the syntactic and lexical reading mechanisms which foster comprehension will generalize across media. Indeed, the signposting aspect of headings may be more critical for CRT texts than for print on paper, and this in turn may have design implications (such as the need to include hierarchical numbering systems) for both the content and the display of such headings. It is even possible that the class of dominant cognitive processes may change across media (e.g., with search and location processes playing a much greater part with electronic displays). If this happens, then no simple generalizations may be possible from studies of print on paper to the other kinds of presentation.

To transpose the methodology and do conventional reading studies of computer-generated displays runs the serious risk of being limited by the currently available technology. This limitation has two facets, one concerning the interface characteristics, the other concerning the users. On the one hand, new systems require technological developments (e.g., new architectures) that are not yet available, although sometimes these can be simulated with Wizard of Oz techniques (e.g., the listening typewriter, Gould, Conti, & Hovanyecz, 1983). On the other hand, new "reading" or other information-handling skills may need to be learned. Therefore the researcher is doubly handicapped in neither having access to a population of readers who have these skills, nor being certain what some of these skills may turn out to be. It follows from this that any research data obtained may not generalize beyond the population tested and the hardware–software package actually used in the study itself. Such problems bedevil the use of rapid prototyping as a design tool. Ergonomists and applied psychologists are familiar with this difficulty and recognize the caution with which conclusions can be drawn. Nevertheless, because of the cognitive changes that may be fostered by interactions with computer-based displays, even greater caution may be necessary when interpreting research dealing with the new information technologies.

Cognitive ergonomists seek to obtain generality at the level of assessing the effectiveness of design options (e.g., headings or numbering systems). But it is far from obvious that such options can be treated as if they were modules that could be pieced together in some future system without there being interaction among the modules themselves (Macdonald-Ross & Waller, 1975). Indeed, the cognitive automatization of processes relating to reading (such as page turning) may result in very different performance characteristics once the technology has been mastered. Lest it be thought that such interactions could be incorporated as part of the research enterprise, there are two major difficulties: firstly, the design space created by all possible permutations of all possible options is simply too large for any unprincipled approach to be feasible; secondly, and standing in the way of the development of such principles, is the difficulty of characterizing texts and reading purposes. There is evidence that reading purpose affects executive processes at the microlevel, such as controlling the distribution of pauses when reading (e.g., Aaronson & Scarborough, 1976) and the amount of incidental information that the reader will acquire (Rothkopf & Billington, 1975). The effects of the organizational structure of the material have been less widely studied, although there is evidence that introducing structural elements into a text (e.g., questions) can change the reading pattern (Rothkopf, 1982).

It is important to know what the effects on reading may be of changing text structures because different academic domains adopt alternative styles of academic writing. For example, long footnotes are common in the humanities, much less so in the sciences. Law texts are glossed with comment and interpretation. In other domains parallel texts in different languages are presented. These stylistic differences in the written material may well be associated with a shift in reading strategies and hence in the preponderance of particular executive control processes. Coping with interruptions to the flow of the main text, and the attendant place-keeping problems, may be a much more highly developed reading skill within some academic domains than in others.

The lack of a principled underlying framework (never mind adequate theories) also hampers the contrastive approach to questions about reading, writing, or information design. Whereas at first glance it might seem both feasible and useful to contrast the merits of print and electronic media for specific reading activities (e.g., proofreading, refereeing, browsing through abstracts), such comparisons can only be considered "fair" if the presentation style adopted within each medium is optimized. It would be clearly a waste of time to compare a superb, multicolor, high resolution CRT display with a poor quality photocopy of a printed journal. Although it may seem unlikely that any investigator would make such a comparison, it is surprisingly easy to find published studies where the inequalities were reversed, i.e., the electronic medium was far from optimal. Without knowing how to optimize within each medium, it may be meaningless to attempt contrastive research. So there seems to be an urgent need for the acceptance of a given medium and an exploration of characteristics and possibilities afforded by that means of communication. This is in accord with the spirit of an argument put forward by Wright and Bason (1982), that the potential and limitations of any new communication medium need to be understood in their own terms, both by designers and by users. Unfortunately for the new information technologies, such research will always risk being limited by the state of the art in technical development.

The advantages and drawbacks of these alternative methodologies have been discussed here, not only to draw attention to the problem in its own right, but also as a mitigation for some of the experimental work to be reported later. Perfect solutions do not yet seem to be on offer. The present studies can only be viewed as preliminary explorations of the impact on readers and writers that the advent of electronic journals may have.

Both the design process and research relating to information design could benefit from being set within a coherent framework. Such a framework would need to characterize in general terms (rather than at the level of specific details) how people interact with information (Wright, 1980a). One such framework has been put forward by Nickerson (1984). He suggests that there are four clusters of issues relating to the acquisition and use of information:

1. the representational form in which the information is displayed;
2. the information seeking behavior of information users;
3. the filtering (disregarding) and evaluation of potentially available information;
4. the organization and manipulation of information in relation to other information.

Undoubtedly all these clusters of issues have relevance to academic communication, but for the present we assume that issues (1) and (4) can be set aside. In the short term at least, the representational form for electronic journals will still be based predominantly on the written word. The wider issues of the organization and management of the information, its storage and retrieval, are relevant but not critical to the present focus on the problems of scholarly reading and writing.

Let us follow Nickerson's procedure of outlining issue clusters. For the purpose of academic reading, there are at least four major decision processes under which other metacognitive processes cluster:

1. decisions about starting to read;
2. decisions about the order in which information will be read;
3. decisions about interrupting the ongoing reading activity—either for further reading, e.g., to compare what is being read with other information in the text, or to write, e.g., making brief marginal annotations or extended comments;
4. decisions about rereading the text.

For each of these decisions, the executive control processes are influenced by presentation factors, some of which are shown in Table 2.1.

Within the simplistic framework outlined in Table 2.1, the research reported here concerns all but the first decision-making stage. This omission of the first stage tends to be an inevitable consequence of using

TABLE 2.1
Executive Control Processes and Some of Their Determinants

---

1. Decisions About Starting to Read

Psychological factors: "Relevance" based on title, author, hearsay, text sampling.

Presentation factors: Length, Legibility.

---

2. Decisions About the Order of Reading Information

Psychological factors: Schema driven by expected structure.
Text driven by internal reference.
Strategies for searching and browsing.
Presentation factors: Index, Headings

---

3. Decisions About Interrupting Reading

Psychological factors:
semantic conflict ————→ check other information
salient point   ————→ reflection / annotation
thematic break   ————→ decision about continuing

semantic difficulty
boredom   } ————→stop reading
content irrelevance

strategies for place-keeping

Presentation factors: cues to structural organization

---

4. Decisions About Rereading

Psychological factors: attention and memory lapses (esp. for details when writing
comments)
comprehension difficulties
enjoyment
strategies for relocating information
Presentation factors: textual access structures

---

5. Recycle

If an affirmative decision is made at 4, the executive control processes may recycle
from 2.

---

laboratory rather than field techniques. In our studies people read the text they were given because they were asked to. Other kinds of investigation are required in order to find out what it is that people choose to read, when, and why. Such studies have been carried out by the Primary Communications Research Centre at the University of Leicester where, understandably, the focus has been on traditional printed media. One notable extension of the field study approach has been the recent large-scale project in the United Kingdom, funded by the British Library Research and Development Department. This project provides the starting point for our consideration of the executive processes that control the activities of reading and writing for electronic journals.

READING ELECTRONIC JOURNALS

The first studies of electronic journals were carried out in the United States, funded by the National Science Foundation during the period 1976–1980. Several reports on the findings from that project, which involved the Electronic Information Exchange System (EIES) centered on the New Jersey Institute of Technology, are available (e.g., Hiltz & Turoff, 1978; Moray, 1980; Senders, 1977). Although the project had envisaged detailed consideration of communication among academics, for a variety of reasons it ultimately focused more on communications outside academic circles. In contrast, in the United Kingdom the British Library Electronic Network Development (BLEND) had as its primary objective "to gain practical experience of how electronic journals can be operated, and to evaluate their potential" in an academic context (Shackel, 1982).

The BLEND project started with two very different communities, one of computer scientists, the other of behavioral scientists. In the course of time the network also came to be used by various "closed" groups of specialists (e.g., 14 library schools, the Further Education Research Network, and a group of biotechnologists who used it for weekly reports). It was always a major part of the project objectives to explore a variety of kinds of "journal," ranging from fully refereed academic research papers to newsletters and reviews. My own involvement was as assistant editor of the refereed journal, and the research studies reported here have therefore tended to focus in the direction of scholarly reports. But before considering these smaller studies, it is of interest to see how the findings from the larger project relate to the outline of executive control processes given in Table 2.1.

Decisions about Starting to Read

The need for specialized support for different kinds of reading became evident from the early stages of the electronic journal. Unlike the sudden arrival of printed documents, it was not automatically obvious when something new to read became available on the system. An alerting device needed to be specially devised. This was done by providing readers, on entry to the system, with a list of all available journals. When one was selected, its contents were displayed and anything new since the reader had last looked at this journal was starred in the contents list.

Although alerted to the existence of something new, it does not follow that the reader will elect to read this article. It soon became apparent that one of the important pieces of information that readers needed was knowledge of how long the article was. Again this illustrates a control process which is less apparent in the medium of print. The solution for the electronic journals on the BLEND system was to provide contents lists, both on entry to the journal and at the start of each article. These lists gave information about length in several different ways. Instead of page numbers, contents lists contained "entry numbers, where an entry was a thematic unit that was shorter than a full page of a CRT screen (24 lines). A typical entry would be just one or two paragraphs. Providing these entries with subheadings facilitated certain search operations. Thus, the presentation system being used for these journals is making serious demands on writers to modify their normal writing style.

Decisions about the Order of Reading and Interruptions

Several readers complained of losing track of where they had been, both when jumping around within a single article and when reading several articles in different journals on the system. This latter activity poses fewer problems in print because readers can move articles from one pile to another as an external memory aid. So the problem of this kind of placekeeping tends to be unnoticed with printed materials. Moving around within a single article poses rather different problems. Some of these are taken up later in a discussion of the functions of color cues in lengthy texts. Some of the problems of moving around will only be solved by the opportunity for personal annotation of the text (perhaps ranging from the electronic equivalent of "dogears," to the freedom to insert amendments or corrections in the text itself).

It has already been suggested that there are numerous very different reading activities. Several of these have design implications for electronic journals. When readers are browsing, they need to have a choice of the information "window" through which they are looking; when they are skimming, they need to be able to control the speed of access to new information, as well as having the opportunity to "gracefully" abort their search through any particular part of the journal; people studying texts in detail need annotation facilities; people in editorial roles need to be able to manipulate the text being read, plus their own notes about that text, together with referees' comments. In the early stages of a project involving new display media, the limitations imposed by currently available hardware and software will inevitably be very real.

The changes required to the structure and format of the refereed articles published in an electronic journal have been discussed by Pullinger (1984a). Here again, the close intertwining of constraints on readers and writers can be seen. It has been mentioned that the reader's need to be able to move about within the text was met in part by a contents list of numbered entries at the start of each article. It is easy to see the opportunity for confusion that arises when authors initially number their main and subordinate headings and subsequently superimpose entry numbers throughout the text. So a formatting constraint had to be accepted by writers in order to meet readers' requirements, given the system characteristics.

One of the advantages of an electronic medium is that it enables public communication between readers and authors. When a text has been electronically "published," it can then be the focus of further comments from the audience. These comments are transmitted electronically and archived with the original report. In this way the change of medium enhances the links between the activities of reading and writing. It is possible that an article in an electronic journal may have more in common with a teleconference on a closely defined topic than it has with the conventional communication style of a published journal article. Nickerson (1984) has pointed out that new modes of interaction will often lead to the emergence of new social structures. It is too early to tell just what changes in the patterns of scientific communication may arise if electronic journals are more widely used by researchers.

STUDIES OF STRATEGIES AND CONTROL PROCESSES
USED BY ACADEMIC READERS

The preceding discussion of electronic journals has considered investigations that have used field study techniques. The researchers created electronic journals that were usable by the academic community. In contrast, the following section discusses the findings from three laboratory-based experiments. Each study focuses on a specific aspect of academic reading.

The first study being reported explores the problems of scientific readers adopting the role of an academic referee on behalf of a scholarly journal. An apparently "contrastive" methodology is employed. However, there is no wish to evaluate which is the more suitable medium for refereeing tasks. The intention is to discover more about how the activity of scholarly refereeing proceeds at present (i.e., with the text on paper). We also hoped to capitalize on the insightful comments of those referees who were already very familiar with using word processors. This might enable contrasts between the requirements for system support of those who were "computer-experts" or "computer-novices," when both were carrying out a familiar task in a relatively novel communication environment.

This study of refereeing indicated that relocating information which had been read was a serious problem. So the issue of relocating information formed the focus of the second study. Again, there was no intention at the outset of making comparisons across presentation media. But the unexpected results of the first study prompted further investigations in order to see whether similar effects would be obtained in another medium.

A rather different aspect of getting scientific reports into print concerns the activity of proofreading. This reading activity was the focus of the third study being reported here. Although this investigation was more inherently contrastive than the other studies, the focus moved to the ease of integrating the activities of reading and writing in different media.

How Do Academics Referee?

One effect that the change of medium had on an activity such as refereeing (reviewing) scholarly papers was seen in the feedback received when I invited eight colleagues to referee four papers on the BLEND system. I drew blanks almost all the way round. "Certainly, if you send a printout" was not an isolated response. There may have been many factors contributing to this reluctance, including limited access to adequate hardware and a need to modify well-established patterns of work. The first of these problems we could do nothing about, but the second was amenable to several lines of investigation. So, in an attempt to understand the causes of this reluctance, we decided to explore what referees actually did when refereeing a typewritten manuscript (Wright & Lickorish, 1984b). At the same time we hoped to get some insights into the kinds of facilities, support systems, and information redesign required by referees working electronically.

The measures that we were interested in were related to the framework outlined in Table 2.1. We wanted to know whether referees made several, perhaps different kinds of, "reads" through the manuscript; how and when they made notes about the text; the nature of their interaction with the manuscript when they were composing their report for the editor. Such research questions sounded sensible enough at the outset.

We monitored experienced referees as they each dealt with two texts, one seen as print on paper and the other presented as white text on a black background on a CRT controlled by an Apple II computer. The CRT display could be paged both forward and backwards. It did not scroll, nor were keyword search facilities available. The order of presenting the texts and the order in which readers encountered particular media were counterbalanced across the eight referees. The two articles were chosen because they were both available in electronic form on BLEND, and they were both discussions of general issues whose content would be relatively novel for the referees (one considered the relative merits of human and computer-based editorial comments, the other was an introduction to electronic journals).

It remains possible that with a large enough sample some of the questions we asked might have interesting answers. But what we found, with the generous assistance of APU colleagues who were all tenured scientists accustomed to acting as referees for learned journals, was a tremendous amount of variability in every measure that we examined. This may not be unusual. Hartley (1984b) reported receiving qualitatively very different comments from nine colleagues whom he had asked to respond to one of his own papers. Some commentators addressed issues of principle, others issues of detail. Such differences might well be reflected in the reading strategies adopted.

In our study few people troubled to skim read the article before starting. Some people said that they normally would skim through first, but in this instance they did not want to prolong the experimental session. It is possible that all the measures we took might be subject to similar kinds of bias toward saving time, but one might expect that such a bias would increase the similarity in the reading procedures adopted. Most people made notes while reading. About half did so on the manuscript itself, and the others wrote on the note pad that was provided for all referees. Table 2.2 illustrates that the variability in reading procedures was reflected in the variability of the assessments made of the manu-

TABLE 2.2
Number of Referees Using Each Evaluation Category

Recommendation on Publication	Text A	Text B	Overall
1. YES, as it stands	2	0	2
2. YES, minor revisions	1	2	3
3. MAYBE, major revisions	2	1	3
4. NO, needs further work	1	3	4
5. NO, not at all	2	2	4
TOTAL:	8	8	16

scripts reviewed. All referees had been asked to make their assessments with respect to the articles' suitability for a journal such as Applied Ergonomics, a journal with which they were familiar although not necessarily regular readers.

It was no surprise to find the data suggesting that the CRT display may have had legibility drawbacks. It certainly slowed referees down: Dealing with the printed texts took 30 minutes, the CRT texts took 36 minutes, 20% longer (fuller details are given in Wright & Lickorish, 1984b). It had been of some interest to see whether the move from print to CRT influenced the referee's evaluation of the text. Given the variability shown in Table 2.2, it was impossible to detect any effect of changing media. A related question is whether reviewers who were severe with one text were also harsh in their evaluation of the other. Again, no clear pattern emerged. Three of the eight reviewers gave the same category evaluation to both papers (categories 2, 4, 5); four of the reviewers rated one paper as being at least two categories better than the other (two used categories 1 and 4, two used categories 3 and 5), but there was no unanimity about which was the better text (analyzed by content, medium, or presentation order). Obviously, the small number of reviewers taking part in this study does not make it easy to discern general trends, but given the variability observed, there seems little incentive for collecting more data of this kind.

One potential limitation of these findings is that the subject matter of the texts being reviewed (electronic journals, computer analysis of texts) did not fall within the specialism of any of the referees. It is quite conceivable that people adopt rather different reading strategies in their own field. Indeed, studies of students who are reading material in other than their first language have shown that, once a threshold of reading ability has been passed, knowledge of the field is a more powerful determinant of comprehension than is language fluency (Mohammed & Swales, 1984). We had hoped to find some nonsubject-specific skills to be common among our referees. For example, following Lesgold (1984), we had hoped that our experts would have some finely tuned "diagnostic schemata" that would be manifest both in the way decisions were reached and in the content of those decisions. Academic referees may have such schemata; the significant effects of factors such as the author's name and institution suggest they do (e.g., Peters & Ceci, 1982). However, we failed to find any evidence of the generality of these schemata at the level of text-processing strategies.

Among the comments made by referees was a complaint that they found it difficult to refer back to material which they had previously read on a CRT screen (decisions 3 and 4 of the outline given in Table 2.1). The problem was not so much with the manipulative aspects of the task;

rather, it was the cognitive problem of not being certain whereabouts to look within the text. It is known that using scrolled presentations tends to impair readers' knowledge of where in a text information has occurred (Lovelace & Southall, 1983), but it had not been appreciated that this could be such a problem with paged displays. There exist studies of search strategies that readers use in data-base environments (e.g., Elkerton & Williges, 1984), but in our next study we sought to examine ways of trying to help people locate information within lengthy texts presented on single-window CRT screens. These problems are reduced by using larger screens (Haas & Hayes, 1985), but it seems likely that many people will be using the more primitive 80-character 24-line CRT displays for several years yet.

Do Color Cues Help Readers Locate Information?

It is not unusual for printed texts, although not academic journals, to have colored sections as a means of helping readers quickly locate particular categories of information. We applied this technique to the articles that had been read by our referees. Each text was subdivided, at thematic boundaries, into five discrete color sections of some four to six 24-line pages. That is to say, although the background was always black, the color of the text was green, yellow, light blue, or white (because of hardware limitations it was only possible to select four colors that maintained good visibility; therefore green was used for both the first and the fifth sections). It was hoped that the use of colored sections, as distinct from relying on a section-numbering system, would facilitate the incidental learning of where information occurred in the text.

This time the reader's task was to read through an entire article once in order to get some idea of where information was in the text, and then answer a series of 10 questions by looking back through the text and specifying the line number on which the answer was given (Wright, Lickorish, & Whalley, 1985).

In a preliminary pilot test, reverse video had also been used to differentiate subheadings and alternate subsections within the text. This seemed to follow the spirit of Shebilske and Rotondo (1981) that typographical cues could enhance readers' memory. However, in our pilot study readers complained that the frequent variation in color was confusing. So a simpler coding system was adopted for the experiment itself.

There were 32 readers, all paid volunteers from the APU's subject panel comprising adult members of the general public. Everyone carried out a similar search task for two texts. One text was presented in monochrome (each of the four colors served as the monochrome version for different readers), and the other was presented in colored sections.

The order in which the texts and the experimental conditions were presented were both counterbalanced separately, as was the order of the 10 questions. The questions were subdivided into "first five" and "second five," with half the testees receiving the "second five" first. The advantage of this control was that it enabled an assessment of how well the structure of the text was being learned during the period of answering questions.

The results showed that dividing a lengthy text on a CRT display into colored sections impaired performance on the information location task, relative to performance with the monochrome CRT versions. The data are shown in Table 2.3, where it can be seen that only with the monochrome displays did people speed up in answering the second five questions.

Two questions arise from these unexpected findings. One is the possibility that perhaps for some reason these texts were unsuitable for the kind of segmentation that was applied to generate the colored versions. These texts were single, coherent, "case history" style reports. Texts that were inherently more segmented might show a different pattern. The other possibility is that there could be something about the present methodology which is failing to pick up the expected advantage from introducing color cues into the text.

To check both these possibilities, the experiment was repeated with another 32 volunteers, and with the major modification of having the texts printed on paper in a format that preserved close similarity with the "page" displays used in the previous study (i.e., identical line-breaks and page-breaks). Because the printed materials were generated by linking a printer to the computer used in the previous study, the color segmentation was achieved by variation in background hue of the paper on which the text was printed. For texts on paper, the pattern of results was rather different from that found with the CRT display. Now the color segmentation resulted in better performance with the colored text than with the

TABLE 2.3
Performance With CRT Text in Either Monochrome
or Colored Sections

	Monochrome	Colored
Time to read text (mins)	14.4	14.7
Time for correct answers (sec)		
1st five questions	78.4	84.3
2nd five questions	69.9	80.0
	($p < 0.01$)	(ns)

TABLE 2.4
Performance With Paper Text in Either Monochrome
or Colored Sections

	Monochrome	Colored
Time to read text (mins)	13.2	13.6
Time for correct answers (sec)		
1st five questions	59.6	63.2
2nd five questions	59.5	51.4
	(ns)	($p < 0.0$)

monochrome text (i.e., the increase in speed of answering the second set of five questions was statistically significant, $p < 0.01$). The details are given in Table 2.4.

Before considering the reasons for the discrepancy between the findings for the same texts on CRT and on paper, it was decided to check the generality of the CRT findings by making a similar comparison with two new texts. This time the texts consisted of discrete sections (one text dealt with various house plants, the other dealt with various travel destinations). These texts were read by another 16 members of the general public. As Table 2.5 shows, the pattern of results was very similar to that of the previous CRT experiment. Color segmentation does not seem to offer assistance to readers trying to locate information on a single-window CRT display, although it can be helpful for texts printed on paper. It now becomes necessary to consider the possible reasons for the discrepancy between the two CRT studies and the print on paper study.

The experimental design, with its comparison between changing color and a range of monochrome texts within a single communication medium (computer based or paper based), rules out the possibility that legibility factors were in any way responsible. The factor most likely to be responsible for the different effects of color variation on CRTs and on paper would seem to be that CRT displays had colored *text*, whereas the

TABLE 2.5
Performance With CRT Sectional Text in Either Monochrome or
Colored Sections

	Monochrome	Colored	
Time to read text (mins)	15.3	15.4	
Time for correct answers (sec)			
1st five questions	69.0	75.6	
2nd five questions	58.9	69.4	($p < 0.05$)

paper displays varied the colored *background* behind the text. One of the advantages of varying the background color of a text on paper is that, even when the pages of the text are closed, the reader is reminded of the order in which the colors occur. This visible framework may make it easier for readers to direct their search task. In the absence of such cues to the serial ordering of the colored sections, readers working with CRT displays may inadvertently sometimes set off in the wrong direction and need to double back when they realize their mistake. Support for this suggestion was found in the CRT experiments. In both studies readers turned significantly more pages while looking for the answer with the color display than with the monochrome display (Experiment 1, $p < 0.02$; Experiment 3, $p < 0.05$). So readers may have been trying to use the color cues but not succeeding.

A visual framework listing the order of the colors could have been provided for the CRT displays. This was not done because it had been assumed (perhaps wrongly) that remembering the serial order of the five colored sections would be a trivially easy task. In a subsequent study, the texts used in Experiment 3 were presented on a CRT screen that had five color patches, corresponding to the section colors pasted above the screen. The data showed that this visual aid eliminated the impairment from using color, but did not produce the enhancement found with colored paper (Wright & Lickorish, 1987).

The amount of incidental information that readers pick up while reading a text has received scant attention from researchers. A notable exception is the work of Rothkopf (1971), who showed that readers tended to remember where on the page they had encountered certain material. If this incidental learning is essentially tied to some kind of "spatial" coding as the work by Lovelace and Southall (1983) on scrolling displays would suggest, then perhaps it was singularly inappropriate for us to try recouping the deficit on a CRT display by using color. Spatial solutions, achieved via multiwindow displays, could potentially offer better incidental retrieval cues for readers (Tombaugh, Lickorish, & Wright, 1987).

For many practical purposes this locative aspect of the memory for a text can be of considerable importance. Sticht (1977) reported that thumbing through a manual was often the preferred way of locating information, rather than using formal access structures such as contents lists and indexes. The opportunity for spatial coding that print on paper affords seems to be missing with CRT displays. Whereas our findings confirm that some alternative cueing system needs to be provided for readers, the present studies serve only to urge caution when looking to color variation to meet this need. The uses of color in multiwindow displays are, of course, related to a separate cluster of issues.

Does Proofreading on a CRT Pose Special Problems?

Another editorial chore associated with academic journal articles, a chore usually shared with the authors themselves, is proofreading. There have been complaints about the legibility of some CRT displays (Hulme, 1984). The character font does not always have adequate ascenders and descenders, although research has established that outline shape is an important contributor to word recognition (Monk & Hulme, 1983; Rudnicky & Kolers, 1984). The interline spacing is often too close for easy reading because of the space constraints of the CRT screen. The text on a CRT screen is often displayed as bright characters on a dark background. The reverse would make for easier reading but for the fact that the early screen technology was such that, with the currently used screen refresh rates, a bright background results in unpleasant flicker. In some studies it has been found that reading long texts on a CRT may take 20 to 30% longer than reading printed versions of the same material (Muter et al., 1982). Given such legibility problems, the task of proofreading might seem to be a fair candidate for one in which the executive processes of reading are impaired when journals change media.

In a first attempt to explore the problems of proofreading electronically displayed text, Wright and Lickorish (1983) noted that people were indeed considerably slower when carrying out a proofreading task on a CRT screen although accuracy was not impaired. However, a subsequent study showed that the dominant factor contributing to this slowness was not legibility, although that did play a part. The major cause of people's slowness was the difficulty of annotating the screen text (Wright & Lickorish, 1984a). One option that was explored had people write notes on a pad, but this involved repeated shifting of the eyes to and from the screen.

Another option explored people's use of an annotation device which enabled symbols to be placed in the margin. This device was based on three clearly labeled keys on the keyboard and was provided specifically for the proofreading study. Proofreaders had both to learn to use the notation system afforded by the device and also to remember to scroll it down line by line to keep level with the text that they were currently reading and that they might want to annotate. In this study, with inexperienced proofreaders, few people continuously scrolled the cursor down the page. So, when working with texts on CRT screens, there was a pause while the marking device was moved from the position in which it had last been used to the location in which it was now wanted. This relates to the control process of Decision 3 in the outline given in Table 2.1, the problems of interrupting reading and resuming again.

We have not yet had the opportunity to see what effect other pointing devices (e.g., mouse, touchscreen, or trackerball) might have on tasks such as proofreading. There seem to be two broad categories of written response that proofreaders make, either very brief marginal annotations or extended verbal comments. It seems possible that other pointing devices might simplify the task of recording where in the text something has gone astray, but it is not obvious that pointing devices alone have much to offer for the task of indicating what corrections are necessary (e.g., corresponding to a marginal sign for deletion). If the pointing devices lead to a menu selection, this may be very disruptive of the ongoing reading processes. Such disruption is a disadvantage that may also accompany the insertion of any keyboarding activity when compared with a highly overlearned skill like handwriting, at least until keyboard skills achieve a comparable level of automaticity.

Voice of course is another possibility. This may be more advantageous for extended comments than for brief marginal annotations. Wright and Lickorish argued that one of the advantages of the traditional handwritten medium might be the possibility of overlapping the tasks of reading and writing. They suggested that the proofreader was often able to continue reading the text while brief marginal annotations were being made. It seems possible that a voice input to a computer-based editing system would afford more interference with continued reading of the text than does the recording of a written symbol.

It should not be thought that the problems of annotation are confined to activities such as proofreading. The desire to make annotations on the text being read featured as a requirement of several referees when reviewing papers submitted to BLEND. It was an activity engaged in by some of the referees in the study reported earlier. Annotation is often used by scholars in reading contexts other than those involving journals. In a questionnaire answered by 81 computer science students, Nielsen (1984) found that over 80% of the respondents used highlighting techniques and made informal additions to their textbooks.

The columns of Table 2.6 summarize how the findings from these studies relate to the kinds of executive control processes outlined in Table 2.1. We have seen that people acting as scholarly referees (at least in our experimental setting) adopt a predominantly linear reading strategy. They may need to relocate specific information but do not reread substantial sections of the text. We have seen that readers have problems remembering where information is, but such problems are not alleviated by dividing the text into colored sections on CRT displays. We have seen that provision for the integration of reading and writing activities is something that paper affords more easily than does the CRT screen at present. Other studies will be needed to furnish the empty cells in Table 2.6. The table itself needs extending to other reading tasks. There is much more we need to know about readers' interaction with electronic texts.

TABLE 2.6
Relation of the Three Experiments to Previous Outline of
Decision Processes

Decisions	Experimental Studies		
	Refereeing	Locating	Proofreading
Starting to read			
Order of reading	linear		linear
Interrupting reading	crossrefs + writing		integrating reading and writing
Rereading	v. little	use of location cues	

Given the findings from these three studies (concerned with refereeing, with locating information, and with proofreading), it is obvious that those colleagues who declined the invitation to electronically referee material for the electronic journal were operating with sound intuitions. They were all busy people and believed it would be much more hassle for them to work electronically. This would undoubtedly have been the case, no matter how convenient their access to the necessary hardware.

The difficulty of knowing the generality of the present findings has already been discussed in relation to research methodologies. The conclusions drawn here are inevitably limited by characteristics of the present hardware and software. It has already been acknowledged that ideally one would wish to frame research questions so that issues can be studied in ways that are relatively independent of system characteristics. Whether such ideals can be realized is less clear. Communication will always be by some "channel," and the characteristics of that channel will significantly influence many aspects of the communication (Twyman, 1982). Recognizing this, and exploring these influences, may not be a waste of time. So it is hoped that the findings from these three preliminary studies, set within the framework outlined in Table 2.1, may offer some insights into the kinds of system developments that are needed if electronic journals are to become a fully acceptable communication mode rather than just a convenient information dissemination facility.

NEW SKILLS NEEDED BY READERS AND WRITERS

Because technical and scientific texts may be read in nonlinear fashion, is there any need for them to be written as linear entities? Computer-held text offers considerable freedom from the constraints of conventional print on paper. There have been several suggestions made concerning the possibilities of completely changing the way texts are structured in an electronic medium (e.g., Weyer, 1982). Pullinger (1984a) spelt out five alternative structures that an electronic journal might have:

1. linear, as in print;
2. tree structure, e.g., with the conventional sections of a scientific report being the main branches of the tree;
3. a relational net, with optional paths between certain sections of the text;
4. a matrix, enabling a choice of vertical or horizontal progression through the text (e.g., with the vertical dimension reflecting differing levels of specificity and the horizontal dimension differing subtopics);
5. free browsing, in which each section of text is accompanied by pointers that would take the reader to all other sections.

With such innovative text structures, contents lists might need to be supplemented or replaced by diagrams showing the author's chosen structure. Navigational hints may be needed for readers. These are uncommon in printed texts, although the subheadings in directories like the Yellow Pages may contain such advice as "See also . . ."

Creating appropriately "networked" texts is not simply a matter of having an editorial system that creates the routes. Writers need to have appreciated that readers will have arrived at particular locations by a variety of different paths. This has serious implications for anaphoric references, both explicit and implicit, within the text. It might even be necessary to adopt notational conventions (such as reserved margins for cross-referencing) in order to preserve the readability of the body of the text while helping readers locate the source of references within the text. Yet, no matter how redesigned, the basic problem of reading and writing academic articles will remain. As noted by Hebb and Bindra (1952), the reader's problem when reading any lengthy account is that of trying to get an overview of a complicated structure that can only be perceived a piece at a time. It is not self-evident how new text structures will help the reader to solve this particular problem. Increased freedom for readers to integrate information in their own preferred order may be beneficial, but only if readers are skillful in selecting their information order.

In the sciences, academic journals contain not only prose text but also diagrams and tabular material. There is evidence that illustrations or tables may need to be drastically revised for screen display (Norrish,

1984). Limitations of space on the CRT screen impose considerable constraints on how much information can be presented at any one time. This problem cannot be solved simply by presenting tabular material as successive sections cut from the larger version (Norrish, 1984). From working with tables displayed on the British viewdata system, PRE-STEL, Norrish concluded that there was a need for completely redesigning the information to make it suitable for an electronic medium. The emphasis was on creating screen-sized modules of information that were semantically coherent in themselves. To each module it was necessary to add signposts indicating where related information could be accessed.

WRITERS' SUPPORT

New developments in computer-based displays may not only assist readers but may also afford some help to writers. It has already been mentioned that there exists a literature concerned with the evaluation of writing tools such as text editors (e.g., Borenstein, 1984). In some writing contexts these tools have undoubtedly had a liberating effect on inexperienced writers (e.g., Levin, Boruta, & Vasconcellos, 1983). As novel resources they are also introducing significant changes in the creation of several categories of technical information (Wright, 1986).

Gradually, the effects on the academic community of developments in the technology of information handling are being documented. Meadows (1978) has noted that one consequence of better text production and reprographic facilities is that an increasing number of preprints are circulated among academics, where the text has only the status of being a draft for comment rather than being the text of an article "in press." There has also been an increase in the number of academic publications requesting camera-ready copy from authors. This puts considerable onus on the editorial skills of the writer. For some writers the exercise of such skills already causes problems. Galbraith (1980) proposed that a major source of writing difficulties could arise from the conflict between the goals of expression and presentation. He suggested that this conflict sometimes leads to difficulties in both generating and revising the text. It is possible that writing for electronic journals may exacerbate such conflicts by increasing the demands on presentation skills. On the other hand, if such demands become considerable, this may lead to their temporal separation.

If forced to deal with issues of content and presentation separately, this may alleviate the difficulties some writers have. The opportunity is now available in several word-processing systems to set up a "style file" which takes over the editorial chore of keeping the major formatting decisions consistent throughout the text. This encourages the separation of activities relating to text generation and text display. Its effect on writers of differing ability has yet to be examined.

Collins and Gentner (1980) have suggested that a writing support system can offer assistance to authors in at least three distinct ways: by indicating writing strategies, by advising on appropriate text structures, and by recommending editorial operations. There do not yet seem to be findings that show what effects such support may have on writers for electronic journals. However, it has been reported that provision of a computer-based Writer's Assistant improved both the length and the quality of output to an electronic classroom newspaper written by third and fourth graders (Levin et al., 1983).

For adult writers there exist sophisticated suites of programs that offer a variety of "editorial" feedback for technical writers. The Writers Workbench, developed by AT&T Bell Labs is one such example. It provides comments on the overall readability of the text, as well as flagging specific items within the text such as long sentences and hackneyed expressions (e.g., Cherry & Macdonald, 1983; Coke, 1982). Many of these systems take linguistic aspects of the text into account, and spelling checkers are now commonplace additions to many word-processing packages. However, Kieras (1985) has emphasized the need for systems that assist writers to be based on what is known about the psychology of comprehension. Coupled with this, Kieras has urged the need to recruit AI techniques in order to process the text in other than superficial ways. Yet, even when powerful expert systems are available as editorial aids, it seems likely that different kinds of feedback will reach the author from computer analysis and from human editors (Hartley, 1984b). Humans, rather than computers, may complain that the enterprise was misguided and the article should never have been written at all.

It is feasible to apply the outline given in Table 2.1, showing readers' decision processes, to the task of writing. As Table 2.7 shows, there are several parallels between the metacognitive processes of reading and writing, although the details of the executive control processes clustering under the major headings will be rather different. Like readers, writers also make decisions about starting, about the order of writing, about interrupting writing (to check information or to get editorial feedback), and about rewriting. In Table 2.7 an attempt is made to suggest some of the factors influencing the strategy selection and the executive control processes of writers, but very little research exists which has focused directly on these factors, particularly as they relate to variation in the stylistic conventions of academic journals.

Of course, there are other approaches to the study of writing processes. Hayes and Flower (1980a) outlined four perspectives: the psycho-

TABLE 2.7
Application of the Schematic Outline of Table 2.1, for Reading, to the
Executive Control Processes for Writing

Executive Processes	Writing	
	Psychological Factors	Presentation Factors
Starting	target goal, time available	length, writing facilities
Sequencing	ease of generating ideas, custom/habit	availability of information (e.g.: already on disc)
Interrupting	check content, dissatisfaction with product	revise verbal style, change format, create illust./tables
Repeating	shift in target, feedback	publication constraints

linguistic, the linguistic, the developmental, and the cognitive-processing approach. These different approaches are not necessarily in conflict with each other, but they do vary in their appropriateness for particular objectives. The present framework was developed because of its applicability to the information design issues raised by electronic journals.

There is evidence that academics vary greatly in the way they go about the task of writing for publication (Hartley, 1984a). It is less clear how this variation relates either to the nature or to the quality of the product. It is possible that writing "blocks," which may prevent the writer starting at all, can sometimes be overcome by the use of computer-based "idea organizers." However, this assumes that the locus of the problem is at the high level of thematic organization. Writing blocks may occur at a number of different levels (Hayes & Flower, 1980b). Indeed, one characteristic of those with writing difficulties is that they succumb to what Collins and Gentner (1980) term *downsliding,* namely, a tendency to become preoccupied by the lower, more local levels of decision making. Other kinds of writing support may be needed to prevent this.

The way authors take decisions about the order of writing, as distinct from the order intended for the finished text, seems to be relatively unexplored. Wason (1970) reported a strong personal preference for writing the first draft of a scientific paper at a single sitting, which tends to imply that he started at the beginning and wrote through to the end. In contrast, Hartley (1984a) found a variety of writing sequences among five of his academic colleagues: One started with the Introduction section, others preferred to leave this to nearer the end. It seems likely that with an increase in the existence of information already in electronic form (e.g., materials or results), there may be a corresponding increase in the nonlinearity of the writing sequence.

The ways in which writers interrupt the writing activity have been examined in experimental rather than in field conditions. For example, Hayes and Flower (1980b) have used techniques of protocol analysis to study transfers of information between the task environment and the processes of text generation. Whereas this is a technique yielding valuable insights into cognitive processes, Waern (1980) has shown that readers are less criticial of a text when they are thinking aloud as they read. The same may be true for writing. Hammerton (1969) has shown that even reciting a familiar sentence (Mary had a little lamb) impaired performance on a sentence comprehension task (the 3-minute reasoning test; Baddeley, 1968). So further investigations, using other techniques, may find a higher incidence of interruptions to the writer's flow of expression.

It is also a little difficult to surmise what effect there might be on a writer's tolerance for interruptions if computer-based support of different kinds were made available. Would authors stop to check a reference more readily if they could do so without leaving their terminal, or is any interruption of the writing flow unacceptable to most authors?

In Table 2.7 it is suggested that dissatisfaction with the product is another reason for interrupting writing. Gould and Boies (1978) showed that novice users of a new authoring system (dictating) tended to be unjustifiably more critical of their output. This may relate to the observation that authors tend to make more revisions when using a text editor (Gould, 1981).

The willingness to rewrite and the ability to completely reorganize the material may well be something that becomes easier when certain computer-based support becomes available. For example, Perlman and Erickson (1984) have discussed the value of providing authors with diagrammatic outlines of the text they have produced. Such diagrams can indicate the various levels of embeddedness in the text and can show how much textual space has been devoted to each part. Comparing alternative arrangements of the text with the aid of such diagrams may be simpler than carrying out a series of cut and paste exercises on the printout.

Perhaps the most exciting developments for the readers and writers of electronic journals will come about when the readers themselves are able to make decisions interactively about the way the information is displayed to them. With advances in the technology of memory storage devices the choice of presentation medium could be very great, including dynamic video images of a quality comparable with film (cf. Cook, 1984).

Gould (1981) has commented on the potential of an audio rather than a visual message being received; but, as Nickerson (1984) pointed out, advances in technology highlight how much more we need to know about the cognitive consequences of different forms of information display, particularly the consequences for subsequent ease of manipulating the information.

In terms of more mundane options available with present technology, factors of economics and expediency may dictate whether the reader is shown a table or a graph. In principle, the readers of a computer-based text could be given the option of selectively transforming the data, in whole or in part, in any way they chose. In this sense, familiarity with the options available to them as writers is reflected in the new demands that people will make as readers. Providing material in a form that facilitates such transformations by readers is a new skill that writers may need to acquire. Similarly, before readers can exercise their new freedom adequately, they may need to develop new, and very different, executive processes from those that are currently within the repertoire of the skilled reader of paper-based materials.

Throughout this chapter, whether discussing the control of reading or of writing processes, very little has been said about the processes of comprehension. This omission was deliberate. Comprehension processes are of great importance, but they have been the almost exclusive focus of much of the research on reading. As Black and Sebrechts (1981) have pointed out, one advantage of applied research is that it leads to new and broader paradigms. The present intention was to emphasize that there are other executive control processes that are also important; strategies and tactics that operate at a higher, more global level than the comprehension of words, sentences, or paragraphs; executive strategies within which the processes of comprehension are nested. Of course, readers need to be able to understand what they read, and writers need to be able to generate written information that can be understood. The desirability of studying such processes is hardly contentious. But in this chapter we have tried to show that more than this is needed. There is little advantage in knowing that readers can understand the information, if in practice they cannot find it. Consideration of the problems of reading and writing for electronic journals serves to emphasize the contribution of these other executive control processes to the activities of reading and writing.

ACKNOWLEDGMENTS

I would like to thank Ann Lickorish for her contribution to the studies reported here, and also I express my gratitude to both Ann and Audrey Hull for their patience in sorting out the references cited in this chapter. My sincere appreciation goes to Professor Brian Shackel for his invitation to participate in the BLEND project, so promoting an interest in the issues discussed here, and to the British Library Research and Development Department who supported this work.

A very special thanks is due to Steve Platt who, as APU computer manager, facilitated access to the electronic journals (courtesy of Chris Idzikowski's software) and subsequently made it possible for a variety of different APU systems to communicate with each other. Without that help, this chapter would be available in electronic form only. Finally, my thanks to Thomas Green, Tom Landauer, and Mike Wilson for generously commenting on earlier drafts of this chapter. Their advice enhanced both the content and presentation of the ideas being put forward, which is not to say that they agreed with all of them.

REFERENCES

Aaronson, D., & Scarborough, H. S. (1976). Performance theories for sentence coding: Some quantitative evidence. *Journal of Experimental Psychology: Human Perception and Performance, 2,* 56–70.

Baddeley, A. D. (1968). A three-minute reasoning test based on grammatical transformation. *Psychonomic Science, 10,* 341–342.

Black, J. B., & Sebrechts, M. M. (1981). Facilitating human–computer communication. *Applied Psycholinguistics, 2,* 149–177.

Borenstein, N. S. (1984). *The evaluation of text editors: A critical review based on new experiments.* Manuscript available from the Computer Science Department, Carnegie–Mellon University, Pittsburgh.

Card, S. K., Moran, T. P., & Newell, A. (1983). *The psychology of human-computer interaction.* Hillsdale, NJ: Lawrence Erlbaum Associates.

Cherry, L. F., & Macdonald, N. H. (1983). The Unix writer's workbench software. *Byte, 8,* 241–248.

Coke, E. U. (1982). Computer aids for writing text. In D. H. Jonassen (Ed.), *The technology of text.* NJ: Educational Technology Publications.

Collins, A., & Gentner, D. (1980). A framework for a cognitive theory of writing. In L. Gregg & I. Steinberg (Eds.), *Cognitive processes in writing.* Hillsdale, NJ: Lawrence Erlbaum Associates.

Cook, P. R. (1984). Electronic encyclopedias. *Byte, 9,* 151–170.

Elkerton, J., & Williges, R. C. (1984). Information retrieval strategies in a file search environment. *Human Factors, 26,* 171–184.

Galbraith, D. (1980). The effect of conflicting goals on writing: A case study. *Visible Language, 14,* 364–375.

Gould, J. D. (1978). An experimental study of writing, dictating and speaking. In J. Requin (Ed.), *Attention and performance* (VII). Hillsdale, NJ: Lawrence Erlbaum Associates.

Gould, J. D. (1981). Composing letters with computer-baed text-editors. *Human Factors, 23,* 593–606.

Gould, J. D. (1982). Writing and speaking letters and messages. *International Journal of Man–Machine Studies, 16,* 147–171.

Gould, J. D., & Alfaro, L. (1984). Revising documents with text editors, handwriting and recognition systems. *Human Factors, 26,* 391–406.

Gould, J. D., & Boies, S. J. (1978). How authors think about their writing, dictating and speaking. *Human Factors, 20,* 495–505.

Gould, J. D., Conti, J., & Hovanyecz, T. (1983). Composing letters with a simulated listening typewriter. *Communications of the ACM, 26,* 295–308.

Haas, C., & Hayes, J. R. (1985). Reading on the computer: A comparison of standard and advanced computer display and hard copy. Tech. Rep. No. 7, Communications Design Center. Pittsburgh: Carnegie–Mellon University.

Hammerton, M. (1969). Interference between low information verbal output and a cognitive task. *Nature, 222,* 196.

Hartley, J. (1984a). Academic writing and postgraduate supervision. In R. M. Beard & J. Hartley (Eds.), *Teaching and learning in higher education.* London: Harper & Row.

Hartley, J. (1984b). The role of colleagues and text-editing programs in improving text. *IEEE Transactions on Professional Communication, 27,* 42–44.

Hayes, J. R., & Flower, L. S. (1980a). Writing as problem solving. *Visible Language, 16,* 388–399.

Hayes, J. R., & Flower, L. S. (1980b). Identifying the organization of writing processes. In L. W. Gregg & E. Steinberg (Eds.), *Cognitive processes in writing.* Hillsdale, NJ: Lawrence Erlbaum Associates.

Hebb, D. O., & Bindra, D. (1952). Scientific writing and the general problem of communication. *American Psychologist, 7,* 569–573.

Hiltz, S. R., & Turoff, M. (1978). *The network nation: Human communication via computer.* Reading, MA: Addison–Wesley.

Hulme, C. (1984). Reading: Extracting information from printed and electronic text. In A. Monk (Ed.), *Fundamentals of human–computer interaction.* London: Academic Press.

Kieras, D. E. (1985). *The potential for advanced computerized aids for comprehensible writing of technical documents.* (Tech. Rep. No. 17, TR-85/ONR-17), University of Michigan.

Lesgold, A. M. (1984). Human skills in a computerized society: Complex skills and their acquisition. *Behavior Research Methods, Instruments, and Computers, 16,* 79–87.

Levin, J. A., Boruta, M. J., & Vasconcellos, M. T. (1983). Microcomputer-based environments for writing: A writer's assistant. In A. C. Wilkinson (Ed.), *Classroom computers and cognitive science.* New York: Academic Press.

Light, L. I., & Anderson, P. A. (1983). Memory scripts in younger and older adults. *Memory and Cognition, 11,* 435–444.

Lovelace, E. A., & Southall, S. D. (1983). Memory for words in prose and their locations on the page. *Memory and Cognition, 11,* 429–434.

Macdonald-Ross, M., & Waller, R. (1975). Criticism, alternatives and tests: A conceptual framework for improving typography. *Programmed Learning and Educational Technology, 12,* 75–83.

Meadows, A. J. (1978). Documentation and the scientific producer/user. *Journal of Documentation, 34,* 324–332.

Mohammed, M. A. H., & Swales, J. M. (1984). Factors affecting the successful reading of technical instructions. *Reading in a Foreign Language, 2,* 206–217.

Monk, A. F., & Hulme, C. (1983). Errors in proofreading: Evidence for use of shape in word recognition. *Memory and Cognition, 11,* 16–23.

Moray, N. (1980). Towards an electronic journal. In P. A. Kolers, M. E. Wrolstad, & H. Bouma (Eds.), *Processing of visible language* (2). New York: Plenum Press.

Muter, P., Latremouille, S. A., Treurniet, W. C., & Beam, P. (1982). Extended reading of texts on television screens. *Human Factors, 23,* 529–540.

Neal, A. S., & Darnell, M. J. (1984). Text editing performance with partial-line, partial-page and full-page displays. *Human Factors, 26,* 431–441.

Nickerson, R. S. (1981). Understanding signs: Some examples of knowledge-dependent processing. *Information Design Journal, 2*, 2–16.

Nickerson, R. S. (1984). *Research needs on the interactions between information systems and their users: Report of a workshop.* Washington, DC: National Academy Press.

Nielsen, J. (1984). *How readers annotate textbooks and manuals.* Computer Science Department, Aarhus University, Denmark. ISSN 0105-8517.

Norrish, P. (1984). Moving tables from paper to CRT screen. *Visible Language, 18*, 154–170.

Perlman, G., & Erickson, T. D. (1984). *Graphical abstraction of technical documents.* Manuscript while the first author was at AT&T, Murray Hill, NJ; now at Wang Institute, Waltham, MA.

Peters, D. P., & Ceci, S. J. (1982). Peer review practices of psychological journals: The fate of published articles submitted again. *The Behavioural and Brain Sciences, 5*, 187–225.

Poller, M. F., & Garter, S. K. (1984). The effect of modes on text editing by experienced editor users. *Human Factors, 26*, 449–462.

Pullinger, D. J. (1984a). Design and presentation of Computer Human Factors journal on the BLEND system. *Visible Language, 23*, 171–185.

Pullinger, D. J. (1984b). Enhancing NOTEPAD teleconferencing for the BLEND electronic journal. *Behaviour and Information Technology, 3*, 13–23.

Rothkopf, E. Z. (1971). Incidental memory for location of information in text. *Journal of Verbal Learning and Verbal Behavior, 10*, 608–613.

Rothkopf, E. Z. (1982). Adjunct aids and the control of mathemagenic activities during purposeful reading. In W. Otto & S. White (Eds.), *Reading expository material.* New York: Academic Press.

Rothkopf, E. Z., & Billington, M. J. (1975). A two-factor model of the effect of goal-descriptive directions on learning from text. *Journal of Educational Psychology, 67*, 692–704.

Rudnicky, A. I., & Kolers, P. A. (1984). Size and case of type as stimuli in reading. *Journal of Experimental Psychology: Human Perception and Performance, 10*, 231–249.

Schank, R., & Hunter, L. (1985). The quest to understand thinking. *Byte, 10*, 143–155.

Senders, J. (1977). An on-line scientific journal. *Information Scientist, 11*, 3–9.

Shackel, B. (1982). The BLEND system—programme for the study of some electronic journals. *Computer Journal, 25*, 161–168. *Ergonomics, 25*, 269–284. *Journal of the American Society for Information Science, 34*, 22–30.

Shackel, B., Pullinger, D. J., Maude, T. I., & Dodd, W. P. (1983). The BLEND–LINK project on "electronic journals" after 2 years. *The Computer Journal, 26*, 247–254.

Shebilske, W. L., & Rotondo, J. A. (1981). Typographical and spatial cues that facilitate learning from textbooks. *Visible Language, 15*, 41–54.

Stewart, T. F. M. (1979). Eyestrain and visual display units: A review. *Displays*, 25–32.

Sticht, T. (1977). Comprehending reading at work. In M. A. Just & P. A. Carpenter (Eds.), *Cognitive processes in comprehension.* Hillsdale, NJ: Lawrence Erlbaum Associates.

Tombaugh, J., Lickorish, A., & Wright, P. (1987). Multi-window displays for readers of lengthy texts. Paper submitted for publication.

Twyman, M. (1982). The graphic presentation of language. *Information Design Journal, 3*, 2–22.

Waern, Y. (1980). Thinking aloud during reading. A descriptive model and its application. *Scandinavian Journal of Psychology, 21*, 123–132.

Waern, Y., & Askwall, S. (1981). On some sources of metacomprehension. *Scandinavian Journal of Psychology, 22*, 21–37.

Waern, Y., & Rollenhagen, C. (1983). Reading text from visual display units. *International Journal of Man–Machine Studies, 18*, 441–465.

Wason, P. C. (1970). On writing scientific papers. *Physics Bulletin, 21*, 407–408.

Wason, P.C. (1980). Conformity and commitment in writing. *Visible Language, 14,* 351–363.

Weyer, S. A. (1982). The design of a dynamic book for information search. *International Journal of Man–Machine Studies, 17,* 87–107.

Wright, P. (1980a). Usability: The criterion for designing written information. In P. A. Kolers, M. E. Wrolstad, & H. Bouma (Eds.), *Processing of visible language* (2). New York: Plenum Press.

Wright, P. (1980b). The comprehension of tabulated information: Some similarities between reading prose and reading tables. *National Society for Performance and Instruction Journal, 19,* 25–29.

Wright, P. (1981). Tables in text: The subskills needed for reading formatted information. In L. J. Chapman (Ed.), *The reader and the text.* London: Heineman.

Wright, P. (1986). Writing technical information. *Review of Research in Education, 14,* in press.

Wright, P., & Bason, G. (1982). Detour routes to usability: A comparison of alternative approaches to multipurpose software design. *International Journal of Man–Machine Studies, 18,* 391–400.

Wright, P., & Lickorish, A. (1983). Proofreading texts on screen and paper. *Behaviour and Information Technology, 2,* 227–235.

Wright, P., & Lickorish, A. (1984a). Ease of annotation in proofreading tasks. *Behaviour and Information Technology, 3,* 185–194.

Wright, P., & Lickorish, A. (1984b). Investigating referee's requirements in an electronic medium. *Visible Language, 18,* 186–205.

Wright, P., & Lickorish, A. (1987). Colour cues as location aids in lengthy texts on screen and paper. Paper submitted for publication.

Wright, P., Lickorish, A., & Whalley, P. (1985). *Experimental comparisons of reading lengthy texts on either CRT screen or paper.* Proceedings of FORUM '85, pp. 105–112. Available from Dantekom, Postbox 146, 7K–3600, Frederikssund, Denmark.

TYPOGRAPHY AND EXECUTIVE CONTROL PROCESSES IN READING 3

James Hartley
University of Keele, U.K.

READING AND EXECUTIVE CONTROL PROCESSES

Reading is a complex cognitive task. The simple word *reading* describes a skill that subsumes a number of different component processes, many of which are discussed in detail in other chapters of this textbook. In this chaper I begin by making a few simple and rather obvious remarks about reading which have relevance for the typographic setting of text. The aim of the chapter as a whole, however, is to suggest how the typographic design of text can support the component processes that readers must perform.

At the molecular level, reading involves discriminating between meaningful marks on paper, marks that come in all shapes and sizes. In addition, reading at the molecular level involves discriminating between the ordering of the marks and their grouping to form meaningful wholes or words. Clearly, the order of letters can have a profound effect on their meaning (compare *god* with *dog*), and so too can their spacing (compare *therapist* with *the rapist*). Punctuation also plays a part (compare *Give experience with dates* and *Give experience, with dates*), and so too does prior knowledge (consider *the young man the jumps* where the verb is *to man* the jumps . . .).

Normally, of course, we carry out these molecular processes unconsciously in pursuing the more global objectives of skilled reading (the search for the important ideas and meaning). We are not often aware of the fixations, the saccades, and the regressions of our eyes when we are reading. We are not concerned with the laborious blending of letters and

Box 1: An illustration of how the smallest of typographic conventions has to be learned.

Ann Henshaw asked 5-year-old children to explain to her why we had periods or "dots" at the end of sentences. A sample of the replies is as follows:

"Well . . . the ones with dots on *should* have dots on. It's the words . . . Well sometimes you *don't* need one. When you've had enough of doing dots you don't do one 'cos then it won't make your arm ache."

"Some words need them. Some words don't."

"It's for if you go off the page and go on to the desk . . . you stop . . . you don't start again . . . you start again after a minute or two."

"It's to tell you when they've finished."

"When they have to finish a page of writing they have them . . . if there's no room and you have to go on to another page they put a fullstop (period) there. Then they put a picture . . . then they go to another page . . . then a picture."

"It stops you from doing writing."

"It's at the end of your work you put one. You get told off if you don't."

"It's to finish a sentence. If you don't put a fullstop and you write a letter people might think you've forgotten to post the other half."

"Look," (reading 'It is another day,') "Then it is the fullstop. See? . . . I miss out a bit of my voice and then I start again."

Extracts from Henshaw, A. (1983) The fullstop. *Times Educational Supplement,* 15.7.83, p. 17. Reproduced with permission of the author.

sounds that so occupies the beginning reader, nor indeed are we concerned with the learning that goes on in connection with the simplest typographic conventions (see Box 1). All of this implies, as we shall see, that much of the discussion by typographers over typographic detailing (e.g., choice of typefaces, typesizes, spacing, etc.) is especially important for texts used by beginning readers.

People come to texts for many different purposes. They may be following instructions, searching for something that they have read before, or looking for something new. They may be skimming a text to get the gist of an argument, or they may be reading deeply so that they can recall and use the material in some forthcoming task. They may be reading for pleasure or because they are bored. Skilled readers may become more aware of using executive control processes when they deliberately search text, when they look for section headings, when they pause to read or reread parts that are more difficult, and when they stop to ask themselves questions about their understanding of the content (Anderson, 1980; Wong, 1985).

Not only do people read for many different purposes, but they also differ in many ways. Readers differ in their skills at reading, in their motivation, and in their cognitive styles. Some readers are more visualizers than verbalizers, some read more deeply than others, and some, if not all of them, adjust their reading methods to match the task they have in hand. And all of them, conceivably, are more skilled at reading particular kinds of materials than other kinds.

So when reading a text the reader (or executive) is faced with a number of activities, all of which compete for time and for resources. Different sets of activities are consequent on decisions about whether to read for gist, or whether to read for detail. In essence, the crucial problem is deciding where to go next. Should one plough on remorselessly, should one skip ahead, should one ignore a particular figure for the time being, and so on.

TYPOGRAPHY AND EXECUTIVE CONTROL PROCESSES

The purpose of this chapter is to indicate how the typography and the layout of a piece of text can help or hinder such executive control processes in reading. I consider how this can be done under four headings: typography, layout, typographic cueing, and "access structures." It is argued that typographic details can assist with the molecular unconscious processing and that layout can facilitate the reader's more global and conscious decision making.

However, before turning to these topics, note that when designing a text a typographic designer is being asked to provide a single solution to serve the multiple goals of, and the multiple differences between, individual readers. The aim, therefore, is to provide an optimal solution, but it has to be acknowledged at its outset that such a solution cannot meet all the requirements all the time for all possible readers. (Indeed, publishers and designers have remained peculiarly resistant to the notion of individual differences in readers.)

To some extent this is an exaggeration. The authors of texts are likely to know (at least roughly) the kinds of readers they can expect, and how they are likely to use the text. This knowledge can be conveyed to designers and they can then work within various constraints—certain page sizes, optimal line lengths, typesizes and interlinear spacing, for instance. However, as we soon see, within these constraints there is considerable room for maneuver. As the text *One Book: Five Ways* (1978) amply shows, there is no *one* agreed way of designing text.

Typography

Obviously, it is not possible in the few pages at my disposal to say a great deal about typography. (Readers interested in a fuller exposition might like to consult one or two of the following books: Berryman, 1984; Hartley, 1985; McLean, 1980; Rehe, 1974; Spencer, 1969; Watts & Nisbet, 1974.) Here, I just want to make some simple points.

Typesizes.   The measurement systems used in typography are varied and complex. Clearly there are many different typefaces and typesizes but, for all practical purposes, typographic designers are likely to choose between half a dozen typefaces and one or two sizes (with some exceptions for headings). Sizes generally vary in fact from around 4 point to around 14 point, but sizes of 8, 9, 10, 11, and 12 point are considered the most effective (see Fig. 3.1). One point in fact measures approximately 0.014 of an inch, and "typesize," in fact, refers to the depth of space required by one line of type "set solid," i.e., set with minimum line-to-line space. When discussing typesizes, it is also important to note that the size of the image conveyed by the same point size of different typefaces can in fact differ (see Fig. 3.2), and that the readers can in fact compensate for differences in typesize by adjusting their focal depth.

Typesize considerations are, however, important when using narrow column widths. Larger typesizes mean fewer words per line, and this may break the sense in these situations. This is an important factor to bear in mind in designing reading books for young children (Hartley, 1985),

8 point typesize affects line length as well as height

10 point typesize affects line length as well as height

12 point typesize affects line length as well as height

FIGURE 3.1   Different typesizes.

Typeface and typesize affects line length (8 point in Times Roman)

Typeface and typesize affects line length (8 point in Univers)

FIGURE 3.2   The same typesize in different typefaces produces different effects.

visually handicapped readers (Prince, 1967), and possibly older readers (Glynn & Muth, 1979).

Typefaces.   Typefaces can be divided into many different categories, but two main ones are serif and sans-serif faces. The text in Fig. 3.1 has been printed in a sans-serif typeface (i.e., without the small finishing strokes at the top and bottom of each letter) to illustrate the effect (and to illustrate how one can use a different typeface to signal a different function). Some researchers believe that serifs help to guide the reader's eye along each letter and word, but there is little conclusive proof for such assumptions (Hartley & Rooum, 1983). My own preference is generally for a serif face, largely because serifs force the letters to be more openly spaced and hence more legible. Words such as "illicit" can look very odd in a sans-serif typeface.

Spacing.   Letter spacing, word spacing, and line spacing are all important issues in designing text. Spacing that is too narrow can make it difficult to discriminate between the letters and the words. And, as we see next, I believe that reading is easier when the word spacing and line spacing are consistent throughout a text (see Fig. 3.3, 3.4, and 3.5).

Typographic Layout

When we turn from a consideration of particular typefaces, typesizes, and spacing to more global issues concerning the spatial arrangement of the text on the page, we are turning to the issues of typographic *layout*. Here it is important to consider at the outset some examples of inappropriate layouts. Inappropriate layouts produce errors in reading. They illustrate, therefore, routine executive control processes in action, albeit inappropriately. Errors illustrate how the readers' expectations can override what is actually present and lead to confusion. Consider the following examples.

Figure 3.6 shows an extract from a newspaper article. The author is describing the experience of driving a brewer's dray. Here the narrow line length and the unfortunate word breaks left me pondering for a moment over the meaning of "sepower" (thus suggesting I paid more attention to the start of the line than to its ending).

In this paragraph the text is
set solid, that is, no extra
space has been set between
the lines. Large amounts of
such text would be difficult
to read.

9 point set solid

In this paragraph one point of
"leading" (space) has been set
between the lines. This improves
the legibility of the text.

9 on 10 point

In this paragraph two points of
"leading" (space) have been set
between the lines. This is
thought of as the optimum amount
of line space.

9 on 11 point

FIGURE 3.3   The effects of interline spacing.

In this paragraph the text is
set solid, that is no extra
space has been added between
the lines. The text is also
"justified," that is it has a
straight left and right hand
margin. To achieve this the
word spacing is inconsistent.

9 point set solid, justified

FIGURE 3.4

In this paragraph the line
spacing is more appropriate.
The text is "unjustified,"
that is it has a ragged
right hand margin. This is
achieved by using consistent
spacing between the words.

9 on 11 point, unjustified

FIGURE 3.5

My first efforts earned John
Lawless's scorn: "Don't whis-
per at them! How do you
expect them to hear you over
all this traffic." The horses
eavesdrop on this banter, their
ears swivelling to catch our
conversation. If they are
disturbed at the feel of a novice
at the helm, they are at least
too well schooled to show it,
confining themselves to an
occasional toss of mane in
gentle protest. The thick
leather reins pull a raw pattern
on bare hands, and my arms feel
inches longer from the effort of
hauling a halt for red traffic
lights. But open air horse-
power does have some advantages over motorized traffic.

FIGURE 3.6

Figure 3.7 shows a table set in the middle of a two-column structure. The question that arises is: "Where do you go next when you arrive at the table?" The problem of where to go if there is a large table in a two-column structure is increased if there are additional small tables confined to the column widths. In this latter situation one skips over the inserts to continue reading: In the former case one expects to do so, but sometimes (as in Fig. 3.7) such an expectation will cause difficulties.

Figure 3.8 shows the design for an index of book reviews in a journal. Readers found this design confusing for it did not follow their expectations about how an index should be printed. This index has three major elements: book titles, authors, and the names of reviewers. Wright and Threlfall (1979) reported that in previous years the titles had been listed vertically in alphabetical order, and the author and the reviewer had been positioned on the same horizontal line to which they applied. However, the journal's indexer had decided that this layout might cause confusion if readers only knew the author or the reviewer and did not know the title. To solve this problem, the indexer alphabetized the information separately in all three columns. The links between the three columns were

(iii) Finally, we may note in this connection a different approach to measuring social desirability. After completing the above questionnaire the college of education students were divided into two groups: one group was asked to fill in the educational media questionnaire as they felt a " good teacher " might fill it in; the other as a " bad teacher " might fill it in. (Only one student queried the phrase a " bad teacher ".) This experiment was partly duplicated with a group of 18 teachers on a counsellors' course at Keele University. Table 5 shows the scores obtained by these subjects relative to the scores obtained when the questionnaire was completed personally. It may be observed that the students were able to

TABLE 5

ORIGINAL SCORES ON THE EUDCATIONAL MEDIA SCALE (22 ITEMS) COMPARED WITH THOSE OF THE " GOOD " AND THE " BAD " TEACHER FOR COLLEGE OF EDUCATION STUDENTS AND COUNSELLORS

		The " bad " teacher	Own score	The " good " teacher	Significance level of difference between own score and " good " teacher
College Students	$\bar{X}$	38·6	85·6	95·0	
	s.d.	11·5	8·7	6·7	$t = 5·4$ $p < 0·01$
	N	25	53	28	
Counsellors	$\bar{X}$		88·7	90·6	
	s.d.	—	6·3	9·7	n.s.d.
	N		18	18	

separate out the " good " and " bad " teachers quite distinctly (there was no overlap of scores), and that their own personal scores were significantly less than their " good " teachers. The personal scores of the counsellors, however, did not differ significantly from their " good " teachers' scores. Such findings as these suggest indeed that the questionnaire is open to pressures of social desirability.

It would seem valid, therefore, to conclude that the scale may be far from useful with regard to our secondary set of aims outlined at the beginning of this report, and that a different approach to the question of measuring teacher attitudes to new educational media might be more profitable. One approach that would take more time but would possibly be more fruitful, would be to attempt to measure what equipment was available in schools, who

used it, how often, etc. The beginnings of research in this direction have been described by Mackenzie, Jones and Payne (1970).

CONCLUDING REMARKS

There are a number of observations that—with the wisdom of hindsight—can be made here.

1. It is questionable whether it is possible to produce a single scale which measures the attitudes of all teachers to all aspects of new educational media. It might have been preferable, but certainly more arduous, to construct separate sub-scales for different media, and to standardise them on certain sections of the educational spectrum. It is interesting to note in this connection, however, that at least one item specific to certain kinds of

FIGURE 3.7 From page 148, Hartley, J., & Holt, J. (1971). Measuring teachers' attitudes to new educational media. *Programmed Learning & Educational Technology, 8,* 3, 143–150.

Book Reviews Index

Key to the Index

The bold number in square brackets after each book title (Column A) is the page number of the journal on which that book was reviewed.

The letter plus number combinations in round brackets which follow the square brackets denote the position down the columns of the author (Column B) and of the reviewer (Column C) of the book.

The letter plus number combinations in round brackets which follow each entry in Columns B and C refer to position down the A column of the book either written (Column B) or reviewed (Column C) by that name.

A	B	C
Book Title	*Author(s)*	*Reviewer*
1. Analysis of Variance in complex experimental designs. [204](B20)(C22)	Baddeley, A. D. (A20)	Annet, J. (A19)
2. Attention and performance V. [593](B13)(B30)(C7)	Beishon, J. (A26)	Atha, J. (A10)
3. Behavioural foundations of system development [336](B23)(C8)	Bell, C. R. (A14)	Brown, I. D. (A22)
4. Behavioural sciences: techniques of application. [201](B36)(C18)	Bignell, V. (A5)	Buzzard, R. B. (A13)
5. Catastrophic failures. [697](B4)(B27)(B29)(C13)	Broadbent, D. E. (A11)	Cherns, A. B. (A26)
6. Designtheorie, Vol. 2. [442](B7)(C10)	Brooke, J. D. (A10)	Corlett, N. (A9)
7. Environmental interaction: psychological approaches to our physical surroundings. [100](B10)(C16)	Bürdeck, B. E. (A6)	Davies, D. R. (A2)(A11)
8. Experimental studies of shift work. [594](B12)(B14)(B19)(B32)(C26)	Bures, J. (A27)	Edwards, E. (A3)
9. Human factors in work, design and production. [595](B22)(B38)(C6)	Buresova, (A27)	Fisher, G. H. (A29)

FIGURE 3.8   A design for a journal index. Reproduced with permission from *Ergonomics* (1977). *20,* 6, p. 709. Copyright © Taylor & Francis.

now provided by reference codes, and an introductory key to the index explained the new arrangement (see Fig. 3.8).

Wright and Threlfall studied users of the original and the revised index. They concluded that, although an attempt had been made to meet the readers' needs, the attempt was not successful because readers started out with different expectations about how the information would be presented.

These three illustrations indicate that problems arise in typography when the layout of the text is inappropriate. This problem has been one of my main concerns over the last 10 years or so. My argument has been that readers need to know (and to be able to tell at a glance) where they are going and where things are. They should never have to ask the question, "Where am I supposed to go from here?"

Rational spacing.   I have developed the case for the rational spacing of text in many places, and I only briefly present it here. (A full account is provided in Hartley, 1985). Essentially my argument is against the use of traditional justified text—that is to say the kind of text we are sharing now. As we can see, justified text has a balanced and a centered approach. Each page has a straight left- and right-hand margin, and each page starts at the same place at the top and stops at the same place at the bottom, regardless of the content.

To achieve horizontal and vertical justification, the space between the horizontal elements (the words) and the vertical elements (the paragraphs, subheading, etc.) is often varied and inconsistent. The approach that I employ uses consistent spacing between these elements. Thus, I use an equal word space between the words and this leads to a ragged right-hand margin. In addition, I use a proportional vertical spacing system between the vertical elements (e.g., one line space between paragraphs, one line space above but no line space below a secondary heading, and two line spaces above and one below a main heading). My system necessitates a "variable" rather than a fixed baseline for each page. The decision where to stop the text on each page is made on the basis of the content—both horizontally and vertically. Horizontally, one can stop at syntactic units (if one wishes). Vertically, one can stop at the end of a paragraph or before a heading if there is only one (or two) line(s) of text to go.

This approach is unlikely to have much effect on the reading and comprehension of text such as that presented in this chapter (so I have not objected to the traditional setting here). This is because this chapter consists mainly of continuous prose (with the occasional illustration). But some instructional text is much more complex than this. Instructions, directions, tabular insertions, lists, and diagrams present great difficulties for the traditional setting. Figures 3.9 and 3.10 provide a "before" and

5 How much change should you get from 50p when you spend: (a) 40p, (b) 20p, (c) 30p, (d) 10p, (e) 45p, (f) 25p, (g) 42p, (h) 38p, (i) 27p, (j) 34p, (k) 22p, (l) 17p?

6 How much change should you get from 100p when you spend: (a) 50p, (b) 70p, (c) 80p, (d) 40p, (e) 95p, (f) 75p, (g) 45p, (h) 25p, (i) 42p, (j) 38p, (k) 58p, (l) 16p?

1 Tom had 5p. He spent 3½p. How much had he left?
2 Jim had 10p. He spent 4½p. How much had he left?
3 Jean had 25p. She spent 6p on chocolate and 5p on sweets.
(a) How much did she spend?
(b) How much had she left?
4 John had 20p. He spent 9p on comics and 2p on sweets.
(a) How much did he spend?
(b) How much had he left?

5 Anne went out with 30p. She spent 8p on cakes and 7p on lemonade.
(a) How much did she spend?
(b) How much had she left?
6 Shirley had 50p. She bought sweets for 12p and biscuits for 9p.
(a) How much did she spend?
(b) How much had she left?

FIGURE 3.9 This shows a page from a junior school mathematics text (slightly reduced in size). On this page the child has first to work *across* from item 5 to item 6, and then *down* to items 1, 2, and 3, etc. Note that in answering questions 5 and 6 the child is likely to have difficulty in knowing exactly where he or she has got to because the subitems (a), (b), and (c), etc. are not clearly differentiated from each other. Similarly, the item numbers (1, 2, 3, etc.) are embedded in the text, and the actual items themselves are not sufficiently separated from each other by appropriate spacing.

"after" illustration to show how the argument for my approach is (at any rate for me) more viable with more complex text. Here, in the revision of the original text, the designer has used consistent horizontal and vertical spacing to make clearer its underlying structure.

My argument is that spacing is an important typographical tool. Appropriate spacing can convey structure at a glance; inappropriate spacing can confuse.

There is some evidence to support these views. Research on the effectiveness of spaced text has been carried out sporadically for some years now. (Overview summaries can be found in Hartley, 1981a, 1985; Keenan, 1984; Stone, 1981). My own (1985) survey concludes that there are sometimes instructional and sometimes financial gains to be achieved by designing text in the ways outlined above.

Typographic Cues to Aid Comprehension

In discussing typographic layout, I have been mainly concerned with the overall spatial arrangement of the text. For me, this is one of the most

5 How much change should you get from 50p when you spend:

a	40p	**e**	45p	**i**	27p
b	20p	**f**	25p	**j**	34p
c	30p	**g**	42p	**k**	22p
d	10p	**h**	38p	**l**	17p

6 How much change should you get from 100p when you spend:

a	50p	**e**	95p	**i**	42p
b	70p	**f**	75p	**j**	38p
c	80p	**g**	45p	**k**	58p
d	40p	**h**	25p	**l**	16p

1 Tom had 5p. He spent 3$\frac{1}{2}$p. How much had he left?

2 Jim had 10p. He spent 4$\frac{1}{2}$p. How much had he left?

3 Jean had 25p. She spent 6p on chocolate and 5p on sweets.
  a How much did she spend?
  b How much had she left?

4 John had 20p. He spent 9p on comics and 2p on sweets.
  a How much did he spend?
  b How much had he left?

5 Anne went out with 30p. She spent 8p on cakes and 7p on lemonade.
  a How much did she spend?
  b How much had she left?

6 Shirley had 50p. She bought sweets for 12p and biscuits for 9p.
  a How much did she spend?
  b How much had she left?

FIGURE 3.10   This shows the same information as that displayed in Figure 3.9, but it has been redesigned in terms of its spatial arrangement. (Figure courtesy of Peter Burnhill.) Source: Hartley, J. (1985). *Designing Instructional Text,* (2nd Ed.), New York: Nichols, p. 41.

important features of printed text, for it is the spacing of the text that conveys its structure. Nonetheless, typographic cues can be used to enhance both the textual and spatial components of the text. *Italic,* **bold** faces, CAPITAL LETTERS, <u>underlining</u>, color, and the like signal to the reader that something needs more of their attention. Such cues can indicate the importance of particular words and concepts, and they can also support the spatial organization of the text.

Readers find such cues helpful during initial reading and during later review sessions. Fowler and Barker (1974) showed that, when authors or designers failed to provide such cues, students generated their own.

Fowler and Barker surveyed 200 randomly selected used textbooks for sale in a college bookshop. They found that approximately 90% of these texts contained cues applied by the previous owners. These included underlining, highlighting in various colors, marginal notes, and boxes. The students had also added asterisks, parentheses, brackets, and exclamation marks!

Underlining.   Interestingly enough, there is a fair amount of research that contrasts experimenter-provided with student-generated underlining (see Anderson, 1980; Hartley, Bartlett, & Branthwaite, 1980; Wollen, Cone, Britcher, & Mindemann, 1985). The evidence suggests that student-generated underlining is *not* more effective than experimenter-provided underlining, and that experimenter or author-provided underlining is only effective when its purpose is explicitly explained to the reader, or when it is incorporated into some such study-scheme as Robinson's SQ3R method (Robinson, 1961) and its purpose is appreciated. Thus, many young children do not grasp the importance of underlining without instruction in its function.

Italic.   There has been very little research on the use of italic (or bold face) as a typographic cue to signal the importance of certain words. Perhaps this is because adults take this obvious function for granted. Research with italic (like that with capital letters) has been mainly confined to demonstrating that text printed in italic is harder to read than text printed conventionally (e.g., see Foster, 1979; Foster & Bruce, 1982; Tinker, 1965). Nonetheless, italic has been successfully used to stress certain words in order to enhance a particular perspective on a passage (Meyer, 1985; Meyer & Rice, 1980; Pratt, Krane, & Kendall, 1981).

One possible source of confusion in instructional text arises when the same cue is used to signify different things. Italic is often used to draw attention to something (e.g., How are the seeds *attached* to it?), to introduce technical terms (What color is the seed coat or *testa*?), to particularize (Can the testa be removed easily with a *dissecting* needle?), to provide a heading (*Feeling the bean*), or to indicate the title of a book (In the *Biology of the Bean,* the author . . .). It seems sensible, as a rule of thumb, to try to restrict the number of things signified by one particular cue, especially in children's texts.

Color.   Color is a major typographic cue that is used in instructional materials for rather different purposes. Color can be used functionally to aid instruction, or decoratively for aesthetic or motivational reasons.

A good example of the functional use of color is provided by the map of the Paris Metro system. Here several different colors are used and each one denotes a different route. (In addition each route is numbered, which provides a back-up facility for the color-blind). Such a use of color is a useful ingredient in line-drawings and illustrations—particularly technical ones (Dwyer, 1978). Again, the conventions that adults accept so naturally have to be taught to children.

In a useful review of the problems of using a second color functionally in printed text, Waller et al. (1982) point out that a second color may be useful:

- where pointer lines linking labels to diagrams might be confusing if only one color is used;
- where a colored grid might be superimposed over a black and white illustration to indicate, for example, some sort of grouping; and
- where there might be two or more levels of text running in parallel (e.g., study guidance being differentiated by color from mainstream subject matter).

It may also be useful—and attractive—to use a second color for headings. Nonetheless, I argue here that if only one or two extra colors are to be used, they must be used consistently and only where it seems necessary to make a point. There is no need to use color on every page simply because it is technically possible to do so.

The debate about whether or not to use color, and if so how many colors to use, arises in situations where color is not absolutely necessary. Particular difficulties arise when using too many colors, and when using too few colors (say, two only) to denote more than two functions. In electronic text, of course, color takes on a more important role. The problems of presenting different colors on different colored backgrounds are discussed by Tinker (1965) for printed text, and by Hartley (1985) for electronic text.

Multiple Cueing.   It is clear from this discussion that there are many ways of cueing important words or phrases, and indeed, many designers are often tempted to use more cues than necessary. We might well ask, for example, if a heading is printed in capital letters, does it also need to be larger, in bold face, and in a different color? What little research there has been on this topic does indeed suggest that multiple cueing can be confusing. Hershberger and Terry (1965) conclude their article by saying "Simple typographic cueing significantly enhances the ratio of important to unimportant content learned without reducing the total amount learned," but "Complex typographic cueing (distinguishing five categories of lesson content) does not appear to benefit the reader in the least."

Access Structures

The term *access structure* was coined by Waller (1979) to describe devices that help the reader gain access to the text and to read it in variety of ways. Access structures use both spatial and typographic cues to group relatively large chunks of text and to sequence them appropriately.

In this section I briefly consider five kinds of access structures: summaries, headings, numbering systems, references, and boxed materials. We need to note here that there are many others: for example, contents pages, lists of tables and figures, page numbers, running headings, footnotes, indexes, different ways of denoting new paragraphs and sections, and so on. I have reviewed the research on these additional devices elsewhere (Hartley, 1985).

In terms of this chapter, it is important to note that there has been very little research on the typographic setting of access structures. There is no research to my knowledge on the effectiveness of different typographic settings for headings, summaries, or boxed materials, although there is a little on the spatial positioning of adjunct questions, headings, and illustrations (see Hartley, 1985).

Summaries. Turning to the more global access structures, it appears that summaries can aid the recall of salient facts, although there is some debate about whether they do this better if they are placed at the beginning or the end of a piece of text (see Hartley & Trueman, 1982). Some authors, of course, distinguish between and use different kinds of summaries. Thus, *overview* summaries presented at the beginning provide a description of what is to follow in general terms, *interim* summaries sum up the argument so far, and *review* summaries, placed at the end, summarize what has gone before, often using the more technical terminology introduced in the text itself.

Headings. My research (and that of others) on the effectiveness of headings and subheadings suggests that headings can aid recall, and in addition, they can help readers find and retrieve information from text (Hartley & Trueman, 1985). There is some debate over issues such as the frequency of headings, their length, their position (marginal or embedded), their style (e.g., headings written in the form of statements vs. headings written in the form of questions), and their quality (poor headings can mislead). I have discussed this research in my (1985) article with David Jonassen.

Numbering systems. Writers often use numbering systems to help sequence their text. Headings and sections in technical materials are frequently numbered 1.00, 1.01, 1.02, 2.00, etc. Some of these numbering systems that are supposed to aid retrieval can be confusing, especially when there are references in the text to other numbering systems—page numbers, chapter numbers, section numbers, table numbers, figure numbers, different appendices, and so on. Figure 3.11 gives an illuminating example.

Lists. The research on the setting of contents pages, references, bibliographies, and indexes is characterized by the fact that each of these devices is a *list-structure*. Each consists of a string of main elements all of which contain a number of subelements. The task of the designer is to display both the main elements and each subelement clearly because different people will want to use the list in different ways. As one of the participants explained in one of my experiments on the design of journal contents pages: "If I am looking to see if X has a paper, then I want to scan the names; if I am browsing through journals to see if there is a topic of interest to me, then I need to skim through the titles; if I am hunting for a specific article, then I need to find the author." The way the designer

26.1.2   A modern coastal environment

The idea of interpreting the past in terms of the present sounds extremely simple, but there are many practical difficulties. An insight into the extent of these can be gained by considering a present-day environment from a geological point of view.

So, you should now read the section in Chapter 13 of *Understanding the Earth* entitled 'environmental analysis—the beach' (pp. 180–5).

When you read this section, examine Figure 14 in Appendix 3 (p. 34), which summarizes information on the sediments and faunas of a modern beach. Plate A and TV programme 26 are about this area. *Make sure you have examined Figure 14 thoroughly and have read pp. 180–5 of* Understanding the Earth *given above before viewing the television programme.* The post-broadcast notes will refer you to Appendix 3 which describes a 'geological model' of this stretch of coast and summarizes the sequence of 'rocks in the making' in this environment.

FIGURE 3.11. An example of a piece of text with multiple numbering systems. For further discussion of this issue, see Waller (1977).

normally solves this problem is to use a judicious mixture of spatial and typographic cues so that the different elements and subelements in the list stand out in some way from each other.

My own research in this area indicates that an important feature in the design of a list-structure is its *spatial* arrangement. Whereas readers prefer a combination of spatial and typographic cues to indicate each element in a particular list-structure, when given a choice between a spatial arrangement without typographic cues and continuous text with typographic cues, readers generally prefer the spatially arranged text

Box 2   The role of boxes

Glynn et al. (1984) point out that authors frequently seek to extend the readers' comprehension of the main ideas in an instructional text by including supporting information such as examples, anecdotes, and bibliographies. Often, one way of handling such material is to treat the information as a figure, and to box it off from the main body of the text and to use a different typeface and/or typographic setting. The idea here, presumably, is that by being separated from the main text the information provided in the box is seen as separate, and adjunct, and that it is less likely to interfere with either the author's presentation or the readers' comprehension of the main ideas.

Some authors have provided interesting comments on the problems of dealing with this ancillary material (e.g., Armbruster & Anderson, 1985; Schumacher, 1985), but I know of no research enquiry into the effectiveness of such procedures. However, if one examines what writers and reviewers of instructional texts have to say, one can discern here how such materials may affect executive processing. Consider, for example, this extract from James Thomas' (1984) review of four introductory psychology textbooks:

> On the negative side, the text includes many boxed inserts presenting "Critical Issues" and "Applications." I object to this common approach for two reasons. First, these inserts disrupt the logical flow of the running text. If the application or issue is important enough to be boxed, why not include it in the running text and avoid breaking the reader's train of thought? Second, the boxed inserts exaggerate the importance of single, non-replicated research findings. In many cases, these boxes report unusual, unexpected, or sensational research or applications that have not been adequately evaluated. Their appearance in an introductory textbook, especially in a highlighted position, seems to legitimize these findings and applications, whereas they should still be regarded as tentative. These concerns apply to three of the texts under review. (p. 631)

(Hartley, 1981b; Hartley & Guile, 1981). The spatial arrangement, of course, needs to reflect the underlying organization of the text and to match readers' expectations (Wright & Threlfall, 1979).

DESIGNING TEXT TO ENCOURAGE DEEPER PROCESSING

As noted previously, typographic designers face a problem in that they have to provide one single optimum solution for different readers and different reading purposes. I conclude this chapter by discussing how the development of reading skills (and thus the use of executive control processes) can be enhanced by writers and designers employing devices that will encourage deeper processing by the reader. Again, however, I know of no research on typographic settings for the ideas I am discussing.

In my introduction I pointed out that readers vary in their reasons for reading, in their ability and motivation, and in their styles of approach. One particular distinction currently receiving much attention is that between "surface" and "deep" approaches to reading (Biggs, 1985; Marton, 1975). The surface reader skims the text, retains isolated facts, and is not concerned with the overall structure or the argument of the text. The deep reader, on the other hand, searches for the underlying structure of the text, questions it, relates ideas in the text to his or her own prior knowledge and experience, and so on. Crudely putting it, the deep approach is seen as superior to the surface approach—especially as far as study skills are concerned (see Marton, Hounsell, & Entwistle, 1984; Schumacher, this volume).

This distinction between "surface" and "deep" approaches is of course only one of many similar ones. Thomas and Bain (1984) point out that parallel notions can be discerned in the distinctions drawn between meaningful and rote learning (Ausubel, 1963), transformational and reproductive learning (Biggs, 1973), generative and reproductive processing (Wittrock, 1974), comprehension and operation learning (Pask, 1976), and elaborative processing and fact retention (Schmeck, 1983).

However, whatever terminology is used, the question is, how can one encourage a deeper approach to reading? One answer might be to identify executive control strategies in reading and persuade readers to practice them. Table 3.1 indicates some of the many variables that have been explored in this respect.

Clearly, I am arguing for instruction in techniques of skilled reading. I am not sure that this would do any harm and conceivably it might do some good. As we have already seen in this chapter, children appear to need instruction in the typographic conventions that adults take for granted.

TABLE 3.1
Some Representative Reviews of Strategies That Encourage Deeper
Text Processing

Studies/Reviews	Readers Were Encouraged/Taught to:
Maxwell, 1972	Skim the text in advance
Jonassen, 1984a	Underline/highlight key points
Davies, 1976	Read with objectives in mind
Robinson, 1961	Read with questions in mind
Robinson, 1961	Turn headings into questions
Hartley & Jonassen, 1985	Construct their own headings
Gagne et al., 1984	Make "elaborations"
Jonassen, 1984a, b	Take notes from the text
Dansereau, 1978 Jonassen, 1984b	Construct cognitive maps (or patterned notes and/or networks)
Davies & Green, 1984	Categorize information (by constructing tables, diagrams, graphs)
Duchastel, 1983	Summarize the text
Brown & Deloache, 1978 Brown et al., 1981	Practice metacognitive skills such as: predicting checking monitoring reality testing
Davies & Green, 1984	Carry out some of the above activities in pairs or small groups as well as individually

In addition, however, many of the strategies listed in Table 3.1 can be built into instructional text so that readers are obliged to carry them out in order to follow the text. Thus, I would like to see (along with Armbruster & Anderson, 1985, and Jones, Friedman, Tinzmann, & Cox, 1984) "coherent texts," texts that are written for specific groups of readers, texts that use language with which readers are familiar, texts that include experiences that readers share, and texts that provide meaningful examples. I would also like to see texts that ask their readers questions as they go along (not just in the headings, or at the end), and texts that provide examples and problems that readers actually have to work through in order to follow the exposition. (I have provided examples of such texts in my chapters in the books edited by Branthwaite & Rogers, 1985; and Gellatly, 1986).

It may be that electronic text can be better developed than printed text in these respects. The kind of text that I am advocating might not always be best presented in the form of continuous prose. With electronic text, it might be easier to slot in different examples and different routes for different readers (Pullinger, 1984). However, such a text would require considerable typographic expertise for its presentation in printed or electronic form. Indeed, effective presentation in the latter would be extremely difficult because electronic text is highly restricted in certain ways (especially in terms of typefaces, line lengths, spacing, and knowing where you are). Electronic text, however, does have color, animated graphics, and possibly sound. And, because electronic text is so "chopped up," there is more emphasis on practicing and using executive control processes in reading it than there is with conventional print.

SUMMARY

1. Poor typographic practice can misdirect and/or slow down executive control processes in reading.
2. Good typographic practice clarifies the underlying structure of a text and assists executive control processes in reading.
3. The typographic layout of the page is of crucial importance in denoting the underlying structure of the text. In complex text the horizontal and vertical spacing should be consistent. The reader should never have to ask, "Where do I go from here?"
4. Typographic cues emphasize the importance of key words or concepts by manipulating the typography of the text.
5. Access structures use both layout and typographic cues to enable readers to gain access to the text at particular points: They also indicate sequence and structure.
6. There has been virtually no research on different typographic settings for access structures, but research with access structures suggests that it is important to teach children to appreciate the typographic conventions that skilled readers take for granted.
7. Text can be designed to encourage deeper processing, but such text will require considerable typographic expertise to ensure its effectiveness. The nature of electronic text may force readers to practice more overtly executive control processes in reading.

ACKNOWLEDGMENTS

I am indebted to Peter Burnhill, David Michael, and anonymous reviewers for helpful comments on an earlier draft of this chapter.

REFERENCES

Anderson, T. H. (1980). Study strategies and adjunct aids. In R. J. Spiro, B. C. Bruce, & W. F. Brewer (Eds.), *Theoretical issues in reading comprehension.* Hillsdale, NJ: Lawrence Erlbaum Associates.

Armbruster, B. B., & Anderson, T. H. (1985). Producing considerate expository text or easy reading is damned hard writing. *Journal of Curriculum Studies, 17,* 3, 247–263.

Ausubel, D. P. (1963). *The psychology of meaningful verbal learning.* New York: Grune & Stratton.

Berryman, G. (1984). *Notes on graphic design and visual communication.* Los Altos, CA: Kaufmann.

Biggs, J. B. (1973). Study behavior and performance in objective and essay formats. *The Australian Journal of Education, 17,* 157–167.

Biggs, J. P. (1985). Student approaches to learning and essay writing. In R. R. Schmeck (Ed.), *Learning styles and learning strategies.* New York: Plenum.

Branthwaite, A., & Rogers, D. R. (Eds.). (1985). *Children growing up.* Milton Keynes: Open University Press.

Brown, A. L., Campione, J. C., & Day, J. D. (1981). Learning to learn: On training students to learn from texts. *Educational Researcher, 10,* 14–21.

Brown, A. L., & DeLoache, J. S. (1978). Skills, plans, and self-regulation. In R. S. Siegler (Ed.), *Children's thinking: What develops.* Hillsdale, NJ: Lawrence Erlbaum Associates.

Dansereau, D. F. (1978). The development of a learned strategy curriculum. In H. F. O'Neil (Ed.), *Learning strategies.* New York: Academic Press.

Davies, F., & Greene, T. (1984). *Reading for learning in the sciences.* London: Oliver & Boyd.

Davies, I. K. (1976). *Objectives in curriculum design.* London: McGraw-Hill.

Duchastel, D. C. (1983). The use of summaries in studying text. *Educational Technology,* June, 36–41.

Foster, J. J. (1979). The use of visual cues in text. In P. Kolers, M. E. Wrolstad, & H. Bouma (Eds.), *Processing of visible language.* New York: Plenum.

Foster, J. J., & Bruce, M. (1982). Reading upper and lower case on Viewdata. *Applied Ergonomics, 13,* 2, 145–149.

Fowler, R. L., & Barker, A. S. (1974). Effectiveness of highlighting for retention of text material. *Journal of Applied Psychology, 59,* 3, 358–364.

Gagne, E. D., Weidemann, C., Bell, M. S., & Anders, T. D. (1984). Training 13-year-olds to elaborate while studying text. *Human Learning, 3,* 4, 281–294.

Gellatly, A. (Ed.). (1986). *The skilful mind.* Milton Keynes: Open University Press.

Glynn, S. M., Britton, B. K., Tillman, M. H., & Muth, K. D. (1984, April). *Typographical cues in text: Management of the readers' attention.* Paper to AERA Convention, New Orleans. (Copies available from S. M. Glynn at the Department of Educational Psychology, University of Georgia, Athens, Georgia, 30602).

Glynn, S. M., & Muth, K. D. (1979). Text learning capabilities of older adults. *Educational Gerontology, 4,* 253–269.

Hartley, J. (1981a). Eighty ways of improving instructional text. *IEEE Transactions on Professional Communication, Vol. PC-24,* 1, 17–27.

Hartley, J. (1981b). Spacing the elements in references. *Applied Ergonomics, 12,* 1, 7–12.

Hartley, J. (1985). *Designing instructional text* (2nd ed.). New York: Nichols.

Hartley, J., Bartlett, S., & Branthwaite, J. A. (1980). Underlining can make a difference— sometimes. *Journal of Educational Research, 73,* 218–224.

Hartley, J., & Guile, C. (1981). Designing journal contents pages: Preferences for horizontal and vertical layouts. *Journal of Research Communication Studies, 2,* 271–288.

Hartley, J., & Jonassen, D. (1985). The role of headings in printed and electronic text. In D. Jonassen (Ed.), *The technology of text* (Vol. 2). Englewood Cliffs, NJ: Educational Technology Publications.

Hartley, J., & Rooum, D. (1983). Sir Cyril Burt and typography. *British Journal of Psychology, 74,* 2, 203–212.

Hartley, J., & Trueman, M. (1982). The effects of summaries on the recall of information from prose: Five experimental studies. *Human Learning, 1,* 1, 63–82.

Hartley, J., & Trueman, M. (1985). A research strategy for text designers: The role of headings. *Instructional Science, 14,* 2, 99–155.

Hershberger, W. A., & Terry, D. F. (1965). Typographical cueing in conventional and programmed texts. *Journal of Applied Psychology, 49,* 55–60.

Jonassen, D. H. (1984a). Effects of generative text processing strategies on recall and retention. *Human Learning, 3,* 4, 241–256.

Jonassen, D. H. (1984b). Developing a learning strategy using pattern notes: A new technology. *Programmed Learning & Educational Technology, 21,* 3, 163–175.

Jones, B. F., Friedman, L. B., Tinzmann, M., & Cox, D. E. (1984). *Content driven comprehension instruction and assessment: A model for army training literature* (Tech. Rep.). Alexandria, VA: Army Research Institute.

Keenan, S. A. (1984). Effects of chunking and line-length on reading efficiency. *Visible Language, XVIII,* 1, 61–80.

Marton, F. (1975). What does it take to learn? In J. Hartley & I. K. Davies (Eds.), *Contributions to an educational technology* (Vol. 2). New York: Nichols, 1978.

Marton, F., Hounsell, D., & Entwistle, N. (Eds.). (1984). *The experience of learning.* Edinburgh: Scottish Academic Press.

Maxwell, M. J. (1972–3). Skimming and scanning improvement: The needs, assumptions and knowledge base. *Journal of Reading Behavior, 5,* 1, 47–59.

McLean, R. (1980). *The Thames and Hudson manual of typography.* London: Thames & Hudson.

Meyer, B. J. F. (1985). Signaling the structure of text. In D. H. Jonassen (Ed.), *The technology of text* (Vol. 2). Englewood Cliffs, NJ: Educational Technology Publications.

Meyer, B. J. F., & Rice, G. E. (1980). *Signaling in text.* Paper to APA Convention, Montreal. (Copies available from the authors, Department of Educational Psychology, Arizona State University, Tempe, AZ 85281.)

One book five ways: The publishing procedures of five university presses (1978). Los Altos, CA: Kaufmann.

Pask, G. (1976). Styles and strategies of learning. *British Journal of Educational Psychology, 46,* 128–148.

Pratt, M. W., Krane, A. R., & Kendall, J. R. (1981). Triggering a schema: The role of italics and intonation in the interpretation of ambiguous discourse. *American Educational Research Journal, 18,* 303–315.

Prince, J. H. (1967). Printing for the visually handicapped. *Journal of Typographic Research, 1,* 1, 31–47.

Pullinger, D. (1984). The design and presentation of the *Computer Human Factors* journal on the BLEND system. *Visible Language, XVIII,* 2, 171–185.

Rehe, R. F. (1974). *Typography: How to make it most legible.* Carmel, IN: Design Research International.

Robinson, F. (1961). *Effective study* (rev. ed.). New York: Harper & Row.

Schmeck, R. R. (1983). Learning styles of college students. In R. F. Dillon & R. R. Schmeck (Eds.), *Individual differences in cognition* (Vol. 1). New York: Academic Press.

Schumacher, G. M. (1985). Reaction to "Americans Develop Plans for Government." *Journal of Curriculum Studies, 17,* 3, 263–267.

Spencer, H. (1969). *The visible word*. London: Lund Humphries.

Stone, J. (1981). The effect of format and the number of arguments on comprehension of text by college undergraduates. In L. J. Chapman (Ed.), *The reader and the text*. London: Heinemann.

Thomas, J. M. (1984). Four introductions to psychology. *Contemporary Psychology, 29*, 8, 629–632.

Thomas, P. R., & Bain, J. D. (1984). Contextual dependence of learning approaches: The effects of assessments. *Human Learning, 3*, 4, 227–240.

Tinker, M. A. (1965). *Bases for effective reading*. Minneapolis: University of Minnesota Press.

Waller, R. H. W. (1977). Notes on transforming No. 4. In J. Hartley (Ed.), *The psychology of written communication: Selected readings*. New York: Nichols, 1980.

Waller, R. H. W. (1979). Typographic access structures for instructional text. In P. A. Kolers, M. E. Wrolstad, & H. Bouma (Eds.), *Processing of visible language*. New York: Plenum.

Waller, R. H. W., Lefrere, P., & Macdonald-Ross, M. (1982). Do you need that second color? *IEEE Transactions on Professional Communication, Vol. PC-25*, 2, 80–85.

Watts, L., & Nisbet, J. (1974). *Legibility in children's books*. London: National Foundation for Educational Research.

Wittrock, M. C. (1974). Learning as a generative process. *Educational Psychologist, 11*, 87–95.

Wollen, K. A., Cone, R. S., Britcher, J. C., & Mindemann, K. M. (1985). The effect of instructional sets upon the apportionment of study times to individual lines of text. *Human Learning, 4*, 2, 89–103.

Wong, B. Y. L. (1985). Self-questioning instructional research: A review. *Review of Educational Research, 55*, 2, 227–268.

Wright, P., & Threlfall, M. S. (1979–80). Readers' expectations about format influences the usability of an index. *Journal of Research Communication Studies, 2*, 99–106.

TYPOGRAPHY AND READING STRATEGY 4

Robert Waller
Institute of Educational Technology
The Open University, U.K.

Typography may be broadly defined as "the visual attributes of written language." Although at a certain level of analysis a spoken sentence may be said to be roughly the same as its written equivalent, it is never exactly the same in substance or effect. Writing both diminishes and enhances: diminshes because it offers only a crude and unreliable version of vocal pitch, timing, gesture, and tone; and enhances through spatial organization, graphic emphasis, and through the clues about its origin offered by the tool used to write, whether an aerosol or a computer display. It is *typography* that has both enhanced and diminished the subtlety of the message.

We can go further and say that there are some kinds of written language that have no spoken equivalent: A table, for example, contains the potential for a large number of interactions between row and column headings. A skilled reader of tables can perceive patterns in the data such as would be impossible should the information be read out aloud—in the case of a large table, a long and tedious process. The reading of tables demands a greatly more active and purposeful involvement of the reader than does the relatively passive process of scanning sequential prose—it is hard to conceive of a bottom-up model of table reading. Instead, as Wright (1981) argues, the reading of a table involves the purposeful application of a conscious strategy by a reader in possession of appropriate skills.

---

*Robert Waller is a lecturer in textual communication research at the Open University. His research interests focus on typography and diagrams and he is editor of *Information Design Journal*.

This chapter discusses some problems of accounting for the role of typography in this exercise of strategy, or *executive control* in reading. This term is used loosely here to refer to those deliberate (although not necessarily articulated) choices that readers must make to read a text in a particular order or at a particular pace, to start reading and to stop, to skip or skim. The importance of strategic skills has been demonstrated by Thomas (1976) and Pugh (1979), who found that readers who employed active reading strategies were more effective in achieving their goals than those who simply read through a text once at an even pace. Active reading strategies include initial skimming, look-backs, rereading, changes of pace, and pauses for thought.

This strategic level of the reading process is usually distinguished from the detailed comprehension or memorizing of text at the clause or sentence level. Active reading strategies are a manifestation of meta-cognitive processes which Brown (1980) describes as the "debugging" as distinct from the "automatic pilot" state of reading. Metacognition means "knowing about knowing"—it involves an awareness of how much you know about a particular subject, how much you don't know, and what you need to find out to achieve a particular goal you may have. Textbook writers need to be aware that very young readers may not have reached the level of development needed to make decisions about the relevance of printed material to particular tasks. The developmental nature of meta-cognitive skills may explain why Hartley, Kenely, Owen, and Trueman (1980) found that, whereas headings worded as statements made little difference in the ability of children to learn from text, headings worded as questions (that is, whose relevance was explicit) did result in increased recall. There is some evidence that the use of punctuation, too, is related to maturity. Baldwin and Coady (1978) found that punctuation was usually ignored as a syntactic cue by young readers. It may be that other perceptual cues such as typography and diagrams are also only appreciated by those who have reached appropriate stages of metacognitive development.

Effective strategy is dependent not only on the reader possessing an appropriate level of skill but also on a text which makes its structure clear enough for strategy to be formulated. Typography is one of a range of cuing systems that authors can use to signal the structure of arguments in text. This chapter explores the kinds of reasoning that readers might use to interpret it.

OBSERVING READING STRATEGIES

As part of a research program on text design, we have at various times collected evidence about the effect of typography on reading strategy.

An Official Form

Figure 4.1 shows two versions of the same form which we developed and evaluated for a British government department (Waller, 1984). In this case our evidence was derived from the location of missed questions on completed forms. A large number of people filling in the first version failed to answer any questions in section 7. They had, it seems, moved straight into 8 from 6, and from there they had moved to the next page. By changing the order of the sections, the problem was solved.

Users of this form seemed to be applying to whole layouts a basic rule that we all use for reading lines of type: Every time you finish a linear segment of the text, you go to the next one below and to the left.

A Health Education Textbook

Figure 4.2 shows a double page spread from a health education textbook aimed at a general adult audience. The publishers used a highly graphic format which it was hoped would be attractive and easy to read.

We recorded the reading strategy of adult subjects using a light-pen apparatus developed originally by Whalley (Whalley & Fleming, 1975). Subjects have to read in a dimly-lit room with a flashlight attached to a joystick suspended from above. The flashlight projects an adjustable rectangular beam slightly wider than the column of type, and about four lines high. The joystick is connected to a microcomputer which records its movement and later prints out a graphic plot of the read, and a table analyzing the time the subject spent in each block of text. Advantages and disadvantages of this apparatus and other ways of recording reading behavior are discussed in more detail by Schumacher and Waller (1985).

In Fig. 4.2, first paragraph of the first column, the author instructs readers to compare three scenarios illustrated in comic strip form. They should then return to the first column and continue reading. We predicted that, if these readers operated the same rule as those who filled in the form, they would fail to return after reading the cartoons and instead go straight to the section below.

A second prediction concerned the relationship between the second and third cartoons. Speech balloons that overlap the following frame are normally used by artists as a horizontal cue to direct the reader sideways. Here they are used incorrectly and the two cartoons are visually merged into one; the illusion is compounded by the insignificant numbering of the cartoons, and the fact that the same characters appear in all three.

In practice, the first problem never occurred and the second was not significant. Although readers used a variety of strategies to integrate their reading of the cartoons with the discussion of them in the text, most succeeded in reading all the cartoons and all the text, and moving

6 Money due to you

- **Are you** (or your partner or children living with you) **owed any money?**
(for example holiday pay, maintenance payments, redundancy pay)

  yes ☐   no ☐

  If you ticked no, go straight to part 7, 'More about money'

  If you ticked yes, tell us how much you are each owed. what it is for and when you expect to get it

  [ ]

7 More about money

- **Do you** (or your partner) **get child benefit?**

  yes ☐   no ☐

  If you ticked yes, say how much you get

  £ [ ] .

- **Do you** (or your partner or children living with you) **get mobility or attendance allowance?**

  yes ☐   no ☐

  If you ticked yes, say which allowance and how much you get

  [ ]   £ [ ] .

- **Do you** (or your partner or children living with you) **get any other social security benefit?**
(such as family income supplement, unemployment benefit, disablement benefit, sickness benefit, maternity benefit, retirement pension)

  yes ☐   no ☐

  If you ticked yes, say which, and how much.

  [ ]   £ [ ] .

- **Do you** (or your partner or children living with you) **have any other money coming in?**
(such as maintenance, court order or pensions from work)

  yes ☐   no ☐

  If you ticked yes, say what it is and how much

  [ ]   £ [ ] .

  Now go to the top of the next column

'More about money' continued

- **Do you** (or your partner) **have any of these?**
You must tick one box for each line

current bank accounts	no ☐	yes ☐	£ .
deposit bank accounts	no ☐	yes ☐	£ .
Post Office or Nat. Savings Bank	no ☐	yes ☐	£ .
building society	no ☐	yes ☐	£ .
premium bonds	no ☐	yes ☐	£ .
shares and unit trusts	no ☐	yes ☐	£ .
cash and other savings	no ☐	yes ☐	£ .
National Savings Certificates	no ☐	yes ☐	issue number / no of units

- **If you have children who live with you, please list their savings here.**

  If they have no savings, tick here ☐

  [ ]

- **Apart from where you live, do you own any property?**
(This includes any property or land owned by you, your partner or children who live with you)

  yes ☐   no ☐

- **Do you** (or your partner or children living with you) **have any life assurance or endowment policies?**

  yes ☐   no ☐

  If you ticked no, go straight to part 8, 'People living with you'

- **Give details of your life assurance or endowment policies**
(List year each policy was taken out and the amounts for which you are assured. If you don't know the amount assured, tell us how much you pay each month)

19	£
19	£
19	£

---

8 People living with you
- **List below all the people living with you.** If none, tick here ☐

	their names	their relationship to you or your partner	their date of birth (or 'over 18')	do you get child benefit for them?	do they get supplementary benefit?
Your partner					yes ☐ no ☐
Children under 16 who live with you				yes ☐ no ☐	
				yes ☐ no ☐	
				yes ☐ no ☐	
				yes ☐ no ☐	
Children over 16 who live with you				yes ☐ no ☐	yes ☐ no ☐
				yes ☐ no ☐	yes ☐ no ☐
Anyone else who lives with you (include boarders and subtenants) If none, tick here ☐				yes ☐ no ☐	yes ☐ no ☐
					yes ☐ no ☐

Now go to the top of the next page

FIGURE 4.1 Two versions of an official form for welfare claimants. When the wide "People living with you" section was at the foot of the page, many respondents missed the right-hand column. Moving it to the top of the page solved the problem. (Draft versions of the B1 Supplementary Benefit Postal Claim Form reproduced with permission of the Controller of Her Majesty's Stationery Office).

6 People living with you

- **List below all the people living with you.**
  If none, tick here ☐

	their full names	their relationship to you or your partner	their date of birth	do you get child benefit for them?	do they get supplementary benefit?
Your wife or partner					yes ☐ no ☐
Children under 16 who live with you				yes ☐ no ☐	
				yes ☐ no ☐	
				yes ☐ no ☐	
				yes ☐ no ☐	
Children 16 or over who live with you				yes ☐ no ☐	yes ☐ no ☐
				yes ☐ no ☐	yes ☐ no ☐
Anyone else who lives with you (say if they are boarders)					yes ☐ no ☐
					yes ☐ no ☐

7 More about money

- **Do you** (or your partner) **get child benefit?**
  yes ☐ no ☐
  If you ticked <u>yes</u>, say how much you get
  £ .

- **Do you** (or your partner or children living with you)
  get mobility or attendance allowance?
  yes ☐ no ☐
  If you ticked <u>yes</u>, say which allowance and how much you get
  £ .

- **Do you** (or your partner or children living with you)
  get any other social security benefit?
  (such as family income supplement, unemployment benefit, disablement benefit, sickness benefit, maternity benefit, retirement pension)
  yes ☐ no ☐
  If you ticked <u>yes</u>, give details below.

which benefit do you get?	
how much do you get?	£ .
how often do you get it?	

- **Do you** (or your partner or children living with you)
  have any other money coming in?
  (such as maintenance, court order or pensions from work)
  yes ☐ no ☐
  If you ticked <u>yes</u>, give details below.

what kind of income?	
how much do you get?	£ .
how often do you get it?	

  Now go to the top of the next column

More about money continued

- **Do you** (or your partner) **have any of these?**
  You must tick one box for each line

current bank accounts	no ☐ yes ☐	£ .
deposit bank accounts	no ☐ yes ☐	£ .
Post Office or Nat. Savings Bank	no ☐ yes ☐	£ .
building society accounts	no ☐ yes ☐	£ .
premium bonds	no ☐ yes ☐	£ .
shares and unit trusts	no ☐ yes ☐	£ .
cash or other savings	no ☐ yes ☐	£ .
National Savings Certificates	no ☐ yes ☐	issue number / no. of units

- **If you have children who live with you, please list their savings below.**
  If they have no savings, tick here ☐

- **Apart from where you live, do you own any property?**
  (This includes any property or land owned by you, your partner or children who live with you)
  yes ☐ no ☐

- **Do you** (or your partner or children living with you)
  have any life assurance or endowment policies?
  yes ☐ no ☐
  If you ticked <u>yes</u>, give details below
  (List the year each policy was taken out and the amounts for which you are assured. If you don't know the amount assured, tell us how much you pay each month)

19	£
19	£
19	£

  Now go to the top of the next page

85

Asserting yourself

Relationships are a matter of give and take. You tell people what you want. You try to understand what they want.

How can you do it without falling into the traps we talk about in the earlier topics? Look at the cartoons on these two pages and decide which is most typical of you when you try to stick up for yourself.

Passive, hostile or assertive?

The first cartoon shows a passive exchange. Mabel approaches Bill timidly. She is apologetic. She is vague about what she wants. Bill hardly bothers to listen. He doesn't even register that there is a problem.

The second cartoon shows a hostile exchange. Mabel is really steamed up. She attacks Bill but she doesn't really say what she wants him to do. The conversation escalates. They exchange insults. Bill slams out of the house.

In the third cartoon strip, Mabel gets what she wants. Bill agrees to 'talk about the problem'. Why? What has happened that is different? Mabel has asserted herself. She has worked out beforehand what she wants to say. She is concrete about exactly what she wants Bill to do. She persists. She is not put off.

Asserting yourself or asserting your rights is part of good, clear communication. People sometimes think that being assertive means being pushy, selfish or manipulative. It doesn't.

You are more likely to be manipulative if you adopt a passive role like Mabel in the first cartoon. This Mabel will probably get back at Bill by sulking, crying or secret acts of revenge. She might 'forget' to wash his socks.

You are more likely to be selfish and pushy if you adopt the hostile approach. The hostile approach assumes that no compromise is possible. The only gains will be those won by force. Blaming, anger and making others feel guilty are the weapons in both cases.

Asserting yourself means first working out what you want, then saying it clearly and negotiating with others. If you are assertive, you retain your dignity and leave others the chance to retain theirs.

What do you do?

Most people have times when they find it difficult to assert themselves. Someone puts you down. Someone takes advantage of you. You get bad service in a shop. You can't stand up to someone in authority. You feel timid, anxious, or shy. You find a 'good reason' for not making a fuss. And you don't get what you want.

Think of some occasions where this sort of thing has happened to you recently. Write them down, on a separate piece of paper, like the example from Mabel below. For each one make sure you write down what happened, who you were with, where you were, when it happened, how often this has happened before.

Think of at least four events of your own to write down.

What happened?	Who with?	Where?	When?	How often has this happened before?
When I made a comment about politics to Jane, Bill said 'Oh Mabel, you don't know what you're talking about'	Bill	At a party	Last week	Every time we meet his friends

FIGURE 4.2   A spread from the Open University course P921 *Health Choices* (a continuing education course for a general adult audience). (© The Open University, 1980.)

For the four events you have written down, tick any of the following feelings you experienced at the time:

	1	2	3	4
sad				
hostile				
bewildered				
frightened				
shy				
resigned				
inadequate				
self-conscious				
stupid				
inferior				

Tick any of the following bodily reactions you felt:

	1	2	3	4
'butterflies in the stomach'				
blushing				
going weak at the knees				
dry mouth				
increased pulse				
heart thumping				
shallow breathing				
hot flushes				
sweating				

And any of the following rationalisations you made to yourself:

	1	2	3	4
it's not worth making a fuss about				
perhaps I'm being selfish				
it's only once				
no-one else is complaining				
it won't make any difference				
I don't want to make a scene				

You now have the information you need to start changing your behaviour to become more assertive. Look through your list of situations. Decide which was the most threatening to you.

Decide which was the least threatening. And which came in between. The more ticks you made on the three checklists above the more threatening or upsetting the situation probably was. Use this as a rough guide to help you judge.

Now pick one of your medium-threat situations. This is the situation you are going to work on for the rest of this topic. If you choose a very threatening situation to work on it is likely to be too upsetting for you to do much about at first. If you pick one with very little threat it will be such a pushover that you won't learn anything.

87

correctly to the next section, headed "What do you do?" Figure 4.3 shows a typical subject's strategy. She reads the first cartoon, returns to the discussion until the second one is mentioned, at which point she reads the other two cartoons.

Figure 4.3 also illustrates a third prediction we made about this page. At the bottom right of the spread is a "student activity" in which students are asked to identify their responses to four events in their lives. It is divided into three sections and so presented in three columns. Below is a single discussion which is also laid out in three columns, but here the column breaks are arbitrary. However, the discussion is separated from the activity by very little space and only a very thin line. We were worried that readers would read straight down each column in turn, ignoring the break between sections.

We were right this time. Almost everyone did read in this manner, sometimes scanning back over previous columns to make sense of what they were reading. Why, though, did our predictions not work out before? The difference is that the author had explicitly instructed readers to return to the first column after looking at the pictures; and because she had mentioned three cartoons, the readers consciously looked for and found three, not two as we predicted. Similarly, we have found that readers are more likely to look at pictures if they are specifically referred to in the text. "Atmosphere" pictures without captions or textual reference are unlikely to be attended to (except perhaps in peripheral vision not picked up by our apparatus).

Interpreting Reading Strategies

In practice, the interpretation of reading strategy data is something of a problem. In some cases you can count looks-back and looks-forward, but where illustrations and activities are integrated into a complex multicolumn layout, the aggregated results hide the variety of individual strategies. It is also difficult to define error at the strategic level of the reading process. We cannot assume that where readers are looking actually reflects what they are thinking about—apparently eccentric strategies may result in perfectly effective reading (that is, the achievement of goals). In fact, Thomas (1976) reported that readers who frequently changes pace, regressed, or looked ahead achieved more than those who progressed at a predictable and even pace.

Considering these examples together, it appears that ambiguous typographic arrangements can be disruptive, but that the risk is lessened if the typography suggests a more "natural" flow through the page or if authors provide explicit verbal instructions. This is consistent with the findings of Whalley and Fleming (1975), who recorded the strategies of readers of

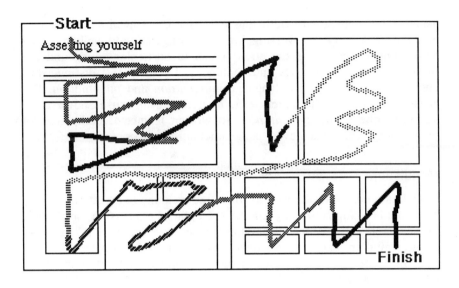

Line style changes every 30 seconds

FIGURE 4.3   The strategy of a typical reader.

illustrated technical magazines. But it would be premature to translate those conclusions directly into prescriptive guidance for writers without attempting first to integrate them into a broader argument about the way readers use typography to form judgments about the nature and structure of text. How, then, does typography relate to other aspects of language?

TYPOGRAPHY AS PARALANGUAGE

The graphic appearance of written language has attracted little comment from linguistic scientists. Indeed, de Saussure (1974), generally regarded as the father of modern linguistics, considered written language to be secondary to spoken language and so off the linguistic agenda: "Language and writing are two distinct systems of signs; the second exists for the sole purpose of representing the first" (p. 23). Those who have noted graphic factors have done so in the context of the more interdisciplinary areas of text linguistics and stylistics (for example, Bernhardt, 1985; Crystal & Davy, 1969). Bolinger (1975) probably reflects the general verdict of linguists when he refers in passing to "paragraphology" in parallel to paralinguistics.

Linguists use the term *paralanguage* to describe things that speakers do that affect the interpretation of what they are saying, but that have not usually been considered strictly linguistic (that is, to do with the structure of sentences). Pointing, winking, waving, shrugging, and smiling are all paralinguistic, and so is the stress given to particular words and the rhythm or tone of phrases and sentences. Lyons (1977) distinguishes between two kinds of paralanguage, *modulation* and *punctuation*. Because Lyons uses the latter term in a technical sense, however, I substitute the term *segmentation*. In written language, both kinds of paralanguage can be achieved using punctuation marks.

Modulation

Modulation describes the way in which the meaning of an utterance may be colored or emphasized by tone of voice, facial expression, or gesture. For example, a sentence like "Don't be boring" may be taken as an insult, a mild protest at an idea rejected, or a joke, depending on how it is said. In written language we can achieve a similar, but still ambiguous, effect by italicizing a word or adding an exclamation mark ("Don't be boring!"). Advertizing copywriters have developed this use of punctuation to a fine art: the period after short headlines, single word sentences, frequent paragraph breaks with excessive indentation. These "score" our reading of the advertisement (the musical term is suggested by Nash, 1980) in imitation of an intimate television voice-over—"Kleeno. Because you care."

Our writing system has normally been considered inadequate, though, by linguists wishing to transcribe speech in its full paralinguistic richness. They have had to invent special notations to give some impression of rises and falls in pitch and the relative stress given to parts of a sentence. It is possible to use italics and bold type to add some vocal quality to writing but it quickly becomes absurd. At the discourse level, though, typographic modulation is common. Textbook designers, for example, often specify different typographic "voices" to distinguish among, say, the main text, quotations, captions, and study guidance.

Segmentation

In writing, punctuation marks developed to score the "performance" of a text by reading aloud. This involved the indication of not only boundaries, but also the way the text should be modulated by tone of voice—question marks, irony marks, and exclamation marks were suggested (they didn't all catch on). During the late 18th and 19th centuries, syntactic theories of punctuation were often preferred to the earlier elocutionary theories (Honan, 1960). Syntactic theories saw punctuation as a means of segmenting sentences in order to make their grammatical structure clear. According to the elocutionary model, the various stops (full point, comma, semicolon, colon, dash) represent different lengths of pause. Taken literally, this might mean that a dramatic mid-sentence pause would require a full point rather than a comma. The syntactic theory explains why this would be an error because a full point marks sentence boundaries; subdivisions of sentences are marked by lesser stops. Most readers and writers today would agree with both views. Full points do bound sentences, but it is still possible to direct the reader's "performance" within the sentence by using a stronger stop—dashes, perhaps—instead of commas.

Typography can be described as a system of "macropunctuation" at the discourse level, where the text still has to be segmented and its status indicated (Waller, 1980). For example, one function of punctuation is to enable the interpolation of a text segment within a larger unit without destroying its continuity. Within the sentence this is normally achieved by parentheses, dashes, or commas. On a larger scale, typographic and spatial distinctions are used—footnotes, boxed panels, or marginalia. Series of items, placed between commas within the sentence, can be indicated by spacing and the use of "bullets" at the level of the page, and by title pages or display headings at the book level. Like sentence-level punctuation, macropunctuation has the dual function of directing the reader's strategy and explaining the structure of a document.

PURPOSES OF TYPOGRAPHIC SEGMENTATION

If the function of punctuation at the sentence level, and typography at the discourse level, is to divide the text into segments and to indicate how those segments are related, the question follows: Why segment the text, and where? What is the reader to construe from the various boundaries marked out on the typographic page—the paragraphs, sections, marginalia, and so on?

Although the sentence is a relatively uncontroversial linguistic unit, basic to our understanding of English syntax, graphically signalled units such as the paragraph have no such solid grammatical foundation. As de Beaugrande (1984) points out: "a 'sentence fragment' is a more reasonable notion than a 'paragraph fragment' " (p. 304). An ungrammatical sentence is judged as such by publicly agreed rules, intuitively obvious to native users of a language; a poor paragraph break is a matter of opinion, easily forgiven, easily corrected. You obviously can't scramble words and expect them to be reassembled into sentences. You can often do it with sentences or paragraphs, particularly if their boundaries coincide with topic or episode boundaries "natural" to the argument being expounded in the text.

Nash (1980) suggests that it is more helpful to think of the paragraph as a rhetorical rather than a grammatical unit. Paragraph breaks may be introduced for a number of reasons, none of which is strictly rule-bound in a grammatical sense. These may include the marking of topic boundaries implicit in the "content" of the text (that is, real stages or subdivisions in something being described), the signalling of rhetorical steps in an expository argument, or the emphasis of a particular point. The fact the paragraphs are not grammatical units does not make them less useful to readers in their effort to understand—rather the opposite, because rhetoric is essentially the tool that writers use to give structure and relevance to their arguments and to comment on that structure through forward reference, summary, and recapitulation.

This distinction between the grammatical sentence and the rhetorical paragraph is in practice somewhat blurred. Writers often manipulate sentence length for rhetorical reasons; and rhetorical structure can create such strong anticipations in the readers that an unexpected turn throws them as much as any grammatical error. This is particularly true of typography, where readers expect an exceptionally high degree of consistency in the way text components are signalled.

De Beaugrande (1984) emphasizes these similarities between sentence structure and paragraph structure through his theory of linear action which, he suggests, accounts for the way writers and readers are able to manage the transition between complex multidimensional "cognitive space" and linear linguistic sequences. He uses the same principles of linearity (see Table 4.1) to explain how both sentences and paragraphs work in sequences, and to account for conventions of punctuation. The importance of de Beaugrande's theory is that it suggests a unified view of a range of textual phenomena that we are accustomed to think about separately. Thus, Table 4.1 extends his linear principles to typography, or macropunctuation.

Authors also cope with the linearity problem by explicitly addressing it. For example, they may voice an anticipated question ("I expect you are wondering . . .") or summarize ("Up to now I have been discussing . . ."). This "metalanguage" provides explicit support for particular components of normal reading by, for example, identifying the topic or the conclusion, enumerating the main points, and drawing connections between different parts of the text. The metalinguistic function is often enhanced through typographic signalling. Some educational materials, for example, contain a second level of commentary that is typographically distinguished from the main argument.

TABLE 4.1.
The first two columns list the seven principles of linearity (de Beaugrande, 1984: p. 153) in tabular form. The third column is my application of them to typographic signalling.

Principle	De Beaugrande's Explanation	My Application to Typography
Core-and-adjunct	distinguishes between core and peripheral entities	Marginalia, typographic cuing
Pause	allows the on-line sequence to be retarded or suspended	Interpolated boxes or inserts, footnotes
Look-back	subsumes all consultations of the prior discourse	Regularity of layout pattern, tabular structure
Look-ahead	subsumes all anticipations of the subsequent discourse	Regularity of layout pattern, tabular structure
Heaviness	concerns gradations of importance, emphasis, focus, length, salience, or novelty, in the sense that these all draw a "heavier" load on processing.	Typographic emphasis, spatial isolation
Disambiguation	deals with excluding alternative patterns, both formal and conceptual	Use of layout to direct reading sequence, to group related items
Listing	handles the enumeration of comparable items in a sequence	Bullets, tabular structure

Segmentation for Accessibility

Although writing, being linguistic, is obviously linear in its most basic format, it is less restricted by this limitation than speech, which is bounded by time. For example, one strategy used by both speakers and writers to cope with the linearity of language is called the *look-back principle* by de Beaugrande; this covers parallel constructions, alliteration and rhyme, anaphoric reference, and other ways in which an audience can be reminded of preceding text. Whereas these things are essential for both readers and listeners, readers have the advantage of being able to check for themselves. They can literally look back to the preceding text, not just to their memory of it. They can do so not just when the writer alludes to it, but when some logical or cognitive problem, unpredicted by the writer, presents itself. This *accessibility* of text liberates the reader from the unidirectional linearity of written language.

Although breaking away from a strict adherence to the author's sequence, the exercise of accessibility is not obstructed by the fact that language is linear. Rather, it relies on the knowledge that there is a reliable linear structure in the text that made sense to the writer. Even the most active reading strategies (for example, of the bookshop browser) still involve periodic compliance with the writer's intended sequence. The ethnomethodologists' concept of turn-taking (Sacks, Schegloff, & Jefferson, 1974) recognizes that there is a limit to the degree to which conversations (or active reading, in our case) can be interactive. For effective communication to take place you have to be quiet, suspend your disbelief, listen to what the other person has to say, and make an effort to understand until some mutually agreed signal allows you to interrupt or take your turn.

This suggests one explanation about why text is chunked at the sentence, paragraph, and chapter (and, perhaps, other) levels. You have to finish the chunk before you can complain that it is erroneous. Each level of chunking, though, is subject to a particular level of error. A single word risks lexical error, a sentence risks grammatical error, a paragraph risks irrelevance, and a chapter risks poor argument. According to this theory, then, the higher level boundaries—between paragraphs, chapters, and similar units of text—are turn-taking cues in the "conversation" between writer and reader.

A form of dialogue is obviously more possible when we use a reference book designed for easy access, but it has been argued that even continuous prose is more conversational than it appears. According to this view, writers "converse" with an imagined reader whose questions and objections must be met. Conversational theories have appeared in the literature of rhetoric (Gray, 1977), applied linguistics (Widdowson, 1979; Winter, 1977), and among literary critics of the "reader-response" school (Tompkins, 1980). Crudely summarized, the conversational view is one in which writers address themselves to an imagined reader (sometimes referred to as a "mock," "virtual," or "implied" reader), whose characteristics and attitudes the real reader is able to perceive and assume. It is argued that just like a participant in a conversation, the imagined reader has particular questions or objections that must be met at the right time. Thus, we are asked to empathize with radically different personalities in order to make sense of books by, say, Austen and Hemingway. As real readers, naturally, we will ask different questions but must suspend our disbelief and hope that they will be answered in the author's good time.

Conversational theories are the subject of vigorous debate and represent only one among a range of theories of author–text–reader relations. However, we need not demand that each theory be exclusive. Readers may simultaneously operate at different levels of analysis, switching among different reader-roles: a close identification with the imagined reader, a goal-directed strategy of their own, and the distanced view required for critical scrutiny.

Authors of instructional texts, like novelists, address themselves to imagined readers—often defined by entry qualifications or evaluation data. Even so, the needs of actual readers are often unpredictable and vary too much to be handled within the linear sequence of normal prose. It is because they must enable readers to control their own access to information that nonfiction texts use typographic and graphic features to a degree rare in fiction. Because such features map out the structure of a text in a visual, accessible way, readers are to some extent freed from the narrative and able to move around the text as they please.

The implications of the accessibility of written and printed text for human culture are momentous, as Eisenstein (1979) and others have documented. The key advantage of the written word is that it enables knowledge to be stored in a publicly accessible form, relieving the memory burden that oral cultures impose. In literate cultures, it is more important to know where information may be located than to know the information itself.

THE PRESUMPTION OF RATIONALITY

Elsewhere (Waller, 1982), I have contrasted syntactic and artifactual typographic effects. Many aspects of typography—for example, the distinction between different categories of information or levels of heading—are under the direct control of the writer and can be considered as reliably meaningful. Others, though, are arbitrary effects of the manufacturing process—the location of page breaks, for example, changes as a book moves from first draft to typescript and into print.

This effect was called *linear interruption* by Twyman (1979) in his schema for describing graphic language. The interruption of the linear flow is of little importance when a text consists largely of typographically simple prose—we regard it as always acceptable to break lines in the middle of sentences, and often in the middle of words. But where the typography has been used to shape or, in effect, to diagram the structure of prose, artifactually imposed boundaries can be more disruptive.

The problem is that although some aspects of typography are thus arbitrary or out of the writer's control, readers cannot necessarily tell which. Although most readers are also writers and know about the arbitrariness of page breaks from personal experience, there is a considerable asymmetry of expertise in more technical aspects of publishing. Few readers have personal experience of the restrictions imposed by different printing equipment on such things as the setting of vertical rules, the choice of typeface and size, the printing of illustrations, and the use of color and tints.

In the absence of this technical insight, readers can only assume that what they see is a unified discourse in which all elements—typographic and linguistic—are marshalled purposefully with communicative intent. They must use what they see as a basis for reasoning about the structure of the writer's message. As Grice (1975) has shown, people are well accustomed to constructing scenarios that make sense of apparently illogical or unconnected data.

Grice's "cooperative principle" has been influential as an account of the role of inference in our interpretation of utterances (and other human acts). Grice points out that apparently illogical conversations are perfectly well understood in everyday situations. For example, why should "We have no potatoes" make sense as a response to "Where are you going?" The answer can be inferred because we assume that other people will cooperate in a conversation. If we therefore believe that the apparently unconnected response is likely to be relevant to the question, we can then search for the intended implication—in this case, "I'm going to the grocery store." At the heart of Grice's theory of conversational implicature are four maxims governing the appropriateness of contributions to a conversation (Grice's elaborations of them are paraphrased here):

Quantity: make your contribution as informative as is required.

Quality: do not say what you do not believe to be true.

Relation: be relevant.

Manner: avoid ambiguity of expression.

By requiring us to take on the character of an imagined reader, the literary author can, in effect, ensure that all of Grice's conversational maxims are satisfied. Writers of functional text, though, cannot address the imagined reader in the same way as the author of fiction, and they may not know much about their real readers. They cannot take responsibility, in particular, for the *relevance* of information for every individual reader and so provide elaborate access structures (indexes, contents lists, headings, and so on) to compensate. The matter of *quantity* is also important; one advantage of literate over oral culture is that authors can develop long and complex arguments that take many hours to study, uninhibited by the readers' limited attention span. If a reliable structure of accessibility is provided, though, the responsibility can be more fairly transferred to the purposeful reader using metacognitive skills.

If Grice accurately describes our normal assumptions about the communicative intent of others, then everything about a page of type is potentially informative, correct, relevant, and clear. On what basis might readers impute rationality to typographic pages?

A GRAMMAR OF TYPOGRAPHY?

One possibility is that typographic pages, like sentences, might be subject to grammatical rules. Indeed, publishers use long and detailed style manuals to guide the presentation of printed matter. Reference texts in particular, such as dictionaries or bibliographies, rely on the strictly consistent use of type variation to indicate the status of text components. But because these conventions are almost invariably explained at the beginning of each text, and because they differ among publishers, they can be better regarded as formalized local systems rather than evidence that there is a natural grammar of typography regulated by usage among a language community.

Popular books on graphic design (an inclusive term for typography, illustration, and other visual arts) often talk as if there is a language of visual imagery that mirrors verbal language. Booth-Clibborn and Baroni (1980), for example, claim that they "have analyzed the graphic language over the last few decades and have found that a universal grammar emerges." Thompson and Davenport (1980) claim similarly that "graphic design is a language. Like other languages it has a vocabulary, grammar, syntax, rhetoric." If there is a grammar of typography, we might expect to be able to recognize the function of various components of a document simply by their typographic treatment. We would expect to be floored by a document that presented information ungrammatically. But a brief analysis of almost any type of document disappoints us.

Figure 4.4 represents the jackets of two books on a nearby shelf as I write. I correctly interpreted the first as a book called *Tom Jones* by an author called Henry Fielding. I may have deduced that either from a typographic rule (that, in the absence of specific linguistic formulation "This is a book called X, written by Y, published by Z," the title is printed larger than the author's name), or from my knowledge that there is a famous 18th-century author called Henry Fielding—although Tom Jones (the singer) might be a more familiar name to those who didn't happen to study Fielding at school. If I applied this typographic "rule" to the next book, I would conclude that it is a book called *Mary Stewart* by an author called The Gabriel Hounds. I didn't, of course, but not because I knew in advance of an author named Mary Stewart (I didn't). I simply knew that dogs can't write. I therefore rejected the typographic rule and added to my general knowledge the fact that there is an author called Mary Stewart who, in the publisher's view, everyone else has probably heard of.

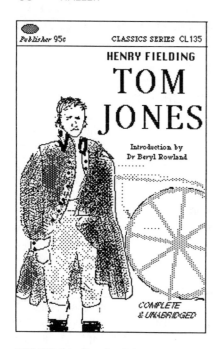

FIGURE 4.4   Two book jackets, redrawn for clarity. The publishers' trademarks have been deleted for copyright reasons.

These two approaches to language interpretation have been described as *linguistic* and *ethnomethodological* (Widdowson, 1979). Whereas a linguist might look for logical rules linking linguistic (or in our case typographic) signals and patterns to meanings, to be shared by the creator and interpreter of a document, the ethnomethodologist is more interested in the practical reasoning that occurs on an actual occasion of language interpretation (e.g., in a bookshop), reasoning that usually goes beyond knowledge of language systems to include all our knowledge of social interaction. We can apply the same principle to the interpretation of a simple sentence such as "The cat is ___ the mat." Our identification of the missing word is not just a matter of parsing the grammar of the sentence. We must also use commonsense knowledge to reject unlikely options. "The cat is on the mat" resembles a reading primer cliché and is selected in preference to, say, "the cat is mending the mat." Had the subject of the sentence been human, this might be as good a guess.

PRACTICAL REASONING

Widdowson's distinction echoes de Saussure's classic definition of *langue* and *parole*—language and speech, or language system and language use

TABLE 4.2
De Beaugrande and Dressler's seven standards of textuality (de
Beaugrande & Dressler, 1981: p. 37) transcribed into tabular form.
The third column is my application to the Mary Stewart book jacket.

Category	De Beaugrande and Dressler's Explanation	My Application to Fig. 4.4
Cohesion	Grammatical dependencies on the (text) surface	Title is usually larger than author, but . . .
Coherence	Conceptual dependencies in the textual world	'The Gabriel Hounds' is less likely to be the author than Mary Stewart. Her name is emphasised because . . .
Intentionality & acceptability	The attitudes of the participants towards the text	We know that the publisher wants to stress the information that will sell most books. We want to choose a book.
Informativity	The incorporation of the new and unexpected into the old and expected	The title or author may or may not relate to our interests, mood, or cultural awareness
Situationality	The setting	The text is on a book which is for sale
Intertextuality	The mutual relevance of separate texts	It looks like other books we have or have not enjoyed (genre of romantic fiction)

(de Saussure, 1974). Similarly, de Beaugrande and Dressler (1981) distinguish between *virtual* and *actual* systems: "Whereas a language is a virtual system of available options not yet in use, the text is an actual system in which options have been taken from their repertories and utilized in a particular structure." They go on to describe seven standards of textuality that characterize actual texts. Table 4.2 lists these in table form to demonstrate why, using practical reasoning, we still understand the cover of the Mary Stewart book in spite of an apparent breakdown of the first standard, cohesion.

These seven factors bring together things found in the text and things that lie outside of it. They thus form a useful account of how we reason about actual texts in a practical or pragmatic way.

The general knowledge and cultural attitudes that we bring to texts can lead to quite definite expectations about the content and design of different types of text. Although the typography of the two book jackets was inconsistent, I had clear expectations of what should be on a book jacket: author, title, publisher, price, "blurb," and so on. It may be that there are *models* for book jackets and other text types.

Because publishers usually treat book jackets as part of a packaging and marketing operation, they have much in common with other examples of packaging. Table 4.3 shows how similar components can be identified in both the book jackets illustrated in Figure 4.4 and two other examples of the "packaging" text type I find near me as I write (Fig. 4.5).

The question arises: How do we identify the text type of a particular document? In rare cases it is explicitly labeled—*notice, warning, advertisement feature, application form*—but often its visual appearance is the first clue. Romantic novels, forms, instruction leaflets, newspapers, technical manuals, legal documents all have distinctive appearances; indeed, most text types have developed special visual styles with which new documents are expected to conform. Although these usually originate with functional reasons connected with manufacturing processes or conditions of use, they can quickly become purely conventional and hard to change. thus, legal documents have to look legalistic in order to be considered with care, warranties have to look valuable in order to be valued—perhaps scholarly books have to look scholarly in order to be respected. Texts, like people, wear uniforms.

By extension, this argument suggests that once readers have identified the appropriate model, they then search for its components and expect to be able to use them in a particular way—or, we might say, according to a particular *script*. Each text type might suggest an appropriate strategy,

FIGURE 4.5 Two typical product packs, redrawn for clarity. The manufacturers' trademarks have been deleted for copyright reasons.

TABLE 4.3
Components of a possible "packaging" text type (see Fig. 4.4 and 4.5).

Topic	Firelighters	Spray Mount	Mary Stewart	Tom Jones
Qualifier	White	Adhesive	The Gabriel Hounds	Henry Fielding
Quantifier	14	391g (414ml)	—	Classics series CL135
Context	Picture of fire	Picture of design studio	Romantic painting	Period picture
Source	Trademark	Trademark	Imprint	Imprint
Technical data	Suitable for use in smokeless zone	Allows for repositioning	—	Introduction by Dr Beryl Rowland
Exhortation	New improved formula	FREE . . .	Ghostly hounds . . .	Complete and unabridged

level of attention, critical stance, and range of responses, modified by the purpose of each individual user.

In the case of the form design project mentioned earlier, for example, we found a strong expectation among users to answer every question, leaving none blank. We had to test several ways of directing people around secondary questions that were only to be answered by certain categories of user. Similarly, users expect to sign a form once. Forms that require two signatures depart from the normal script and so need special design attention.

PERCEPTUAL REASONING

Templates and Grids

On all the examples described in Table 4.3, it is noticeable that the source (manufacturer or publisher) is at an extreme edge of the display (usually at the top), the topic identifier was above the middle or in the top half, and the "flash" was, on both product packages, at an angle and at the edge. It may be that typographic models include not only inventories of components but visual *templates* for their disposition on the page. To decide this issue would require an exhaustive survey and classification of examples. Walker (1982) has proposed a methodology for this and demonstrated it with a survey of children's layout when letter writing.

Whether or not there are universal templates, there are certainly local ones. Typographers use the term *grid* to refer to the basic page plan they draw up at the outset of a text design task. Grids can be simple indications of a single-column type area, but the term comes from the complex multicolumn layouts that have become popular during the last few decades.

Although there are precedents, particularly in newspaper and magazine design, multicolumn grids have been most self-consciously used and discussed by Swiss typographers of the last three decades (see review by Kinross, 1984). The problem of laying out three or four languages in parallel led to the development of a system of multicolumn design where text components are aligned on (unseen) vertical and horizontal grid lines. The grid is simply a means of dividing the page into slots which may be filled by the various components of the text.

The grid gives visual order to the page, which in classic Swiss typography is reinforced by the practice of using plain sans-serif typefaces and minial typographic signaling. Taken to extremes, this can result in designers giving visual order priority over usability; complex information is simply tidied away. Indeed, one writer (Bonsiepe, 1968) proposed a method of quantifying the orderliness of typography (analogous to readability indices for prose) that was, in effect, a measure of visual simplicity—giving high marks to pages with the fewest alignments. Being totally content free and backed by no empirical evidence about the reaction of readers, his index remains little used.

Text as Diagram

I have described typographic segmentation as one of a range of ways in which writers can compensate for the linearity of prose. Some texts go further than simple segmentation and use the two-dimensional surface of the page to break through the barrier of linearity and establish spatial relationships. Tables, discussed in the introduction of this chapter, are one example. Figure 4.6 illustrates another.

Even before you start reading this page, the structure of its argument is apparent: There are three sections, each divided into three. A closer look at the headings shows *how* the visual pattern relates to the argument. It discusses three aspects of diet, and approaches each in the same way ("Why?" "By how much?" "Watch these foods"). In conventional prose this advance warning of structure would have to be made explicitly: "There are three targets for a healthier diet—fats, sugar, and fibre. We will examine each in turn."

In such typographically structured pages, parallelisms can be literally, not only metaphorically, parallel. The principles described by de Beaugrande are exhibited in the reader's strategy rather than in the text itself. We cannot identify a particular textual device at the macrolevel to control, for example, looking forward and looking back. Instead of using the techniques of prose to provide explicit references forward or back, the writer has used the techniques of diagramming to communicate holistic, nonlinear aspects of the text. This use of layout to shape arguments has been called text-as-diagram (Waller, 1982); elsewhere I have provided critiques of further examples of pages designed in this way (Waller, 1985).

The text-as-diagram metaphor expresses the view that typography is a two-dimensional, perceptual phenomenon which shares many of the characteristics of diagrams. Diagrams represent conceptual relationships through perceptual principles (such as proximity, similarity, and closure, described by the Gestalt psychologists), through visual metaphor, through cultural conventions and special notations. *Graphic language,* as it has been termed, is a very extensive resource, but space does not permit a full discussion here. Twyman (1979, 1983) has classified and described a wide range of examples.

Target – eat less fats

Why?
Cholesterol is the main constituent of fatty deposits in arteries and of gallstones. Excess amounts are made in the body when high fat foods are eaten. Particularly food rich in 'saturated' fat mainly found in animal foods. Other fats in the diet – called 'poly-unsaturated' fats – tend to reduce cholesterol in the body. This type of fat is found in many foods, particularly in corn oil, sunflower seed oil and soya oil. (NB some vegetable oils and margarines are, in fact, rich in saturated fat.)
As far as general health is concerned it is more important to reduce the total amount of all fats rather than just to swap animal fats for special vegetable oils or margarine

By how much?
We get more than 40% of the calories we need from fats. It would be better to reduce fats to 30–35%. This is difficult to calculate. You almost certainly need to cut down if you often do one or more of these things. Eat fried food. Put butter or margarine on cooked vegetables. Spread butter thickly on your bread. Eat a lot of the foods listed in the next column. Provided you keep the total amount low you do not need to cut out completely your favourite butter, cream or fried food. If you are not prepared to cut down on the total amount of fat in your diet you should change to special vegetable oils and low fat spreads

Watch these foods
Fat is a major part of: cakes, pastries, biscuits and chocolates, sausages, salami, pork, lamb, cheese, cream, butter and margarine, cooking oils and fat.
If you love the taste of butter, really savour it on a plain slice of bread and butter.
Change your cooking habits by
○ Grilling instead of frying
○ Using non-stick pans
○ Using recipes which use less fat
○ Using skimmed (low fat) milk instead of ordinary milk in recipes

Target – eat less sugar

Why?
A high sugar diet encourages dental decay. Sweet foods can spoil the appetite for more nourishing foods. Sugar only provides energy which is also provided by, for example, potatoes and wholemeal bread. Because we become addicted to sweet things we are tempted to overeat and so may put on weight

By how much?
Most people get one fifth of their energy needs (calories) from sugar. About half of this is from the use of packet sugar and jams. The other half might be thought of as 'hidden sugar' which is added to many manufactured foods. *We do not need any sugar at all*

Watch these foods
Sugar is the major part of sweets, soft drinks, cakes, biscuits, puddings and jams. It is also added to many manufactured foods like tomato ketchup, tinned fruit, ice cream and frozen foods. Reading the label will tell you which have sugar added to them. If you have a sweet tooth you could have an occasional treat, eg, jam on your bread or a piece of chocolate

Target – eat more fibre

Why?
There are probably a dozen different kinds of fibres, all with different roles to play. Therefore cereal foods *and* fruit and vegetables are equally important. Extra bran is not the same as 'high fibre diet' and is only good for helping constipation. 'High fibre diets', which may offer protection from a number of digestive ailments, are also low in fat and animal protein

By how much?
You can't really eat too much when it is a natural part of food. You could eat too much bran – but you would be hard put to swallow it. You are probably eating enough if you have regular bulky, but not hard, bowel movements

Watch these foods
Eat more of the bulky foods listed in 'fillers' *and* a variety of fruit and vegetables
○ Eat breakfast cereals made from the whole grain
○ Try brown rice or wholemeal pasta
○ Eat wholemeal or brown bread
○ Eat the skins of old potatoes as well as new ones

FIGURE 4.6 A page from the Open University course P921 *Health Choices*. (© The Open University, 1980.)

CONCLUSION

Typography is a ubiquitous but poorly understood aspect of language. Its interpretation is not well understood but seems to combine the same kind of logical and pragmatic reasoning that we use for prose with an extra perceptual dimension. The spatial metaphors that are so common in ordinary language can thus be realized in its written shape.

Paralanguage in speech is relatively natural, acquired through social interaction with others. It is also informal and its conventions can change even during a single conversation interaction. Typography, however—paralanguage in text—has to be more formal, deliberate, and consistent. Furthermore, typographic skills are extremely specialized and quite rare. They are normally acquired from long apprenticeship and the exercise of a sensitive and critical judgment. However, recent advances in personal computing are now replacing typewriters with laser systems capable of sophisticated typography—complex typography is now directly accessible to large numbers of writers.

Typographic teachers and researchers are currently much concerned by this new accessibility of typography, combined with the challenge of adapting typographic conventions developed for printing to the electronic media. But before new "grammars" can be established, and before empirical research can be useful—before our concept of literacy can be thus extended—we need a deeper understanding of typography as an integral part of written language.

REFERENCES

Baldwin, R. S., & Coady, J. M. (1978). Psycholinguistic approaches to a theory of punctuation. *Journal of Reading Behaviour, 10,* 363–376.

Beaugrande, R. de (1984). *Text production: Towards a science of composition.* Norwood, NJ: Ablex.

Beaugrande, R. de, & Dressler, W. (1981). *Introduction to text linguistics.* London: Longman.

Bernhardt, S. A. (1985). Text structure and graphic design: The visible design. In J. D. Benson & W. S. Greaves (Eds.), *Systemic perspectives on discourse* (Vol. 2). Norwood, NJ: Ablex.

Bolinger, D. (1975). *Aspects of language* (2nd ed.). New York: Harcourt Brace Jovanovich.

Bonsiepe, G. (1968). A method of quantifying order in typographic design. *Journal of Typographic Research, 2,* 203–220.

Booth-Clibborn, E., & Baroni, D. (1980). *The language of graphics.* London: Thames & Hudson.

Brown, A. (1980). Metacognitive development and reading. In R. J. Spiro, B. C. Bruce, & W. F. Brewer (Eds.), *Theoretical issues in reading comprehension.* Hillsdale, NJ: Lawrence Erlbaum Associates.

Crystal, D., & Davy, D. (1969). *Investigating English style*. London: Longman.

Eisenstein, E. L. (1979). *The printing press as an agent of change* (2 volumes). Cambridge, England: Cambridge University Press.

Gray B. (1977). *The grammatical foundations of rhetoric*. The Hague: Mouton.

Grice, H. P. (1975). Logic and conversation. In P. Cole & J. Sadock (Eds.), *Syntax and semantics III: Speech acts*. New York: Academic Press.

Hartley, J., Kenely, J., Owen, G., & Trueman, M. (1980). The effect of headings on children's recall of prose text. *British Journal of Educational Psychology, 50,* 304–307.

Honan, P. (1960). Eighteenth- and nineteenth-century punctuation theory. *English Studies, 40,* 92–102.

Kinross, R. (1984). Emil Ruder's *Typography* and "Swiss typography." *Information Design Journal, 4,* 147–153.

Lyons, J. (1977). *Semantics* (Vol. 1). Cambridge, England: Cambridge University Press.

Nash, W. (1980). *Designs in prose*. London: Longman.

Pugh, A. K. (1979). Styles and strategies in adult silent reading. In P. Kolers, M. Wrolstad, & H. Bouma (Eds.), *Processing of visible language* (Vol. 1). New York: Plenum.

Sacks, H., Schegloff, E. A., & Jefferson, G. (1974). A simplest systematics for the organization of turn-taking in conversations. *Language, 50,* 696–735.

Saussure, F. de (1974). *Course in general linguistics*. London: Fontana.

Schumacher, G. M., & Waller, R. H. W. (1985). Testing design alternatives: A comparison of procedures. In T. M. Duffy & R. H. W. Waller (Eds.), *Designing usable texts*. Orlando, FL: Academic Press.

Thomas, L. (1976). *The self-organized learner and the printed word*. Uxbridge, England: Brunel University Centre for the Study of Human Learning.

Thompson, P., & Davenport, P. (1980). *The dictionary of visual language*. London: Bergstrom & Boyle.

Tompkins, J. P. (1980). *Reader-response criticism*. Baltimore: The Johns Hopkins University Press.

Twyman, M. (1979). A schema for the study of graphic language. In P. Kolers, M. Wrolstad, & H. Bouma (Eds.), *Processing of visible language* (Vol. 1). New York: Plenum.

Twyman, M. (1983). The graphic presentation of language. *Information Design Journal, 3,* 2–22.

Walker, S. (1982). Describing verbal graphic language: Practicalities and implications. *Information Design Journal, 3,* 102–109.

Waller, R. H. W. (1980). Graphic aspects of complex texts: Typography as macropunctuation. In P. Kolers, M. Wrolstad, & H. Bouma (Eds.), *Processing of visible language* (Vol. 2). New York: Plenum.

Waller, R. H. W. (1982). Text as diagram: Using typography to improve access and understanding. In D. Jonassen (Ed.), *The technology of text* (1). Englewood Cliffs, NJ: Educational Technology Publications.

Waller, R. H. W. (1984). Designing a government form: A case study. *Information Design Journal, 4,* 36–57.

Waller, R. H. W. (1985). Using typography to structure arguments. In D. Jonassen (Ed.), *The technology of text* (2). Englewood Cliffs, NJ: Educational Technology Publications.

Whalley, P. C., & Fleming, R. W. (1975). An experiment with a simple recorder of reading behaviour. *Programmed Learning and Educational Technology, 12,* 120–124.

Widdowson, H. G. (1979). *Explorations in applied linguistics*. Oxford: Oxford University Press.

Winter, E. O. (1977). A clause relational approach to English texts. *Instructional Science, 6,* 1–92.

Wright, P. (1981). Tables in text: The subskills needed for reading formatted information. In L. J. Chapman (Ed.), *The reader and the text*. London: Heinemann.

EXECUTIVE CONTROL IN STUDYING 5

Gary M. Schumacher
Ohio University

The process of studying presents researchers and educators with a puzzling dilemma. It is widely accepted that studying is a crucial factor in the success of most students in most educational settings. Rohwer (1984), for example, notes that studying is considered one of the prime ingredients in school success (particularly for students beyond the early elementary years). Indeed, if high school or college students are found to be struggling in their academic work, parents and teachers are likely to turn early to a consideration of the quality of the student's studying processes. As Rohwer notes, studying is a major variable in our intuitive theory of the determinants of academic success.

Yet, when we turn to the psychological literature for insight on the process of studying, we are soon dismayed. There is little coherent research on the topic. Whereas there is research on numerous facets of studying such as underlining (Hartley, Bartlett, & Branthwaite, 1980), the use of text aids (Mayer, 1984), notetaking (Kiewra, 1985a, 1985b), and individual differences in studying (Gettinger, 1984), there is little effort to build this research into a coherent theory of studying. This state of affairs has led Rohwer (1984) to call for the initiation of an educational psychology of studying. This is a desirable and laudable aim and one that is long overdue.

Rohwer suggested a tentative framework to guide research on studying. This framework delineated three major characteristics which impact on students' achievement levels and which need to be investigated. These are course and task characteristics, student characteristics, and study activities. By taking this approach, Rohwer establishes not only a specific framework for investigating studying, but also a general mindset or orientation regarding how to approach the investigation of studying; that is, the object of the investigation, the focus of the enterprise, becomes the *act of studying*.

This may well be a useful and effective orientation for it should lead to a number of relevant investigations. But we should be aware that this is not the only orientation we can take to this area of concern. For just as there is an act of studying, there is a person who studies—the studier. By changing the focus from the act of studying to the studier, we obtain a different perspective on many issues. Sometimes this difference in perspective is of little consequence, whereas at other times it is highly significant. For example, from both perspectives there is interest in understanding the various studying activities such as underlining and notetaking. From the act of studying viewpoint, the major emphasis often is whether the carrying out of these activities leads to a significant improvement in achievement and whether there are certain course characteristics that interrelate with these studying activities (e.g., does notetaking work best in courses with large amounts of factual information?). From the viewpoint of the studier, however, we may wonder whether a group of studiers know how to carry out a particular studying activity and under what conditions the studiers choose to carry out that activity. In this view our emphasis is primarily on the numerous cognitive characteristics of the studiers, and how changing task and course settings influence these studiers to modify their cognitive activities. Topics that may be of special concern, then, are the specific cognitive structures and processes available to the studier for carrying out the tasks necessary in studying, and how these structures and processes are orchestrated and controlled for this particular function.

One criticism of this approach is that it is calling for nothing more than additional research on human cognitive abilities. This would, however, be misunderstanding the principal thrust of an approach emphasizing the studier. This point needs further elaboration. In the past decade, one central theme running through much of cognitive psychology has been the importance of context in human functioning. For example, researchers in the area of problem solving have shown that, by a simple recasting of a problem description, a very difficult problem can be made trivial (Hayes, 1978); developmental psychologists have found that children egocentric in one setting will not be so in another (Donaldson, 1978); psycholinguists have noted that the same phoneme is produced in a much different fashion depending on the context in which it is produced (MacNeilage & DeClerk, 1969); and researchers interested in prose comprehension have found that the same passage may be interpreted in a very different fashion, depending on the context in which it is set (Moates & Schumacher, 1980).

This heavy context dependency in human cognition suggests that it is unlikely that researchers will be able to determine general laws of cognitive functioning that extend over a wide range of contexts. Mishler (1979) convincingly argues this case in his critique of much social science research. He concludes by recommending an alternative goal for such research, namely, one in which the task of the research endeavors should be to specify the boundary conditions under which functional relationships hold between variables.

For our sake, then, in attempting to understand the studier and the studying process, it would be necessary to investigate the types of cognitive activities, processes, strategies, and structures that individuals use in varying studying contexts. The goal would be to establish the boundary conditions under which certain studying activities are called into use and to discover what conditions lead to successful employment of the activities.

The purpose of the present chapter is not to detail the specific characteristics of this alternative approach to the investigation of the studier. That is far too ambitious a project for this setting. Rather, the emphasis here is on one particular aspect of this formulation that plays an important role in understanding how the studier interfaces with the studying task and its contextual setting. This is the issue of executive control processes.

Executive control processes deal with how individuals plan and direct, select and orchestrate the various cognitive structures and processes available to them for attaining some goal. Thus, we are dealing with executive control issues when we address how individuals decide in a laboratory investigation to combine their rehearsal and imaging processes to help remember a long list of words, or how a child fails to employ newly learned capabilities of labeling to remember a set of pictures. In the context of studying, executive control issues deal with such questions as why an individual may use underlining or notetaking in one setting but not in another, and why individuals find it particularly difficult to effectively monitor their comprehension process in one study setting but not in another.

WHY EXECUTIVE CONTROL?

Is there any reason to believe that placing an emphasis on executive control might prove fruitful in understanding aspects of studying? In fact, it is possible to suggest at least four reasons. First, researchers in both adult cognitive functioning and in cognitive development have found it necessary to consider issues of executive control to explain cognitive functioning on numerous tasks. In adult cognition the problem of executive control has long been recognized. Early cognitive psychologists struggled with the knowledge to action gap, a classic criticism by behaviorists of cognitive theories. The crux of this criticism is captured by the following question: If experience with the world leads to knowledge and not direct responses, how is it that the organism converts its knowledge to action? Miller, Galanter, and Pribram's (1960) famous book, *Plans and the Structure of Behavior,* is in large measure an attempt to answer this question. These researchers postulated *plans* and *TOTE* (Test, Operate, Test, Exit) units as key concepts in bridging the knowledge to action gap. In that sense the principal concern of their book was that of executive control.

In a similar manner the numerous variations of information-processing theories have all attempted to address executive control in some fashion or another with concepts such as executive routines and monitors. The vagueness of a number of these concepts attests to the difficulty in developing viable models of human cognition that adequately address the issue of executive control. Probably the most ambitious model of human cognition that attempts to address executive control is John Anderson's (1983) computer-based model of cognition—ACT*. This complex and detailed model has gone far in advancing our thoughts about the issues of executive control and is a major focus later in this chapter. Thus, cognitive psychologists have made significant strides in understanding human cognition by directly tackling the issue of executive control.

Similarly, psychologists interested in cognitive development have made substantial progress by considering issues of executive control. In this case the principal emphasis has centered on the concept of metacognition. Metacognition refers to the knowledge individuals have about their own cognitive processes and how this knowledge is involved in controlling which cognitive activities are carried out at which time. Since the introduction of the concept of metacognition, an extensive research literature has developed attempting to explicate the role of metacognition in children's cognitive functioning. The concept is not without its critics (see Cavanaugh & Perlmutter, 1982), but it has raised interest regarding issues of executive control and has suggested some fruitful avenues that research might follow. The extensive work of Ann Brown and her colleagues (Baker & Brown, 1984; Brown, Armbruster, & Baker, 1985; Brown & Campione, 1978) has introduced the concept into the area of studying.

A second reason why an emphasis on executive control may be fruitful in understanding studying comes directly from observations on the current research on studying. The reviews of research on studying all seem to point to a similar conclusion—the link between studying and achievement has not been strongly established. Rohwer (1984), for example, comments that: "the results of research on studying have failed to provide convincing demonstrations of its role as a major determinant of academic achievement" (p. 3). Speaking more specifically about studying techniques, Anderson and Armbruster (1984) state that: "Unfortunately, empirical research fails to confirm the purported benefits of the popular strategies. So far, the effort to find the one superior method has not been successful; the few studies that have been done present a confusing array of inconsistent results" (p. 665).

The failure to find a consistent pattern of results in an area usually indicates that some key variable or variables are not being controlled in the research. This appears to be the case in the studying research. Of course, the failure to find consistent results does not directly support the need for consideration of executive control. However, one possible reason for the inconsistent results may be the failure to understand how studiers orchestrate (i.e., control) the numerous processes and structures available to them to meet their academic goals.

The third reason that an emphasis on executive control may be useful is related to the large role that context factors play in research on studying. Consider, for example, the research on two variables that may be thought to play significant roles in studying—the readability of the materials to be studied and the act of notetaking.

The readability level of materials would be expected to play a significant role in the ease of comprehension and retention of prose materials. However, this has not always been found to be the case. By altering the contextual setting in which the materials are studied, the impact of readability level has been found to change significantly. Fass and Schumacher (1978), for example, found that by manipulating the motivational level of the subjects the impact of readability changed substantially. Retention of nonhighly motivated subjects was improved by the use of more readable versions of a text passage. This was not the case in highly motivated subjects. Klare (1984), in fact, discussed several factors that interact with readability to influence comprehension.

Perhaps an even more impressive indication of the impact of contextual factors on the role of readability level is seen in a study by Klare and Smart (1973). Whereas laboratory investigations have shown mixed results of readability on comprehension and retention, Klare and Smart demonstrated that readability can have dramatic effects in a real-world setting. These researchers investigated the relationship between readability levels of materials used in armed services correspondence courses and course success and found strong correlations between readability level and course completion rates. Students receiving more difficult materials were substantially less likely to complete a course than those who received more readable materials.

The research on notetaking shows similar effects of contextual variables. Whereas some reviews of notetaking report positive relationships between studying and academic achievement (Kiewra, 1985a), other reviews are far more cautious in their conclusions. Anderson and Armbruster (1984), for example, claim that most studies fail to establish any significant advantage for taking notes. However, the large majority of the investigations of studying have been carried out in laboratory settings using relatively short passages. In addition, Nye, Crooks, Powley, and Tripp (1984) note that most laboratory investigations of notetaking also have one or more of the following characteristics:

1. Students took notes and were tested on material irrelevant to their studies.
2. Only one instructor or one passage of written material was used.
3. The period of notetaking was very brief.
4. Students were aware that they were participating in an experiment about notetaking.
5. Some or all of the students were asked to adopt strategies which were foreign to them.
6. Retention was tested immediately, or after very restricted access to the notes. (p. 86)

Nye et al. claimed these contextual variables could have significant impact on the effectiveness of notetaking. In order to test this notion, they obtained complete sets of notes from 38 students on a psychology course involving 75 lectures and 10 instructors. They systematically sampled notes from these students and analyzed them for such variables as the total number of words recorded during a lecture, the number of highlights and underlinings, and the number of words added to the lecture notes after the lecture. They then obtained scores of the students on a two-part final examination for the course (a 3-hour essay exam and a 3-hour multiple choice exam) and correlated characteristics of the student notes with the examination performance. The results were stunning. The total number of words in the students' notes correlated .58 with scores on the essay exam and .70 with scores on the multiple choice exam. Even more striking was the correlation between the total number of words and the exam total for the top 8 students in the sample, .97. These results are quite exceptional, of course, but they do suggest that in some contextual settings there may be a strong relationship between notetaking and academic achievement.

This research investigating contextual variables in studying indicates that how students employ the various processes, strategies, and structures available to them is markedly influenced by contextual variables. A better understanding of the issues of executive control may provide insight into how these numerous contextual variables impact on the studying process.

A systematic analysis of studying suggests a fourth reason why investigating executive control may be a fruitful approach. Studying involves the potential use of a wide-ranging number of processes (e.g., retrieval, rehearsal, generation, comparison), using numerous tasks (e.g., underlining, notetaking, question answering), all aimed at varying goals (e.g., preparation for different kinds of tests, gaining a preliminary understanding, preparing to write a paper), carried out under disparate conditions (e.g., quiet–noisy room, short–long time span, crucial–unimportant test) on materials of varying difficulty. Anderson and Armbruster (1984) nicely capture one aspect of the difficult processing demands of studying: "In realistic studying situations, this processing demand is very heavy. For example, it is not unusual for a single page of expository text to have at least 50 idea units which could be interrelated in a vast number of ways. In a chapter of text, the number of ideas and relationships is mind-boggling indeed" (p. 660).

Studying, then, presents the studier with an exceptionally difficult and complex problem of how to wed numerous cognitive features into coherent action. It is a classic example of the issue of executive control. Is it any wonder why children are ineffective at studying, and in fact why studying is frequently a difficult and ineffective activity even in adults? Therefore, approaching the area of studying through the question of executive control may prove very fruitful.

But if executive control is a major issue in studying, how can we approach this concept in a beneficial manner? This question necessitates a consideration of the current models of cognition which address the issue of executive control, and how these models might be applied to an understanding of executive control in studying.

MODELS OF EXECUTIVE CONTROL

There appear to be three major types of models which address the issue of executive control in cognition in at least some fashion. The goal of this section is to characterize these models in some detail and then to attempt to specify how these models might be particularized to the area of studying.

Information-Processing Models

The first type of model discussed is perhaps best described under the general label of information-processing models. Information-processing models usually postulate various stages of processing between the incoming stimulus and outgoing response. They also maintain that the stimulus is transformed as it is processed through these stages, and that there is one or more stages in the model in which capacity limitations restrict how much information can be processed (Howard, 1983). These models may be of a general form that specify how information is processed through a wide variety of cognitive tasks (e.g., see Howard, 1983). Or the models can be more specific and apply to a particular area of cognition (e.g., see the Flower & Hayes (1981) model of writing).

An Information-Processing Model of Studying.   Although there has been little effort to generate information-processing models of studying that specify how executive control might be conceptualized, the Flower and Hayes writing model suggests one way such a model might be structured. In this section a preliminary version of a studying model adapted from the Flower and Hayes model is described. The major features of the model include how it handles the issue of executive control. The section ends with a discussion of the types of research questions this model brings forth.

The major features of the model are shown in Fig. 5.1. The basic form of the model is similar to the Flower and Hayes model, although there are some important differences. The model describes three major elements that are thought to be important in the studying process. In its present formulation the model is specified primarily for studying textual materials, although this is not viewed as a major restriction.

The first major element in the model is the task environment in which the act of studying is carried out. This refers to characteristics outside the individual that may influence the studying activity. This includes two major characteristics: text characteristics and the study situation. Under text characteristics come numerous factors: the type of text materials (e.g., text book, written notes); the readability level of the materials; the organizational structure of the text (e.g., expository vs. narrative structure, well or poorly structured presentation); the existence or nonexistence of various adjunct aids (e.g., inserted questions, advanced organizers) and text access structures (e.g., table of contents, side bar headings); and the typographical layout of the text.

The study situation refers to a number of factors which set the immediate context for the studying activity. These include the time available for study, whether the current interaction with the text is a first-time interaction or last-minute preparation, the noise level in the surrounding environment, and all other environmental conditions that could potentially impact on the study situation (e.g., room temperature, available space). Both the text characteristics and study situation may substantially influence the ease and manner of studying and may markedly affect how executive control routines are carried out.

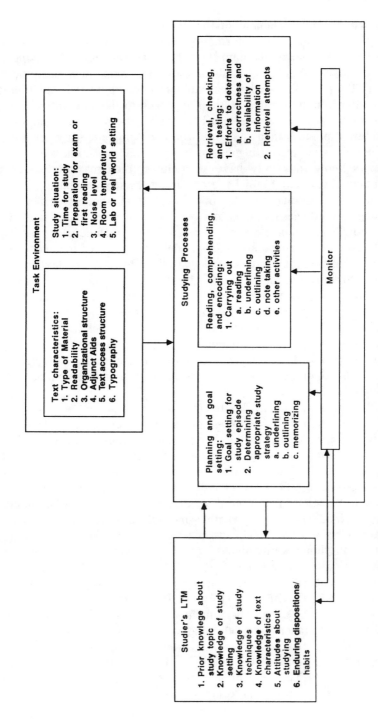

FIGURE 5.1 Information-processing model of studying. Adapted from Flower and Hayes (1981).

The second major element in the model is the studiers' long-term memory. This refers to any information that is part of the studiers' long-term knowledge that might impact on how the process of studying is carried out. Several different kinds of knowledge must be included here. Certainly the prior knowledge that studiers have about the topic being studied substantially impacts on their approach to the studying process. Someone who has substantial knowledge about the topic may employ a very different process than someone who is a complete novice. Knowledge about the studying setting may also impact on how studiers proceed. If studiers know they only have 30 minutes, they may initiate very different activities than if they have 4 hours; if the studying must be done in a noisy room, studiers may be more likely to take notes to generate a permanent record that can't be lost because of unpredictable interruptions. Knowledge about the effectiveness of study techniques or reading capabilities may determine how studiers decide to proceed in a particular studying situation. Similarly, knowledge about how to use text access structures or how certain text structures organize different kinds of information may determine how studiers decide to attack different sets of study materials. In a different fashion, the attitudes that studiers have about studying (e.g., studying is distasteful, difficult, helpful) establish a mindset that can significantly influence the success of a particular studying episode. Finally, the enduring dispositions or habits studiers have may lead to a generally rigid or flexible approach to studying which influences the likelihood of success.

It is the third major element of the model that the processing aspects of studying are emphasized. Three aspects of processing are identified: planning and goal setting; reading, comprehending, and encoding activities; and retrieval, checking, and testing activities. Planning and goal-setting activities include establishing desired outcomes for a particular studying episode (e.g., I just want to determine what this chapter is about, or I need to be able to recall the three major characteristics of democracies). It also includes planning whether one will study for an hour now and then take a break, whether to use a particular studying activity (e.g., outlining, underlining, or mapping), or whether to call someone else to set up a group-studying situation.

Reading, comprehension, and encoding activities involve the carrying out of a variety of activities primarily aimed at understanding and storing information from the texts. These include straight reading activities but also may include underlining, outlining, and notetaking. The efforts are aimed at finding or building structural relations among ideas and concepts and linking these notions with concepts already stored in the studier's long-term memory. This may involve attempts to draw analogies between what is being studied and what is already known. It may also involve the use of mnemonic devices or other techniques aimed at improving memorability of the information.

The retrieval, checking, and testing activities involve efforts by the studier to determine the correctness and availability of information that has been read and encoded. It includes attempts to determine if retrieval is possible. This may include actual practice attempts at retrieving by the use of self-testing procedures, or it may involve the use of available text characteristics such as inserted questions.

It is important to note that these three major processing elements may not necessarily (or even likely) go on in a linear fashion; that is, studiers do not always first systematically plan and set goals, then attempt to comprehend and encode, and finally test and evaluate their success. These processes are likely to intertwine with each other in a quite complex manner. For example, studiers may initiate reading without setting goals and then test themselves to determine how they are proceeding. If they feel that they are not making progress, they may then establish goals and a plan to achieve them. Sometimes studiers may intersperse self-testing activities periodically throughout their encoding efforts to determine what progress is being made. At other times studiers may reserve self-testing efforts for a separate study session.

It is also clear that some studiers make little or no use of planning or self-testing activities at all. This failure to plan or self-test may be a context-sensitive practice (e.g., the upcoming history test is of so little value that I won't bother), or it may be a habitual practice because the studier is unaware of the usefulness or importance of these practices.

There is one final element of the studying model that has not been elaborated—the monitor. The monitor serves as a studying overseer. It is that aspect of the model responsible for determining which of the major elements of the studying process are carried out at each point in time. It serves to orchestrate the numerous processes and activities involved in the act of studying and thus performs the major functions involved in executive control. The monitor is influenced by numerous variables from the task environment (e.g., readability level of the text, studying for a quiz instead of a final examination), as well as long-term memory factors (e.g., prior knowledge about the material being studied, habits that the studiers have developed). There are likely developmental changes in the functioning of the monitor with children being substantially less effective in coordinating the complex activities involved in studying.

It should be obvious that this information-processing model of studying has many similarities to the writing model of Flower and Hayes. This suggests that many of the same elements impacting on writing are a part of the studying process. Although the Flower and Hayes model has turned out to be very fruitful in aiding the investigation of writing, could a studying model such as the one described be useful in aiding studying research? It is too early to tell at this moment, but ssome reflection on the questions and issues which are generated by this model may help provide some insight on that question.

Research Issues and Questions

The preceding model emphasizes the usefulness of a different general methodological approach to research on studying. In particular, instead of studies that primarily involve manipulating characteristics of the text or studying activity and then measuring the changes in performance on a test over the material, the model stresses the importance of investigating the studiers' cognitive and decision processes, especially in everyday studying situations. This calls for the use of procedures such as verbal protocols during studying (Afflerbach & Johnston, 1984; Holland & Redish, 1981); macroeye-movement procedures that allow for direct monitoring of a studier's pattern of text usage (Hout Wolters, 1982; Schumacher, Moses, & Young, 1983; Schumacher & Waller, 1983, 1985; Wollen, Cone, Britcher, & Mindeman, 1985); microeye-movement procedures that allow for very specific observation of processing activities (Just & Carpenter, 1980; McConkie et al., 1979); user edits (Atlas, 1981); and macroprocessing procedures that monitor how studiers read large blocks (e.g., chapters, books) of text (Whalley, 1981, 1982). Each of these methods places emphasis on investigating the cognitive processes involved in interacting with text materials. A number of them are particularly adaptable to investigating how a studier approaches the studying process in naturally occurring contexts. This is an important issue if researchers are to be able to systematically explore the impact of various contextual variables on studiers' processes and how they control them.

Some particular questions that arise from this model are as follows:

1. What contextual variables impact on when studiers employ notetaking, underlining, or outlining activities to prepare for examinations?

2. What types of cognitive processes (e.g., planning how to proceed, practicing retrieval) do subjects carry out during pauses in studying? What impact do various kinds of text features have on the duration of study pauses and the kinds of cognitive processes reported during these pauses? Two techniques that might prove very useful in investigating these types of questions are used by researchers in writing. Swarts, Flower, and Hayes (1984) used protocol analysis techniques to track cognitive processes during writing. Schumacher, Klare, Cronin, and Moses (1984) used a pausal procedure to explore the types of cognitive activities subjects reported carrying out during pauses in writing. Both

procedures would be readily adaptable to investigating cognitive processes in studying.

3. What type of task environment is most likely to lead to high levels of planning activities in studying? For example, are studiers more likely to set overt goals for studying difficult or easy materials, for important or unimportant exams?

4. Do individuals differing on various learning style measures (e.g., Schmeck's, 1983, deep processing or methodical studying factors) show a different pattern of studying processes?

5. Do study skills courses lead to changes in the patterning of the various studying processes?

6. Do studying processes change substantially between laboratory settings and field settings?

From these questions it is apparent that an information-processing model of studying leads us to consider issues that are rarely raised by existing models of studying. Emphasis is placed on the processes that studiers engage in and how various text, setting, and knowledge variables impact on these processes and their selection and control. Although this model introduces the issue of executive control in studying, it does so in a rudimentary way. The next model deals more directly with executive control, particularly as it relates to the studier's knowledge of studying and studying processes.

A Metacognitive Model of Studying

The information-processing model described previously grew out of the adult cognitive process research and emphasized the processes involved in carrying out a particular task. The metacognitive model described here has its origins in the research on cognitive development in children and emphasizes the knowledge the individual has about the task, particularly what has come to be called "metacognitive knowledge."

Because the concept of metacognition is relatively fuzzy and has attracted considerable criticism (e.g., see Cavanaugh & Perlmutter, 1982), it is useful to begin by clarifying what the term means. Flavell (1981) defined metacognition as "knowledge or cognition that takes as its object or regulates any aspect of any cognitive endeavor" (p. 37). Examination of this definition indicates that there are two principal sets of attributes involved in metacognition. The first is concerned with the individual's *knowledge* about his or her own cognitive processes and about how various materials and settings influence the memory process. Thus, the emphasis is on whether one set of words will be easier to recall than another, or whether one strategy is useful in one setting but not in another.

The second set of attributes deals with the issue of regulation or *control* of the procedures used by individuals while attempting to solve problems. The emphasis in this case falls on how individuals check on their progress toward a solution for a problem, monitor the ongoing activity, and evaluate and revise their activities to more effectively attain their goals (Baker & Brown, 1984). It is this latter aspect that comes closest to the issue of executive control that is the prime concern here.

The fact that the concept of metacognition involves both aspects of knowledge and control does potentially raise some difficult issues, particularly if these two aspects are not kept clearly distinct. Cavanaugh and Perlmutter (1982) make this point very forcefully:

> Unfortunately, calling both what the person knows and how she or he uses it "metamemory" reflects a failure to make an explicit distinction between knowledge about memory and processes orchestrating this knowledge. Such conceptual confusion and overconcentration on knowledge use can result in an inability to explain performance. For example, one can never be certain whether impaired performance is due to faulty or absent use of well-articulated memory knowledge or "efficient" use of inadequate knowledge. (pp. 15–16)

It is important to keep this problem in mind as we consider what metacognitive models can tell us about executive control in studying.

Recently, Flavell (1981) has attempted to develop a model of how individuals monitor and regulate a number of cognitive tasks such as communication. For example, how is it that individuals regulate what they say, when they say it, and how they phrase what they say? Flavell's model uses the concept of metacognition as one of its principal components in trying to treat such problems of control. Although this model is not specifically aimed at modeling the studying process, it is cast in a manner that makes it very applicable to this situation. In describing this model I show how it might apply to investigating studying and the processes of executive control involved in studying.

A schematic outline of the model is shown in Fig. 5.2. The model involves four principal components: cognitive goals, metacognitive knowledge, metacognitive experiences, and cognitive actions. The arrows in the model indicate how these various components interact with each other.

Cognitive Goals.   According to Flavell, cognitive goals refer to the implicit or explicit objectives that are involved in initiating or moderating the cognitive processes of the individual. These goals may vary dramatically

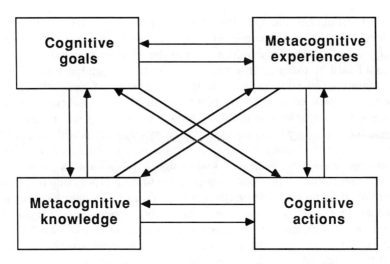

FIGURE 5.2   Components of Flavell's cognitive monitoring model (from Flavell, 1981).

from one situation to another. The goals we have on seeing a math problem on a test are probably much different from seeing that same problem in a popular magazine. Some activities we engage in have very specific goals (e.g., convincing a friend to go out for lunch at Sam's delicatessen), whereas others have very general goals (e.g., wanting to do well in college). Some activities we carry out may involve several goals (e.g., playing tennis may be aimed at getting some exercise, getting away from work, beating a friend, and improving the skill of your game), whereas other tasks may have a single goal.

In studying situations this same variety of goals appears to exist. We may have long-range goals for our studying (e.g., getting a degree), short-range goals (e.g., passing a test), and multiple goals (e.g., preparing for an exam, seeing one's studying partner, improving our knowledge for playing Trivial Pursuit). Our goals may change by the setting we are in (e.g., just trying to pass the course in a required class but trying to develop particular skills in a key professional course), by the time available (e.g., the test is in 2 weeks or 20 minutes), and by external conditions (e.g., the desks are very close together in the testing room, so no one could see me look at my neighbor's paper during the test).

Metacognitive Knowledge.   The second major component of Flavell's monitoring model—metacognitive knowledge—includes a number of distinct categories of knowledge. One of these Flavell labels "sensitivity." This refers to an understanding of when it is necessary to use intentional acts to improve performance on a given task. In studying, this might include a realization that the type of material that is currently being studied will necessitate a different kind of processing activity if it is to be understand and remembered. Although this type of sensitivity is most likely to be missing in children, it may be missing in adults too. The lament heard by many college professors from their students that "I read the material for your exam four times but still I failed your exam" conveys a lack of sensitivity as to the need for a different kind of processing (of course, it *is* possible that the exam really was unfair).

Another category of metacognitive knowledge deals with knowledge about people (including the self) as processors of information. Flavell labels this category "variable knowledge." It includes knowledge at several levels including aspects specific to our own processing (e.g., I am better at studying mathematics than biology), our processing as compared to others (e.g., Kathy seems to understand these philosophical arguments better than I do), and the processing of people in general (e.g., people understand some ideas better than others). Flavell contends that the latter of these types of person knowledge may be of special importance in understanding cognitive processes. This also seems to be the case in studying, particularly in the area of executive control of studying processes. Knowledge about how we generally function as processors of information would appear to play a fundamental role in the regulation of our studying activities. If studiers know that simply reading a book does not guarantee its understanding, or that it is possible to get the wrong message from a book that is being studied (that is, that we may *mis*understand rather than fail to understand), then this knowledge may lead to better control mechanisms to assure that such outcomes do not occur. Unfortunately, relatively few investigations of studying at the adult level have dealt with this aspect of metacognitive knowledge.

A third category of metacognitive knowledge deals with what the individual knows about the impact of certain task variables. There appear to be two identifiable components involved here. One deals with the individual's knowledge about how changes in the material to be processed or conditions of presentation influence the ease of processing. Examples here might include how the individual knows that high-imagery words are easier to recall than low-imagery ones, or that information presented in a distracting environment will be more difficult to comprehend than that presented in a nondistracting setting. The second deals with knowledge about the demands of the task being carried out. This might include knowledge that recalling information is more difficult than recognizing it, or that applying information in a novel setting will be more difficult than reusing it in a familiar setting. Each of these types of task variables has obvious implications in the case of studying. It is important for the studier to understand that poorly organized material, material with low readability level, or material with poor access structures will present a more formidable challenge than materials on the opposite ends of these dimensions. Such knowledge is a necessary first step in setting up appropriate cognitive activities to successfully process such material. Similar arguments could be made for the importance of the studiers' knowledge that essay exams or exams that stress application of knowledge place substantially different loads on the studier than do multiple choice or fact recall exams. Studiers unaware of these differences will be at a substantial disadvantage.

The final category of metacognitive knowledge is concerned with the knowledge that the individual has about the effectiveness of various strategies in meeting the individual's cognitive goals. Studiers who know that outlining or mapping are effective in helping them grasp the argument structure in a difficult text or that mnemonic devices may effectively aid in the retention of list-type information (e.g., muscle names in anatomy) are at a substantial advantage over the studiers who lack such knowledge. Further discussion of this topic is presented in the section on cognitive actions.

Metacognitive Experiences.   The third major component of Flavell's cognitive monitoring model is concerned with the metacognitive experiences—the feelings, sensations, and realizations the individual has in the midst of carrying out cognitive operations. These include such experiences as a realization that what a person is saying to us will be important to tell a friend, that we are dubious about the argument being made by a speaker, or that we have a sinking feeling that we will not be able to perform adequately on an upcoming test (I remember vividly the feeling the night before my doctoral comprehensives that it was not possible for the testing committee to ask a question I could answer). Such metacognitive experiences are a common occurrence in studying activities. They may arise as we are studying a very difficult text section and we suddenly realize that we are understanding little of what is written, when we are reading a text section and it strikes us that this material is the kind the instructor likes to test, or when we realize during a conversation that our friend understands far better than we do some important topic for an upcoming test. Flavell captures this great diversity of metacognitive experiences in the following quote describing the family of feelings that may arise during a comprehension activity:

> I do not know, and could not ever, understand this. I do not now but conceivably/probably/definitely could understand this with more time and work. I may understand it, probably understand it, definitely understand it,

and can prove it. I just failed to understand something because my mind wandered/because of that one puzzling sentence/because this part seems inconsistent with that part/because I do not understand the overall purpose or relevance of the information/and I have no idea why. (p. 49)

Flavell contends that such metacognitive experiences are most likely to occur when a studier is doing a lot of conscious processing and when there appears to be some problem or difficulty with our cognitions. Such situations, of course, are prime ingredients of studying. Studiers are often actively comparing, translating, storing, and retrieving information. This provides a diversity of settings for such experiences to arise. Similarly, during studying, particularly of difficult material, we are likely to encounter ideas we do not understand, to be introduced to new material that slows processing, or to find that previous knowledge we had is incorrect.

This high incidence of metacognitive experiences in studying, combined with the fact that such experiences often signal a need for modification or initiation of specific cognitive activities, indicates that these experiences may play an important role in executive control. I address this issue in more detail when I consider the interactions among the various components of the cognitive monitoring model.

Cognitive Actions.   The fourth and final component of Flavell's model involves the cognitive actions that individuals use to reach their goals. This component may include any number of activities that make the accomplishment of a goal more likely. Thus, a listener may ask a speaker to reiterate a comment she made, a reader may skim over chapter headings to find a particularly interesting one, a problem solver may compare a problem facing him with one that was solved before, or a person attempting to remember a list of words may generate an image linking a to-be-remembered word to a well-known location. In studying, a studier may (1) underline key terms to make them easier to review, (2) take notes to help encode key concepts, (3) practice retrieval to get ready for a test, or (4) look back in a text to find the answer to a question inserted in the text. These actions constitute the prime means by which studiers realize the various goals they have set for themselves.

Interactions Among Components.   It is in the interactions among the components of the monitoring model that the issues of executive control become most prominent. In the discussion of these interactions emphasis is placed on the studying process, although Flavell's model is structured in a more general fashion.

The goals of the studier impact on each of the other components of the model, and each of these interactions has some effect on the control of studying. For example, a studier who forms the goal of understanding a particularly difficult mathematics chapter may activate some prior metacognitive knowledge about her ability to handle difficult mathematical concepts. That goal may also activate metacognitive knowledge that the only strategy that was effective in the last similar study situation was to map out each mathematical relationship and then write them in her own words.

Goals also have substantial impact on the cognitive actions that the studier carries out. If the studier's goal is to quickly refresh the major issues for a test that will be given in an hour, the actions carried out may involve a skimming of the text with a quick review of underlined information or a practice retrieval of the definition of bold-face terms. On the other hand, if the goal is to prepare for a term paper on the nonviolence approach of Gandhi, the studier may also skim a chapter but this time decide to jot down all useful phrases or quotes.

The formation of goals may also trigger metacognitive experiences that play important roles in the control of the studying process. The formation of a goal by studiers to do library research for a term paper may activate a metacognitive experience that the last time they had such a goal they failed to jot down the references for the articles read. Later when completing the reference list, they were forced to reread several articles to find the source of a particular quote. Or the formation of a goal to do better on the next psychology test may remind the studier that he was very embarrassed when he received a D+ on the last exam.

Not all goals, of course, are concerned with establishing desirable outcomes of studying. Some may involve attempting to monitor more effectively how we are progressing toward achieving some objective. Thus, a studier may have a goal of determining how the preparation for a crucial exam is progressing. This *monitoring* goal may result in triggering metacognitive experiences at several spots in the preparation for an exam. Thus, studiers may set up goals to determine how confident they feel at 2 weeks, 1 week, and 1 day before an exam.

A studier's metacognitive knowledge also influences each of the other components of the model with resultant impact on executive control. If part of a studier's knowledge is that she is generally good at mathematical tasks, she may be led to consider a goal involving a career in accounting or computer science. A studier who realizes he has a poor set of memory strategies may decide not to take a course in anatomy involving the memorization of muscle groups. Because a studier believes that she is better at synthesis tasks than at analytical ones, she may volunteer to handle that aspect of a group oral presentation in a speech class. These examples indicate that the metacognitive knowledge individuals have about their capabilities has substantial impact on the goals they set for themselves. Such knowledge also influences the actions that studiers carry out. If a studier knows that he overestimates how well he understands material, he may set up a group-study session with a friend who will quiz him on the material. Similarly, a studier who knows that she remembers names very well but easily forgets dates may create a mnemonic system for the dates but not for the names. Finally, metacognitive knowledge may also be linked to metacognitive experiences. A recollection by a studier that he sometimes tightens up on an exam may regenerate the panic experience he had on a history exam; knowledge that a studier has about her ability to solve organic chemistry problems may lead to a confident feeling that she will do well on an upcoming chemistry exam.

The metacognitive experiences that occur while studying may have a significant impact on the studier's goals, metacognitive knowledge, and actions. A feeling of poor comprehension on a studier's part after repeated attempts to read a physics article may lead him to alter his goal of reporting on that article before his class. In contrast, a feeling of excitement on listening to a lecturer in psychology may lead a studier to set a goal of becoming a psychology major. Such metacognitive experiences may also result in changes in the studier's metacognitive knowledge. A constant failure to understand how to capture depth illusions in an art class may lead a studier to conclude that her ability to learn how to draw is very limited. A successful paper in a technical writing class may lead a studier to alter his previous view that he was a poor writer. Of course, the existence of metacognitive experiences may also lead to changes in cognitive actions. The same feelings of noncomprehension that led to a change in goals for the student reading a difficult physics article may lead instead to discussions with the instructor that help clarify the meaning of the article. The same experience that led the student writer to revise his thoughts about his writing ability may lead to an intensive search of job positions for technical writers or intensive efforts to practice his ability on technical writing by writing descriptions of mousetraps or computer printers.

Finally, the cognitive actions the studier carries out also influence each of the other three components of the model. A studier who is attempting to answer a set of inserted questions in a text may experience frustration or success. These metacognitive experiences may then play an instrumental role in further goal-setting activities or in modification of the studier's metacognitive knowledge. In a similar manner, a studier attempting to carry out a mapping of a text may experience frustration in that she realizes she doesn't understand how to carry out the mapping activity after all. Such a metacognitive experience could be instrumental in seeking further instruction on how to carry out this type of studying strategy. Cognitive actions influence goals because the actions are the principal means for attaining those goals. A studier with a goal to obtain an A on a sociology exam may have carried out the actions of outlining the text, taking notes over the lectures, and attempting to answer a set of practice questions at the end of the text chapters. Similarly, a studier with a goal of improving his speaking ability before a class may practice his delivery before a videotape machine or his roommate. Cognitive actions influence metacognitive knowledge because, by carrying out an action, a studier may obtain information about her own skills and abilities. A studier who thinks she has a good set of abstract reasoning skills may find herself unable to successfully answer a set of reasoning exercises. The inability to carry out the action may lead to a change in her beliefs about her abilities. In contrast, a studier who successfully uses a mnemonic strategy to remember a list of names may revise her estimate of her memory abilities (Flavell, 1981).

The Cognitive Monitoring Model of Studying: Some Observations

Flavell's cognitive monitoring model, as it is made specific to the task of studying, is of obvious use in understanding executive control issues in studying. The numerous interactions among the various components of the model suggest a number of questions about control which have been little considered, let alone investigated. In addition, the model brings new perspectives that are not found in the other models. Specifically, by explicitly emphasizing the aspects of the studier's goals, a key component is foregrounded in understanding executive control that has been given too little attention. The goals of the studier must play a fundamental role in the regulation and control of studying activities. A deeper understanding of how goals are formed, modified, and implemented may help explain the numerous inconsistent results that have been reported in investigations of studying behavior. It is to be expected, for example, that the effectiveness of a studying strategy such as notetaking would be heavily influenced by the studier's goals. The studier whose goal is simply to pass a course probably receives less benefit from notetaking than one who wishes to obtain an A for a course. Another characteristic that is emphasized uniquely by the cognitive monitoring model is the demarcation of the studier's metacognitive experiences. This is an aspect of cognitive activities that has received very little attention in prior models. Such an experiential component could play a key role in understanding how the studier regulates his cognitive activities by serving as a signaling device when activities are proceeding well or poorly.

It is unfortunate that the cognitive monitoring model does not specify precisely how the various characteristics of the studier impact on the regulation of studying; that is, the model is silent on the mechanisms or procedures by which the characteristics such as goals and metacognitive experiences influence control. For example, whereas the studiers' goals are likely to impact on which actions they choose to carry out, how are these decisions made? Why does one goal control the action whereas another similar goal calling for a different set of actions not control the action? Or why does the metacognitive experience of failing to comprehend result in a modification of goals in one setting and a change of cognitive actions in another? These types of questions have bedeviled cognitive psychologists for years and are not unique to those who are trying to understand executive control in studying. In fact, these questions are variants of the old knowledge to action question we noted earlier.

In summary, the cognitive monitoring model of Flavell does provide a significant step forward in understanding the issues of executive control in studying. It has made clear a number of factors that have to be considered if researchers are to establish a more accurate understanding of executive control in studying. It falls short in suggesting a way to handle how these factors might operate in a studying situation. I consider next a model that suggests one way this control might be carried out. Before doing that, however, it is useful to specify some questions about executive control that are generated from the perspective of the cognitive monitoring model.

Research Questions

The cognitive monitoring model suggests a number of ways that control of studying might be influenced by events occurring before and during studying. Some examples of questions suggested by this model include the following:

1. How do the goals of studiers with extensive knowledge about the topic being studied differ from those with little knowledge?
2. Do subjects frequently think about their goals during the act of studying?
3. How frequently do metacognitive experiences become conscious during the act of studying? Does this vary depending on the type of cognitive action being carried out?
4. Do changes in metacognitive knowledge occur after major metacognitive experiences (e.g., does a failure in an exam lead to changes in person, task, or strategy knowledge)?

5. Do studiers consciously think about goals before beginning to study?
6. Do studiers who vary on individual differences measures of studying establish different goals, employ different cognitive actions, or experience a different set of metacognitive experiences?
7. What types of studying situations are most likely to involve conscious monitoring of metacognitive experiences?
8. Can studiers be taught to monitor more closely their metacognitive experiences or cognitive goals?

As we saw with the research questions that arose from the information-process model, it is apparent that a large number of the questions that arise from the cognitive monitoring model necessitate research paradigms in which the emphasis is on monitoring the activities going on during the act of studying. These are in contrast to those that simply look at the outcome of the studying activity. Thus, techniques such as protocol analysis and pausal analysis would also be called for here.

Act* and the Executive Control of Studying

Studying involves choice. In a way, that simple three-word sentence captures the essence of the issue of executive control in studying. Effective studying may involve choosing to read one passage of material very carefully whereas only skimming another, choosing one analogy to understand an idea whereas rejecting another, choosing to underline one sentence but not another, choosing to take notes in one setting while listening carefully in another, and choosing one interpretation of a complex topic and ignoring another. It would be possible to continue this litany for a very long time, but even this short list captures the essence of the importance of choice in studying. To understand how studiers make their choices is to go far in understanding a key factor in the regulation and executive control of studying. The models of studying considered to this point have raised the issue of executive control (and implicitly choice) and some of the factors that influence executive control. They have not, however, attempted to provide an explicit model which explains how the control of studying is effected. In this section I briefly describe a theory that attempts to speak directly to the issue of control. It is not a theory of studying or the studier but rather a theory of human cognition in general—the ACT* theory of human cognition (Anderson, 1983). The following section provides a brief description of the theory with special emphasis on how it applies to studying and executive control. The characterization presented here is drawn from Anderson (1983).

Anderson's ACT* theory is a third-generation computer simulation theory of human cognition. ACT*, which replaces two earlier versions of the theory labeled HAM and ACT, is a broad-based theory whose aim is to explain all of human cognition. It purports, therefore, to explain the underlying functioning of language, problem solving, perception, memory, and by extension, studying.

The key concept in understanding ACT* is the production. The production is a condition—action pair. The condition details a set of data patterns and the action specifies what the individual will do if information relevant to the data patterns is available to the individual. For example, the following production might control your eating activities:

If you are hungry
and you have some coins
and there is a vending machine in the building
and the machine is functioning
and the machine holds food items
then get a food item from the vending machine.

The number of conditions that can be specified for a production can vary dramatically from a few to a large number. The conditions can also vary from those specifying internal states (e.g., being hungry) to those specifying certain environmental conditions (e.g., the existence of a vending machine in the building). The conditions may also include certain goals that the individual wishes to accomplish. The actions may vary from those involving motor behavior (e.g., getting food from a vending machine) to those involving a categorization of information (e.g., if a plant has three leaf clusters and a red stem, then it must be poison ivy). Productions are thought to play a fundamental role in all cognition, are the mechanism by which the theory links knowledge to action, and are fundamental to understanding how executive control is conceptualized in ACT*.

To understand the role of productions in cognition in general and in studying in particular, it is necessary to sketch a general overview of the structure of ACT*. The general structural properties of ACT* are shown in Fig. 5.3. ACT* involves three different memory systems: working memory, declarative memory, and production memory. Working memory holds all the information that ACT* can access at any given point in time. Most of the processes that occur in ACT* do so in working memory. The encoding process puts information from the environment into working memory (see arrows in Fig. 5.3). The storage process may deposit some of this information in declarative memory, whereas the retrieval process

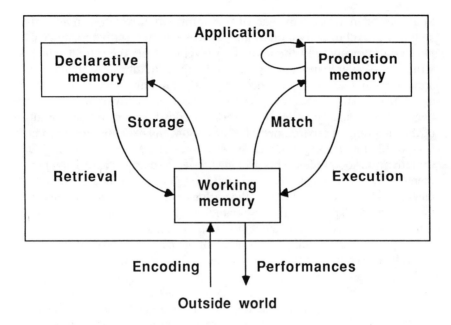

FIGURE 5.3   Components of Anderson's ACT* model (from Anderson, 1983).

brings information from declarative memory to working memory. The match process involves comparing information in working memory to the conditions of productions in production memory. The execution process involves placing the action of a production whose conditions have been matched into working memory. The performance process converts actions active in working memory into actual behavior. The arrow labeled application refers to the entire process of production matching followed by execution. The fact that it points back into production memory indicates that new productions are built from the application of existing ones.

Declarative memory refers to knowledge that individuals have about their world. According to ACT* this knowledge is organized into one of three types of cognitive units: temporal strings, spatial images, or propositions. These units are thought to be linked into a network structure which is referred to as a tangled hierarchy. It is possible to think of this hierarchy as a network of nodes representing various concepts, images, or strings connected to each other by links. Thus, the node for table might be linked to nodes for chairs, places to sit at a restaurant, and an image of a table. The information that is in declarative memory can be in various states of activation. This activation defines working memory and is fundamental to understanding executive control in ACT* because productions can be matched only against that information which is in an active state. The level of activation of any structure in declarative memory can vary continuously, and the activation level controls the rate at which a structure is matched against a production's conditions. Activation can spread from one node to another along the links connecting them, allowing for many nodes to achieve some degree of activation. Activation begins from a source node; these source nodes become sources because of the encoding of environmental information, the execution of a production, or the functioning of goals. When a node stops being a source node, its activation soon fades. This provides a way to dampen activation in the memory system and also a way to limit the total amount of activation that can exist in the system. Finally, the various nodes in declarative memory have a particular strength associated with them. This strength is a function of how frequently a cognitive unit is used.

Production memory is composed of all the productions available to the individual. Anderson estimates that there are tens of thousands to tens of millions of productions. These productions have strengths associated with them; each production's strength increases every time it is successfully applied. Stronger productions can be matched more rapidly than weaker ones. New productions are created through composition which involves the collapsing of a sequence of productions into one, or by proceduralization which involves the elimination of long-term memory retrievals of old productions. Finally, new productions can also be created by the tuning of old productions through processes of generalization and discrimination. There are a number of other features of declarative and production memory that are not detailed here. Those individuals interested in more detailed information should see Anderson (1983).

It is appropriate to pause briefly to discuss how the various components of ACT* described thus far might be applied to studying. Some of the information available in declarative memory deals with the characteristics of various fields of study (e.g., science, mathematics, history), conditions of various study settings (e.g., quiet, noisy, warm, cold), properties of texts (e.g., difficult,, easy, two-column format, small print size), time availability (e.g., the test is tomorrow or next week), the standing in a course (e.g., a studier is currently receiving a D or an A), and difficulty of certain kinds of tests (e.g., essay versus multiple choice, Professor Jones' tests). These various kinds of information may also be part of the conditions for productions related to studying. For example, one such production that a studier might have is as follows:

> If the material being studied is science
> and the professor in the course is Dr. Jones
> and the test being prepared for is an essay test

and the text is very difficult
and the exam is one week away
and the current course grade is a D
and the room is noisy
then outline the material.

As the studier who has this production interacts with her environment, the information relevant to numerous conditions of this production may be activated and a match with the conditions results. When this match occurs, the behavior indicated in the action would be executed and the individual would carry out the outlining behavior.

There are, of course, productions at many other levels that are relevant to the studying activities of individuals. Among these are productions that result in the instigation of different reading behaviors in the midst of studying (e.g., if feelings of noncomprehension arise during reading, and this material is for an important exam, and the material is considered important, then reread slowly the relevant material); productions that are involved in understanding specific content areas (e.g., if an algebra problem involves a verbal description, and the problem relates how fast two individuals can carry out a task, and the problem asks how long it would take the two individuals working together to complete the task, then make use of reciprocals to solve the problem); and productions that influence broad-based study behavior (if my goal is to become an engineer, and a course is a key skill course such as differential equations, then concentrate study time on this course).

These example productions indicate that ACT* might provide another way to view the linkage between environmental contexts, organismic variables, and the behaviors involved in studying. However, the issues of regulation or executive control of studying have not yet been specified. That is the topic of the next section.

Conflict Resolution and Executive Control

The characteristics of ACT* described so far are the foundation of the theory. These components and processes, however, do not address the primary issue regarding the regulation or executive control of cognitive acts (including studying). How is it that the studier decides on one production rather than another? According to ACT*, as the studier interacts with the environment, various aspects of that environment are encoded into working memory and this activates various modes in declarative memory. Through spread of this activation, numerous other nodes are also activated. This activated information is matched to the conditions of productions in production memory readying various productions to be executed. But it is clear that the conditions of many different productions are receiving activation simultaneously and are thus being readied. How is it decided which production is executed? What if productions result in antagonistic actions? To speak to these issues it is necessary to consider the principles of conflict resolution.

Anderson (1983) proposed five principles that guide the individual in the decisions of which productions apply in which situations. These are (1) the degree of match of the conditions of competing productions, (2) the strength of each competing production, (3) data refractoriness, (4) the specificity of competing productions, and (5) goal-dominance. Before considering each of these, it is necessary to consider an important distinction between data-driven (or bottom-up) and goal-directed (top-down) processing. Data-driven processing begins with information from the environment and attempts to match that information to higher level structures. In perception, for example, data-driven processing involves extensive pattern analyses on environmental information in an attempt to match this information with higher-level memory structures. An example of data-driven activation would be an individual sitting in a quiet room, who without any prior warning hears someone yell, "Help!" Relevant memory structures are activated in this case entirely from analyses of incoming environmental information (Moates & Schumacher, 1980).

In contrast, goal-directed or top-down processing involves attempts by the individual to match already activated higher level structures to the incoming information. Thus, a memory structure activated by spread of activation from other memory structures is attempted to be fit to incoming information. Such top-down activation is a crucial part of the numerous expectations that play such an important role in human cognition. Investigations, for example, have demonstrated that an individual who has been shown a kitchen scene is more likely to recognize a picture of a mail box with its door open as a loaf of sliced bread than is an individual who has been shown a blank scene (Palmer, 1975). This distinction between data-driven and goal-directed processing is important in understanding executive control, for it indicates that the conditions of various productions can be activated not only from environmental information but also from goal-related information. This aspect is made clearer when the fifth principle of goal-dominance is discussed.

Degree of Match.   A crucial factor involved in determining which production is executed is how well the conditions of the production are matched against the information from declarative memory that is active in working memory. According to ACT*, it is not necessary that there be a complete match for a production to be executed; partial matches are sufficient.

Anderson argues that it is necessary to allow for partial matches because many times in real-world settings behavior is necessary with less than complete information. In addition, humans frequently make mistakes in carrying out inappropriate productions, suggesting that partial matches may be operative. Of course, if the conditions of two productions both receive some activation, that production whose conditions are more fully matched will be the one that is executed.

The principle of the degree of match suggests one way that executive control is implemented in a studier. Imagine a studier with the following two productions available:

1. If the book being studied is a history book
   and the exam being studied for is an essay test
   and the test is a week away
   then take detailed notes while reading the whole chapter.
2. If the book being studied is a history book
   and the exam being studied for is a multiple choice test
   and the test is 1 day away
   then skim the section headings and read the summaries.

If the studier is preparing to study for a history test that is 1 week away, then the degree of match is better for production 1 than for production 2, and we should expect the studier to take detailed notes. Of course, in a real-world setting there will be many productions vying for execution, including those that do not involve studying. Thus, a studier may also have the following production:

If I am hungry
and there is no food in the house
and I have a car
and the pizza shop is open
then take the car and get a pizza.

If the conditions of this production are well matched, it may be executed instead of production 1 and thus studying behavior would cease.

Production Strength. As just noted, production strength is associated with the frequency with which that production has been successfully executed previously. The strength of a production is a factor in determining whether one production will be executed rather than another. A production with a higher strength level will be executed more quickly and reliably than one with lower strength.

The impact of this principle on executive control in studying might be seen when a studier has always consistently and closely monitored her comprehension of material being studied. Assuming this to be the case, the following production may have great strength and be very likely to be executed if its conditions are matched.

If I am studying a class text
and I finish reading a text section
and I am unable to summarize it easily
then skim the section looking for its main points.

This principle suggests that practice plays an important role in the development of effective study skills. Such practice could provide the studier with readily available and reliably applied procedures in given study situations.

Data Refractoriness.   This principle indicates that the same data elements cannot function in two productions at the same time. Anderson notes that this principle operates in many settings. In perception, for example, it accounts for the fact that the different interpretations of ambiguous figures cannot be seen simultaneously. We either see one interpretation or the other, but we don't see both at the same time. He also claims it accounts for the phenomenon of functional fixedness seen in problem-solving tasks. Functional fixedness refers to the finding that problem solvers have a difficult time using some tool or implement in one way to solve a problem when these objects have another apparent use in another part of the problem. Thus, subjects in a study by Glucksberg and Danks (1968) found it difficult to use the blade of a screwdriver as an electrical conductor to complete a circuit because they apparently viewed the screwdriver as a tool.

How might this principle function in the control of studying behavior? One way in which it applies is that a particular study technique employed for one purpose may be difficult to apply to another. For example, a studier who carefully reads a text chapter and then uses text summaries to review the text material may find it difficult to use summaries as a way to provide a scaffolding structure for the next chapter.

In a slightly different manner, a studier of a particular piece of literature might find it difficult to comprehend the piece because it necessitates realizing that the characteristics which make the protagonist in a story a hero can also be viewed as casting him as the archvillain. Keeping these two different characterizations in mind make this studying task very difficult.

Specificity.   The fourth conflict resolution principle indicates that if the conditions of two productions match the same data, the production that has the more specific set of conditions is the one that will be executed. Anderson claims that there are two ways in which one production may be more specific than another. In the first case, a production may have more tests than another production for the same set of data. Thus, in the case of studying, a production may include a condition testing for aspects of the text design. One production may test for several aspects of text design, including print size, type of text layout (e.g., one- or two-column format), and type font, whereas another production may have only tests for one aspect of text design. The second way in which productions can be more specific is by the existence of additional conditions. Whereas one production may have conditions for text style, type of test, and type of material, another may include additional conditions related to the type of professor, importance of the test (e.g., it's worth 10% or 40% of the grade), and prior performance on other tests. According to the principle of specificity then, assuming the existence of small print size in the text, the first production (following) would be executed before the second because it includes more specific tests.

1. If I am studying a psychology text
   and the text has a 2-column format with small print
   and the material is for an important course
   and the test will be multiple choice
   then highlight important concepts.
2. If I am studying a psychology text
   and the text has a 2-column format
   and the material is for an important course
   and the test will be multiple choice
   then write notes in the margin.

Goal-dominance.   The four principles of conflict resolution that we have discussed to this point are primarily concerned with data-driven activation of the conditions of productions. The fifth principle, in contrast, emphasizes top-down or goal-directed activation of productions. Goal elements in ACT* are high-level sources of activation which, unlike other activation sources, provide a constant source of activation. In fact, a goal will continue to be a source of activation until it is changed. In ACT* goals may be ordered into a hierarchical pattern such that some goals have subgoals, and these goals may themselves be subgoals of even larger goals. In the functioning of ACT*, when one goal is attained the system will move on to the next goal in the hierarchy. In addition, when all the subgoals of a goal are attained, the goal itself is attained and the next higher-level goal is than sought. In this fashion the actions of the productions are instrumental in leading the individual to attain whole sets of goals in a systematic fashion.

ACT* has a couple of additional goal-related features that make it an even more powerful model of cognition. The first of these relates to planning activities. The goal structures discussed to this point emphasize direct actions by the individual. But in many cognitive situations, individuals do not execute activities directly but rather generate plans from which the individual selects the best one. Anderson gives as an example the chess player who generates several different attack plans for his current position and selects the one from among them that gives the greatest likelihood of success. Such planning activities are an important part of cognition in almost any setting. The second feature that expands ACT*'s capability involves the concept of intention. In many situations there will be too little information available for the achievement of a particular goal. Under this circumstance individuals must either come to a halt in their efforts to achieve this goal or proceed without the relevant information with the intention to deal with the missing information later. Again, Anderson (1983) provides an instructive example in this case involving his son J. J., who likes to put together small jigsaw puzzles. J. J's approach is to put the peripheral pieces in first and then the center pieces. If he tries a center piece and it fits, he places it; if he can't place it, he sets that piece aside and appears to create an intention to place it later when the conditions are appropriate.

This goal-directed principle plays an important role in understanding executive control in studiers. The goals that a studier sets help to orchestrate sets of productions to obtain these goals. The following three productions carry some of this flavor that might be expected to appear in studying situations. Note also the use of planning and intention processes in these study-related productions.

1. If my goal is to obtain an A in this course
     and the course is a history course
     and the instructor is a tough grader
     and the course involves a paper
     then start reading for this paper in the second week.
2. If my subgoal is to do well on this paper
     and the paper involves a complex argument
     and the argument involves several different facets
     then consider several different ways to sequence the paper and choose the best.
3. If my subgoal is to write the subsection on the causes of WWII
     and there are three issues to discuss

and I've left my notes on the first one at home
then write the last two sections and return to the other when the
notes are available.

This brief and admittedly cursory consideration of ACT* does indicate
that the model may be particularly useful in speaking to the issues of
executive control in studying. In contrast to the earlier information-
processing and metacognitive models, it suggests a specific way in which
to conceptualize how executive control is accomplished. This is an
especially important contribution. The model thus provides insight into
why studiers carry out different studying activities in seemingly very
similar situations.

The model also emphasizes the role that goals play in studying, an
important feature because goals appear to play such a crucial role in
studying. It seems unlikely, for example, that we will obtain a complete
understanding of studying until we better understand how goals intertwine to control the activities in which studiers engage.

For the ACT* model to become a significant force in research on
studying, however, it will be necessary to determine what sets of productions different groups of studiers have available. It will also be necessary
to determine what goals individuals have and what goal structures inter-
link these goals. Finally, in order to test the concept of conflict resolution
principles, it will be necessary to determine what environmental information is being encoded and matched to production conditions and what
levels of strength various productions have.

In summary, it is apparent that there is significant promise in the ACT*
model to aid our understanding of studying. However, several issues need
to be addressed before this promise can be fulfilled.

Research Questions

One test of the usefulness of a model is whether it generates new and
important questions that enable us to better understand a phenomenon. In
great measure ACT* passes this test. By making the process of executive
control more explicit, a number of questions are raised whose answers
would significantly aid our understanding of control in studying. Some
examples of such questions are the following:

1. Do studiers have specific studying strategies linked closely to
varying study conditions; that is, in the same manner that chess experts
appear to have specific moves associated with particular chess positions,
do studiers have specific studying strategies associated with particular
study settings? Would a studier, for example, be likely to think "Oh, this

upcoming test is a short-answer type and the only technique that works is to outline it." A number of studies might generate useful results here. For example, would expert studiers who are given brief glances of different text types be more able than novice studiers to determine key structural characteristics of the text, remember more major elements, or identify effective study strategies?

2. What types of changes in contextual variables or text characteristics lead to shifts in studying activities? Would observing studiers in normal settings in which close monitoring of environmental conditions is also recorded allow researchers to ascertain which shifts in environmental variables result in or are correlated with shifts in study activities? Would verbal protocol studies provide evidence that indicates when control of studying shifts from one production to another?

3. Can useful indices of production strength be ascertained through questionnaire or interview procedures, and would such measures predict the speed or reliability with which certain productions are implemented?

4. What measures of studier-environmental interaction would allow researchers to predict which conditions of productions are being matched and consequently which productions are most likely to be executed? For example, would eye-movement measures indicate which text properties are being checked or which portion of a written set of instructions for a term paper are being attended to and thus allow researchers to predict which productions are most likely to be executed?

5. How does the length of the study period influence the type of study activities carried out? Does the probability of certain study activities decline as the length of a particular study period increases?

6. Are there stable individual differences in the types of control decisions that are made by different studiers? For example, are some studiers more likely than other studiers to shift from one study activity (e.g., outlining) to another with minor changes in study setting or text characteristics?

From these questions it is apparent that ACT* does provide another window on the role of executive control in studying. By focusing attention on how choice may be conceptualized in studying it provides another set of issues and questions that may help us make better progress in understanding studying and its control.

SUMMARY AND CONCLUSIONS

I argued at the beginning of this chapter that it might be very beneficial to view studying through the perspective of the studier with special emphasis on executive control. It was argued that understanding executive control has been crucial to understanding most cognitive activities in which individuals engage. It was also suggested that an understanding of executive control might prove helpful in explaining the inconsistencies in studying research and the powerful role that contextual factors play in studying activities. In addition, it was noted that the numerous processes involved in carrying out studying necessitate an understanding of how they are orchestrated into a coherent process.

The major portion of the chapter considered three major ways of conceptualizing executive control: an information-processing model, a cognitive monitoring model, and a computer simulation model. Each of these was interpreted from the point of view of studying, and research questions that arose from each model were suggested. What conclusions seem appropriate at this point and where might we go from here?

First, it is even more apparent after reviewing these models and their implications that the time is ripe for a more thorough consideration of the role of executive control in studying. The models reviewed provide potential insights into understanding why there is little coherence in studying research. They also suggest how researchers might better approach the issue of context. Rather than viewing context as error which complicates and obfuscates, it becomes an important factor in explaining how control is effected. In doing this it makes us more optimistic that a systematic, generalizable view of studying may be fashioned.

Second, it is clear that there is an important need for certain kinds of research on studying which to this point has not been regularly carried out. There is a need for research in naturalistic settings so that the role of contextual variables, important in everyday studying, can be better understood. For example, we need to better understand how time factors (e.g., how long before an exam), text characteristics (e.g., text structure), and exam type (e.g., multiple choice, essay) impact on the type of study activities carried out. We also need more process-oriented research in studying, much as has been occurring recently in the study of writing. There is a need for investigations such as protocol analyses, observational studies, and macroeye-movement studies to track the processes involved in studying and how the studier controls and uses these processes. Similarly, there is a need for investigations in which the outcome of studying is measured in ways different from simple tests of comprehension or memory. For example, we need to know how studying influences a studier's knowledge structures. The impact of studying on knowledge structures is important because executive control may be substantially different when studiers are attempting to become experts in an area than when they are trying to perform successfully on an exam.

Third, the models of executive control considered in this chapter provide differing views of executive control in studying. Each of these models emphasizes different aspects of how the studier interacts with the studying task. Further research is necessary to determine if one or the other of these models is the most fruitful one to develop.

Finally, one last observation seems appropriate. Understanding how executive control in studying is obtained will be a very difficult task. It will involve a significant shift in focus in terms of both research and theorizing. The consequences of significant progress in achieving this end, however, may be a far more coherent understanding of studying. Such an understanding could provide the basis for more effective ways of improving how students carry out and control the act of studying.

REFERENCES

Afflerbach, P., & Johnston, P. (1984). On the use of verbal reports in reading research. *Journal of Reading Behavior, 16,* 307–322.

Anderson, J. R. (1983). *The architecture of cognition.* Cambridge, MA: Harvard University Press.

Anderson, T. H., & Armbruster, B. B. (1984). Studying. In P. D. Pearson (Ed.), *Handbook of reading research* (pp. 657–679). New York: Longman.

Atlas, M. A. (1981). The user edit: Making manuals easier to use. *IEEE Transactions on Professional Communication, PC-24,* 28–29.

Baker, L., & Brown, A. L. (1984). Metacognitive skills and reading. In P. D. Pearson (Ed.), *Handbook of reading research* (pp. 353–394). New York: Longman.

Brown, A. L., Armbruster, B. B., & Baker, L. (1985). The role of metacognition in reading and studying. In J. Orasanu (Ed.), *Reading comprehension: From research to practice.* Hillsdale, NJ: Lawrence Erlbaum Associates.

Brown, A. L., & Campione, J. C. (1978). The effects of knowledge and experience on the formation of retrieval plans for studying from texts. In M. M. Gruneberg, P. E. Morris, & R. N. Sykes (Eds.), *Practical aspects of memory* (pp. 378–384). London: Academic Press.

Cavanaugh, J. C., & Perlmutter, M. (1982). Metamemory: A critical examination. *Child Development, 53,* 11–28.

Donaldson, M. (1978). *Children's minds.* New York: W. W. Norton.

Fass, W., & Schumacher, G. M. (1978). Effects of motivation, subject activity, and readability on the retention of prose materials. *Journal of Educational Psychology, 70,* 803–807.

Flavell, J. H. (1981). Cognitive monitoring. In W. P. Dickson (Ed.), *Children's oral communication skills* (pp. 35–60). New York: Academic Press.

Flower, L., & Hayes, J. R. (1981). A cognitive process theory of writing. *College Composition and Communication, 32,* 365–387.

Gettinger, M. (1984). Individual differences in time needed for learning: A review of the literature. *Educational Psychologist, 19,* 15–29.

Glucksberg, S., & Danks, J. H. (1968). Effects of discriminative labels and of nonsense labels upon availability of novel function. *Journal of Verbal Learning and Verbal Behavior, 7,* 72–76.

Hartley, J., Bartlett, S., & Branthwaite, A (1980). Underlining can make a difference— sometimes. *Journal of Educational Research, 73,* 218–224.

Hayes, J. R. (1978). *Cognitive psychology: Thinking and creating.* Homewood, IL: Dorsey.

Holland, V. M., & Redish, J. C. (1981). *Strategies for understanding forms and other public documents*. (Document Design Project Tech. Rep. No. 13). Washington, DC: The American Institutes for Research.

Hout Wolters, B. van. (1982). Methoden voor procesgericht onderzoek tijdens het besturen van studieteksten. In M. van de Kamp & L. van de Kamp (Eds.), *Methodologie van de onderwijsresearch*. Lisse, The Netherlands: Swets en Zeitlinger.

Howard, D. V. (1983). *Cognitive psychology: Memory, language, and thought*. New York: MacMillan.

Just, M. A., & Carpenter, P. A. (1980). A theory of reading: From eye fixations to comprehension. *Psychological Review, 87,* 329–354.

Kiewra, K. A. (1985a). Investigating notetaking and review: A depth of processing alternative. *Educational Psychologist, 20,* 23–32.

Kiewra, K. A. (1985b). Providing the instructor's notes: An effective addition to student notetaking. *Educational Psychologist, 20,* 33–39.

Klare, G. R. (1984). Readability. In P. D. Pearson (Ed.), *Handbook of reading research* (pp. 681–744). New York: Longman.

Klare, G. R., & Smart, K. (1973). Analysis of the readability level of selected USAFI instructional materials. *Journal of Educational Research, 67,* 176.

MacNeilage, P. F., & DeClerk, J. L. (1969). On the motor control of coarticulation in CVC monosyllables. *Journal of the Acoustical Society of America, 45,* 1217–1233.

Mayer, R. E. (1984). Aids to text comprehension. *Educational Psychologist, 19,* 30–42.

McConkie, G. W., Hogaboam, T. W., Wolverton, G. S., Zola, D., & Lucas, P. A. (1979). *Toward the use of eye movements in the study of language processing*. (Center for the Study of Reading Tech. Rep. No. 134). Champaign, IL: University of Illinois.

Miller, G. A., Galanter, E., & Pribram, K. H. (1960). *Plans and the structure of behavior*. New York: Holt, Rinehart, & Winston.

Mishler, E. G. (1979). Meaning in context: Is there any other kind? *Harvard Educational Review, 49,* 1–19.

Moates, D. M., & Schumacher, G. M. (1980). *An introduction to cognitive psychology*. Belmont, CA: Wadsworth.

Nye, P. A., Crooks, T. J., Powley, M., & Tripp, G. (1984). Student notetaking related to university examination performance. *Higher Education, 13,* 85–97.

Palmer, S. E. (1975). The effects of contextual scenes on the identification of objects. *Memory and Cognition, 3,* 519–526.

Rohwer, Jr., W. D. (1984). An invitation to an educational psychology of studying. *Educational Psychologist, 19,* 1–14.

Schmeck, R. R. (1983). Learning styles of college students. In R. F. Dillon & R. R. Schmeck (Eds.), *Individual differences in cognition* (Vol. 1, pp. 233–279). New York: Academic Press.

Schumacher, G. M., Klare, G. R., Cronin, F. C., & Moses, J. D. (1984). Cognitive activites of beginning and advanced college writers: A pausal analysis. *Research in the teaching of English, 18,* 169–187.

Schumacher, G. M., Moses, J. D., & Young, D. (1983). Students' studying processes on course related texts: The impact of inserted questions. *Journal of Reading Behavior, 15,* 19–36.

Schumacher, G. M., & Waller, R. (1983, April). *Recording study behavior on normal text: A methodological comparison*. Paper presented at the American Educational Research Association, Montreal.

Schumacher, G. M., & Waller, R. (1985). Testing design alternatives: A comparison of procedures. In T. Duffy & R. Waller (Eds.), *Designing usable texts* (pp. 377–403). New York: Academic Press.

Swarts, H., Flower, L. S., & Hayes, J. R. (1984). Designing protocol studies of the writing process: An introduction. In R. Beach & L. S. Bridwell (Eds.), *New directions in composition research* (pp. 53–71). New York: The Guilford Press.

Whalley, P. C. (1981). *Macrolevel recording of reading behavior.* Paper presented at the Conference of the European Group for Eye-Movement Research, Bern, Switzerland.

Whalley, P. C. (1982). *Argument in text and the reading process.* Unpublished paper. Institute of Educational Technology, Open University, Milton Keynes, England.

Wollen, K. A., Cone, R. S., Britcher, J. C., & Mindeman, K. M. (1985). The effect of instructional sets upon the apportionment of study time to individual lines of text. *Human Learning, 4,* 89–103.

THE ACTIVATION AND USE
OF SCRIPTED KNOWLEDGE
IN READING ABOUT
ROUTINE ACTIVITIES 6

Frank R. Yekovich *and* Carol H. Walker
The Catholic University of America

One of the hallmarks of skilled reading is the ease with which a person comprehends the meaning of a text. Much of the credit for this apparent effortlessness is traceable to the executive control processes that coordinate the functioning of the human cognitive system. Control functions are aspects of cognitive processes that contribute to the achievement of particular reading goals. One such control function is monitoring an ongoing component process in order to assure its successful completion. Another control function is the initiation of a different component process when the current goals of processing either are not being achieved or could be achieved more efficiently. These examples illustrate that executive control functions exhibit *sensitivity* during reading comprehension and they also have certain *responsibilities*. The sensitivity of the control system is a function of a reader's goals (e.g., skimming for theme v. learning details), reader skill (e.g., the degree of automaticity of the component processes), and a text's characteristics (e.g., its local coherence). This sensitivity can be seen operating by observing modulations in reading speed (e.g., Cirilo & Foss, 1980), gaze durations on individual words, and/or regressive fixations (see Just & Carpenter, 1980 for a discussion).

Control functions also have numerous responsibilities, such as the coordination of the component reading processes (e.g., prioritizing word identification over lexical access), the coordination and allocation of cognitive resources (e.g., optimizing the use of short-term memory), and the selection and use of knowledge to fill gaps in text (e.g., inserting knowledge into a composite representation of the text and subsequently using this knowledge for inferencing or reasoning). This last issue, the selection and use of knowledge, is an important feature of any comprehensive theory of reading, and it is the issue with which this chapter is concerned.

Most theorists agree that an understanding of knowledge selection and use is critical (see van Dijk & Kintsch, 1983). Unfortunately, little work has seriously attempted to study the processes by which the cognitive system activates knowledge from long-term memory and makes it available for on-line use during reading. Two reasons underlie why so little work has been done. First, in order to understand knowledge selection and use, one must have an explicit model of the organization of the knowledge structures that reside in long-term memory. Such models of memory are required in order to predict how a piece of incoming text is likely to affect the activation of knowledge in memory. The lack of consensus among memory models attests to the fact that the knowledge issue is both nontrivial and unresolved (see Anderson, 1983a). Second, research that has concerned itself with knowledge-based issues (e.g., the effects of context on lexical access) has generally relied on small text segments such as individual sentences, or at most, two-to-three-sentence texts (e.g., Swinney, 1979). Whereas this approach has yielded valuable information about reading components, it has not provided data about large-scale knowledge use during extended reading situations. So, for example, little is known about the time course of knowledge activation during text comprehension (except see Dell, McKoon, & Ratcliff, 1983; Foss, 1982).

The purpose of the present chapter is to describe our first attempt at tackling the problem of knowledge selection and use during reading. Because so little previous work has been concerned with knowledge-based effects, the first task involves defining the organization of a knowledge structure that has tractable characteristics. In the next section, we describe our view of the organization of one such knowledge structure, a *script*. Subsequently, we sketch how portions of this long-term knowledge are selected and inserted into a working memory trace during the reading of a text that describes the scripted activity. In the last major section, we describe a program of research aimed at understanding the effects of this process on text comprehension and memory.

THE ORGANIZATION OF SCRIPTED KNOWLEDGE

Most current models of reading comprehension have been developed using text segments drawn from popular reading sources such as *Reader's Digest* or *Scientific American*. For the most part the content of these text segments is relatively unfamiliar to the reader. One consequence of using this type of material is that charting knowledge selection and use becomes difficult because such text favors bottom-up processes rather than top-down or knowledge-driven ones. Thus, although many reading models are based on "naturally" occurring types of texts, these same texts are not optimal for the systematic study of knowledge-based contributions to reading.

In order to study knowledge-based contributions, we and others (see especially Graesser & Clark, 1985) have begun using segments of discourse that maximize top-down or knowledge-driven processes during comprehension. The texts we have chosen to use are based on knowledge structures that have received a moderate amount of empirical attention. Specifically, we have selected *scripted* knowledge structures and have used scripted texts. A script represents a person's prototypical knowledge of a routine activity, such as PAINTING A ROOM or GOING TO A RESTAURANT. Scripted knowledge has two features that make it useful for studying knowledge-based contributions to reading. First, a script, by definition, is culturally uniform and represents "expert" knowledge about human behavior in a routine situation. The clear implication of this uniformity is that the organization of scripted knowledge will not vary markedly across individuals within a given culture (Bower, Black, & Turner, 1979). Second, scripts generally have well-defined goal structures and predictable temporal properties. The implication of this is that the relations among scripted components are well specified and unambiguous. Taken together, these two features suggest that scripted knowledge has tractable characteristics, that is to say, its organization can be specified. Once this organization is specified, the effects of this structure on reading can be studied. For instance, a researcher might activate a particular portion of a scripted knowledge structure using textual input that corresponds to that portion of the structure, and systematically monitor the effect of that input on other parts of the knowledge structure. Although reading a text that describes the performance of a routine activity may not be very interesting or informative for the reader, using this type of text in reading experiments does provide an opportunity for studying the knowledge components that are used during comprehension.

The issue of how scripts are represented in memory has received considerable attention in recent years (see, for example, Abbott, Black, & Smith, 1985; Bower et al., 1979; Galambos & Rips, 1982; Graesser, 1981; Graesser & Clark, 1985; Mandler & Murphy, 1983; Schank & Abelson, 1977; Walker & Yekovich, 1984, 1986; Yekovich & Walker, 1986). Although some progress has been made on this topic, no consistent view has emerged regarding the representational properties of scripts. Our own work has led us to adopt a model of script representation that is consistent with production system architecture (see Anderson, 1983a). According to this view, scripted knowledge is comprised of separate *procedural* and *declarative* memory components. Each of these memory components contributes knowledge to the final memory trace of the text. In the next two sections, we describe the procedural and declarative components of scripts.

Procedural Representation of Scripts.   The procedural component of a script (i.e., knowledge of how to do the activity) is comprised of productions, which are formalized as sets of IF–THEN contingency rules (see Anderson, 1982; Lewis & Anderson, 1985). To illustrate one such procedural rule, consider a production associated with PAINTING A ROOM (adapted from Anderson, 1983a):

> IF   The goal is to paint X
> And X is too high to reach
> THEN   Use the ladder method
> And set as subgoals to
>   1. Get the paint
>   2. Use the ladder
>   3. Apply the paint to X

The production has two major components, conditions and actions.[1] The conditions (i.e., the clauses associated with IF) specify the state that must exist for the production to apply, and the actions (i.e., the clauses associated with THEN) specify the cognitive or physical behavior that will be executed when the conditions are met. In this production, X is a variable that represents any paintable object beyond reach (e.g., ceiling, light fixture) and thus makes the production more flexible. The conditions of this production will be satisfied when they can be matched against information active in working memory.

In a reading situation concerned with PAINTING, the preceding production would apply if a reader encountered, *Next, Phil decided to paint the ceiling. However, the handle on his roller was so short that he could not reach the ceiling.* The propositional textbase of this segment would include (PAINT, PHIL, CEILING) and (NOT REACH, PHIL, CEILING), which would match the conditions of the production. The application of the production would lead the reader to generate expecta-

---

[1]Notice that the production has a goal and several subgoals in it. This feature is used to produce a goal hierarchy in a set of productions. The goal structure is assumed to be inherent and is responsible for the control of cognitive or physical behavior.

tions about ladders, which would be realized as an increase in activation on the concept LADDER, and associated memory nodes. Theoretically, the application of the production should facilitate comprehension of upcoming text that has ladder-related content because ladder-related concepts are now more active in declarative memory. The exact concepts that are affected by the production's execution depend on the organization of those concepts (i.e., which concepts are connected to which others). Thus, to understand knowledge selection, we must consider the structure of scripted concepts in declarative memory.

Declarative Representation of Scripts.   The declarative representation of a script may be characterized as a semantic network which represents factual knowledge as conceptual nodes and relational links. For purposes of the present discussion, these concepts and relations are assumed to represent context-specific meanings. Figure 6.1 depicts a portion of the hypothetical structure for a PAINTING A ROOM script. The script header is illustrated as two connected but separate concepts, and its status as a header is shown by the elipse encircling the two concepts. The script-specific associations are shown as the solid lines that connect the concepts. For the sake of simplicity we have depicted the obvious relations only. For example, the figure illustrates that PAINTER (i.e., one who uses tools for the purpose of covering some object with paint) and BRUSH (i.e., a tool used for covering some object with paint) are connected by the relation USE. The figure does not depict the directionality or the strength of the associations.

The major purpose of the figure is to demonstrate the likely organization of the scripted concepts. Note that some concepts (e.g., WALLS) are associated with many other concepts, whereas other concepts (e.g., WATER) have few script-specific associations. This characterization of organization argues that scripted concepts have different degrees of *associative relevance* or *centrality* within the script. Concepts with high associative relevance are likely to be necessary, useful, and important to the successful completion of the routine activity. In contrast, concepts with fewer associations are less relevant to the successful completion of the activity. Thus, a concept such as WALLS is depicted as highly relevant or central to the PAINTING routine. WATER, on the other hand, is depicted as less important although still related to the routine. In previous work, we have referred to these two types of concepts as central and peripheral, respectively. For continuity that same terminology is used here. Further, although centrality varies continuously, for present purposes we consider the two extremes.

The depiction in Fig. 6.1 is assumed to be a context-specific one; that is, this representational pattern applies only when the PAINTING A

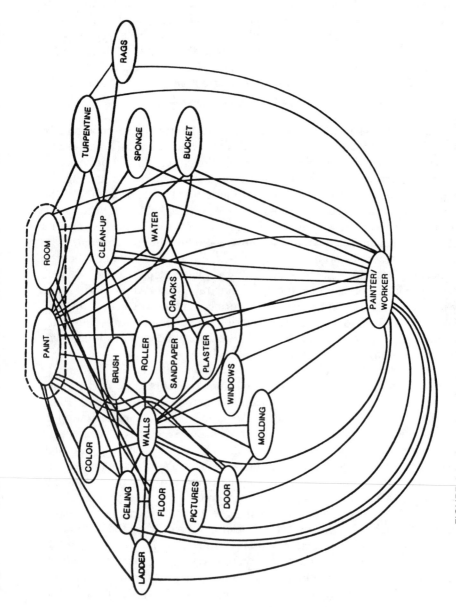

FIGURE 6.1 A portion of a hypothetical declarative representation for PAINTING A ROOM.

150

ROOM script becomes activated for use. Thus, the pattern of associations illustrated for a particular concept is in effect only when that particular script is active. The concept, WATER, is a particularly good example of this assumption because in the PAINTING context WATER is peripheral, whereas in a SWIMMING or CAR WASHING context WATER would be a central concept.

The declarative representation in Fig. 6.1 derives its organization from repeated exposures to the PAINTING routine. Similarly, the associative strength of each connection is determined by these exposures. Thus, the associative network develops through experience (see Schank's descriptions of his child's development of the RESTAURANT script; Schank & Abelson, 1977). Being a member of a particular culture affects the uniformity of these experiences, and thus the eventual organization of declarative knowledge.

Having outlined a hypothetical organization of the semantic content of scripted knowledge, the next issue involves how portions of this knowledge are selected and used in text comprehension. The next section spells out in some detail how this occurs.

INSERTING SCRIPTED KNOWLEDGE
INTO THE COMPOSITE TRACE

When a text is read, an episodic memory representation is formed. This representation is a composite trace. Two information sources that contribute to this composite trace are the text and the reader's knowledge. Exactly how does reader knowledge get inserted into the composite trace? We believe that *activation-based* mechanisms are responsible. Essentially, activation accrues on nodes in memory and these activated nodes are inserted into the memory trace of the text. Four factors affect the level of activation on a node (see Just & Carpenter, 1980). First, perceptual encoding raises the level of activation of a memory node (e.g., reading the word *brush* directly activates BRUSH in memory). Second, the output of a component process can affect the level of activation of a node. For instance, during lexical access of the word, *brush,* at least two meanings will be activated initially; (a) an implement used on one's hair, and (b) a tool used for a work-related purpose such as painting. However, according to Swinney (1979), one meaning will be deactivated very quickly and the other meaning selected for insertion into working memory. Thus, the final product of lexical access will be one set of active nodes and a separate set of deactivated nodes. The third factor that affects level of activation on a memory node is the node's baseline level, which roughly corresponds to the context-free normative frequency of use of the concept (e.g., BRUSH has a higher baseline level of activation than SANDPAPER because *brush* has a word frequency of 44 whereas *sandpaper* has a frequency of 1, according to Kucera and Francis (1967)). The fourth factor is the spread of activation through the declarative network. For example, if the concept BRUSH is activated through the perceptual encoding of *brush*, residual or indirect activation will spread from the source node, BRUSH, to its associated or secondary nodes (e.g., PAINT, ROLLER, WALLS in Fig. 6.1). The amount that is spread to each secondary node will be directly related to associative strength of the connection between the source node and the secondary node and inversely related to number of secondary nodes connected to the source. In scripted knowledge structures, central concepts have more opportunities to receive indirect activation than peripheral concepts because central concepts have a larger number of associations.

Level of activation, whether from direct or indirect excitation, is the primary criterion for a memory node being inserted into the composite memory trace. Once a concept has been inserted, its level of activation does not remain constant. Instead, it continues to vary as a function of the four factors described earlier. Concepts that are maintained at high levels of activation are accessible in the composite; concepts whose levels of activation decay are less accessible. Accessibility of a concept is an indicator of its utility during comprehension and its availability at retrieval.

It is instructive to consider an illustration of how the concepts of a scripted knowledge structure become activated during reading. The purpose of the description that follows is threefold. First, it provides a flavor of the semantic content of a composite representation as it develops. Second, the description provides face validity for our view of the organization of semantic content associated with scripted knowledge. In other words, the illustration points out the heuristic value of the assumption of associative relevance. Third, the example demonstrates that relatively few concepts receive indirect activation repeatedly by virtue of the organization of declarative knowledge.

For this illustration consider another well-known script, GOING TO A RESTAURANT (Schank & Abelson, 1977). Suppose that a person read the following prototypical text:

> Jack and his girlfriend Chris decided to go out to a nice restaurant. They called to make a reservation and then they drove to the restaurant. When they arrived, Jack opened the door and they walked inside. Jack gave his name to the hostess at the reservation desk. Because they were a little too early to be seated, they decided to go in the bar for a drink. When their table was ready, Jack and Chris went into the dining room. They were seated at a

table near the window. The waiter came over and introduced himself. He gave Jack and Chris their menus. They discussed the menu. Soon, they were ready to order. After they ordered, Jack and Chris talked and admired the view. When Jack and Chris were served, they ate their meal leisurely, savoring every bite. Later they decided to splurge and have dessert. Jack and Chris ate most of their dessert, but by now they were getting full. It was late, so Jack asked for the check. The service had been good, so they left a big tip for the waiter. They paid the check and got their coats. Jack and Chris walked out of the restaurant and drove home.

The preceding text presents a fairly routine description of a couple going out to dinner, and in fact the description "seems" rather complete. Few American adults have trouble comprehending descriptions about such routine activities. Yet, in many ways the *written words* themselves do not capture the phenomenological richness of meaning that a person experiences when reading the restaurant description. Phenomenologically, knowledge of going out to dinner focuses on images of being served a meal at a private table, of paying for the experience, and on concepts such as MEAL, WAITER, TABLE, and CHECK. Although these concepts are mentioned explicitly in the text, so are less prototypical concepts such as DESK and COATS. However, few people would include DESK and COATS in their recollections of this text, whereas almost everyone would include MEAL, WAITER, TABLE, and CHECK. Thus, the memorial or phenomenological importance of the prototypical concepts is not realized within the propositional textbase alone. Put another way, a person's memory of the text automatically preserves the central elements of the routine even though the text itself does not emphasize these concepts. What we want to demonstrate is how one's knowledge of GOING TO A RESTAURANT interacts with the preceding text to produce this phenomenologically complete memory representation.

To demonstrate this interaction, two simple rules are used to expand the text's content into a memorial version that includes the reader's declarative knowledge of the routine. First, assume that a reader makes the lexical inferences required to fill the case slots associated with each verb in a text (see also Corbett & Dosher, 1978; McKoon & Ratcliff, 1981; Singer & Ferreira, 1983). For instance, in the sentence, "They called to make a reservation and then they drove to the restaurant," the verb *call* requires an agent, a recipient, and an instrument. The agent *They* is specified but neither the recipient (i.e., someone at the restaurant) nor the instrument (i.e., the telephone) is. We assume that knowledgeable readers typically make these lexical inferences, at least about routine activities. According to this assumption, the expanded sentence would resemble the following:

> They called (on the telephone) (to someone) (at the restaurant) to make a reservation and then they drove (in a car) to the restaurant.

The content in parentheses refers to the lexical inferences required to fill the case slots.

The second expansion rule states that in a scripted context all concepts will activate script-specific definitions, and these definitions will be incorporated into the expanded memory representation. To illustrate, consider the noun *reservation* in the previously mentioned sentence. *Reservation* can be defined in a number of ways (e.g., a tract of land set aside, as for the use of Indians; a specific objection about a finding; an arrangement to hold a table for one's use). In the context of the RESTAURANT script, only the script-specific definition (ARRANGEMENT TO HOLD A TABLE FOR ONE'S USE) will be inserted into the expansion. The net effect is that mention of *reservation* spreads indirect activation to the definitional concepts in memory (e.g., TABLE). Using this rule, and combining it with the case-filling rule, the following expanded sentence results:

> They (CUSTOMERS OR ONES THAT PURCHASE) called (on the telephone) (to someone) (at the restaurant (PLACE WHERE CUSTOMERS CAN PURCHASE AND BE SERVED A MEAL)) to make a reservation (ARRANGEMENT TO HOLD A TABLE FOR ONE'S USE) and then they (CUSTOMERS OR ONES THAT PURCHASE) drove (in a car) to the restaurant (PLACE WHERE CUSTOMERS CAN PURCHASE AND BE SERVED A MEAL).

We have included definitional expansions only for script-relevant concepts in order to keep the illustration simple. Further, we recognize that the choice of a stopping point for the expansion procedure here is arbitrary. We could repeat the two rules again, but the result would be an expansion into concepts that are not script specific. This would resemble a form of semantic decomposition, and several theorists argue against extreme forms of semantic decomposition (e.g., Kintsch, 1974).

Using these two rules, we have expanded the entire GOING TO A RESTAURANT passage and have included the expanded version in the appendix. From the sample sentence, and the entire passage, a number of interesting phenomena emerge. First, the expansion procedure produces a highly enriched version of the script. This result is in keeping with the phenomenological richness of one's memory for such texts, which has been documented several times (Abbott et al., 1985; Bower et al., 1979; Graesser, Gordon, & Sawyer, 1979).

Second, by considering each sentence individually as it would be read, one can see how unstated but script-relevant concepts become incrementally activated. For example, the expanded sentence demonstrates that MEAL is indirectly activated twice and TABLE once, even though neither is mentioned.

Third, the expanded version is better than a traditional text-based analysis of the passage at capturing the relative importance of concepts in the script. Table 6.1 provides a frequency count of 15 script-relevant concepts that occur in the expanded version of GOING TO A RESTAURANT. The table displays separate columns for explicit occurrences, lexically based implications, and definitional expansions. Note how only a few concepts have high total occurrences. Note also that these high totals are due primarily to implications and definitions rather than textual redundancy. These two contributors reflect the organization of the declarative representation in memory. Consequently, one can argue that the counts associated with these contributors are an indicator of the associative relevance or centrality of the scripted concepts in one's knowledge of the RESTAURANT routine.

In summary, the expansion example accounts qualitatively for the rich memory representation that results from reading the RESTAURANT text by illustrating how portions of one's knowledge are incorporated into a composite trace as the result of specific textual input. Additionally, the example demonstrates how important but infrequently mentioned concepts can be incrementally activated by implication or through the definitional expansion of words in the text.

Our activation-based analysis makes numerous predictions about the probability of inserting scripted knowledge into the composite memory trace and the accessibility of that knowledge during and immediately after comprehension. For example, one straightforward prediction is that even when central and peripheral concepts are in the composite by virtue of direct activation (i.e., a single perceptual encoding), the maintenance of activation should differ for the two types of concepts because of differing amounts of indirect activation. This in turn should produce different degrees of accessibility that result in different recognition patterns. A second and somewhat similar prediction is that central concepts have a higher probability of being inserted into the composite trace than do peripheral concepts when neither is actually mentioned in a text. This argues that central concepts should have a higher false alarm rate on a recognition task than peripheral concepts, even when textual features are controlled. A third prediction is that the resolution of anaphora should proceed more smoothly when central concepts are involved when peripheral concepts are involved because of the accessibility advantage of central concepts. We tested these predictions in three sets of experiments (Walker & Yekovich, 1984, 1986; Yekovich & Walker, 1986). The next section describes this work.

TABLE 6.1

Occurrence Counts for 15 Concepts in the Expanded Version of GOING TO A RESTAURANT

Concept	Explicit mentions	Verb-based implications	Definitional expansions	TOTAL
RESTAURANT	3	4	0	7
(CUSTOMERS) (DINERS)	0	0	0 (40)	0 (40)
RESERVATIONS	2	0	0	2
HOSTESS	1	1	0	2
DINING ROOM	1	0	2	3
WAITER	4	5	0	9
MENU	2	2	0	4
MEAL	1	4	31	36
DESSERT	2	0	0	2
CHECK (PURCHASE)	2	0	1 (35)	3 (38)
SERVICE	1	0	1	2
TABLE	2	3	13	18
TIP	1	0	0	1
DRINK	1	0	1	2
BAR	1	0	0	1

Note: Concepts in parentheses never appear in the text explicitly. Counts in parentheses correspond to the number of times those concepts appear in definitional expansions.

KNOWLEDGE-BASED EFFECTS
ON COMPREHENSION AND RETRIEVAL

In this section, we describe a program of research that has systematically investigated the text and knowledge-based components of the composite trace that is formed when a person reads a text about a familiar, routine activity. The research can be thought of as studying two aspects of the composite, its content and composition *immediately after* reading, and its form *during* reading. The first two sets of studies focus on the trace as it exists immediately after reading, and the last set of studies investigates the content of the trace as it exists on-line. Before discussing the research itself, we present a brief overview of the methodological approach.

Methodological Overview

Materials.   Eight scripted activities were selected for use, GOING TO A RESTAURANT, GOING TO THE DOCTOR, PAINTING A ROOM, SHOPPING FOR GROCERIES, GOING TO THE LIBRARY, APPLYING FOR COLLEGE, GETTING UP IN THE MORNING, and ATTENDING A LECTURE. For each script, a prototypical description was constructed based on materials from previous research (Bower et al., 1979; Galambos & Rips, 1982; Graesser et al., 1979). Each prototype was subjected to the expansion procedure described earlier, and the expanded versions were propositionalized (Turner & Greene, 1978). From each expanded version, a list of scripted concepts was extracted. The centrality of each concept was defined as the number of total occurrences in the expanded version. Two additional checks on centrality were performed. First, a group of undergraduates rated a large list of scripted nouns for each routine. The nouns were rated for centrality, which was defined as "importance with respect to the successful completion of the activity." The resulting ratings were highly correlated with the occurrence counts obtained from the expansion procedure.

Second, a separate group of students generated lists of nouns associated with each of the routines. Two results of the free generation data are noteworthy. First, the originally extracted concepts were in fact a subset of the generated nouns. Second, the generation frequency of the nouns correlated significantly with both the occurrence counts and with the centrality ratings. Given that the occurrence counts, the centrality ratings, and the generation frequencies were all correlated, we used the ratings to select central and peripheral target concepts for each script.

For each experiment, small numbers of central and peripheral concepts ($n = 2$ of each type) were selected as targets. Subsequently, each prototypical description was rewritten in order to control the text features associated with the target concepts. For example, in one set of recognition studies, the texts were altered so that a target concept was mentioned only once in the text and was not referenced or implied (i.e., through unfilled case slots) at all. This alteration had the effect of controlling the number of processing cycles or episodes in which a concept participated (see Kintsch & van Dijk, 1978 for a description of a cyclic processing model). In general, by controlling number of mentions and number of implications, we were better able to observe the effects of the organization of the semantic network itself. In other words, we could get a view of the "definitional expansion" effect independent of the text.

Another major control in the materials involved matching central and peripheral concepts for normative word frequency. Because normative word frequency is known to be an important variable that affects reading performance, and because this factor is often associated with text-driven component processes, we wanted to control its potential effect. In one experiment, we systematically varied normative word frequency of the targets in order to determine the influence of this variable. In all other experiments word frequency was controlled.

Procedure.   Each subject sat in front of a video display terminal and read each scripted text one sentence at a time. (S)he was instructed to read at a normal pace, and (s)he controlled the advancement of the sentences by pressing a button. On completion of each passage, the subject took a word recognition test. The subject was instructed to make each decision based on whether or not the item was actually present in the text just read. The composition of the test list varied across experiments although all test lists included both the target scripted nouns (central and peripheral) and nouns unrelated to the script. The experiments were computer controlled. (Note: Complete details of materials and procedures can be found in Walker & Yekovich, 1984, 1986; Yekovich & Walker, 1986).

Retrieving Studied Concepts from the Composite Trace

According to our analysis, central concepts have greater numbers of associations or links emanating from them than do peripheral concepts (see Fig. 6.1). Assuming that this analysis is valid, central nodes in memory should enjoy an activation advantage over peripheral nodes during and immediately after reading a description of a routine activity. This advantage should occur because an increased number of links produces more opportunities for central concepts to receive indirect activation. So, for example, if a reader encounters *meal* and *hostess* once each while reading the RESTAURANT text, the MEAL node in the composite trace will still have a higher level of activation than HOSTESS because MEAL is central whereas HOSTESS is peripheral. Consequently, on an immediate recognition test, the activation difference should produce judgment time differences for the two types of concepts. Specifically, central nouns should be judged faster than peripheral nouns as having just been read, even though both nouns were actually mentioned the same number of times in the text. Similarly, hit rates ought to favor central nouns over peripheral nouns.

We tested this idea in two separate experiments (Yekovich & Walker, 1986). In both experiments the procedure was the same. Undergraduates read eight scripted texts that had been written so that in each text four target nouns (two central and two peripheral) were each mentioned once. The texts were also worded so that unfilled case slots would not be filled by inferring the target concepts. Immediately after each text, a 20-item recognition test was presented. The test list was comprised of script-relevant and script-irrelevant nouns. The script-relevant nouns included the four targets and four other nouns that had appeared in the text. Twelve script-irrelevant nouns were chosen from a large pool of unrelated nouns. The order of items within the list was constrained so that no two script-relevant nouns occurred consecutively. This ordering reduced possible priming effects.

Subjects were instructed to read each sentence of each text at a normal pace and to expect a test after completing each text. They were also told that the test involved judging whether or not the nouns in the test list had actually appeared in the text. Note that because of the exact composition of the list, all script-relevant nouns had appeared whereas none of the irrelevant nouns had. This particular combination of items maximizes the likelihood that subjects will adopt a judgment strategy that relies largely on the level of activation of the nodes in the composite memory trace (cf. Anderson, 1983b; Reder, 1982; Reder & Ross, 1983). This type of judgment strategy is exactly the one that should produce the recognition differences described earlier.

Across the two experiments we varied the normative word frequency of the target nouns. In Experiment 1, central (C) and peripheral (P) nouns were of moderate frequency (the means were 90.31 and 99.5, respectively, based on the Kucera and Francis, 1967, norms). In the second experiment, both frequent (F) and infrequent (I) nouns were used (the means were 104.1, 108.1, 6.63, and 6.81 for CF, PF, CI, and PI targets, respectively). The purpose of this variation was to see whether or not a word level effect would moderate the knowledge-based effect of centrality.

The results of the experiments are summarized in Table 6.2. A number of interesting findings occurred. First, we found a consistent retrieval

TABLE 6.2
Mean Correct Judgment Times in Msec and Hit Rates (in
Parentheses) for the Central and Peripheral Targets in the Two
Experiments

Experiment/ Normative Word Frequency	Type of Target Concept	
	Central	Peripheral
Experiment 1		
Frequent	697 (.98)	852 (.85)
Experiment 2		
Frequent	867 (.98)	1024 (.83)
Infrequent	869 (.96)	914 (.92)

advantage of central over peripheral concepts, for both judgment time and hit rates. These results supported the predictions made earlier, and suggested that even when central and peripheral concepts were mentioned equally often in a text, the central concepts still had an accessibility advantage due to their higher level of activation. In terms of reader knowledge, the organization of declarative memory provided more opportunities for the indirect activation of central or important information.

Second, the normative word frequency of the target nouns did moderate the knowledge-based effects of centrality. As Table 6.2 shows, the results of Experiment 2 indicated different retrieval patterns for central and peripheral nouns as a function of word frequency (the interaction effects for subjects and items, respectively, were $F(1, 19) = 8.21, p < .01$ and $F(1, 53) = 1.84, p > .10$ for judgment times, and $F(1, 19) = 10.72, p < .01$ and $F(1, 53) = 4.76, p < .05$ for hit rates). For central nouns, varying word frequency had no effect on judgment time or hit rates. In contrast, the peripheral nouns were affected by the frequency variable. Peripheral infrequent nouns were judged more quickly and with higher hit rates than peripheral frequent nouns. The results for peripheral nouns paralleled the traditional word-frequency effect obtained in reading and recognition paradigms (e.g., Mandler, Goodman, & Wilkes-Gibbs, 1982; Murdock, 1974). Thus, the interaction showed that the central concepts in a knowledge structure are highly active after reading, regardless of the word-level properties associated with those concepts. On the other hand, peripheral concepts in a knowledge structure are more reliant on word-level properties during immediate recognition, suggesting that the level of activation on these nodes fluctuates as a function of text-driven or bottom-up influences.[2]

---

[2]We have also observed this interaction when target concepts are mentioned five times in a text.

It is appealing to interpret this interaction as a knowledge by text one, or more simply, a top-down by bottom-up interaction. The shape of the interaction suggests that when readers encounter a familiar prototypical text, selective portions of knowledge (i.e., central) become so active that those portions are inserted automatically into the composite representation, regardless of the exact content of the text. However, for other portions of the knowledge base (i.e., peripheral portions), text-based factors (e.g., word frequency) essentially determine the degree of accessibility of those nodes in memory. In this latter case, the exact content of a text becomes a powerful determiner of whether or not peripheral knowledge is inserted into the composite memory trace.

Retrieving Unstated but Inferred Concepts from the Composite

Suppose that certain scripted concepts are *not* mentioned in a text that describes a routine activity. Are those unstated concepts likely to be inserted into the memory trace of the text? According to our view, the major factor that determines whether or not a concept will be added to memory is the level of activation of the concept. If a concept is not mentioned, level of activation will be determined by the indirect activation that accrues on the memory node. The amount of indirect activation that accrues will be directly related to the number of associations or links that the concept possesses. Thus, unstated central concepts should receive more indirect activation than unstated peripheral concepts, and consequently should have a higher probability of being inserted into the composite. In immediate recognition, this difference should be observable in two ways. First, the probability of false alarming should be greater for unstated central nouns than for unstated peripheral nouns. Second, correctly rejecting unstated central concepts should be more difficult than rejecting unstated peripheral concepts. This difficulty should produce rejection time differences with central being slower than peripheral (see Yekovich & Walker, 1986, for a discussion of the factors responsible for this difficulty).

To test these two predictions, we performed a pair of experiments (Walker & Yekovich, 1984). In the experiments subjects read scripted texts in which four target nouns (2 central, 2 peripheral) were deliberately left out of each passage. In Experiment 1, the unstated targets were implied either 1 or 5 times. In Experiment 2, the unstated targets were implied either 0 or 3 times. The implication manipulation was achieved by using verbs for which a case slot was left unfilled. For example, in the RESTAURANT passage, the original sentence, *They ate their MEAL leisurely,* was changed to *They ate leisurely,* to produce one implication of MEAL (see the original paper for a complete description of the materials).

The purpose of varying the number of implications was threefold. First, these unfilled case slots are really lexical inferences which readers may or may not draw, and so in one sense the experiments tested whether or not lexical inferences are made when reading familiar material. Second, if such inferences occur during reading, then varying the number of implications is one way to vary the number of processing cycles in which unstated concepts participate. Number of processing cycles is a text-based factor that influences the likelihood that an unstated concept will be inserted into the composite (Kintsch & van Dijk, 1978). Third, by crossing the centrality variable with number of implications, we can explore another aspect of knowledge by text interactions.

Procedurally, subjects read each text sentence by sentence and immediately afterward they were tested for noun recognition. Each recognition list was comprised of eight script-relevant nouns and 12 irrelevant nouns. Of the eight relevant nouns, four were unstated but differentially implied targets and four were nouns that had actually appeared in the text. This combination of nouns requires subjects to discriminate between stated and unstated concepts, and this need to discriminate produces a more complex judgment strategy than the thematically based strategy described earlier (see especially Reder & Ross, 1983; Yekovich & Walker, 1986). Subjects were again instructed to read normally and to make recognition judgments about whether or not each noun had actually appeared in the preceding text.

The results of these experiments are summarized in Fig. 6.2 and Table 6.3. Figure 6.2 depicts the false alarm rates as a function of the number of text-based implications. The results showed that unstated central concepts were more likely to be in the composite trace than unstated peripheral concepts, thus supporting one of our major predictions. The other interesting result in the figure is the obvious interaction between centrality and number of implications. The false alarm rate for unstated central items was always above 50% and was essentially independent of

TABLE 6.3
Mean Correct Rejection Times in Msec for Unstated Central and
Peripheral Targets as a Function of Number of Implications

Type of Concept	Number of Implications		MEAN
	Few	Many	
Central	2538	2467	2502
Peripheral	1697	2171	1934

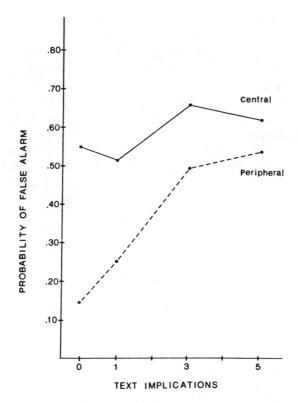

FIGURE 6.2   Mean proportions of false alarms for unstated central and unstated peripheral concepts as a function of the number of text-based implications of those concepts.

number of implications. In contrast, the false alarm rate for unstated peripheral nouns increased linearly from 0 to 3 implications and then levelled off from 3 to 5 implications. Clearly, this interaction is parallel to the one described in the previous section involving word frequency. Thus, we have demonstrated again that some parts of a reader's pre-experimental knowledge are likely to be highly active regardless of a text's exact content, whereas other parts of the knowledge base depend on the text for activation.

Because the false alarm rate was so high for central nouns, the correct rejection rate (i.e., correctly responding NO to the unstated concepts) was relatively low, thus complicating the time analysis. In order to get stable means, we collapsed 0 and 1 implications into FEW and 3 and 5 implications into MANY. Table 6.3 presents the resulting mean judgment times for correct rejections. As predicted, unstated central nouns were considerably more difficult to reject than unstated peripheral nouns.

Further, the degree of difficulty was independent of number of text implications for the unstated central nouns but was a direct function of number of implications for the unstated peripheral nouns. Thus, the interaction between centrality and number of implications also obtained for rejection time.

Using unstated concepts on a recognition test provides an opportunity for studying another assumption of our activation-based view, namely, that *level* of activation rather than *directness* of activation is the mechanism responsible for concepts being available in the composite memory trace. According to our reasoning, a concept may never be mentioned in a text but may still achieve a high level of activation through the accrual of indirect activation. In fact, this level may actually be similar to the level of activation of a concept that is explicitly mentioned in the text. In our studies, central concepts appear to be good candidates for testing this assumption because they are likely to be in the composite trace regardless of the text's properties.

In the Yekovich and Walker (1986) studies, we ran an experiment in which central nouns were either mentioned once or not at all. For current purposes, the interesting prediction concerns a comparison of the judgment times for central stated nouns that are correctly identified with the judgment times for central unstated nouns that are incorrectly accepted (i.e., false alarms). These two conditions test concepts that are part of the composite, but for different reasons. The level of activation on central stated concepts will be high by virtue of direct activation, whereas the level of activation on central unstated concepts will be the result of indirect activation only. If these two levels are similar, the judgment times should be similar. In fact, in the experiment the mean correct identification time was 1093 msec for central stated nouns and the mean false alarm time was 1124 msec for central unstated nouns. The 31 msec difference did not approach significance, suggesting that the levels of activation were approximately the same for stated and unstated central concepts in the composite memory trace of the text.

We believe that the recognition studies summarized here provide convincing evidence for an activation-based view of knowledge selection and use in reading. Further, we think that the joint effects of knowledge and various text-based variables expose in a new way the interactive character of the cognitive processes that produce successful comprehension. However, in order to claim that these effects have a direct impact on reading, we need converging evidence from on-line paradigms. In other words, if activation-based mechanisms are responsible for the recognition memory effects we have observed, those same mechanisms should be at work *during* reading. The suggestion from this assumption is that central and peripheral concepts should be (a) differentially active during reading, and (b) differentially affected by text-based manipulations. The next section describes a set of experiments that tested whether or not these conditions exist during on-line comprehension.

THE ACTIVATION OF SCRIPTED ANTECEDENTS IN ANAPHORIC REFERENCE

One important set of issues concerns how a reader's world knowledge contributes to comprehension as it occurs in real time. For example, an intuitive hypothesis is that if a reader's knowledge of a topic is active during reading, then the increased accessibility of that knowledge should have positive effects on the component processes that underlie successful comprehension. Thus, one might suppose that if the RESTAURANT routine has been activated, concepts such as MEAL and WAITER will be active and accessible for use in word identification or perhaps as memory antecedents in anaphoric reference.

We recently completed a set of experiments that studied the accessibility of scripted concepts during reading (Walker & Yekovich, 1986). The experiments were designed to study anaphoric reference, a linguistic device for connecting or integrating two phrases or sentences. In anaphoric reference, a referent or antecedent is established in memory, usually through the use of a noun phrase containing an indefinite modifier (e.g., "a" table), and subsequently the text refers back to that antecedent through the use of a definite phrase (e.g., "the" table) known as the anaphor. For instance, in the sentence pair, *Jack and Chris were seated at a table. The table was near a window, a table* is the antecedent and establishes the referent for the anaphor *The table* in the second sentence. This form of referring back to previously mentioned information is one way to produce a coherent semantic representation of the text. The cognitive processes which control the completion of anaphoric reference have been called integrative processes by a number of researchers (e.g., Just & Carpenter, 1980; Kieras, 1981) and are generally considered complex text-based processes.

Creating a connection between an antecedent and an anaphor depends on the accessibility of the antecedent in working memory. When an antecedent is easily accessible, as in the preceding example, the sentence containing the anaphor can be integrated rapidly into the working memory trace that is being constructed. In contrast, when a referent either has not been established or is no longer active, integrating an anaphoric sentence requires a long-term memory search and/or the construction of an inferential bridge. These extra operations are time and resource consuming. So, for example, in the sentence pair, *Jack and Chris were led into the dining room. The table was near the window,* a bridging inference such as "The dining room has tables" would presumably have to be generated in order for the second sentence to be integrated with the first. The widely held belief is that the *text alone* is responsible for establishing a referent as an antecedent in working memory (e.g, Haviland & Clark, 1974).

In contrast, we believe that the ease of accessing an antecedent is a direct function of the antecedent's *level of activation* in memory (see also Dell et al., 1983). A highly active antecedent is more accessible than an antecedent with a lower level of activation. Throughout the chapter we have pointed out that perceptual encoding and indirect activation via the organization of declarative memory are two ways for a scripted memory node to achieve a high state of activation. Accordingly, we propose that a scripted antecedent will be accessible as a referent when the antecedent is mentioned explicitly *or* when the antecedent is not mentioned but its node in memory receives a substantial amount of indirect activation from associated nodes.

To test this proposal, we created scripted texts in which target anaphoric sentences were immediately preceded by a sentence expressing one of three possible antecedent conditions. In the first antecedent condition, a scripted concept was explicitly introduced for the first time in the antecedent sentence, and the antecedent–anaphor relation was achieved through a noun repetition across the two sentences. In the second antecedent condition, the first sentence did not mention the antecedent, but implied it through a verb with an unfilled case slot. Thus, the antecedent–anaphor link across the sentences required a lexical inference. In the third condition, the antecedent sentence was deleted (hereafter called No Referent), and thus, integrating the anaphoric sentence involved construction of a proposition that linked the No Referent sentence back to the preceding text. For the Explicit and the Implied antecedent conditions, the sentences were worded so that the scripted antecedent in each was "new" information. In all the anaphoric target sentences, the scripted concept was mentioned as "given" information, thus presupposing the existence of a definite referent (see Haviland & Clark, 1974; Yekovich & Walker, 1978). A sample from the RESTAURANT passage involving the central concept, TABLE, follows:

> . . . Because they were a little early, they decided to go in the bar for a drink. Soon the hostess led Jack and Chris into the dining room.

Explicit	She seated them at a table.
Implied	She seated them.
No Referent	
Target	The table was near a window.

We also varied the centrality of the scripted concepts; half were central and half were peripheral. The nouns that represented the concepts were controlled for normative word frequency and for syllabic length. Reading time for anaphoric sentences was the measure of interest.

An activation-based view predicts an interaction between the text variable and the knowledge variable for reading time of the targets. Consider targets with central concepts first. Because a central concept has many associative links emanating from it, the explicit mention of any associate will result in indirect activation accruing on the central node. In a fairly prototypical description of a routine, many of the associated concepts are likely to be mentioned, and consequently the amount of indirect activation on a central node should be high. This suggests that a central concept will be accessible in working memory as a referent regardless of whether the concept appears explicitly as an antecedent or not. Because comprehension time of a target anaphoric sentence is directly related to the accessibility of an antecedent in memory, central target sentences should take the same amount of time to comprehend, regardless of the type of antecedent sentence that precedes them (i.e., Explicit = Implied = No Referent).

Peripheral concepts, on the other hand, are not likely to accrue much indirect activation, because of the smaller number of associative links emanating from those nodes. As a consequence, the type of antecedent sentence that precedes a peripheral anaphoric target should have a larger effect on the referent's accessibility in working memory, and thus, comprehension time of the target. Explicit mention of a peripheral concept in an antecedent sentence should result in rapid comprehension of the subsequent target. Implication of a peripheral concept in an antecedent sentence may produce target comprehension times either equivalent to or slower than the Explicit condition. The time will be equivalent if subjects draw lexical inferences at the time they are reading the antecedent sentence, and it will be slower if subjects do not draw these inferences. Finally, comprehension time to a peripheral target preceded by No Referent should be slow because the peripheral concept that acts as a potential referent will not be active in working memory (i.e., Explicit < Implied < No Referent).

In the first experiment of this set, subjects read each of eight scripted texts, one sentence at a time. The subjects were told to read at a normal pace and to be sure that they understood each sentence before advancing to the next one. Sentence reading times were recorded. Each text contained six target anaphoric sentences (three central, three peripheral) with each one preceded by one of three possible antecedent sentences. Each text contained one complete replication of the design. Immediately after each text, subjects took a sentence judgment test which required them to decide whether each of 12 sentences was thematically consistent

TABLE 6.4
Mean Reading Times (Upper Panel) and Judgment Times (Lower
Panel) in Msec for the Central and Peripheral Targets as a Function of
Antecedent Condition

Experiment/	Type of Antecedent		
Type of Concept	Explicit	Implied	No Referent
Sentence Reading Time			
Central	1824	1824	1856
Peripheral	1727	1829	2007
Word Relatedness Judgment			
Central	947	—	1033
Peripheral	989	—	1312

with the text just read. The purpose of the test was to urge subjects to attend to the reading task.

The upper panel of Table 6.4 displays the reading times for the six experimental cells. The results of the experiment are straightforward. Reading time for central anaphoric targets did not vary as a function of the type of antecedent sentence, whereas reading time for peripheral anaphoric targets did.[3] For peripheral targets, the Explicit and Implied antecedent conditions are marginally different and the Implied versus No Referent difference is highly significant.

These results have several implications. First, activation differences between central and peripheral knowledge components are evident during reading, just as they were evident immediately after reading. Second, central concepts appear to be active in working memory, regardless of whether they are mentioned or not in a prototypical text. In contrast, peripheral concepts are not automatically accessible in working memory. Rather, their activation level and consequently their accessibility depends on the text's properties. Third, the different reading time patterns for central and peripheral targets across antecedent conditions produce another example of a knowledge by text interaction. The present interaction shows that central concepts in a knowledge structure can actually moderate text-based integrative processes. This is strong evidence for an interactive characterization of reading comprehension. Finally, lexical inferences appear to be made during the reading of scripted texts, though the tendency appears to be stronger for central than for peripheral concepts.

---

[3]Although the peripheral EXPLICIT condition appears faster than the central conditions, the peripheral targets are slightly shorter than the central targets. When the means are adjusted for syllabic length, the difference disappears.

One criticism of sentence reading time as a dependent measure concerns its inability to pinpoint processing ease or difficulty. In the present case, we are unable to determine if the reading-time patterns for central and peripheral anaphoric sentences are due to the processing difficulty caused by the accessibility of the concepts themselves or to some other factors (e.g., wrap-up processing that has been deferred to the final word of the anaphoric sentence; cf. Just & Carpenter, 1980). Our activation-based arguments would be more convincing if we could demonstrate, for example, that the reading-time difference between the Peripheral–Explicit and the Peripheral–No Referent conditions was due largely to processing differences localized at the peripheral concept in the anaphoric sentence. Such processing differences would provide evidence for the differential accessibility of peripheral concepts as referents in working memory.

To test this idea, we modified the reading-time experiment in the following way. First, we eliminated the Implied antecedent condition but retained the Explicit and No Referent conditions. Second, rather than measure sentence reading time, we devised a task in which subjects were occasionally interrupted while reading and required to make judgments about whether or not a test word was thematically related to the content of the text. Judgment time was the measure of interest because it has been shown to be a reflection of the accessibility of a concept in working memory (see also Fletcher, 1981). The test words were either script related or unrelated, and the related nouns were central, peripheral, or filler. The test points were identical to the points where the anaphoric sentences had occurred in the previous experiment. For instance, a subject might read, *She seated them at a table,* and then be immediately tested with *Table.* Once the subject made a judgment about the word's relatedness to the passage, the anaphoric sentence appeared and reading continued.

The lower panel of Table 6.4 displays the mean judgment times for our first 20 subjects. In general, the times are consistent with the idea that central and peripheral concepts were differentially accessible. Central nouns were judged as related nearly as quickly when No Referent had been mentioned as when the referent had been Explicitly mentioned in the antecedent sentence. Although the two conditions differ by 86 msec, much of the difference is probably attributable to the existence of surface feature traces in the Explicit condition. The more interesting result is the 323 msec difference between the peripheral antecedent conditions. This finding parallels the difference found in the sentence reading-time experiment and suggests that a large part of that difference is localized on the peripheral anaphor. Apparently, when subjects read the peripheral anaphor, they immediately try to find its antecedent, and the antecedent's accessibility in the peripheral condition is controlled by the text (in this case, the antecedent sentence). Processing of the peripheral anaphor occurs rapidly when the antecedent has been Explicitly introduced, but processing takes more time when No Referent has been supplied.

The results of the on-line experiments parallel the findings of the recognition studies. Essentially, central concepts appear to be activated to a level that results in their automatic insertion into the compositive memory trace of a text. The result is that central concepts are easily accessible for use in processing, regardless of the text's properties. Peripheral concepts, on the other hand, depend on the text for activation, and consequently for their presence in the composite trace. Thus, the accessibility of these concepts is governed by text-based factors.

CONCLUDING REMARKS

In this chapter we have presented an outline of how the organization and activation of one's knowledge contributes to the construction of a composite memory trace of a text that describes a familiar routine. Additionally, we have presented evidence that supports the basic assumptions of this outline. Taken together, our research findings present a coherent view of how portions of a reader's knowledge base are selected and used when he or she reads text on a familiar topic. In essence, the organization of a declarative knowledge structure about a particular topic, and the direct and indirect activation of nodes within the structure are jointly responsible for the insertion of concepts into a composite memory trace. Because the organization of the knowledge structure naturally favors concepts with a high degree of associative relevance, these concepts are incorporated virtually automatically into the composite because of the large amount of indirect activation that accrues on them. On the other hand, concepts with a lower degree of associative relevance within the context depend on the text for activation and eventual incorporation into the composite representation.

Finally, we have demonstrated the truly interactive character of reading. Models of reading comprehension that purport to be interactive, but rely on text-driven factors alone, seriously underestimate the effects that domain knowledge has on comprehension. In our studies of knowledge-based comprehension and memory, we have shown that the central components of a declarative knowledge structure can moderate or override the effect of text-based variables that are normally associated with text-driven component processes. For example, the lack of a word-frequency effect in the recognition of central concepts suggests that the duration of word-recognition processes are sometimes controlled by one's knowledge rather than the text. Similarly, the findings concerning lexical inferencing of central concepts demonstrate that the time course of processes associated with syntactic and semantic analysis are sometimes controlled by knowledge. Along the same line, the reading-time and word-relatedness results argue that the integrative processes associated with anaphoric reference are greatly affected by one's knowledge of a topic. Thus, our data suggest that a reader's knowledge can dramatically affect the duration of many of the component processes which underlie success-ful reading comprehension. Truly interactive models of reading will eventually need to account for findings such as these.

APPENDIX

GOING TO A RESTAURANT

Expanded version including verb-based implications (in parentheses) and definitional expansions (IN CAPS AND IN PARENTHESES)

Jack and his girlfriend Chris decided to go out to a nice restaurant (PLACE WHERE CUSTOMERS CAN PURCHASE AND BE SERVED A MEAL). They (CUSTOMERS OR ONES THAT PURCHASE) called (on the telephone) (to someone) (at the restaurant (PLACE WHERE CUSTOMERS CAN PURCHASE AND BE SERVED A MEAL)) to make a reservation (ARRANGEMENT TO HOLD A TABLE FOR ONE'S USE) and then they (CUSTOMERS OR ONES THAT PURCHASE) drove (in a car) to the restaurant (PLACE WHERE CUSTOMERS CAN PURCHASE AND BE SERVED A MEAL). When they (CUSTOMERS) arrived (at the restaurant (PLACE WHERE CUSTOMERS CAN PURCHASE AND BE SERVED A MEAL)), Jack (CUSTOMER) opened the door (of the restaurant (PLACE WHERE CUSTOMERS CAN PURCHASE AND BE SERVED A MEAL)) and they (CUSTOMERS) walked inside (the restaurant (PLACE WHERE CUSTOMERS CAN PURCHASE AND BE SERVED A MEAL)). Jack (CUSTOMER) gave his name to the hostess (WOMAN IN PUBLIC DINING ROOM WHO SEATS DINERS) at the reservation (ARRANGEMENT TO HOLD A TABLE FOR ONE'S USE) desk. Since they (CUSTOMERS) were a little too early (for the reservation (ARRANGEMENT TO HOLD A TABLE FOR ONE'S USE)) to be seated (at their table (PLACE TO ASSEMBLE IN ORDER TO EAT A MEAL)), they (CUSTOMERS) decided to go in the bar (COUNTER WHERE ALCOHOLIC BEVERAGES ARE SERVED) for a drink (ALCOHOLIC LIQUOR). When their (CUSTOMERS') table (PLACE TO ASSEMBLE IN ORDER TO EAT A MEAL) was ready, Jack and Chris (CUS-TOMERS) went into the dining room (ROOM USED FOR THE TAKING OF MEALS). They (CUSTOMERS) were seated (in chairs) (by the hostess (WOMAN IN PUBLIC DINING ROOM WHO SEATS DINERS)) at a table (PLACE TO ASSEMBLE IN ORDER TO EAT A MEAL) near the window. The waiter (MAN WHO WAITS ON TABLE AND SERVES MEALS) came over (to the table (PLACE TO ASSEM-BLE IN ORDER TO EAT A MEAL)) and introduced himself (MAN WHO WAITS ON TABLE AND SERVES MEALS) (to Jack and Chris (CUSTOMERS)). He (MAN WHO WAITS ON TABLE AND SERVES MEALS) gave Jack and Chris (CUSTOMERS) their menus (LISTING OF MEALS THAT CAN BE ORDERED). They (CUSTOMERS) dis-cussed the menu (LISTING OF MEALS THAT CAN BE ORDERED) (with each other (CUSTOMERS)). Soon, they (CUSTOMERS) were ready to order (their meal (PORTION OF FOOD TAKEN TO SATISFY APPETITE)) (from the menu (LISTING OF MEALS THAT CAN BE ORDERED)) (from the waiter (MAN WHO WAITS ON TABLE AND SERVES MEALS)). After they (CUSTOMERS) ordered (their meal (PORTION OF FOOD TAKEN TO SATISFY APPETITE)) (from the menu (LISTING OF MEALS THAT CAN BE ORDERED)) (from the waiter (MAN WHO WAITS ON TABLE AND SERVES MEALS)), Jack and Chris (CUSTOMERS) talked (to each other (CUSTOMERS)) and (they (CUSTOMERS)) admired the view (out the window). When Jack and Chris (CUSTOMERS) were served (their meal (PORTION OF FOOD TAKEN TO SATISFY APPETITE)) (by the waiter (MAN WHO WAITS ON TABLE AND SERVES MEALS)), they (CUSTOMERS) ate their meal (PORTION OF FOOD TAKEN TO SATISFY APPETITE) leisurely, savoring (TASTING OR SMELLING WITH PLEASURE) (they (CUSTOMERS)) every bite (AMOUNT OF FOOD TAKEN AT A BITE) (of the meal (PORTION OF FOOD TAKEN TO SATISFY APPE-TITE)). Later (AFTER THE MEAL (PORTION OF FOOD TAKEN TO SATISFY APPETITE)), they (CUSTOMERS) decided to splurge and have dessert (A COURSE SERVED AT THE CLOSE OF A MEAL). Jack and Chris (CUSTOMERS) ate most of their dessert (A COURSE SERVED AT THE CLOSE OF A MEAL), but by now (AFTER THE MEAL (PORTION OF FOOD TAKEN TO SATISFY APPETITE)) they (CUSTOMERS) were getting full (SATISFIED, ESPECIALLY WITH FOOD AND DRINK). It was late, so Jack (CUSTOMER) asked (the waiter (MAN WHO WAITS ON TABLE AND SERVES MEALS)) for the check (SLIP THAT INDICATES THE AMOUNT DUE). The service (of the waiter (MAN WHO WAITS ON TABLE AND SERVES MEALS)) had been good, so they (CUSTOMERS) left a big tip (% OF THE CHECK (SLIP THAT INDICATES THE AMOUNT DUE) TEN-DERED FOR A SERVICE PERFORMED) (on the table (PLACE TO ASSEMBLE IN ORDER TO EAT A MEAL)) for the waiter (MAN WHO WAITS ON TABLE AND SERVES MEALS). They (CUSTOMERS) paid the check (SLIP THAT INDICATES THE AMOUNT DUE) (to the waiter (MAN WHO WAITS ON TABLE AND SERVES MEALS)) and (they (CUSTOMERS)) got their coats. Jack and Chris (CUSTOMERS) walked out of the restaurant (PLACE WHERE CUSTOMERS CAN PURCHASE AND BE SERVED A MEAL) and (they) drove (in a car) home.

REFERENCES

Abbott, V., Black, J. B., & Smith, E. E. (1985). The representation of scripts in memory. *Journal of Memory and Language, 24*, 179–199.

Anderson, J. R. (1982). Acquisition of cognitive skill. *Psychological Review, 89*, 369–406.

Anderson, J. R. (1983a). *The architecture of cognition.* Cambridge, MA: Harvard University Press.

Anderson, J. R. (1983b). A spreading activation theory of memory. *Journal of Verbal Learning and Verbal Behavior, 22*, 261–295.

Bower, G. H., Black, J. B., & Turner, T. J. (1979). Scripts in memory for text. *Cognitive Psychology, 11*, 177–220.

Cirilo, R. K., & Foss, D. J. (1980). Text structure and reading time for sentences. *Journal of Verbal Learning and Verbal Behavior, 19*, 96–109.

Corbett, A. T., & Dosher, B. A. (1978). Instrument inferences in sentence encoding. *Journal of Verbal Learning and Verbal Behavior, 17*, 479–491.

Dell, G., McKoon, G., & Ratcliff, R. (1983). The activation of antecedent information during the processing of anaphoric reference in reading. *Journal of Verbal Learning and Verbal Behavior, 22*, 121–132.

Fletcher, C. R. (1981). Short-term memory processes in text comprehension. *Journal of Verbal Learning and Verbal Behavior, 20*, 564–574.

Foss, D. J. (1982). A discourse on semantic priming. *Cognitive Psychology, 14*, 590–607.

Galambos, J. A., & Rips, L. J. (1982). Memory for routines. *Journal of Verbal Learning and Verbal Behavior, 21*, 260–281.

Graesser, A. C. (1981). *Prose comprehension beyond the word.* New York: Springer–Verlag.

Graesser, A. C., & Clark, L. F. (1985). *Structures and procedures of implicit knowledge.* Norwood, NJ: Ablex.

Graesser, A. C., Gordon, S. E., & Sawyer, J. D. (1979). Recognition memory for typical and atypical actions in scripted activities: Tests of a script pointer + tag hypothesis. *Journal of Verbal Learning and Verbal Behavior, 18*, 319–332.

Haviland, S. E., & Clark, H. H. (1974). What's new? Acquiring new information as a process in comprehension. *Journal of Verbal Learning and Verbal Behavior, 13*, 512–521.

Just, M. A., & Carpenter, P. A. (1980). A theory of reading: From eye fixations to comprehension. *Psychological Review, 87*, 329–354.

Kieras, D. E. (1981). Component processes in the comprehension of simple prose. *Journal of Verbal Learning and Verbal Behavior, 20*, 1–23.

Kintsch, W. (1974). *The representation of meaning in memory.* Hillsdale, NJ: Lawrence Erlbaum Associates.

Kintsch, W., & van Dijk, T. A. (1978). Toward a model of text comprehension and production. *Psychological Review, 85*, 363–394.

Kucera, H., & Francis, W. N. (1967). *Computational analysis of present-day American English.* Providence, RI: Brown University Press.

Lewis, M. W., & Anderson, J. R. (1985). Discrimination of operator schemata in problem solving: Learning from examples. *Cognitive Psychology, 17*, 26–65.

Mandler, G., Goodman, G. O., & Wilkes-Gibbs, D. L. (1982). The word-frequency paradox in recognition. *Memory and Cognition, 10*, 33–42.

Mandler, J. M., & Murphy, C. M. (1983). Subjective judgments of script structure. *Journal of Experimental Psychology: Learning, Memory and Cognition, 9*, 534–543.

McKoon, G., & Ratcliff, R. (1981). The comprehension processes and memory structures involved in instrumental inference. *Journal of Verbal Learning and Verbal Behavior, 20*, 671–682.

Murdock, B. B. Jr. (1974). *Human memory: Theory and data*. Hillsdale, NJ: Lawrence Erlbaum Associates.

Reder, L. M. (1982). Plausibility judgments versus fact retrieval: Alternative strategies for sentence verification. *Psychological Review, 89,* 250–280.

Reder, L. M., & Ross, B. H. (1983). Integrated knowledge in different tasks: Positive and negative fan effects. *Journal of Experimental Psychology: Learning, Memory, and Cognition, 9,* 55–72.

Schank, R. C., & Abelson, R. (1977). *Scripts, plans, goals, and understanding*. Hillsdale, NJ: Lawrence Erlbaum Associates.

Singer, M., & Ferreira, F. (1983). Inferring consequences in story comprehension. *Journal of Verbal Learning and Verbal Behavior, 22,* 437–448.

Swinney, D. A. (1979). Lexical access during sentence comprehension: (Re)Consideration of context effects. *Journal of Verbal Learning and Verbal Behavior, 18,* 645–659.

Turner, A., & Greene, E. (1978, August). The construction of a propositional text base. *JSAS Catalog of Selected Documents in Psychology.*

van Dijk, T. A., & Kintsch, W. (1983). *Strategies of discourse comprehension*. New York: Academic Press.

Walker, C. H., & Yekovich, F. R. (1984). Script-based inferences: Effects of text and knowledge variables on recognition memory. *Journal of Verbal Learning and Verbal Behavior, 23,* 357–370.

Walker, C. H., & Yekovich, F. R. (1986). *Activation and use of script-based antecedents in anaphoric reference*. Manuscript in submission.

Yekovich, F. R., & Walker, C. H. (1978). Identifying and using referents in sentence comprehension. *Journal of Verbal Learning and Verbal Behavior, 17,* 265–277.

Yekovich, F. R., & Walker, C. H. (1986). Retrieval of scripted concepts. *Journal of Memory and Language, 25,* 627–644.

KNOWLEDGE ACQUISITION FOR APPLICATION:
Cognitive Flexibility and Transfer in Complex Content Domains

Rand J. Spiro, Walter P. Vispoel, John G. Schmitz,
Ala Samarapungavan, and A. E. Boerger
University of Illinois at Urbana-Champaign

OVERVIEW

A fundamental tenet of all recent theories of comprehension, problem solving, and decision making is that success in such cognitive arenas depends on the activation and appropriate application of relevant preexisting knowledge. Despite the substantial agreement on this general claim, we know very little about the organization of background knowledge and the method of its application to the understanding of new situations when, because of a combination of the breadth, complexity, and irregularity of a content domain, formulating knowledge in that domain to explicitly prescribe its full range of uses is impossible. We call knowledge domains of this type *ill-structured* and contrast them with more routinizable knowledge domains that we refer to as *well-structured*.[1] What does one do when relevant prior knowledge is not already organized to fit a situation (as will frequently be true in ill-structured domains, by definition) and so must be assembled from different knowledge sources in memory? This is a problem of knowledge *transfer*. We address a crucial issue in transfer: How should knowledge be acquired and organized to facilitate a *wide range* of future applications?

The principle contentions developed in this chapter are:

---

[1]These terms receive further explication later in the chapter and are clarified in a more general manner by their *use* throughout the chapter—as "family resemblance" concepts, part of their definition can be no more than implicit in a complicated network of similarities and differences across uses (Wittgenstein, 1953).

1. that theories in the cognitive sciences have produced a far better understanding of cognitive process in well-structured domains (WSDs) than in ill-structured domains (ISDs);

2. that theories apprropriate for WSDs are in many ways inappropriate for ISDs—that, in fact, optimal conditions of learning and instruction in the two kinds of domains are *opposite* in several important respects;

3. that one of the most serious problems with treating ISDs as if they were WSDs is an inability to establish a basis for knowledge transfer, for the application of preexisting knowledge to new situations;

4. that transfer in ISDs is best promoted by knowledge representations that possess the following features: multiple interconnectedness between different aspects of domain knowledge, multidimensional or multiperspectival representation of examples/cases, and allowance for various forms of naturally occurring complexity and irregularity;

5. that in order for knowledge structures to possess the characteristics described in 4, emphasis must shift from the *retrieval* of a precompiled schema to the *assembly* of a situation-sensitive schema from knowledge fragments—the features described in 4 and 5 are characteristics of what we call *cognitive flexibility;*

6. that the best way to learn and instruct in order to attain the goal of cognitive flexibility in knowledge representation for future application is by a method of case-based presentations which treats a content domain as a landscape that is explored by "criss-crossing" it in many directions, by reexamining each case "site" in the varying contexts of different neighboring cases, and by using a variety of abstract dimensions for comparing cases.

Our primary claim is that in situations where complete comprehension or solution paths are neither inherent in the task or its description (i.e., are not implicitly or explicitly prescribed), nor anticipatable in the natural course of earlier learning and concomitant knowledge representation (either by explicit mention or by generative rule), then the key factors affecting the success with which prior knowledge is used to improve performance in a new situation will be the *flexibility* with which the relevant prior knowledge is represented in memory, and the mastery or *control* the individual has over those flexible representations (the ability to recombine elements of the representations, reorder the importance of elements in different contexts, and so on).

When knowledge cannot be routinized, mechanized, or automatized, it must be flexibly controlled. And control is not solely a process issue, independent of content. Executive control *strategies* require flexible knowledge *structures* to operate upon. In turn, control over flexible representations will give an individual more control over a content domain; rather than monolithic prepackaged knowledge structures constraining an individual to apply knowledge in a fixed and limited manner, the individual controls the knowledge; that is, a great variety of nonpredetermined ways to adapt knowledge to the task and content elements involved in the new situation are available. This chapter presents a theory of learning and instruction, of knowledge representation and application, for the flexibility-based control that enables transfer. The goal of the program of research that we discuss is the validation of a set of basic principles and related instructional practices that will allow students to better apply the knowledge they acquire from formal schooling to new, real-world cases—knowledge that is built for *use*, not for imitative reproduction in artificial school or laboratory settings.

SCHEMA-THEORETIC KNOWLEDGE REPRESENTATION AND THE PROBLEM OF TRANSFER

It is hard to imagine a more valued intellectual ability than that of *independent thought*—the ability to "think for yourself" when applying the necessarily limited knowledge acquired in formal schooling and training to the wide variety of situations in which that knowledge is relevant—the ability to use one's knowledge flexibly and to efficiently adapt it to varying contexts. Of what value is knowledge if its potential for application is much more limited than the range of uses to which it needs to be put? Very little, most would agree.

Nevertheless, a class of very influential contemporary approaches to knowledge representation, schema, frame, and script theories (e.g., Minsky, 1975; Rumelhart & Ortony, 1977; Schank & Abelson, 1977) have had four interrelated shortcomings related to the problem of transfer. (As we see later, many of the following criticisms also apply to another class of approaches to knowledge representation: prototype and exemplar theories; e.g., Rosch & Mervis, 1975.)

First, because these kinds of knowledge structures are frequently *prepackaged* (precompiled), they tend to be overly *rigid*. As a result, they provide very little opportunity for adaptation to diverse contexts of use.

Second, these modes of representation tend to isolate or *compartmentalize* aspects of knowledge that, in use, need to be interconnected. Again, the result is a limited potential for transfer.

Third, they have frequently treated complex subject matter as if it were simpler than it really was; complexities that transfer depends on have been *artificially neatened*.

Fourth, they have often implicitly assumed that knowledge domains possess more *regularity* or consistency across cases of application than they actually do.

These four characteristics of the recently predominant modes for representing knowledge, antithetical to the flexibility needed for wide application, are essentially simplifying assumptions: It is assumed that knowledge domains are *simpler* and more *regular* than they in fact are; these assumptions lead to representational approaches that are more rigid and compartmentalized than they ought to be. Historically, the assumptions of simplicity and regularity are strategically understandable and justifiable: Progress in new fields comes much more slowly without simplifying assumptions. And there has been very considerable progress in cognitive science. However, when progress has been as slow as it has been on so important a topic as transfer, then it is time to drop those simplifying assumptions that are causing progress to be impeded.[2]

The simplifying assumptions of cognitive science apply as well to dominant modes of education. Simplification of complex subject matter makes it easier for teachers to teach, for students to take notes and prepare for their tests, for test-givers to construct and grade tests, and for authors to write texts. The result is a massive *"conspiracy of convenience."* To take one example of the consequences of this tendency, Spiro, Feltovich, and Coulson (in preparation) have identified more than a dozen serious errors in the concepts held by a majority of medical students tested. Each of the errors was connected to a different kind of cognitive or educational oversimplification.

The overall effect of the simplifying features of knowledge representation systems and instructional strategies mentioned previously is a leveling tendency, a tendency towards *monolithic* approaches. Understanding is seen as proceeding in essentially the same way across instances of the same topic. Our view is different: The conditions for applying old knowl-

---

[2]It should be noted that the relatively harsh tone taken toward schema-type theories throughout this chapter should be understood in the qualified sense in which it is intended. Rather than a blanket condemnation of these theories, we intend only to point out their shortcomings in enabling transfer in certain fairly common situations characterized by irregular complexity. Much of our earlier work has been in the schema theory tradition, and we are well aware of the importance of schema-type approaches. Again, our claims against those approaches are limited, namely to aspects of knowledge domains that are "ill-structured" (keeping in mind that even when well-structured knowledge is involved, the context of its *application* is frequently ill-structured). The next step after the kind of work that we describe in this chapter will be to *combine* schema-type representations with the more flexible kind we are developing, because the two approaches seem to be natural complements, possessing compensating strengths and weaknesses. Also, the fact that we emphasize the less studied ill-structured domains does not imply that we discount the existence of domains with substantial regularity—they are just not the focus of our research.

edge are subject to considerable *variability,* and that variability in turn requires *flexibility* of response. Monolithic representations of knowledge will too often leave their holders facing situations for which their rigid "plaster-casts" simply do not fit. The result is the often heard complaint of students: "We weren't taught that." By which they mean that they weren't taught *exactly* that. They lack the ability to use their knowledge in new ways, the ability to think for themselves. Our research focuses on fostering the kinds of flexible knowledge representations that would free students and trainees from the limitations of having to use the information they receive in instruction in only that way in which it was originally instructed (rigid knowledge structures that need to be applied rigidly).

To achieve this goal we systematically depart from the four interrelated simplifying assumptions of the schema-type theories that we identified earlier (which, again, are also common assumptions in schooling).

• Rigid, monolithic, prepackaged knowledge representations are replaced by flexible representations in which fragments of knowledge are moved about and *assembled* to fit the needs of a given *context* of application. Instead of prepackaged schemata, purpose-sensitive situational schemata are constructed, thus allowing knowledge to be used in different ways on different occasions for different purposes. The emphasis is shifted from prepackaged schemata to the ingredients for many potential schemata; schema selection is devalued in favor of schema assembly; storage of fixed knowledge is devalued in favor of the *mobilization of potential knowledge*. One cannot have a prepackaged schema for everything.

• We replace highly compartmentalized knowledge representations with structures characterized by a high degree of *interconnectedness*. Appropriate compartmentalization of knowledge in one situation may not be appropriate in another. Multiple interconnectedness permits (a) situation-specific categorization, (b) multiple access routes to relevant case precedents in long-term memory from the details of new cases, and (c) the development of a reservoir of potential analogies when case precedents are less literally relevant.

• Instead of inappropriate simplification, we work with complex subject matter (e.g., historical topics, military strategy, biomedical concepts), acknowledging and teaching towards the *complexity* inherent in them. (Later in this chapter we address the issue of how learners can be aided in managing difficult complexities.) And just as subject matter is frequently more complex than is realized, so too are the real cases to which knowledge about that subject matter has to be applied. Cases or examples must be studied as they really occur, in their natural contexts, not as stripped down "textbook examples" that conveniently illustrate some principle. The application of knowledge in new situations will be thwarted if the contingencies for application are more complex than the knowledge brought to bear.

• We relax the often unrealistic assumption of regularity, of routiniza-bility, of well-structuredness—the assumption that subsets of individual cases (applications, examples) in a knowledge domain are sufficiently alike that they may be covered in common by a self-consistent system of general principles or rules. Thus, where schema-type theories tend to be overly general and to abstract away from individual cases that are classified in the same way, our approach sticks closer to the specific details and characteristics of individual cases. The consequences of treating ill-structured material as if it were well-structured are knowledge representations that are inapplicable in transfer situations or that produce inaccuracy. (Note that although complexity is highly related to irregular-ity, they are not the same thing. For example, the facade of the Old Executive Office Building next to the White House has a highly complex but regular structure. We work with domains that are complex and ill-structured.)

A NOTE ON RELATED RESEARCH

Our approach has many connections to prominent thematic strands of current theoretical interest. However, the manner in which we instantiate these strands, especially the way they are configured in our overall approach, is novel. Therefore, because the main thing in common be-tween what we do and the research of others involves overlap in subsets of the constituent themes emphasized rather than in the specifics of how those themes are applied and combined, we simply point to those the-matic areas of overlap here: analogy (e.g., Carbonell, 1983; Gentner & Gentner, 1983; Gick & Holyoak, 1980, 1983; Rumelhart & Norman, 1981; Winston, 1983); learning from examples (e.g., Anderson, Kline, & Beas-ley, 1979; Carnine, 1980; Medin & Schaffer, 1978); reminding (e.g., Kolodner, 1980; Ross, 1984; Schank, 1982); connectionism, parallel dis-tributed systems, "society of mind" (e.g., McClelland & Rumelhart, 1985; Minsky, 1979; Waltz & Pollack, 1985); tutorial guiding (Collins & Stevens, 1983); constructivity (e.g., J. Anderson, 1983; R. Anderson, 1977; Barsalou, in press; Bartlett, 1932; Spiro, 1977, 1980a, 1983); cogni-tive complexity (e.g., Scott, Osgood, & Peterson, 1979; Streufert, 1981); automatic versus controlled processing (e.g., Shiffrin & Schneider, 1977; Schneider & Shiffrin, 1977); efficiency and cognitive economies in mental processes (e.g., Spiro, 1980b; Spiro & Esposito, 1981; Spiro, Esposito, & Vondruska, 1978); metacognition and learning to learn (e.g., Brown,

Campione, & Day, 1981); perceptual and experiential aspects of conceptual memory (e.g., Bartlett, 1932; Spiro, 1983; Spiro, Crismore, & Turner, 1982); contextual encoding variability (Smith, Glenberg, & Bjork, 1978); linear separability (Medin & Schwanenfluegel, 1981); fluid task environments (Lenat, Hayes-Roth, & Klahr, 1983); structural analysis of content-area text (e.g., Britton & Black, 1985; Spiro & Taylor, in press).

A good example of a researcher whose work incorporates many of the same themes that we do is Barsalou. As we are, he is centrally concerned with contextual variability in conceptual structure, cognitive flexibility, and temporary concept construction under contextual constraint (Barsalou, in press). Even here though, the similarities are not as instructive as they might at first appear because of the difference in the kind of domains studied. Barsalou works with relatively low-level concepts and categories. There are many fundamental differences in both internal structure and the cognitive processes that must operate on that structure between concepts like "Birds" and "Fruit" (or even "Places To Go On A Vacation"), on the one hand, and complex *topics* such as "20th-Century History" or "Military Battles," on the other hand. There are also big differences between semantic memory tasks and the application of knowledge to real cases. All the problems with concepts and categories addressed by researchers like Barsalou (e.g., graded structure; contextual variability; see also Medin & Smith, 1984; Smith & Medin, 1981) are so greatly exacerbated by dealing with knowledge application in real-world content domains that are made up of *many concepts*, that new issues of learning, representation, and transfer are inevitably introduced. The theoretical and empirical solutions corresponding to these issues produce a picture that overlaps very little between simple concepts and complex topical domains.

So, as promised earlier, because of the novel way we apply the preceding headlined themes, we move on to further discussion of the nature of our own approach. However, before proceeding we should explicitly acknowledge the most pervasive influence on our theoretical orientation and empirical procedures, the later work of Wittgenstein (1953). Our treatment of complex topical knowledge was inspired by prominent Wittgensteinian metaphors for knowledge organization and learning, especially the metaphor of the "criss-crossed landscape." These and other debts to Wittgenstein (e.g., the reliance on approximate processes of family resemblance and the role of visual–perceptual forms of representation in attaining *synoptic* conceptual understandings) will be obvious in the following section and throughout the chapter.

ILL-STRUCTUREDNESS, LEARNING FROM CASES, AND THE INSTRUCTIONAL METAPHOR OF THE "CRISS-CROSSED LANDSCAPE": A PRESCRIPTION FOR TRANSFER

Ill-structuredness

In many domains, if one compares the features of large numbers of cases, a subset of the following conclusions may be drawn:

- There are no rules or principles of sufficient generality to cover most of the cases, nor defining characteristics for determining the actions appropriate for a given case.
- Hierarchical relations of dominance and subsumption are inverted from case to case.
- Prototypes tend to often be misleading.
- The same features assume different patterns of significance when placed in different contexts.
- An explosion of higher order interactions among many relevant features introduces aspects of case novelty.

It is such failures of general principles as these that we designate by the family label *ill-structuredness*. As will be seen later, this failure of general principles in ill-structured domains is directly related to the most sweeping recommendation that will emerge from our theoretical orientation: an emphasis in learning and instruction upon *multiplicity*. Instead of using a single knowledge structure, prototype, analogy, and so on, multiple knowledge precedents will need to be applied to new situations (multiple schemas, several past cases, overlapping analogies). Under conditions of ill-structured complexity, single approaches provide insufficient coverage.

"Ill-structured Complexity in the Domain 20th-Century History." How would the events and phenomena of the 20th century be classified and presented in typical instruction? Some abstract system for organizing material would be developed. One likely approach would be to identify several themes of the 20th century to serve as organizing compartments (chapters, subheads), and then individual examples would be slotted where they seemed to best fit. "Moral Relativism" and "Knowledge Specialization" might both be discussed in a chapter on "Fragmentation as a Theme of 20th-Century Life"; a chapter about "Irrationality and Uncertainty in 20th-Century Ideas" might refer to "Freud's Psychological Theory of Unconscious Control of Motivation and Behavior" and

"The Uncertainty Principle in Physics"; there might be a chapter on "Alienation" that would cite "Massive Bureaucracies Dwarfing the Individual" and "Mass Media Brainwashing"; and so on. Notice the implicit assumption of well-structuredness: Cases are taken as (often interchangable) instances or illustrations of abstract themes. "The Advent of Nuclear Weapons" and "Existentialist Philosophy" both illustrate irrational aspects of the era, and it is the latter, more abstract, point that is taken as the important lesson.

However, think some more about the examples. Is not existentialist philosophy an example of alienation as well as a demonstration of the recent trend away from Cartesian views of rational man? Are there not advantages to grouping Freud's theories with the subliminal influences of mass media to bring out a point about how influences we are not aware of have come to increasingly control 20th-century life? In fact, any single organizational scheme for presenting examples from 20th-century history will suffer from two important shortcomings: (a) It will not be possible to present together all the cases that it would be *instructive* to present together, and cases that are not in the same physical vicinity in text will tend not to be closely connected in memory; and (b) much of the multifacetedness of the individual case will be lost as its significance is *narrowed* to the abstract point that the case is presented as an illustration of. Similar problems would arise if some other system were used to represent the 20th-century cases. For example, if events were presented in chronological order, connections between temporally distant events would be likely to be missed. Similar consequences would ensue from a division along lines like politics, economics, and culture. *Any* single system for organizing material would not establish enough connections along enough dimensions to prepare one to deal with the great varieties of discourse about the 20th century that a learner is likely to encounter.

The Importance of Cases

It is partly because of such ill-structuredness that classroom instruction in professional fields (e.g., medicine, business) is so often augmented by considerable *case experience* (and that instruction in basic, nonapplied fields of knowledge ought to be). Lectures and textbooks tend to stress generalizations, commonalities, and abstractions over cases. Such approaches are clearly very effective when cases tend to be pretty much alike in how they have to be analyzed and responded to (i.e., in well-structured domains). Unfortunately, it is too often true that such assumptions are unwarranted, and the greater convenience associated with the traditional pedagogies is negated if they are ineffective.

How is successful performance possible in the absence of generalizability across cases? The answer is by focusing analysis and knowledge representation more at the level of the individual case (example, occasion of use, event, or other cognate terms) and by guided experience with large numbers of cases. If cases come in many forms, one needs to see many cases in order to represent their varieties of contextual influences and configurations of features. In a well-structured domain, cases (examples, etc.) are luxuries, helpful in illustrating general principles and then discardable; the principles can stand for all their subsumed, interchangable cases. In ill-structured domains, crucial information tends to be uniquely contained in individual cases—examples are not just nice, they are necessary. Our approach to knowledge acquisition is highly case-based.

The problem is compounded, however, by the fact that ill-structuredness has a limiting effect on case-based training as well as on the more abstract approaches: Just as there are no homogeneous systems of principles or rules that can be generally applied, there are *no generally applicable prototype cases*. Ill-structuredness means that there cannot be *any* recourse to homogeneity, to any single course of action across instances, whether it involves a single guiding principle, a single organizational scheme, or a single prototype case. (Of course, in relatively well-structured domains like "Trips to Fancy Restaurants," a single conceptual macrosystem can be very effective.) Real-world cases tend to possess a multifaceted complexity and thus need to be represented in lots of different ways in order to bring out those multiple facets. Then, instead of a single case being the basis for case-based cognitive processing, *aspects* of different cases need to be *combined*, and it is the resulting assemblages, made up of fragments of different cases, that underlie an important part of case-based reasoning. The *re*construction of knowledge requires that it first be *de*constructed—flexibility in applying knowledge depends on both schemata (theories) and cases first being disassembled so that they may later be adaptively reassembled. (Of course, some integral, nondecomposed case information must also be retained for guidance in ecologically realistic case assembly.)

Thus, two kinds of flexibility are needed in knowledge structures for ill-structured domains, each of which is a central feature of the mental representations we attempt to build:

1. Each complex real-world case needs to be decomposed and represented along many partially overlapping dimensions (i.e., the same information must be represented in lots of different ways).

2. Many connections must be drawn across the decomposed aspectual

fragments of the cases in 1, thus establishing many possible routes for future assembly and creating many potential analogies useful for understanding new cases or making new applications; it is for this reason that our instructional system emphasizes connections between apparently dissimilar cases (and aspects of cases)—connections among obviously similar cases are much more likely to be noticed without special training, and thus not cause transfer problems.

Nonlinear and Multidimensional Arrangement of Cases

An example of how the two preceding theoretical commitments imply instructional methodologies is the use in our program of *rearrangements of case presentation sequences* so that the same case occurs in the context of various other cases. This enables different features of the individual multifaceted cases to be highlighted, depending on the characteristics of the other cases they are juxtaposed to, while simultaneously establishing multiple connections, including distant ones.

The discussion of case rearrangement brings us to the dominant metaphor employed in our theory of flexible knowledge representation and case-based instruction. Following the lead of Wittgenstein (see, for example, the preface to the *Philosophical Investigations*), we think of an ill-structured knowledge domain as akin to a *landscape*. Landscapes are often complex and ill-structured. No two sites are exactly alike, yet all sites possess many (but not all) of the salient features of the total landscape. The same could be said of landscape regions made up of several sites. The best way to come to understand a given landscape is to explore it from many directions, to traverse it first this way and then that (preferably with a guide to highlight significant features). Our instructional system for presenting a complexly ill-structured "topical landscape" is analogous to physical landscape exploration, with different routes of traversing study-sites (cases) that are each analyzed from a number of thematic perspectives.

The notion of "criss-crossing" from case to case in many directions, with many thematic dimensions serving as routes of traversal, is central to our theory. The treatment of an irregular and complex topic *cannot be forced in any single direction* without curtailing the potential for transfer. If the topic can be applied in many different ways, none of which follow in rule-bound manner from the others, then limiting oneself in acquisition to, say, a single point of view or a single system of classification, will produce a relatively *closed* system instead of one that is open to context-dependent variability. By criss-crossing the complex topical landscape, the twin goals of highlighting multifacetedness and establishing multiple connections are attained. Also, awareness of variability and irregularity is heightened, alternative routes of traversal of the topic's complexities are illustrated, multiple entry routes for later information retrieval are established, and the general skill of working around that particular landscape (domain-dependent processing skill) is developed. *Information that will need to be used in a lot of different ways needs to be taught in lots of different ways.* Real cases (events, uses, etc.) have multiple slants, and, because the goal of widespread transfer must be to be ready for anything that realistically is likely to arise, learning and instruction must anticipate using many of these many slants in the ways they tend to occur.[3] Criss-crossing a topic in many directions serves this purpose. It builds flexible knowledge. Accordingly, we construct *nonlinear* and *multidimensional* acquisition texts.

Empirical Paradigms for Testing the Theory

The acquisition phase of a typical experiment involves presenting cases in an experimental condition that, in general, involves manipulations of acquisition texts that, by using the kind of landscape criss-crossing orientation we have discussed, promote awareness and representation of complexities, ill-structuredness, and multiple potential connections across cases. Our control conditions tend to simplify, to present the same case material according to a single well-structured system ("textbookization"), and to minimize case interconnectedness across the compartments of classification employed in the acquisition text.

Subjects always take at least two kinds of test, one that involves fairly literal understanding and reproductive recall of information from the acquisition text, and the other involving some sort of transfer (see following). Differences between experimental and control conditions are measured in terms of how much transfer they produce, but also in terms of the efficiency with which information stored in memory produces the potential for transfer. We call the amount of transfer enabled by equivalent amounts of old knowledge in long-term memory a measure of *transfer punch*.

There is a basic set of predictions in experiments testing the "Landscape Criss-Crossing" theory. Control conditions are expected to have

---

[3]It is not necessary that criss-crosses of the landscape be exhaustive to produce generative structures. Rather, if enough of the topical landscape is portrayed, accurate anticipations of the structure of nonportrayed aspects will be possible. This can be seen by analogy to a situation in which one is presented with pictures of a man's face only when he has expressions of anger or happiness; one would be able to fairly accurately anticipate what that person would look like if he were sad, grateful, sleepy, and so on.

mnemonic advantages that result in the rapid and accurate memorizability of the material presented in the acquisition phase of the experiments (compared to experimental conditions)—clear-cut "scaffoldings" are most effective for supporting reproductive, fact-retention-type memory (Anderson, Spiro, & Anderson, 1978; Ausubel, 1968). However, it is also expected that control conditions will produce overly inflexible, closed down representations that will result in less transfer than the experimental conditions. (This should especially be so at later stages of practice, because the highly interconnected representations produced by the experimental manipulations probably require some "critical mass" of information before the assembly processes they depend on can begin to operate.)

Results of Preliminary Tests of the Theory. Data from two experiments using high school subjects have been analyzed. Both experiments produced results that conformed to our theoretical predictions. In the first experiment, 24 prominent and characteristic examples of 20th-century events and phenomena were selected. These cases included such developments as the advent of nuclear weaponry, the development of rapidly transmitted mass communications, and the loss of individuality caused by dealing with impersonal and massive bureaucracies. A paragraph was written about each case/example. In the control condition, each of the paragraph-long case descriptions was placed in a chapter corresponding to one of three abstract themes it *best illustrated* (e.g., "Chaos, Uncertainty, and Irrationality," "Fragmentation of Old Unities," and "New Freedoms Mix With Powerful New Controls on the Individual"). This seductive nesting of examples under an abstract point or general principle was intended to parallel the unidimensional treatment of cases and the abstraction-centered organization typical of textbooks and training manuals. In the experimental condition, after subjects read the control text, the same case-paragraphs (with minor modifications) were re-presented in a completely different context: each case was paired with one from a *different chapter*. The intent was to bring out the multifacetedness of the individual case and to demonstrate that the deceptively simple and neat structure of the control text is not an accurate reflection of the domain's actual organization. Both groups had the same amount of study time.

The second experiment paralleled the first one, with the exception that the 20th-century cases were not re-paired in the experimental condition. Instead, the cases were presented in the same order as in the control condition but with individualized case-to-case linkages substituting for more abstract superodinate linkages of several cases. In other words, an experimental *case-centered* presentation scheme was contrasted with an *abstraction-centered* approach to the exact same material.

These early studies did not provide ideal tests of the theory. It would have been desirable to allow longer study time to process the complex materials and, especially, to permit more re-pairings of the cases, more criss-crosses of the topical landscape. Yet, even these first attempts, under far from satisfactory conditions, produced the predicted results. In the first experiment, subjects in the "textbookized" control condition outscored those in the "criss-crossed" experimental condition on a reproductive memory test for the gist of the material as it was presented. The neat, well-structured scaffolding of the control condition provided better support for encoding and retrieving details than did the more complex scheme of the experimental condition. However, when the knowledge from the acquisition text had to be applied in some new way, performance in the experimental conditions of both experiments exceeded that of controls on six out of six transfer measures employed.

The following six transfer tests were used in the two experiments (three in each):

1. and 2. Two different tests of integrative comprehension of new 20th-century texts that were only minimally related to the acquisition materials and that were drawn from books about the 20th century (i.e., the kind of naturally occurring new texts that you would like instruction to transfer to).

3. Comprehension of new texts constructed to link information on the topic of three of the cases from the acquisition text.

4. An essay on a topic (art) that was not mentioned at all in the acquisition text (a picture of an abstract expressionist composition by Kandinsky was presented with the question "How is this painting typical or not of trends of the 20th century?").

5. A remote associations test requiring subjects to draw meaningful connections between randomly paired 20th-century events and phenomena that had not been previously paired in the acquisition phase.

6. A test requiring the selection of a correct description of a prominent (but unfamiliar to high schoolers) 20th-century icon or symbol. For example: "Giacometti's sculptures of walking men have been taken by many to be symbols of the 20th-century's *Existential Man.*' Were these walking men portrayed as (a) excruciatingly thin or (b) grotesquely fat?" Notice how this question has a correct answer (they were thin; and these sculptures have actually been chosen to represent existentialist aspects of the modern condition, for example, on the cover of Barrett's famous book on that topic, *Irrational Man*); note as well that it is possible to develop chains of reasoning that allow that answer to be figured out, but that there is no single, determinate path to that answer.

These preliminary results suggest that there is a fundamental choice in methods of learning and instruction. Conventional methods seem to produce superiority when measured by conventional tests that stress reproductive, fact-retention types of memory. The methods developed from Landscape Criss-Crossing Theory are not as successful at producing mindless, imitative recall. However, if one agrees that the goal of learning and instruction should be the acquisition of generative knowledge with wide application in novel but partially related contexts, then it would seem that methods like ours are far preferrable to the conventional ones.

Toward a Science of Instructional Sequencing, Case Selection, and Case Arrangement

There is no science of instruction from cases. The best we have are occasional useful recommendations (e.g., Collins & Stevens, 1983). Where case-based instruction is practiced (mainly in professional schools and in some training programs), procedures tend to be haphazardly determined by the intuitions of curriculum planners. When there is a systematic basis for case selection, that basis is probably misguided: Cases tend to be picked when they neatly illustrate some instructional point that is being covered. The same features that make such "textbook cases" desirable for formal teaching (the way they form a clear-cut illustration of a topic that is being covered) are also likely to impede transfer, because in ill-structured domains true textbook cases are rare, and the intermediate, across-topic character of typical cases will be missed.

As important, there is currently no systematic basis for case sequencing. Whatever effects there are of learning individual cases, carry-over learning from case to case can vary in its quality. Clearly, not all case arrangements are equivalent in the intercase learning they promote. Why not just allow for a random order of cases, as naturally occurs in the accrual of real-world experience? The answer is that you do not want to have to wait so long for experience to accrue. It is very possible that with the right system of case arrangement, learning from examples can be made far more rapid, accurate, and efficient than with haphazard presentation orders. The development of basic principles of case sequencing could substantially shorten the acquisition time and number of cases needed to support widespread transfer.

Well- to ill-structured Versus Ill- to Well-structured Sequences. Part of conventional wisdom is that you start from the simple and then work toward the more complex (Glaser, 1984). In the terms of this chapter this would translate into a recommendation to first present material according to some well-structured abstract organizations, followed by the later introduction of complexities and irregularities. There are two dangers in this approach. First, it may inculcate a false impression that the domain is fundamentally simple and well-structured. Second, it may result in initial representations that are so neatly self-contained that they rigidly resist the complicated restructurings necessary to mirror the irregular contours of the domain. The problem with starting with an ill-structured presentation, on the other hand, is that it may be unrealistic to expect that subjects will be able to deal with complexity in material they are not sufficiently familiar with—the ingredients for flexible idea combination have to be established in memory before such combinatorial play can operate.

These two instructional orders for teaching the same material can be contrasted with a third approach, an intermediate degree of well-struc-turedness of initial presentations. We expect this to be the most effective in promoting transfer, because it is not subject in extreme degree to the problems that result from having one of the two approaches dominate early instruction. A mixture of well- and ill-structuredness in the early stages of learning should allow sufficient prerequisite material to become well learned prior to operating in a complicated fashion on that material, and at the same time avoid the establishment of an overly rigid represen-tation that would be difficult to dislodge.

Before proceeding it is very important to note that although we entertain different options for instructional sequencing, our position on the *goals* of learning is unequivocal. An *advanced stage of knowledge acquisition* will always be reached where learning criteria should no longer involve the demonstration of a superficial familiarity with subject matter and the memorization of some definitions and facts. Instead, at these more advanced stages, a learner should be required to get ideas *right* (even if that is hard to do) and to be able to appropriately apply those ideas (even if there are no simple formulas that they can memorize for doing so). If extra difficulty and confusion are the price of this shift in criteria, that is unfortunate but not an excuse for oversimplifying instruc-tion. Ways must be found to reduce the difficulties of the learner as much as possible without sacrificing the integrity of the subject matter being learned.

Algorithms for Case-to-Case Sequencing for Transfer.   What is the most efficacious ordering of cases to produce knowledge representations that maximize transfer (i.e., structures that are multiply interconnected along multiple dimensions)? It should first be noted that the many available discourse or text analysis schemes provide little guidance here. Succes-sive cases are unlike successive parts of a text in that each case is an integral entity, rather than a continuation of the preceding case. In this sense, each case is like a new text. Thus, structural analysis models employing, say, linear cohesion principles are inappropriate for analyzing intercase structure. Instead, we argue that several strands of thematic interconnectedness between cases must be considered in evaluating across-case structure. The metaphor of the "line" of development is then superceded by such others as "multistranded weaves," by the degree of overlap of many thematic elements (Wittgenstein, 1953).

Our starting point for identifying optimal case-arrangement algorithms involves the notion of intermediately related cases, of *partial overlap* across cases. We believe that it is important to neither group the cases that are most alike (and thereby promote the formation of spurious generalizations), nor to group cases in a way that maximally highlights their differences (thereby causing those regularities that do exist to be missed). Rather, we believe once again, as with case selection, that an intermediate course is to be preferred. We first seek a balance between continuity and discontinuity; some thematic features would overlap across adjacent cases and some would not; and which features overlap across cases would vary from one pair of cases to the next. Because ill-structured domains do not, by definition, permit single (or even small numbers of) connecting threads to run continuously through large numbers of successive cases, the notion of intermediateness of connection is intended as a first approximation to an alternative metric of strength of connection: "woven" interconnectedness. In this view, strength of connection derives from the partial overlapping of many different strands of connectedness across cases rather than from any single strand running through large numbers of the cases (Wittgenstein, 1953).

By comparing the overlap of thematic features for each adjacently presented case, an index can be calculated of the extent to which cases will appear to be relatively similar (and thus expendable—abstraction away from the cases would be thought to be possible) or dissimilar (in which case attempts at abstractive generalization would be perceived as futile). This is the first part of a "Partial Overlap Index." According to our theory, this Index should optimally have a value between its mathematically derivable maximum and minimum. The second part of the Partial Overlap Index is calculated at a higher level of abstraction by looking at the relationships between the adjacent overlap relationships; successive case pairs should have an intermediate degree of overlap in the specific thematic features that they share (e.g., perhaps half of the overlapping themes for Cases 1 and 2 should be overlapping themes for Cases 2 and 3). The highest values of the Index will be attained when both individual case information and abstract perspectives retain their viability, but without either achieving dominance—they both add something, but neither can supplant the other.

Intermediate values on these two components of the Partial Overlap Index will allow important information about individual cases to be maintained and some partial abstractions to be formed. By maximizing the *joint function of case uniqueness and abstractability away from cases* (that is by treating cases as separate but overlapping), the best of both worlds is attained and the characteristics of complex real-world domains is most accurately mirrored.

Perhaps more importantly, high values of the Index (i.e., intermediate degrees of overlap) should produce mental representations that maximize the potential paths for going from case to case in trying to assemble an appropriate set of precedents from prior knowledge to most closely fit the needs for processing some new case in the future. Because transfer/application in domains that lack rules or general principles of wide application is dependent on such situationally dependent adaptive assembly processes, intermediate degrees of adjacent case overlap should be ideal.

Another model of case sequencing is similar in many respects to the Partial Overlap model. It seeks primarily to highlight points of difficulty and confusion in a knowledge domain (which is, of course, where transfer is hardest to effect), especially those points where inappropriate abstraction is likely to mask useful case information. In this model cases are juxtaposed in such a manner as to achieve a balance between calling attention to (a) differences in superficially similar cases (to avoid having the complexities of individual cases lost due to a reductive assimilation to their apparently common features), and (b) similarities between apparently dissimilar cases (to avoid overly separating the mental representations of cases that may jointly figure as precedents for the analysis of some future case or that may be usable as analogies, one for the other).

Learning as a Cycle of Successive "Mutual Bootstraps" Between Case Knowledge and Abstract Domain Knowledge. Implicit in the ideal, discussed earlier, of intermediate degrees of overlap between cases is the value of maintaining a balance between cases considered as unique and to be subjected to close analysis, on the one hand, and systems for representing the partial abstractions that characterize the across-case domain, on the other hand. This suggests another approach to sequencing: A cyclical alternation between abstraction-centered presentations, in which cases illustrate or concretize the abstractions, and case-centered presentations, in which the same abstractions are now used in combined form to describe the cases. So, for example, the abstract theme of Fragmentation in the 20th century, illustrated by such cases as "Increases in Specialization" and "Multiple Influences from Media Exposure" in an abstraction-centered approach, would alternately be treated as an attribute, as part of the adjectival descriptor vocabulary for characterizing individual cases in a case-centered approach (i.e., "fragmentation" is a feature of the phenomenon of "Increasing Specialization," rather than the latter merely illustrating the former).

Each of these two kinds of systems should be able to help develop the other (hence the use of the expression, "mutual bootstraps"). As knowledge grows about how the complexities of individual cases are structured, that information should be useful in forming better abstract representational schemes for the domain that is the union of those cases. In other words, the more you know about cases in a domain, the better should be your systems for representing information about the domain that is itself, of course, constituted by those cases. At the same time, knowledge advances at the level of the entire domain should provide information useful in deriving insights for the development of better systems for representing the individual case (i.e., building a more adequate *mathesis singularis*). For example, the more you know about trends in the relationships between cases in a domain, the more ideas you will have for how to study and represent an individual case. Therefore, in this instructional approach, new information about the overall, macrostructure of a domain feeds into a next cycle of studying how best to represent the complexities of individual cases already studied, and so on, continuing the cycle. Again, the conjecture is that the two systems may be able to iteratively serve as "mutual bootstraps," each improving the other. Because both systems contribute to novel transfer/application, a self-perpetuating cycle of increasingly finer tuned improvements in the two systems would have obvious learning value.

The Role of Visual–Perceptual Representations and Adjunct Aids in Transfer

As is well known, the human perceptual system is very successful at representing large amounts of highly complex multivariate information at a glance (imagine all the information contained in an image of, say, a face), and storing that information in memory with great accuracy and durability. Studies have shown that hundreds of visual scenes presented in a short amount of time are recognized at very high levels of accuracy (Shepard, 1967; Standing, Conezio, & Haber, 1970). Furthermore, representations of visual information are rapidly comparable using an approximate, "family resemblance" type recognition processes. So, the perceptual system is ideally suited to facilitating the representation of multidimensional complexity in individual cases, the subsequent recall of those cases, and the recognition of approximate family resemblances across cases. Because of these advantages, it may be beneficial to recode ill-structured representations into inputs acceptable for the perceptual system to operate upon, thereby reducing mnemonic overloads and fostering recognition-based assembly processes (Spiro & Myers, 1984).

A means for effecting this perceptual recoding is available in the work on integral visual displays for observation of complex data. For example, we are exploring the use of one of these display systems, Chernoff Faces (Chernoff, 1973), in our own work. Case information is coded along multiple thematic dimensions, and a partly arbitrary code maps thematic features to different features of the visual display (i.e., different features of emotionally neutral Chernoff Faces; more important conceptual features are assigned to more salient facial features). Thus, large amounts of case information are presented in a single integrated picture that can be grasped at a glance. Furthermore, the rapidity of perceptual processing means that large amounts of case information should be learnable in a much shorter time than would otherwise be possible. And a variety of resemblances across cases can be detected using the common human ability to recognize family resemblances across faces.

Discovery Learning in Well-structured Domains

The knowledge gained from studying ill-structured domains should be extendable to discovery learning in well-structured domains. From the perspective of the learner, well-structured domains are ill-structured until the principles of well-structuredness are discovered. Therefore, our principles of flexibly interconnected knowledge representation should increase the chances of *noticing* likely candidate systems of organization for the domain and should permit sufficient old information to still be available in memory to develop and test those candidate systems.

CONCLUDING REMARKS

We have discussed various issues in an area of cognition and instruction that are currently poorly understood: how to get people to independently go beyond their specifically instructed knowledge. In response to this gap in knowledge, we offered a theory of case-based learning for transfer in ill-structured knowledge domains and suggested methods of case-based instruction to produce flexible knowledge representations.

From a practical point of view, the approaches we propose are not easy, and they may result in some increases in the time and effort required in initial instruction in a domain. However, we also expect that that investment will be more than justified by the fact that it will not be wasted instruction, limited in application to situations that happen to fit some narrow range of explicitly established preparedness. Wasted either because the instruction was too narrow in the case prototypes used, thus limiting applicability to resemblant cases; or wasted because oversimplified general principles and rules were taught, accounting for too little of the relevant variability in the knowledge domain. Systems of instruction must be developed that produce knowledge that can be flexibly adapted to the wide variety of new situations to which it will need to be applied, even at some additional early cost.

We know of no area of human endeavor that lacks an ill-structured aspect. Success in ill-structured areas tends to come only with a considerable accumulation of actual case experience. Application of the learning principles we have proposed has the potential to take material that is either taught poorly or not taught at all (and thus left to the vagaries of haphazard acquisition from "experience" over long periods of time) and, for the first time, make that material directly instructable.

ACKNOWLEDGMENTS

This research was supported in part by Contract No. 400-81-0030 from the National Institute of Education and by Contract No. MDA903-86-K-0443 from the Army Research Institute for the Behavioral and Social Sciences. The senior author would like to express his gratitude to Dr. Paul Feltovich for many helpful discussions related to the topic of this chapter. Correspondence concerning this article should be addressed to Rand J. Spiro, Center for the Study of Reading, 51 Gerty Dr., Champaign, IL 61820.

REFERENCES

Anderson, J. R. (1983). *The architecture of cognition*. Cambridge, MA: Harvard University Press.

Anderson, R. C. (1977). The notion of schema and the educational enterprise. In R. C. Anderson, R. J. Spiro, & W. E. Montague (Eds.), *Schooling and the acquisition of knowledge*. Hillsdale, NJ: Lawrence Erlbaum Associates.

Anderson, R. C., Spiro, R. J., & Anderson, M. C. (1978). Schemata as scaffolding for the representation of information in discourse. *American Educational Research Journal, 15,* 433–440.

Anderson, J. R., Kline, P. G., & Beasley, C. M. (1979). A general learning theory and its applications to schema abstraction. In G. H. Bower (Ed.), *The psychology of learning and motivation* (Vol. 13). New York: Academic Press.

Ausubel, D. P. (1968). *Educational psychology: A cognitive view*. New York: Holt, Rinehart & Winston.

Barsalou, L. W. (in press). The instability of graded structure: Implications for the nature of concepts. In U. Neisser (Ed.), *Concepts reconsidered: The ecological and intellectual bases of categories*. Cambridge: Cambridge University Press.

Bartlett, F. C. (1932). *Remembering*. Cambridge: Cambridge University Press.

Bransford, J. B. (1979). *Human cognition: Learning, understanding, and remembering*. Belmont, CA: Wadsworth.

Britton, B. K., & Black, J. B. (1985) *Understanding expository text*. Hillsdale, NJ: Lawrence Erlbaum Associates.

Brown, A. L., Campione, J. C., & Day, J. (1981). Learning to learn: On training students to learn from texts. *Educational Researcher, 10,* 14–21.

Carbonell, J. G. (1983). Derivational analogy in problem solving and knowledge acquisition. *Proceedings of the International Machine Learning Workshop*, Champaign, IL.

Carnine, D. (1980). Three procedures for presenting minimally different positive and negative instances. *Journal of Educational Psychology, 7,* 452–456.

Chernoff, I. (1973). The use of faces to represent points in k-dimensional space graphically. *Journal of the American Statistical Association, 68,* 361–368.

Collins, A., & Stevens, A. L. (1983). Goals and strategies of inquiry teachers. In R. Glaser (Ed.), *Advances in instructional psychology* (Vol. 2). Hillsdale, NJ: Lawrence Erlbaum Associates.

Gentner, D., & Gentner, D.R. (1983). Flowing waters or teeming crowds: Mental models of electricity. In D. Gentner & A. L. Stevens (Eds.), *Mental models.* Hillsdale, NJ: Lawrence Erlbaum Associates.

Gick, M. L., & Holyoak, K. J. (1980). Analogical problem solving. *Cognitive Psychology, 12,* 306–355.

Gick, M. L., & Holyoak, K. J. (1983). Schema induction and analogical transfer. *Cognitive Psychology, 14,* 1–38.

Glaser, R. (1984). Education and thinking: The role of knowledge. *American Psychologist, 39,* 93–104.

Kolodner, J. L. (1980). *Retrieval and organizational strategies in conceptual memory: A computer model* (Research Rep. 187). Dept. of Computer Science, Yale University, New Haven, CT.

Lenat, D. B., Hayes-Roth, F., & Klahr, P. (1983). Cognitive economy in fluid task environment. *Proceedings of the International Machine Learning Workshop,* Champaign, IL.

McClelland, J. L., & Rumelhart, D. E. (1985) Distributed memory and the representation of general and specific information. *Journal of Experimental Psychology: General, 114,* 159–188.

Medin, D. L., & Schaffer, M. H. (1978). A context theory of classification learning. *Psychological Review, 85,* 207–238.

Medin, D. L., & Schwanenflugel, P. J. (1981). Linear separability in classification learning. *Journal of Experimental Psychology: Human Learning and Memory. 7,* 355–68.

Medin, D. L., & Smith, E. E. (1984). Concepts and concept formation. *Annual Review of Psychology, 35,* 113–138.

Minsky, M. (1979). The society theory. In P. Winston (Ed.), *Artificial intelligence: An MIT perspective.* Cambridge, MA: MIT Press.

Rosch, E. H., & Mervis, C. B. (1975). Family resemblances: Studies in the internal structure of categories. *Cognitive Psychology, 7,* 573–605.

Ross, B. H. (1984). Remindings and their effects in learning a cognitive skill. *Cognitive Psychology, 16,* 371–416.

Rumelhart, D. E., & Ortony, A. (1977). The representation of knowledge in memory. In R. C. Anderson, R. J. Spiro, & W. E. Montague (Eds.), *Schooling and the acquisition of knowledge.* Hillsdale, NJ: Lawrence Erlbaum Associates.

Rumelhart, D. E., & Norman, D. A. (1981). Analogical processes in learning. In J. R. Anderson (Ed.), *Cognitive skills and their acquisition.* Hillsdale, NJ: Lawrence Erlbaum Associates.

Schank, R. C. (1982). *Dynamic memory.* Cambridge: Cambridge University Press.

Schank, R. C., & Abelson, R. P. (1977). *Scripts, plans, goals, and understanding.* Hillsdale, NJ: Lawrence Erlbaum Associates.

Schneider, W., & Shiffrin, R. M. (1977). Controlled and automatic human information processing: I. Detection, search, and attention. *Psychological Review, 84,* 1–66.

Scott, W. A., Osgood, D. W., & Peterson, C. (1979). *Cognitive structure: Theory and measurement of individual differences.* Washington, DC: Winston.

Shepard, R. N. (1967). Recognition memory for words, sentences, and pictures. *Journal of Verbal Learning and Verbal Memory, 6,* 156–163.

Shiffrin, R. M., & Schneider, W. (1977). Controlled and automatic human information processing: II. Perceptual learning, automatic attending, and a general theory. *Psychological Review, 84,* 127–190.

Smith, E. E., & Medin, D. L. (1981). *Categories and concepts.* Cambridge, MA: Harvard University Press.

Smith, S., Glenberg, A., & Bjork, R. A. (1978). Environmental context and human memory. *Memory and Cognition, 6,* 342–353.

Spiro, R. J. (1977). Remembering information from text: The "State of Schema" approach. In R. C. Anderson, R. J. Spiro, & W. E. Montague, (Eds.), *Schooling and the acquisition of knowledge.* Hillsdale, NJ: Lawrence Erlbaum Associates.

Spiro, R. J. (1980a). Accommodative reconstruction in prose recall. *Journal of Verbal Learning and Verbal Behavior, 19,* 84–95.

Spiro, R. J. (1980b). Constructive processes in prose comprehension and recall. In R. J. Spiro, B. C. Bruce, & W. F. Brewer (Eds.), *Theoretical issues in reading comprehension.* Hillsdale, NJ: Lawrence Erlbaum Associates.

Spiro, R. J. (1983). Subjectivity and memory. In W. Kintsch & J. Le Ny (Eds.), *Language comprehension.* The Hague: North–Holland.

Spiro, R. J., Crismore, A., & Turner, T. J. (1982). On the role of pervasive experiential coloration in memory. *Text, 2,* 253–262.

Spiro, R. J., & Esposito, J. (1981). Superficial processing of explicit inferences in text. *Discourse Processes, 4,* 313–322.

Spiro, R. J., Esposito, J., & Vondruska, R. (1978). The representation of derivable information in memory: When what might have been left unsaid is said. In D. L. Waltz (Ed.), *Theoretical issues in natural language processing (TINLAP-2).* New York: Association for Computational Linguistics and Association for Computing Machinery.

Spiro, R. J., & Myers, A. (1984). Individual differences and underlying cognitive processes in reading. In P. D. Pearson (Ed.), *Handbook of research in reading.* New York: Longman.

Spiro, R. J., & Taylor, B. M. (in press). On investigating children's transition from narrative to expository discourse: The multidimensional nature of psychological text classification. In R. Tierney, J. Mitchell, & P. Anders (Eds.), *Understanding readers' understanding.* Hillsdale, NJ: Lawrence Erlbaum Associates.

Standing, L., Conezio, J., & Haber, R. N. (1970). Perception and memory for pictures: Single-trial learning of 2500 visual stimuli. *Psychonomic Science, 19,* 73–74.

Streufert, S., & Streufert, S. C. (1978). *Behavior in the complex environment.* Washington, DC: Winston.

Waltz, D. L., & Pollack, J. (1985). Massively parallel parsing, *Cognitive Science, 9,* 51–74.

Winston, P. H. (1983). Learning by augmenting rules and accumulating censors. *Proceedings of the International Machine Learning Workshop,* Champaign, IL.

Wittgenstein, L. (1953). *Philosophical investigations.* New York: Macmillan.

INSTRUCTIONAL VARIABLES THAT INFLUENCE COGNITIVE PROCESSES DURING READING. 8

Richard E. Mayer
University of California, Santa Barbara

THEORY

Meaningful Learning from Expository Prose

Suppose that I asked a group of people to read a passage on how the Nitrogen Cycle works. Further, suppose that I subsequently tested the readers on retention and application. For retention, I could ask about important conceptual information (conceptual retention) and about unimportant details (other retention); also, I could measure whether students remember the word-by-word verbatim aspects of the passage (verbatim retention). For application, I could ask questions that require putting several pieces of information together (far transfer) or that require using one piece of information directly from the passage (near transfer). Examples are shown in Table 8.1.

For some readers, I leave the passage in its normal form (control), but for others I try to manipulate how the reader will process the information in the passage (treatment). In comparing the test performance of the control versus treatment groups, several different patterns are possible. First, the treatment group might perform worse than the control group on all tests. We could then say that the treatment results in "less learning." Alternatively, the treatment group might perform better than the control group on all tests. We could then say that the treatment results in "more learning." In contrast to these overall differences—suggesting more or less learning—the groups could differ in the pattern of performance—suggesting qualitative differences in learning (Mayer, 1979). For example,

TABLE 8.1
Example Test Items

Conceptual Retention

In response to instructions to recall the passage, the subject writes:
"Atmospheric nitrogen is converted into ammonia by the process of fixation, ammonia is converted to nitrate by the process of nitrofication, nitrate is converted to protein by assimilation or into atmospheric nitrogen by denitrification, and protein is converted into ammonia by ammonification."

Other Retention

In response to instructions to recall the passage, the subject writes:
"Molecular nitrogen makes up about 78% of the earth's atmosphere. It is the fourth major element found in living tissues after carbon, oxygen, and hydrogen."

Verbatim Retention

Which of the following sentences appeared word-for-word in the passage that you just read?
1. "Overfertilized lakes may become entirely clogged by dense concentration of algae."
2. "When a lake is overfertiled, it may become completely clogged by heavy concentration of algae."

Far Transfer

Why do farmers rotate crops?

Near Transfer

What is the result of the fixation process?

---

the treatment group might perform better than the controls on retention of specific information (as measured by verbatim retention and other retention) but worse on important conceptual information (conceptual retention); similarly, the treatment group may outperform the controls on answering questions like those in the passage (near transfer) but underperform the controls on applying what they have learned to new problems (far transfer). This pattern suggests that the treatment results in what we can call *rote learning*. Finally, the treatment group might perform better than the controls on conceptual retention and far transfer but worse on verbatim retention, specific retention, or near transfer. This pattern suggests that the treatment produces what we can call *meaningful learning*. Examples of these patterns of test performance are given in Table 8.2

The distinction between rote and meaningful learning has a long history. The Gestalt psychologists, for example, were the most vigorous in their study of this distinction (Katona, 1940; Kohler, 1925; Wertheimer,

TABLE 8.2
Four Possible Patterns of Performance

	Conceptual Retention	Other Retention	Verbatim Retention	Far Transfer	Near Transfer
More Learning					
Treatment group	+	+	+	+	+
Control group	−	−	−	−	−
Less Learning					
Treatment group	−	−	−	−	−
Control group	+	+	+	+	+
Rote Learning					
Treatment group	−	+	+	−	+
Control group	+	−	−	+	−
Meaningful Learning					
Treatment group	+	−	−	+	−
Control group	−	+	+	−	+

Note: Plus sign (+) indicates superior performance. Minus sign (−) indicates inferior performance.

1959). In their classic studies, rote learning (or learning by memorizing) generally referred to arbitrarily memorizing some procedure or facts, whereas meaningful learning (or "learning by understanding") involved "structural insight"—understanding how the parts fit together into some coherent organization. According to the Gestaltists, the payoff for learning by understanding is superior transfer performance. Although the Gestaltists did not study reading comprehension, their theory of problem solving may be relevant. Of particular interest are the emphasis on internal cognitive processes (e.g., structural insight) and on dependent measures that are appropriate for evaluating understanding (e.g., far transfer rather than verbatim retention).

Conditions for Meaningful Learning from Expository Prose

What are the conditions for meaningful learning from prose passages? In a previous review (Mayer, 1984), I suggested a cognitive theory of reading comprehension that requires focusing on relevant cognitive processes. Figure 8.1 presents a simplified version of an information-processing system, which suggests several processes that may be relevant to reading comprehension. The figure contains four memory stores: sensory memory (SM), which temporarily holds incoming sensory information such as images of printed symbols; short-term memory (STM), which temporarily

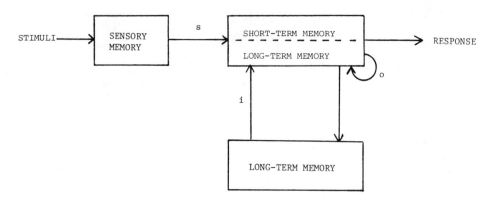

FIGURE 8.1   Human Information Processing System

Note: s refers to the selection process, *o* refers to the organization process, and *i* refers to the integration process.

holds information that has been attended to such as words; working-memory (WM), in which information from STM can be manipulated or rearranged; and long-term memory (LTM), which is a permanent store for information. First, the to-be-learned information must enter short-term memory (STM). This selection process is indicated by the arrow from sensory memory to STM. Second, connections must be built among the key ideas while the information is held in STM/WM. This process is indicated by the arrow from working memory to working memory. Third, connections must be built between the new knowledge in STM and existing knowledge in long-term memory. This integration process is indicated by the arrow from long-term memory to working memory.

The arrow from WM to LTM represents the transfer of the learning outcome to LTM for permanent storage. Figure 8.2 suggests three kinds of learning outcomes that might occur. First, what happens if a reader fails to pay attention? In this case, no information enters STM, so no learning can occur, and there can be no transfer of information from WM to LTM. Second, what happens if the reader pays attention to relevant information but fails to organize the information or fails to integrate the information? In these cases, information enters STM but it is not organized and integrated in WM, so the result is a rote learning outcome that is transferred to LTM. Finally, meaningful learning requires that all three processes successfully occur; that is, selection of conceptual information, organization of the information, integration with appropriate knowledge from LTM. If these three conditions are met, then a meaningful learning outcome is built in WM and can be transferred for permanent storage in LTM.

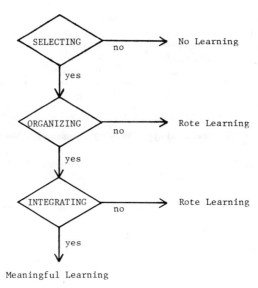

FIGURE 8.2   Three Processes for Meaningful Learning

Theoretical Framework

In the remainder of this section, I present an analysis of the task of reading comprehension into four kinds of variables: instructional variables (which can be thought of as independent variables), cognitive process variables and cognitive structure variables (which can be thought of as internal variables that cannot be directly observed), and performance variables (which can be thought of as observable dependent variables). This framework is summarized in Table 8.3.

Table 8.4 summarizes two different approaches to the study of how instructional variables influence reading comprehension. One straightforward approach is to focus on the effects of instructional variables on performance variables, as shown in the top of Table 8.4. This behavioral approach generates research questions such as, "Do advance organizers increase retention?" or "Does notetaking enhance test scores?" In summary, research questions take the form, "Does instructional manipulation X affect performance variable Y?" Although the behavioral approach has generated a large body of research findings in educational psychology, it has not produced a theory that allows for prediction or for strong pedagogic guidelines.

In contrast, the cognitive approach to research on reading comprehension includes a theory of the learner—that is, an understanding of the cognitive processes and cognitive structures in the learner during reading.

TABLE 8.3
Framework for Research on Reading Comprehension

Instructional Variables	Cognitive Processes	Cognitive Structure	Performance Variables
TEXT-BASED	Selecting	Nonlearning	Conceptual retention
Objectives	Organizing	Rote learning	Other retention
Signaling			
Concrete organizers	Integrating	Meaningful learning	Verbatim retention
READER-BASED			Far transfer
Shadowing			Near transfer
Schema training			
Elaborating			

TABLE 8.4
Two Approaches to Research on Reading Comprehension

Behavioral Approach

Instructional _____→ Performance
variables   variables

Cognitive Approach

Instructional _____→ cognitive _____→ cognitive _____→ Performance
variables   processes   structure   variables

As shown in the bottom of Table 8.4, the cognitive approach focuses on the relationship between instructional variables and internal cognitive variables, and on the relationship between internal cognitive variables and performance variables. This approach generates research questions such as, "Do advance organizers help readers to relate presented information with existing knowledge?" or "Does notetaking help learners to process to-be-learned information more deeply?" In summary, the form of the research question is, "How does instructional manipulation X affect internal cognitive processes that affect the pattern of performances on a series of Y's?" The cognitive approach is intended to develop a theory of the reader's cognitive processes and structures that will allow for predictions and for bringing some order to the growing body of research findings.

Instructional Variables.   The first variables listed in Table 8.3 are instructional variables. Instructional variables refer to observable manipulations that are intended to influence the reading process. In an earlier review, Mayer (1984) distinguished among three kinds of goals for instructional manipulations: guiding selective attention, building internal connections, and building external connections. First, the goal of an instructional variable may be to guide the reader's selective attention, that is to say, to help the reader pay attention to certain information in the passage. Second, the goal might be to help the reader build internal connections, in other words, to organize the conceptual information into a coherent structure. Third, the goal might be to build external connections, that is, to integrate incoming information with existing knowledge.

As noted in an earlier review by Cook and Mayer (1983), two general categories of instructional variables are text-based manipulations and reader-based manipulations. Text-based manipulations refer to alterations in the text, whereas reader-based manipulations refer to changes in the reader's activities. Weinstein and Mayer (1985) have used the term *learning strategy* to refer to reader-based manipulations. Examples are listed in Table 8.5.

Cognitive Process and Cognitive Structure Variables.   The middle portion of Table 8.3 presents two internal cognitive variables: cognitive process and cognitive structure variables. As previously described, three important cognitive processes are paying attention to incoming information, organizing incoming information into a coherent structure, and integrating incoming information with existing knowledge structures. These processes result in cognitive structures that differ in terms of the number of nodes as well as in internal and external connections. Rote outcomes do not contain adequate internal and external connections, whereas meaningful outcomes do contain them. In contrast, the traditional distinction between more versus less learning is based mainly on the number of nodes acquired.

Performance Variables.   The rightmost portion of Table 8.3 lists five performance variables, already described and exemplified in Table 8.1: retention of conceptual information, retention of other information, retention of information in verbatim form, near transfer, far transfer. These

TABLE 8.5
Instructional Treatments by Category

	Text-Based	Reader-Based
Guide attention	Behavioral objectives	Shadowing
Build internal connections	Signaling	Schema training
Build external connections	Advance organizers Conceptual models Conceptual emphasis	Notetaking Elaboration Conceptual pretraining

variables are useful in identifying "rote learning" and "meaningful learning" as suggested by the cognitive approach. In contrast, the traditional measure of overall retention, i.e., total amount recalled or recognized, would be useful in identifying "more learning" or "less learning" under the behavioral approach.

RESEARCH

Experimental Tests Concerning Cognitive Process Manipulations

In this section, I examine the results aimed at testing the predictions for more versus less learning and meaningful versus rote learning as summarized in Table 8.2. In particular, I focus on prose processing studies carried out in our labs over the past 12 years, using data from 16 published research articles (see reference section). These studies have been concerned with the effects of treatments (such as behavioral objectives, signaling, advance organizers, etc.), which are aimed at influencing a person's cognitive processing during reading.

First, each experiment in each article in our data base was broken down into pairwise comparisons between a treatment group and a control group on the following measures: (a) recall of conceptual versus other information, (b) problem solving on near versus far transfer items, and/or (c) recognition or recall in verbatim form. Conceptual information was defined as principles or prerequisite knowledge needed for making inferences in far transfer. Other information was defined as a category of information that was not central to the solution of far transfer problems, such as facts or introductory comments at the beginning of the passage. Near transfer was defined as problems identical or very similar to those in the passage; far transfer was defined as problems that required making inferences that went beyond the information in the passage. Verbatim recognition involved identifying which of a pair of similar statements occurred word-for-word in the passage; verbatim recall was evaluated by determining the length of the verbatim word strings in the recall protocols. Difference scores were computed for each comparison based on the formula: Difference Score = (Treatment Group Score–Control Group Score)/Control Group Score.

Second, Table 8.5 shows how each treatment condition in each experiment was categorized as either a text-based or reader-based technique and as aimed at manipulating selective attention, building internal connections, or building external connections.

Techniques for Guiding Selective Attention

One text-based technique for guiding attention is the use of behavioral objectives, i.e., statements of what the learner should be able to do following instruction. For example, Mayer (1975a) asked students to read a series of lessons on statistics. Before each of the first six lessons, a set of sample problems was given—problems requiring numerical computation (calculation problems), problems requiring a definition (definition problems), or problems requiring relating information to concrete examples (model problems). After the seventh and eighth lessons, students were tested on all three types of problems. As shown in Table 8.6, subjects who were given nonconceptual objectives (samples of definition problems or calculation problems) performed better on retention of those kinds of information but worse on retention of the conceptual information as compared to control subjects. This pattern is most consistent with rote learning. Subjects given conceptual objectives (model questions) excelled on retention of all types of information—a pattern most consistent with more overall learning.

A reader-based technique for guiding attention is shadowing, that is, asking the subject to repeat aloud the information that is being presented. This activity should focus the subject's attention on the verbatim details of the material rather than on the higher order principles. Mayer and Cook (1980) asked students to shadow a passage on radar. Then, students were asked to recall the information or to answer near and far transfer

TABLE 8.6
Tests of Predictions Concerning Manipulations to Guide Attention

Experimental Comparison	Retention			Application	
	Conceptual	Other	Verbatim	Far	Near
Text-based manipulations:					
Behavioral objectives					
Mayer (1975a, Expt. 1)					
Calculation vs. Control	−58	+43			R
Definition vs. Control	−39	+45			R
Model vs. Control	+77	+36			O
Reader-based manipulations:					
Shadowing					
Mayer & Cook (1980, Expt. 1)					
Shadow vs. Control			+7	−40 −4	R*
Mayer & Cook (1980, Expt. 2)					
Shadow vs. Control	−27	+103			R

Note: R indicates rote learning, R* indicates close to rote learning, O indicates more learning overall.

questions. As shown in Table 8.6, shadowing greatly reduced performance on far transfer but not on near transfer, and shadowing reduced
performance on recall of conceptual information but helped on recall of
unimportant details. Finally, shadowing resulted in slightly better verbatim retention of the information. This pattern corresponds most closely
with rote learning.

In summary, techniques for guiding students' attention toward nonconceptual aspects of the passage—either via behavioral objectives or shadowing—tended to result in a pattern of performance most consistent with
rote learning.

Techniques for Building Internal Connections

One text-based technique for building internal connections is signaling:
using an outline and headings to spell out the organization of the passage.
For example, Loman and Mayer (1983) and Mayer, Dyck, and Cook
(1984) asked students to read signaled or normal versions of passage and
then take a series of tests. As can be seen in Table 8.7, students reading a
signaled version of the passage recalled more of the conceptual information and less of other types of information as compared to students
reading a normal version of the passage. Similarly, students reading
signaled versions of the passage performed much better on tests of far
transfer than subjects reading the normal passage; there was some
evidence that signaling slightly aided near transfer as well, but this was
not tested in several of the studies. Verbatim retention was slightly
decreased for signaled groups in three of the four comparisons.

A reader-based technique for building internal connections is schema
training: training students how to recognize different kinds of expository
prose structures and how to outline for each type of structure. For
example, Cook (1982) provided schema training to some students and no
training to others. Students took tests before and after training; the tests
involved reading a passage and then recalling the information and answering near and far transfer questions. Table 8.7 shows that the trained
subjects recalled more conceptual information but less other information
as compared to the control subjects; however, the trained group showed
large improvements in both near and far transfer problems.

In general, the patterns of performance are most consistent with
meaningful learning.

Techniques for Building External Connections

One text-based technique for building external connections is using a
concrete advance organizer, that is, a description of a concrete model of

TABLE 8.7
Tests of Predictions Concerning Manipulations
to Build Internal Connections

Experimental Comparison	Retention			Application		
	Conceptual	Other	Verbatim	Far	Near	
Text based manipulations:						
Signaling						
Loman & Mayer (1983, Expt. 1)						
Signaled vs. Control	+57	−33	−3	+60	+2	M*
Loman & Mayer (1983, Expt. 2)						
Signaled vs. Control	+11	−81	+5	+300	+17	M*
Mayer, Dyck & Cook (1984, Expt. 2)						
Signaled vs. Control	+73	−35	−14	+43	—	M
Signaled-Enhanced Vs. Control	+48	−18	−7	+52	—	M
Mayer, Dyck & Cook (1984, Expt. 3)						
Signaled vs. Control	+13	−50	—	+163	—	M
Signaled-Plus vs. Control	+33	−65	—	+194	—	M
Reader-based manipulations:						
Schema training						
Cook (1982, Expt. 2)	+43	−11	—	+92	+68	M*
Schema Trained vs. Control						

Note: M indicates meaningful learning; M* indicates close to meaningful learning.

the system being explained in the text. For example, in a series of studies we asked students to read a passage on computer programming, but for some students we first presented a concrete model of the computer (Mayer, 1978, 1980, 1983; Mayer & Bromage, 1980). As can be seen in Table 8.8, subjects given the model before reading the manual performed better on recall of conceptual information but worse (or about the same) on recall of other information and verbatim retention, as compared to control subjects. Similarly, the advance organizer greatly enhanced far transfer but either hurt or did not strongly affect near transfer. This pattern is most consistent with meaningful learning. In addition, similar patterns were obtained for two other text-based manipulations for building external connection: incorporating a concrete model within the text (conceptual model within text) or incorporating familiar prerequisite experiences early in the passage and emphasizing this conceptual information within the text (conceptual emphasis).

A reader-based technique for building external connections is conceptual elaboration: restating the conceptual information in terms of some familiar situation or model. For example, students were asked to read computer programming manuals; some students were asked to restate the information in terms of a familiar concrete model after reading about each command (Mayer, 1976, 1980). As can be seen in Table 8.8, conceptual

TABLE 8.8
Tests of Predictions Concerning Manipulations to Build
External Connections

Experimental Comparison	Retention			Application		
	Conceptual	Other	Verbatim	Far	Near	
Text-based manipulations:						
Conceptual emphasis						
Mayer & Greeno (1972, Expt. 1)						
Concepts vs. Formula	—	—	—	+ 93	− 49	M
Mayer & Greeno (1972, Expt. 2)						
Concepts vs. Formula	—	—	—	+ 15	− 63	M
Mayer & Greeno (1972, Expt. 3)						
Concepts vs. Formula	—	—	—	+ 14	− 33	M
Mayer & Greeno (1972, Sup. Study)						
Concepts vs. Formula	—	—	—	+ 84	− 50	M
Mayer (1974, Expt. 1, Open Book)						
Concepts vs. Formula	—	—	—	+ 45	− 7	M
Mayer (1974, Expt. 1, Closed Book)						
Concepts vs. Formula	—	—	—	+ 70	− 6	M
Mayer (1974, Expt. 2)						
Concepts vs. Formula	—	—	—	+ 2	+ 1	X
Mayer (1974, Sup. Study 1, Power)						
Concepts vs. Formula	—	—	—	+ 32	− 9	M
Mayer (1974, Sup. Study 1, Speed)						
Concepts vs. Formula	—	—	—	+ 40	+ 0	M*
Mayer (1974, Sup. Study 2)						
Concepts vs. Formula	+ 47	− 35	—	—	—	M
Mayer, Stiehl & Greeno (1975, Expt. 1)						
Concepts vs. Formula	—	—	—	+ 117	− 15	M
Mayer, Stiehl & Greeno (1975, Expt. 2)						
Concepts vs. Formula	—	—	—	+ 0	− 23	M*
Conceptual model within text						
Mayer (1975b, Expt. 1)						
Model vs. Rule	—	—	—	+ 52	− 2	M
Mayer (1975b, Expt. 2)						
Model vs. Rule	—	—	—	+ 145	− 43	M
Mayer (1976, Expt. 1)						
Model vs. Rule	—	—	—	+ 18	− 39	M
Bromage & Mayer (1981, Expt. 2)						
Explanation vs. Description	+ 13	− 10	—	+ 29	+ 2	M*
Conceptual advance organizer						
Mayer (1978, Expt. 1)						
AO vs. Control	—	—	—	+ 31	− 18	M
Mayer (1980, Expt. 1)						
Before vs. After	—	—	—	+ 105	+ 5	M*
Mayer (1980, Expt. 4)						
AO vs. Control	—	—	—	+ 200	+ 8	M*

(continued)

TABLE 8.8 *(Continued)*

Experimental Comparison	Retention			Application		
	Conceptual	*Other*	*Verbatim*	*Far*	*Near*	
Mayer (1980, Expt. 5)						
AO vs. Control	+32	−41	—	—	—	M
Mayer & Bromage (1980, Expt. 1)						
Before vs. After	+43	−33	—	—	—	M
Mayer & Bromage (1980, Expt. 2, Immediate)						
Before vs. After	+44	− 4	—	—	—	M
Mayer & Bromage (1980, Expt. 2, Delayed)						
Before vs. After	+24	+ 2	—	—	—	M*
Mayer (1983, Expt. 1)						
AO vs. Control	+34	+ 4	−13	+83	—	M*
Mayer (1983, Expt. 2)						
AO vs. Control	+102	−25	—	—	—	M
Reader-based manipulations:						
Notetaking						
Peper & Mayer (1978, Expt. 1)						
Notes vs. No Notes	—	—	—	+70	−20	M
Peper & Mayer (1978, Expt. 2)						
Notes vs. No Notes	—	—	—	+22	−56	M
Peper & Mayer (1978, Expt. 3)						
Notes vs. No Notes	+53	+0	—	—	—	M*
Peper & Mayer (1986, Expt. 1)						
Notes vs. No Notes	—	—	−10	+24	−10	M
Peper & Mayer (1986, Expt. 2)						
Notes vs. No Notes	—	—	− 3	+24	−36	M
Summary Notes vs. No Notes	—	—	− 5	+55	− 7	M
Peper (1979, Expt. 3)						
Notes vs. No Notes	− 8	+ 1	—	—	—	X
Summary Notes vs. No Notes	−20	−30	—	—	—	X
Elaboration						
Mayer (1976, Expt. 1)						
Activator vs. No Activator	—	—	—	+165	−29	M
Mayer (1976, Expt. 2, Subject Control)						
Activator vs. No Activator	—	—	—	+105	+21	O
Mayer (1976, Expt. 2, Experimenter Control)						
Activator vs. No Activator	—	—	—	+ 73	+19	O
Mayer (1980, Expt. 2)						
Elaboration vs. Control	—	—	—	+ 67	− 2	M
Mayer (1980, Expt. 3)						
Elaboration vs. Control	—	—	—	+137	−36	M
Mayer (1980, Expt. 4)						
Elaboration vs. Control	—	—	—	+ 20	+ 4	M
Comparative Elab. vs. Control	—	—	—	+ 13	+12	O
Mayer (1980, Expt. 5)						
Elaboration vs. Control	+77	−22	—	—	—	M
Comparative Elab. vs. Control	+76	+32	—	—	—	O

(continued)

TABLE 8.8 (Continued)

Experimental Comparison	Retention			Application	
	Conceptual	Other	Verbatim	Far	Near
Peper & Mayer (1986, Expt. 2)					
Meaningful Elab. vs. Control	—	—	− 13	+ 26	− 60 M
Conceptual pretraining					
Mayer, Stiehl & Greeno (1975, Expt. 2)					
Pretrain vs. Control	—	—	—	+ 14	− 6 M
Mayer, Stiehl & Greeno (1975, Expt. 4)					
Pretrain vs. Control	—	—	—	+ 24	− 13 M
Mayer, Dyck & Cook (1984, Expt. 1)					
Pretrain vs. Control	+ 144	− 51	− 26	+ 45	− 6 M
Mayer, Dyck & Cook (1984, Expt. 3)					
Pretrain vs. Control	+ 12	− 20	—	+ 58	— M

Note: M indicates meaningful learning; *M** indicates similar to meaningful learning; *O* indicates more learning overall; *X* indicates no clear pattern.

elaboration tends to greatly enhance performance on far transfer and conceptual retention but to reduce or only slightly enhance performance on near transfer and other retention. This pattern is consistent with either meaningful learning or overall more learning. In addition, research on notetaking, (i.e., asking students to put the information into their own words) and on conceptual pretraining (i.e., teaching definitions of key words in terms of a concrete model) tends to produce patterns of test performance that are consistent with meaningful learning.

In summary, elaboration activities, notetaking activities, and pretraining can foster a pattern of results most consistent with meaningful learning. In all cases, these reader-based activities involved asking the learner to connect the presented information to a familiar concrete model or experiences.

CONCLUSION

This chapter summarized a series of research studies of the effects of instructional manipulations on learner's cognitive processing of expository prose. Three cognitive processes required for meaningful learning are paying attention to conceptual information, building internal connections, and building external connections. Meaningful learning is characterized by a pattern of performance in which subjects perform better than controls on retention of conceptual information and on far transfer, but worse on retention of certain other information, retention of information in verbatim form, and near transfer. Rote learning is characterized by the reverse pattern.

Techniques for guiding attention included a text-based manipulation—behavioral objectives—and a reader-based manipulation—shadowing. Both manipulations produced test performance patterns most consistent with rote learning, suggesting that behavioral objectives and shadowing can serve to focus readers' attention on nonconceptual aspects of a passage.

Techniques for building internal connections included signaling as a text-based manipulation and schema training as a reader-based manipulation. Both manipulations produced test performance patterns most consistent with meaningful learning. Apparently, students can be encouraged to actively build a coherent structure for incoming information.

Techniques for building external connections included advance organizers, concrete models, and conceptual emphasis as text-based manipulations and conceptual elaboration, notetaking, and pretraining as reader-based manipulations. All manipulations involved encouraging the reader to actively connect the incoming information to familiar experience or concrete models. These manipulations produced test performance patterns most consistent with meaningful learning.

These results provide some examples of how it is possible to influence the reader's cognitive processing and the quality of the resultant learning outcome. Some techniques seem to reduce cognitive processes needed for meaningful learning (e.g., behavioral objectives that focus on low-level aspects of the passage), whereas others foster cognitive processing needed for meaningful learning (e.g., schema training or concrete advance organizers). If our research studies had focused only on the question of whether instructional manipulations affect how much is learned, we would have found very few effects. However, when we focus on the pattern of performance—with special attention to different patterns for meaningful versus rote learning outcomes—some fairly consistent effects emerge.

REFERENCES

Bromage, B. K., & Mayer, R. E. (1981). Relationship between what is remembered and creative problem solving in science learning. *Journal of Educational Psychology, 73,* 451–461.

Cook, L. K. (1982). *Instructional effects of text structure-based reading strategies on the comprehension of scientific prose.* Doctoral dissertation, University of California, Santa Barbara.

Cook, L. K., & Mayer, R. E. (1983). Reading strategy training for meaningful learning from prose. In M. Pressley & J. R. Levin (Eds.), *Cognitive process research: Educational applications.* New York: Springer–Verlag.

Katona, G. (1940). *Organizing and memorizing*. New York: Columbia University Press.

Kohler, W. (1925). *The mentality of apes*. New York: Harcourt, Brace & World.

Loman, N. L., & Mayer, R. E. (1983). Signaling techniques that increase the understandability of expository prose. *Journal of Educational Psychology, 75*, 402–412.

Mayer, R. E. (1974). Acquisition processes and resilience under varying testing conditions for structurally different problem-solving procedures. *Journal of Educational Psychology, 66*, 644–656.

Mayer, R. E. (1975a). Forward transfer of different reading strategies evoked by test-like events in mathematics text. *Journal of Educational Psychology, 67*, 165–169.

Mayer, R. E. (1975b). Different problem-solving competencies established in learning computer programming with and without meaningful models. *Journal of Educational Psychology, 67*, 725–734.

Mayer, R. E. (1976). Some conditions of meaningful learning for computer programming: Advance organizers and subject control of frame sequencing. *Journal of Educational Psychology, 68*, 143–150.

Mayer, R. E. (1978). Advance organizers that compensate for the organization of text. *Journal of Educational Psychology, 70*, 880–886.

Mayer, R. E. (1979). Can advance organizers influence meaningful learning? *Review of Educational Research, 49*, 371–383.

Mayer, R. E. (1980). Elaboration techniques that increase the meaningfulness of technical text: An experimental test of the learning strategy hypothesis. *Journal of Educational Psychology, 72*, 770–784.

Mayer, R. E. (1983). Can you repeat that? Quantitative and qualitative effects of repetition and advance organizers on learning from science prose. *Journal of Educational Psychology, 75*, 40–49.

Mayer, R. E. (1984). Aids to prose comprehension. *Educational Psychologist, 19*, 30–42.

Mayer, R. E., & Bromage, B. (1980). Different recall protocols for technical text due to advance organizers. *Journal of Educational Psychology, 72*, 209–225.

Mayer, R. E., & Cook, L. K. (1980). Effects of shadowing on prose comprehension and problem solving. *Memory & Cognition, 8*, 101–109.

Mayer, R. E., Dyck, J., & Cook, L. K. (1984). Techniques that help readers build mental models from science text: Definitions training and signaling. *Journal of Educational Psychology, 76*, 1089–1105.

Mayer, R. E., & Greeno, J. G. (1972). Structural differences between learning outcomes produced by different instructional methods. *Journal of Educational Psychology, 63*, 165–172.

Mayer, R. E., Stiehl, C. C., & Greeno, J. G. (1975). Acquisition of understanding and skill in relation to subjects' preparation and meaningfulness of instruction. *Journal of Educational Psychology, 67*, 331–350.

Peper, R. (1979). *The effects of elaborative activities on cognitive structures: Notetaking, summary notetaking, meaningful adjunct questions*. Doctoral dissertation, University of California, Santa Barbara.

Peper, R., & Mayer, R. E. (1978). Notetaking as a generative activity. *Journal of Educational Psychology, 70*, 514–522.

Peper, R. & Mayer, R. E. (1986). Generative effects of notetaking during science lectures. *Journal of Educational Psychology, 78*, 34–38.

Weinstein, C. E., & Mayer, R. E. (1985). The teaching of learning strategies. In M. C. Wittrock (Ed.), *Handbook of research on teaching (3rd ed.)* New York: Macmillan.

Wertheimer, M. (1959). *Productive thinking*. New York: Harper & Row.

HOW IS READING TIME INFLUENCED BY KNOWLEDGE-BASED INFERENCES AND WORLD KNOWLEDGE? 9

Arthur C. Graesser
Memphis State University

Karl Haberlandt
Trinity College

David Koizumi
Catholic University

A satisfactory model of executive control processes during reading must account for inference generation. Unfortunately, however, cognitive psychologists do not have a fine-grained understanding of inference generation, compared to their understanding of processing components that are directly linked to explicit text. This chapter reports some data and aspires to clarify two important questions regarding the relationship between inference generation and executive control processes. First, how do variations in executive control processes influence the generation of knowledge-based inferences during reading? Second, what is the impact of inference generation and world knowledge on reading time?

There are several alternative ways that executive control processes may influence inference generation. Perhaps variations in the readers' goals and conscious reading strategies determine what inferences are generated and how much processing resources are allocated to different categories of inferences. If this is the case, then researchers need to identify different categories of inferences and to explain how variations in executive control processes systematically map onto the cognitive resources allocated to the different categories. Alternatively, perhaps executive control processes merely determine the overall amount of cognitive resources allocated to inference generation, without any selective allocation to specific inference categories. In other words, variations in executive control processes might determine the amount of cognitive resources allocated to inference generation as a whole, but not the pattern of resources allocated to different inference categories. As yet a third alternative, perhaps variations in executive control processes have no impact on inference generation. This would occur if inference generation is confined to a mechanism which is entirely insulated from the readers' goals and conscious reading strategies.

Before we can investigate the impact of executive control processes on inference generation, we need to examine the prerequisite question of how reading time is influenced by inference generation and world knowledge. This question is far from settled. Indeed, this chapter reports some data that is incompatible with some prevailing beliefs among researchers in discourse processing, cognitive psychology, and reading.

KNOWLEDGE-BASED INFERENCES AND WORLD KNOWLEDGE

This chapter focuses on knowledge-based inferences that are generated during the comprehension of narrative text. Knowledge-based inferences are inherited from the reader's knowledge about physical, social, cognitive, and emotional phenomena. We assume that this world knowledge is embodied in a large set of *generic knowledge structures* (GKSs) and *specific knowledge structures* stored in long-term memory. For example, suppose that a reader comprehends a story about a dragon kidnapping some daughters of a Czar. Some GKSs that are relevant to the story are DRAGON, KIDNAPPING, CZAR, and FAIRYTALE. These structures would be activated during comprehension through pattern recognition mechanisms and would provide the data base for constructing inferences. The reader might also activate a specific knowledge structure, such as a movie about a dragon and a princess that the reader had viewed 2 years ago. We assume that the knowledge-based inferences generated during text comprehension are furnished by the GKSs and specific knowledge structures that are relevant to the text. Moreover, these knowledge-based inferences are outside of the province of theories in formal logic and text linguistics (see Brown & Yule, 1983; Clark & Clark, 1977; Crothers, 1979; Graesser & Clark, 1985; Kempson, 1977; Meyer, 1985; Schank & Abelson, 1977; van Dijk & Kintsch, 1983). Consequently, we are not directly concerned with the rules of valid inference in a formal propositional calculus (e.g., modus ponens, modus tollens, de Morgan's rule). Similarly, we are not directly concerned with the rules of computing presuppositions according to some formal or quasiformal theories in text linguistics.

We assume that the reader constructs a structure of propositional units (called nodes) during comprehension. Some of these nodes are explicitly mentioned in the text, whereas other nodes are inferences. The comprehender needs to construct *bridging* inferences in order to establish conceptual connectivity between an incoming explicit statement and prior passage context. The reader may also generate *elaborative* inferences which embellish the text structure but are not really needed for establishing conceptual connectivity. For example, consider the following two explicit statements (which were embedded in a passage):

1. The dragon dragged off the daughters.
2. The daughters cried.

These two statements are not directly related; dragging someone off does not automatically result in the person crying. The following bridging inferences would probably be generated in order to conceptually connect explicit nodes 1 and 2:

3. The daughters thought the dragon would do something bad to them.
4. The daughters were frightened.
5. The daughters wanted someone to help them.

Listed next are some elaborative inferences which readers might generate but are not needed for establishing conceptual connectivity between nodes 1 and 2.

6. Tears ran down the daughters' eyes.
7. The dragon used his claws (when dragging the daughters off).
8. Some heroes killed the dragon (an expectation about the subsequent plot).

The bridging inferences "fill the gaps" between explicit propositions, whereas the elaborative inferences "radiate from" the bridges and explicit nodes.

THREE HYPOTHESES ABOUT THE RELATIONSHIP BETWEEN PROCESSING TIME AND NUMBER OF INFERENCES

As discussed earlier, we are interested in the relationship between reading time and the number of inferences that are constructed during comprehension. Suppose that we had a direct window to the reader's inference mechanism and could compute the *number of inferences* that the reader constructed at the end of each clause in the text. We know from previous research that many inferences are constructed at the end of clauses and sentences (Just & Carpenter, 1980). Suppose further that we had a direct window to the amount of *processing time* that is devoted to the inference processes at the end of clauses. The processing time for a given component can be estimated from gaze durations, sentence reading times, and word reading times. What is the relation between number of inferences and processing time? Is there a positive correlation, a negative correlation, or no systematic relation at all?

There are three hypotheses that make radically different predictions about the relationship between number of inferences and processing time. We refer to these hypotheses as the *strenuous inference generation* hypothesis, the *automatized knowledge package* hypothesis, and the *scanty knowledge-base* hypothesis. All three hypotheses have theoretical foundations that are psychologically plausible, but they end up leading to different predictions.

The Strenuous Inference Generation Hypothesis

According to this hypothesis, the process of generating an average inference is a comparatively strenuous activity that takes a measureable amount of time to accomplish. The strenuous inference generation hypothesis predicts a positive correlation between reading time and the number of inferences constructed during comprehension.

The strenuous inference generation hypothesis has been adopted by most researchers who conduct psychological research on discourse processing. One notable example is Clark's early pioneering research on bridging inferences (Clark, 1977; Clark & Clark, 1977). In most of the reported studies, reading times were collected on pairs of sentences. The reading time for the second sentence of a pair increased as a function of the number of theoretical bridging inferences that were needed to connect sentence 2 to sentence 1. For example, one class of bridging inferences involves anaphoric reference, as illustrated in sentences 1a, 1b, and 2 following:

1a. Jack fired an employee yesterday.
1b. Jack fired Bill yesterday.
2. Bill had been coming in late consistently.

Sentence 2 should take more time to read if it is presented after sentence 1a than after sentence 1b. Sentence 2 takes more time to read after 1a because a referential bridging inference needs to be constructed, namely,

Bill is the employee; such a bridging inference does not need to be constructed when sentence 2 is read after sentence 1b. Clark has reported several experiments demonstrating an increase in reading time as a function of the number of theoretical bridging inferences that readers need to construct (see also Keenan, Baillet, & Brown, 1984).

Some critics of Clark's sentence reading-time research have argued that the reported patterns of reading time cannot unequivocally be attributed to the number of bridging inferences that comprehenders construct. For example, McKoon and Ratcliff (1981) pointed out that target sentences (e.g., sentence 2) tend to be more difficult to interpret when they are placed after context sentences (e.g., 1a and 1b) that call for bridging inferences. In other words, there is a positive correlation between (a) the number of bridging inferences that are theoretically generated by a target sentence and (b) the difficulty of interpreting the target sentence. Therefore, it is unclear whether Clark's reading-time data are best explained by number of bridging inferences or the difficulty of interpreting the target sentence.

Readers normally read passages rather than sentence pairs. Therefore, the question arises as to whether there is any research on longer text which has uncovered a positive correlation between number of inferences and reading time. There are a number of studies that indirectly suggest a positive correlation. For example, Kintsch and Van Dijk (1978) reported that passage reading times increase as a function of the number of inferences that need to be constructed. Just and Carpenter (1980) reported that the gaze durations of end-of-clause words are longer when the reader needs to generate an inference. However, these studies are based on some theories that specify what inferences the reader *should* generate in order to establish text coherence. These inferences did not include the broad profile of knowledge-based inferences that readers normally construct during comprehension (see Graesser & Clark, 1985). For example, in both Kintsch and van Dijk's model and Just and Carpenter's model, a reader would generate an inference whenever an incoming clause failed to have an argument (e.g., noun) that matched an argument in the previous text. Clearly, there are more occasions for generating inferences than failures to establish referential coherence (Black & Bern, 1981; Graesser, 1981; Haberlandt & Bingham, 1978; Van Dijk & Kintsch, 1983).

Some recent studies by Olson have directly investigated the relationship between reading time and number inferences in text (Olson, Duffy, & Mack, 1984, 1985). Most of Olson's studies included two conditions. In a *reading* condition, sentence reading times were collected as subjects read passages at their own pace. Mean sentence reading times were scored for each sentence. In a *think aloud* condition, the subjects would think aloud or ask questions as each incoming sentence was comprehended. These verbal protocols exposed many of the knowledge-based inferences that comprehenders potentially construct as sentences in text are incrementally comprehended. Olson scored the number of unique inferences that the subjects generated for each sentence. These scores were then correlated with the sentence reading times collected in the reading condition, using multiple regression techniques to partial out effects from some extraneous variables (e.g., number of words in the sentence). Olson reported that reading times were significantly predicted by the number inferences in the narrative passages that he investigated (but not the expository passages). The inference component showed a positive regression coefficient in the regression equations. Such an outcome supports the strenuous inference generation hypothesis.

The Automatized Knowledge Package Hypothesis

The automatized knowledge package hypothesis assumes that many generic knowledge structures (GKSs) become automatized through extensive use. For example, an adult reader has encountered the concepts of DAUGHTER, DRAGGING, and CRYING on thousands of occasions; these GKSs would be automatized. When a GKS is automatized, the nodes in its knowledge structure are processed in a wholistic, unitary fashion (see Laberge & Samuels, 1974). The activation and use of an automatized GKS impose comparatively little or no demands on the cognitive system. Consequently, hundreds of nodes may be directly available when an automatized GKS is activated. Regarding passage comprehension, hundreds of inferences may be constructed at very little cost to the cognitive system.

The automatized knowledge package hypothesis challenges the generality of the strenuous inference generation hypothesis. For example, consider a passage that contains familiar content words and messages, such as a passage describing a scripted activity (e.g., eating at a restaurant, washing a car). Such a passage would activate many automatized GKSs and many inferences would be generated at very little cost to the cognitive system (Abelson, 1981; Bower, Black, & Turner, 1979; Graesser & Nakamura, 1982; Schank, 1982; Schank & Abelson, 1977; Walker & Yeckovich, 1984). In contrast, consider a passage that contains rare words, unfamiliar messages, and few automatized GKSs. Such a passage would generate few inferences but would be very taxing on the cognitive system. The automatized knowledge package hypothesis predicts that the correlation between processing time and number of inferences critically depends on the degree of automatization of the GKSs which furnish the knowledge-based inferences.

The Scanty Knowledge-base Hypothesis

According to this hypothesis, comprehension is easy when there is a rich knowledge base that may be tapped for "explaining" the incoming sentences (Collins, Brown, & Larkin, 1980; Graesser & Clark, 1985). When the text activates a large set of GKSs and the GKSs contain many nodes, then there is a rich foundation of knowledge that may be sampled in the process of constructing inferences. At the opposite end of the continuum, consider the situation in which the knowledge base is impoverished. When the text activates very few GKSs and the GKSs contain very few nodes, the comprehender must resort to constructing meaning from a vacuum. Comprehension is difficult and time consuming when the reader's knowledge base is scanty.

The scanty knowledge-base hypothesis predicts a negative correlation between processing time and number of inferences. Sentences that activate many inferences are products of rich knowledge structures and should be processed faster than sentences that activate few inferences. There is some evidence that supports this prediction of the scanty knowledge-base hypothesis. Graesser (1981) has reported that approximately four times as many inferences are generated during the comprehension of narrative text as that of expository text. Graesser used a question-answering task for uncovering inferences that subjects potentially generate during comprehension. The details of this Q/A method are covered later in this chapter. Whereas narrative text generates many more inferences than expository text, an average narrative passage takes approximately half the time to read (Graesser, Hoffman, & Clark, 1980; Graesser & Riha, 1984). This negative correlation between number of inferences and reading time is consistent with the scanty knowledge-base hypothesis and is incompatible with the strenuous inference generation hypothesis.

OVERVIEW OF A STUDY INVESTIGATING THE RELATIONSHIP BETWEEN READING TIME AND INFERENCE GENERATION

The research and hypotheses in the previous section inspired us to investigate the relationship between reading time and the number of inferences generated in narrative text. Subjects supplied word reading times for the four narrative passages that are presented in Table 9.1. Word reading times were collected by a moving window method. In this method the reader views one word at a time on a computer monitor. The reader presses a button when finished processing the word and then the compu-

TABLE 9.1
Passages Investigated in the Word Reading-Time Study

The Czar and His Daughters

Once there was a *Czar** who had three lovely *daughters.* One day the three daughters went walking in the *woods.* They were enjoying themselves so *much,* that they forgot the *time* and stayed too *long.* A dragon kidnapped the three *daughters.* As they were being dragged *off,* they *cried* for *help.* Three heroes heard the *cries* and set *off* to rescue the *daughters.* The heroes *came* and fought the *dragon* and rescued the *maidens.* Then the heroes returned the daughters to their *palace.* When the Czar heard of the *rescue,* he rewarded the *heroes.*

The Ant and the Dove

A thirsty ant went to a *river.* He became carried away by the rush of the *stream* and was about to *drown.* A dove was sitting in a *tree* that was overhanging the *water.* The dove plucked a *leaf* and let it *fall.* The leaf fell into the *stream* and the ant climbed onto *it.* The ant floated safely to the *bank.* Shortly afterwards a birdcatcher *came* and laid a trap into the *tree.* The ant saw his *plan* and stung him on the *foot.* In pain, the birdcatcher threw down his *trap.* The noise made the bird fly *away.*

John at Leone's

John went to New *York* by *bus.* On the bus he talked to an old *lady.* When he left the *bus,* he thanked the *driver.* He took the *subway* to *Leone's.* On the subway his pocket was *picked.* He got off the *train* and entered *Leone's.* He had some *lasagna.* When the check *came,* he discovered he couldn't *pay.* The management told him he would have to wash *dishes.* When he *left,* he caught a *bus* to New *Haven.*

The Boy and his Dog

A boy was holding a dog by a *leash* when the leash *broke.* The dog ran *away* and the boy *fell.* A rabbit looked at the *dog* as the dog ran past *him.* When a fox saw the *dog,* the fox and the dog started *fighting* and the rabbit started *running.* The fox chased the *dog* and the dog chased the *rabbit.* The rabbit jumped into a *hole.* Then the dog jumped into the *hole* to *safety.* Soon the rabbit met the *dog.* Some rabbits gave the dog *carrots* and rode on *him.* When the dog *left* the rabbits *cried.* The dog returned to the sad *boy.* The boy hugged the *dog* and they were happy to be together *again.*

*End-of-clause words are in italics.

ter displays the subsequent word in the text. The words are displayed on the monitor in a format that corresponds to the display format of printed text. Further details about this paradigm are presented in the next section.

Although the moving window method provided reading times for all of the words, we were particularly interested in the final words of the clauses and sentences (i.e., the *end-of-clause* words). Previous research on the moving window method (Haberlandt & Graesser, 1985) and eye movements (Just & Carpenter, 1980) have revealed that many of the semantic processes and inference mechanisms are executed at the end of clauses (and sentences). Therefore, we examined whether the end-of-clause processing time could be predicted by the number of inferences that subjects normally generated at the end of clauses.

We varied the comprehension goals of the readers who read the passages. Half the readers were assigned to a *comprehension* condition, whereas the other half were assigned to a *recall* condition. The readers in the comprehension condition expected a subsequent test that quizzed them on how well they comprehended the passages. The subjects in the recall condition expected a later recall test in which they would write as much information about each passage as they could remember. Generally speaking, the recall task encouraged readers to establish a well-organized representation that is easy to access from memory. Readers would presumably devote more efforts at integrating information from different clauses and at generating more inferences. We varied the readers' goals in order to assess the extent to which inference mechanisms are under the executive control of the reader.

We adopted a question-answering methodology for exposing the knowledge-based inferences that readers potentially generate during comprehension. A group of subjects were probed with *why, how,* and *what-happened-next* (WHN) questions as clauses from the four passages were comprehended in an incremental fashion. For example, suppose that the first clause in a passage was *John went to New York.* The subjects would answer the following three questions: *Why did John go to New York?, How did John go to New York?,* and *What happened next?.* Then the next clause in the passage would be presented and probed. The answers to these questions included a broad profile of knowledge-based inferences that readers potentially generate during comprehension. The answers include (a) goals, motives, and actions of animate agents, (b) states and events that initiate goals, (b) state/event chains in the social, physical, and mental worlds of agents, (d) the style in which actions and events occur, and (e) expectations about subsequent occurrences in the plot.

Graesser and Clark (1985) have previously reported an extensive set of analyses of the question-answering protocols collected on the four narrative passages. In the present study, we used the data reported by Graesser and Clark for scaling clauses on number of inferences. In essence, the present study examines whether the inferences exposed in the Graesser and Clark study (via the question-answering methodology) can predict the word reading times of the readers in the comprehension and recall conditions.

Graesser and Clark (1985) presented a model of comprehension and several analyses of the question-answering protocols. A detailed analysis of the question-answering protocols permitted them to trace the dynamic construction of passage structures as clauses are comprehended incrementally (from the first clause to the last clause in the passage). Graesser and Clark also mapped out the content and structure of the GKSs that were relevant to the four narrative passages. These GKSs furnished approximately 75% of the passage inferences. It is well beyond the scope of this chapter, however, to discuss their model and supporting data. Instead, we focus directly on the problem of relating inference generation with reading time.

One of the central issues about inference mechanisms addresses the distinction between comprehension-generated inferences and inferences that are not generated during text comprehension. When considering the answers exposed in the question answering protocols, some answers would probably be comprehension-generated inferences whereas other answers would not. Graesser and Clark (1985) specified which answers would *probably* be comprehension generated. Specifically, bridging inferences are usually comprehension generated, whereas elaborative inferences do not tend to be comprehension generated. Graesser and Clark also discovered that most of the answers to why-questions are bridging inferences, whereas most of the answers to how-questions and WHN-questions are elaborative inferences. Some of Graesser and Clark's claims were tested further in this chapter by examining the extent to which specific categories of inferences can predict reading time.

METHODS, MEASURES, AND MULTIPLE REGRESSION

This section begins with a description of our methods of collecting reading times and question-answering protocols. We subsequently discuss our use of multiple regression techniques for assessing the relationship between number of inferences and reading time. Finally, we list and operationally define the predictor variables in these regression analyses.

Word Reading Times and the Moving Window Method

Word reading times were collected from 30 college students. Half the readers were assigned to a comprehension condition and half to a recall condition. The subjects in the comprehension condition expected to complete a comprehension test later in the session. They were instructed that the comprehension test would involve answering questions about the characters, setting, and plot in the narrative passages. The subjects in the recall condition were instructed that they would later recall the passages in writing.

The word reading times were collected according to the moving window method (Haberlandt & Graesser, 1985). When the reader first viewed the computer screen, there was a display of dashes (–) and spaces. There was a dash corresponding to each letter and punctuation mark in the text. There were spaces between the dashes, just as there are spaces between words. The display of dashes and spaces directly corresponded to the spatial arrangement of the text (if it were presented on the computer screen). When the reader was ready to read the text, the reader pushed a response key and the first word of the text was presented on the screen; there were dashes corresponding to all the other words in the passage. The reader then pushed a response key when finished reading the first word, and the word reading time was recorded at millisecond accuracy. The computer subsequently presented word 2 on the screen and replaced the letters in word 1 with dashes; all other words also had dashes. This procedure continued until the reader was finished reading all the words in the passage. At any point in the text, only one word was presented to the reader. However, the surrounding display of dashes and spaces conveyed the spatial layout of the text.

There are three additional points that we should mention about the collection of word reading times. First, the readers read three practice passages before the four narrative passages. The subjects became acclimated to the moving window method while they read the three practice passages. Second, titles of the passages were presented before the passages were read. Word reading times were collected on the words in the titles, but these times were not analyzed. Third, the analyses reported in this chapter focus on the content words (nouns, pronouns, verbs, adverbs, and adjectives). We did not analyze the function words (determiners, prepositions, connectives) unless the function word was the final word in the clause. Among the four narrative passages that we analyzed, there were 208 content words and 74 end-of-clause words.

The moving window procedure provides data that are similar to eye movement data. In fact, there is a substantial correlation between the word reading times in the moving window procedure and the gaze durations for words when eye movements are recorded (Just, Carpenter, & Woolley, 1982).

Passages

Table 9.1 shows the four passages that we analyzed. They consisted of a heterogeneous sample of short narrative passages that have been analyzed by other researchers. *The Czar and His Daughters* (C & D) is a prototypical fairytale that has been parsed by several story grammars (Mandler & Johnson, 1977; Rumelhart, 1977). *The Ant and the Dove* (A & D) was generated by TAILSPIN, a computer program that generates simple stories (Meehan, 1977). The A & D passage can be accommodated by some, but not all story grammars. *John at Leone's* (J & L) is a script-based passage that was analyzed by Schank and Abelson's (1977) computer model of comprehension. The J & L passage and the subsequent passage are difficult to parse by most story grammars. *The Boy and his Dog* (B & D) is a passage that has been analyzed by Kintsch (1977). The B & D passage conveys a series of episodes that are not well integrated.

It is possible to order the four passages on a dimension of cohesiveness (Graesser & Clark, 1985). A cohesive narrative passage has a plot with episodes that are well motivated and that hang together conceptually. A very noncohesive passage has a random sequence of episodes that occur "out of the blue." The four passages would be ordered as follows on a scale of cohesiveness: C & D > A & D > J & L > B & D.

Clause Units

Most of the clause units consisted of a single action or event in the plot. An action is defined here as an intentionally motivated behavior of a character in a passage (e.g., the dragon kidnapped the daughters, the heroes went to the dragon). An event is a change of state that causally unfolds but is not intentionally inspired (e.g., the heroes heard the cries, the daughters forgot the time). Any given clause had at most one action or event. However, a single clause could have several atomic propositions that modify elements in the clause (e.g., there were three daughters, X occurred *one day*). Among the 74 clauses, 61 conveyed a single action or event that was modified by 0 to 3 atomic propositions.

The remaining 13 clauses were not single actions or events. Some were completely static clauses that were part of the setting of the narrative (e.g., once there was a Czar, the Czar had three lovely daughters). Some clauses referred to goals (e.g., the daughters cried *for help*). A few clauses referred to methods of travel. For example, in the expression *John went to New York by bus,* the phrase *by bus* was scored as a clause that could be paraphrased as "John took a bus."

Our definition of a clause is based more on semantic/conceptual criteria than on linguistic criteria. However, the four simple narrative passages showed a substantial correlation between our semantic-based clausal units and linguistic-based clausal units (see Halliday & Hasan, 1976; Van Dijk & Kintsch, 1983). Two of the authors of this study segmented the passages into clausal units. Each of these clauses had a final end-of-clause word; the 74 end-of-clause words are presented in italics in Table 9.1.

Number of Inferences and Question-Answering Protocols

Question-answering protocols were collected in order to expose empirically the knowledge-based inferences that readers generate during comprehension. As we mentioned earlier, the question-answering data were available from a previous study by Graesser and Clark (1985). Question-answering (Q/A) protocols were collected after each clause in the four narrative passages in Table 9.1. The clauses were presented and probed in the order that they appeared in the text. Therefore, when a particular clause was probed, the subject knew about the target clause and the previous passage context, but not the subsequent passage context. The subjects gave written answers to three questions when a given clause was probed: why, how, and what-happened-next (WHN). All 74 clauses were probed with why, how, and WHN questions.

Forty college students provided the Q/A protocols in this study. Ten subjects were assigned to each of the four narrative passages. The answer protocols were segregated into statement node units, which are roughly propositions (see Graesser & Clark, 1985). Associated with each clause was a list of unique answers that the subjects produced. There was a frequency score for each answer, which consisted of the number of subjects out of 10 who produced the specific answer for the particular clause. An answer was eliminated from subsequent analyses if it was produced by only one subject. The *answer distribution* of a clause was defined as the set of answers that were elicited by at least two subjects when the clause was probed by our Q/A method.

The answers in the answer distributions may be categorized on a number of dimensions. One dimension segregates new nodes from old nodes. A new node exists in the answer distribution of clause N, but not in the answer distributions of clauses 1 through N-1. In other words, a new node is constructed for the first time in the passage structure. In contrast, an old node in the answer distribution for clause N was also in an answer distribution of a previous clause in the passage. We define the *new inference node distribution* for clause N as the set of inference nodes in the answer distribution that are new nodes. As it turned out, the new inference node distribution for a clause provided the critical data for scaling clauses on number of generated inferences. The *number of new inferences* generated by clause N is the number of unique answers in the new inference node distribution for clause N.

We found it useful to segregate the inference nodes into subcategories. Specifically, we segregated the inferences into four *content categories*. These content categories are listed next, as well as some example node descriptions:

1. *Goals and intentional actions.* The heroes wanted to kill the dragon, the heroes killed the dragon
2. *Events (unintentional).* The heroes heard the cries, the leaf fell into the stream.
3. *States.* The dragon had claws, the heroes knew where the cave was.

4. *Style specifications*. The heroes ran *quickly,* the heroes stabbed the dragon *with a knife*.

The preceding labels and examples should convey the essence of these four categories. Graesser and Clark (1985) define these categories in more detail. Previous research and theory provided the rationale for segregating the inferences into these content categories. For example, there is some evidence that state and style inferences have a lower likelihood of being generated during comprehension than do goal, action, and event inferences (Graesser & Clark, 1985; Robertson, Black, & Lehnert, 1985).

There is one other important dimension for categorizing inferences. It is important to segregate *bridging* inferences from *elaborative* inferences. As we mentioned earlier, bridging inferences fill the conceptual gaps between an incoming clause and the previous passage structure; elaborative inferences embellish the explicit nodes and their bridges. According to Graesser and Clark's model of comprehension, the bridging inferences tend to be generated during comprehension, whereas the elaborative inferences do not tend to be comprehension generated. If this claim is correct, then reading times should be predicted by the bridging inferences to a greater extent than by the elaborative inferences. Of course, a test of this claim requires some defensible criteria for segregating bridging inferences from elaborative inferences. Graesser and Clark provide such criteria.

According to the analyses reported by Graesser and Clark (1985), there is a comparatively simple way of operationally defining the distinction between bridging inferences and elaborative inferences. Answers to why-questions tend to include bridging inferences, whereas answers to how-questions and WHN-questions tend to include elaborative inferences. Graesser and Clark estimated that 72% of the answers to why-questions are bridging inferences; the corresponding percentages for answers to how-questions and WHN-questions were 16% and 12%, respectively. Therefore, we defined the bridging inferences for clause N as those inferences that were answers to why-questions. Elaborative inferences are those inferences that were generated by how-questions and WHN-questions, but not by why-questions. This operational definition does not perfectly segregate bridging inferences from elaborative inferences, but it is rather robust.

When Graesser and Clark traced the dynamic construction of passage inferences, some incoming explicit clauses simply confirmed an inference/expectation that had already been constructed in the passage structure. Other clauses provided entirely new information rather than substantiating prior inferences. Obviously, reading times should be shorter for the expected clauses than for the unexpected clauses. We therefore segregated the explicit clauses into two subcategories: expected clauses versus unexpected clauses. Clause N was an *expected* clause if it confirmed an inference node that had already been constructed in the old passage structure (i.e., clauses 1 through N and their associated inferences). Otherwise, clause N was scored as unexpected.

The question-answering methodology provided a very rich data base for studying inferences in narrative comprehension. Graesser and Clark (1985) reported a model of comprehension and dozens of analyses which addressed the assumptions of the model. However, all their analyses were confined to a data base involving verbal protocols. If Graesser and Clark's qualitative analyses of inferences are valid and useful, then the data from these analyses should predict the word reading-time data.

Applying Multiple Regression Techniques to Reading-Time Data

During the last few years, cognitive psychologists have come to appreciate the use of multiple regression and other multivariate statistical techniques in their research. In the context of reading, multiple regression techniques have been applied to eye movement data (Just & Carpenter, 1980), sentence reading times (Graesser et al., 1980; Graesser & Riha, 1984; Haberlandt, 1984; Kieras, 1981; Olson et al., 1984, 1985), phrase-by-phrase reading time (Mitchell & Green, 1978), and word reading times (Aaronson & Scarborough, 1977; Haberlandt & Graesser, 1985). These researchers scale units in the text on several dimensions and then assess the extent to which reading times can be predicted by the dimensions (either individually or collectively). For example, consider word reading times. The time to process a given word is clearly influenced by several variables. There is word length, word frequency, word imagery, the content/function word distinction, and several other variables. Regression analyses permit the researcher to assess whether a particular variable (e.g., imagery) can predict reading time after statistically controlling for the other predictor variables. The researcher can assess how much reading-time variance is explained by a particular regression equation; this equation contains a set of regression coefficients corresponding to the set of predictor variables. The researcher can also assess statistical interactions between and among predictor variables.

There are several advantages to using multiple regression techniques to study reading. However, it is beyond the scope of this chapter to point out the virtues and the liabilities of multiple regression. Like all statistical and methodological tools, multiple regression techniques have both strengths and weaknesses. One of its weaknesses is that there will always be potential third variables that may be confounded with the predictor variables. Nevertheless, when it comes to studying the relationship between reading time and inference generation, the strengths of multiple regression analyses outweigh the weaknesses. Specifically, the multiple regression approach permits us to investigate inference processing in natural text. We can investigate the knowledge-based inferences that the reader normally generates in an ecologically valid setting. We are convinced that this approach has important advantages over the alternative approach, in which the investigator invents and investigates sentence sets that in theory vary on some dimension of inference processing. When researchers construct and manipulate their stimulus sentences, they often systematically impose constraints on the material that they never intended; the unintended constraints are often responsible for the reported data rather than the variables of interest. Once again, however, this chapter is not directly concerned with the strengths and weaknesses of different methodologies. We have simply adopted the multiple regression approach because it is particularly suited to the phenomenon under investigation.

Predictor Variables

We assessed the impact of several predictor variables on word-reading times. We were intrinsically interested in some of these predictor variables because they were directly related to inference mechanisms. Other predictor variables were not directly pertinent to inference processing, but they were included in the regression equation because (a) they had a substantial impact on reading times, and (b) we wanted to insure that these variables were not confounded with the variables reflecting inferences.

Consider first the three predictor variables related to inference generation. We assessed whether these variables predicted reading times for end-of-clause words. The means and standard deviations of these variables are presented in Table 9.2.

Number of New Inferences. This variable is the number of new nonreferential inferences that are generated when clause N was comprehended. As we discussed earlier, the Q/A protocols served as the data base for computing the number of new inferences. According to Table 9.2, an average clause yielded approximately 21 new inferences. In some regression analyses, we segregated the inferences into different subcategories in order to isolate those inferences that were truly comprehension generated. We segregated the inferences into bridging inferences (which were theoretically comprehension generated) versus elaborative inferences (which theoretically were not comprehension generated). We segregated

TABLE 9.2
Means and Standard Deviations of Predictor Variables

	End-of-Clause Words		All Content Words	
	Mean	SD	Mean	SD
Number of observations	74		208	
Word length	4.84	1.68	4.77	1.99
Word frequency (natural logarithm)	6.43	2.28	6.63	2.27
Word Repetition	.43	.50	.44	.50
Word imagery	3.19	.96	2.92	1.02
End-of-clause	—	—	.36	.48
Number of GKSs in clause	2.69	1.03		
Clause expectation	.51	.50		
Number of new inferences	21.23	9.07		
Bridging inferences	7.58	3.70		
Goals	2.37	2.49		
Events	1.47	1.82		
States	3.74	2.62		
Elaborative inferences	13.65	7.28		
Goals	6.70	3.93		
Events	2.51	2.23		
States	1.18	1.45		
Style specifications	3.26	3.18		

the inferences according to node content, i.e., goal/action, event, state, versus style specifications. It should be noted that none of the style inferences were bridging inferences. Table 9.2 shows means and standard deviations for these subcategories of inferences.

Clause Expectation.　A clause received a value of 1 if it was expected and 0 if it was unexpected. Clause N was expected if it confirmed an inference node that was activated by a previous clause in the passage (i.e., clauses 1 through N-1).

Number of GKSs in the Clause.　This variable was the number of GKSs (generic knowledge structures) that would participate in the interpretation of the clause. In most clauses, the GKSs included the main verb, the arguments that were explicitly mentioned, and modifying adjectives and adverbs. For example, the clause *the heroes returned the daughters to their palace* contains four GKSs: HERO, RETURNING, DAUGHTER, and PALACE. However, sometimes an argument noun-phrase was ellipti-cally deleted in the text, e.g., the heroes came and *fought the dragon*. We included GKSs that were elliptically deleted.

Several predictor variables were not of interest in the present context because they were not directly related to inference processing. Some of these uninteresting variables robustly predict reading time, according to previous studies involving eye movements, sentence reading time, and word-reading time. We included a set of variables that Haberlandt and Graesser (1985) reported to be significant predictors of word-reading time. These predictors included *word length, word frequency, word imagery, word repetition,* and the *end-of-clause* variable. Table 9.2 presents means and standard deviations for these five predictor variables. Word length was simply the number of letters in the word. Word frequency was the natural logarithm of the normative frequency of usage in the English language. Previous studies have reported that there is a linear relationship between reading time and the logarithm of word frequency (Graesser & Riha, 1984; Just & Carpenter, 1980). Two judges scaled the content words on word imagery, using a 4-point scale that varied from 1 (concept evokes little or no mental image) to 4 (concept evokes a vivid mental image). When the word was a pronoun, the rating was based on the referent of the pronoun. Regarding the repetition variable, the word received a score of 1 if it was mentioned previously in the passage and a score of 0 if it was mentioned for the first time in the passage. The end-of-clause variable specified whether the word was at the end of a clause (a score of 1) or not at the end of the clause (a score of 0). Haberlandt and Graesser (1985) segregated end-of-sentence words from end-of-clause words in their analysis of reading times. However, the present study did not capture this distinction because there were fewer data points and we needed to minimize the number of predictor variables.

In some regression analyses we included categorical variables that are not presented in Table 9.2. There was a passage variable that involved four "dummy-coded" predictors, corresponding to the four passages. The dummy-coded passage variable permitted us to assess whether word reading times vary among the four passages. There was a word category variable that had dummy-coded predictors that specified the part of speech of the word (i.e., noun, pronoun, verb, other). For example, if the word was a noun, the noun variable received a score of 1 and the other variables received scores of 0.

Some additional predictor variables were tested in preliminary analyses, but they were not significant predictors of reading time. First, there was no effect of syntactic complexity on reading time. This outcome did not surprise us because the syntactic formats of the sentences and clauses in our passages were uniformly simple; our passages did not provide a sensitive variation of syntactic complexity. It is interesting to note, however, that syntax variables have also failed to predict reading times in several published studies that investigate naturalistic prose (Graesser & Riha, 1984; Haberlandt & Graesser, 1985). Second, reading times were not significantly affected by the number of atomic propositions in the clause. Haberlandt and Graesser (1985) also failed to find significant effects of this proposition variable when they analyzed word-reading times. In contrast, reading times for sentences are significantly affected by number of atomic propositions (Graesser & Riha, 1984; Haberlandt, 1984). Unfortunately, we have no explanation for this discrepancy. Third, reading times were not significantly affected by the serial position of the clauses in the text. Previous studies have presented an inconsistent picture of the impact of serial position on reading time.

PRELIMINARY ANALYSIS OF CONTENT WORDS

We need to report some preliminary analyses before we analyze the relationship between number of inferences and reading times for end-of-clause words. In this section, we report some multiple regression analyses for all the content words in the text, not just the end-of-clause words. There are two major reasons for reporting these preliminary analyses. First, we wanted to assess whether most of the clausal processing actually occurred when end-of-clause words were read in the passages that we studied. Previous research on eye movements (Just & Carpenter, 1980) and word-reading times (Haberlandt & Graesser, 1985) has revealed that inference processing and the semantic interpretation of clauses predominately occurs when the end-of-clause words are read. Second, we wanted to assess whether our passages yield data that are consistent with the Haberlandt and Graesser study.

Reading Times for Content Words

We computed mean reading times for the 208 content words, averaging over readers. Separate means were computed for readers in the comprehension condition and the recall condition. The mean of the mean word-reading times was 513 milliseconds in the comprehension condition (SD = 182 milliseconds), whereas the mean was 598 milliseconds in the recall condition (SD = 263 milliseconds). Readers in the recall condition spent significantly more time processing the content words than did the readers in the comprehension condition. This outcome was expected because the readers in the recall condition presumably executed additional processes that organized the material for later recall.

Correlation Matrix

Table 9.3 presents a correlation matrix that includes the two reading-time variables (i.e., comprehension versus recall condition) and five of the predictor variables that had been investigated in the Haberlandt and

TABLE 9.3
Correlation Matrix for Content Words

| | Reading Times | | | | | |
	Comprehension	Recall	L	F	R	I
Reading time (recall)	.80*					
Word length (L)	.19	.15				
Word frequency (F)	−.14	−.17	−.57*			
Word repetition (R)	−.03	−.08	−.22*	.09		
Word imagery (I)	−.06	−.01	−.02	−.06	−.51*	
End-of-clause	.54*	.46*	.03	−.07	−.01	.19

*Correlation is significant at $p < .01$.

Graesser (1985) study. These five predictor variables include word length, word frequency, word repetition, word imagery, and the end-of-clause specification.

The correlations in Table 9.3 support four major conclusions. First, there was a very high correlation between the reading times in the comprehension condition and those in the recall condition ($r = .80$). It appears that a substantial amount of the reading-time variance is not influenced by variations in the comprehenders' goals. Second, the end-of-clause variable clearly had a more robust correlation with the reading times than did the other four predictor variables. This outcome is consistent with previous studies that have shown that the end-of-clause words have a privileged status regarding inference processing and the semantic interpretation of the clauses (Haberlandt & Graesser, 1985; Just & Carpenter, 1980). Third, the end-of-clause variable was not intercorrelated significantly with the other predictor variables. Thus, the semantic/conceptual processes that contribute to end-of-clause reading times cannot be explained by the lower level variables of word length, word frequency, word repetition, and word imagery. Finally, the directions of the correlations are consistent with the Haberlandt and Graesser (1985) study. The reading times increased as a function of word length and end-of-clause but decreased as a function of word frequency, word repetition, and word imagery.

Multiple Regression Analyses

We performed separate multiple regression analyses on the reading times in the comprehension condition versus the recall condition. In each analysis we included the five predictor variables captured in Table 9.3. We also included two other sets of predictor variables. There were four passage variables (one variable per passage) and four word category variables (noun, pronoun, verb, and other). Therefore, there were 13 predictor variables altogether.

Both of the multiple regression analyses indicated that the best fit regression equation significantly predicted the word-reading times. The regression equation predicted 41% of the reading-time variance in the comprehension condition, $F(13, 194) = 10.37$, $p < .01$, and 33% of the reading-time variance in the recall condition, $F(13, 194) = 7.45$, $p < .01$. Table 9.4 presents the regression coefficients for the 13 predictor variables. A regression coefficient reflects the amount of processing time (in milliseconds) that is associated with one unit of change on the predictor variable. For example, if the word-length variable shows a slope of 26, then it takes 26 milliseconds to process an average letter in a word. The asterisks (*) specify whether each predictor variable had a significant semipartial correlation. A significant semipartial correlation indicates that the predictor variable had a significant unique impact on the reading times, after partialling out contributions from all other predictor variables.

The regression coefficients of the first five predictor variables in Table 9.4 are consistent with Haberlandt and Graesser's analysis of word-reading times. Word-reading times increased as a function of word length and end-of-clause, whereas they decreased as a function of word fre-

TABLE 9.4
Regression Coefficients in the Analysis of Content Words

Predictor Variable	Comprehension Condition	Recall Condition
Word length	26**	18***
Word frequency	−1	−27***
Word repetition	−26	−69*
Word imagery	−24**	−41***
End-of-clause	209***	277***
Word Category		
Noun	117*	137
Pronoun	177**	359***
Verb	27	82
Other	31	102
Passage		
The Czar and His Daughters (C & D)	−121***	−171***
The Ant and the Dove (A & D)	−60***	−122***
John at Leone's (J & L)	−41*	−75*
The Boy and His Dog (B & D)	0	0

Significance of semipartial correlation
   ***$p < .05$, two-tailed test.
   **$p < .10$, two-tailed test.
   *$p < .20$, two-tailed test.

quency, word repetition, and word imagery. For the most part, these five predictor variables were significant predictors of reading time.

Both the correlation matrix and the regression analyses revealed that the end-of-clause variable was the most robust predictor of reading times among the five predictor variables. According to the regression coefficients in Table 9.4, the subjects in the comprehension condition spent an additional 209 milliseconds reading the end-of-clause words compared to the content words that were not at the end-of-clause positions. The subjects in the recall condition devoted an additional 277 milliseconds to end-of-clause words. The patterns of mean reading times were compatible with the regression coefficients. In the comprehension condition, the mean reading times for end-of-clause words versus other content words were 645 and 440 milliseconds, respectively (a difference of 205 milliseconds). In the recall condition, the corresponding times were 759 and 509 milliseconds (a difference of 250 milliseconds). The end-of-clause effect was clearly a very robust predictor of word-reading times.

Table 9.4 revealed that word-reading times varied as a function of word category. The regression coefficients showed the following ordering among the word categories: pronoun > noun > other > verb. The pronouns required substantially more processing time than the other word categories. On the average, a pronoun required 185 milliseconds more processing time than the other word categories. This outcome is consistent with several models of comprehension which assume that additional processing time is needed to compute the referent of a pronoun (Clark, 1977; Clark & Clark, 1977; Sanford & Garrod, 1981). According to these models, the process of resolving a pronoun's referent is equivalent to establishing a bridging inference (i.e., pronoun refers to referent). From this perspective, we have identified one class of inferences that is consistent with the strenuous inference generation hypothesis.

The regression coefficients in Table 9.4 showed significant differences among the four passages. If we were to rank order the passages according to reading time, there would be the following ordering: B & D > J & L > A & D > C & D. This rank ordering is negatively related to text cohesiveness. As we discussed earlier, the four passages varied in cohesiveness according to the following ordering: B & D < J & L < A & D < C & D. Not surprisingly, therefore, the cohesive passages tended to be read faster.

ANALYSIS OF END-OF-CLAUSE READING TIMES

This section examines the relationship between word-reading time and number of inferences. The analyses in the previous section were consistent with the claim that semantic processing and inference generation tend to occur at the end-of-clause positions. If this claim is correct, then the number of inferences generated by a clause should significantly predict end-of-clause reading times.

Predictor Variables.

There were only 74 words in the end-of-clause positions so we needed to be economical in selecting the predictor variables. The regression analyses included the word length, word frequency, word repetition, and word imagery variables. These four predictors proved to be significant in the previous analyses of the content words. We did not include the word category variable in the subsequent regression analyses because (a) nearly all the end-of-clause words were nouns or verbs (rather than adjectives, adverbs, pronouns, and other categories), and (b) the word category predictor was nonsignificant when we included this component in the regression equation. We also reduced the number of predictor variables by collapsing the four passage variables (which had been dummy coded) into a single quantitative variable, called *passage cohesiveness*. The words in the B & D, J & L, A & D, and C & D passages received scores of 1, 2, 3, and 4, respectively. We felt justified in adopting this passage cohesiveness variable because the coefficients of the four passage variables in Table 9.4 were nearly equidistant from each other when ordering them from highest to lowest. In summary, the regressions reported in this section always contained the following five predictor variables: word length, word frequency, word repetition, word imagery, and passage cohesiveness.

The remaining predictors in the regression analyses were more interesting from the standpoint of the present study. The additional variables included (a) the number of new inferences generated by the clause, (b) the number of GKSs in the clause, and (c) clause expectation (i.e., whether or not the clause was expected). These predictor variables were operationally defined earlier in this chapter. In some analyses we segregated the inference predictor into subcategories. We contrasted bridging inferences and elaborative inferences. We also segregated goals, events, and states.

Intercorrelations Among Predictor Variables

We prepared a correlation matrix that assessed the extent to which the predictor variables were intercorrelated. The correlation matrix did not show any problems of collinearity among the predictor variables. Number of new inferences had low correlations with the other predictor variables, varying from $-.19$ to $.33$. There were also low correlations when we assessed potential collinearity problems for number of GKSs (r's varying from $-.25$ to $.33$) and for clause expectation (r's varying from $-.33$ to $.16$). There were no problems of collinearity (or multicollinearity) in the subsequent regression analyses.

Regression Analyses

We performed four sets of regression analyses altogether. The regression equation was significant in all these analyses ($p < .01$). The different sets of regressions reflected variations in the inference component. In the first set of regressions, the number of new inferences variable included all of the new nonreferential inferences associated with a clause (i.e., both bridging and elaborative). In the second set of regressions, we segregated the bridging inferences from the elaborative inferences. The third set included the bridging inferences, but not the elaborative inferences. The fourth set segregated bridging inferences that were goals, events, versus states. Table 9.5 summarizes the results of the four sets of regression analyses. It includes (a) the regression coefficients of the interesting predictor variables, (b) a specification as to whether each predictor variable is significant, and (c) an R^2 value, which indicates the proportion of reading time variance that is explained by the regression equation. This table does not include data on the word-level predictor variables (e.g., word length, word frequency, etc.)

Consider the first set of regressions in Table 9.5. In both reading conditions, the reading times significantly *decreased* as a function of the number of new inferences associated with the clause. This outcome supports the scanty knowledge-base hypothesis rather than the strenuous inference generation hypothesis. Clauses that produce many new inferences tend to have shorter end-of-clause reading times.

The scanty knowledge-base hypothesis is supported further by the negative regression coefficient associated with the number of GKSs in the clause. The coefficient was negative in all the regression analyses, although the coefficient was not always significant in the comprehension condition. Clauses with many GKSs have a richer knowledge base from which to construct inferences. The rich knowledge base speeds up the generation of inferences that are needed for understanding the text.

The fact that the clause expectation variable had a negative coefficient is consistent with most models of comprehension. Clauses that confirm prior inferences and expectations are read faster than clauses that supply new information. We do not discuss this clause expectation variable any further in this section because it confirms virtually every theory and everyone's intuition.

The first set of regressions in Table 9.5 revealed that reading times decreased as a function of the number of new inferences generated by the

TABLE 9.5
Regression Coefficients in the Analyses of the
End-of-clause Reading Times

	Predictor Variable[a]	Comprehension Condition	Recall Condition
	Clause Expectation	−78*	−105*
Regression 1	Number of GKSs in clause	−21	−82**
	Number of New Inferences	−6**	−8**
	R²	.28	.29
	Clause Expectation	−88*	−132*
	Number of GKSs in clause	−22	−86***
Regression 2	Number of bridging inferences	−10*	−18*
	Number of elaborative inferences	−5	−5
	R²	.29	.29
	Clause Expectation	−91*	−135*
Regression 3	Number of GKSs in clause	−30*	−93***
	Number of bridging inferences	−12*	−20**
	R²	.27	.29
	Clause Expectation	−102**	−144*
	Number of GKSs in clause	−35*	−103***
Regression 4	Number of bridging goals/actions	−27***	−41***
	Number of bridging events	−14*	−31*
	Number of bridging states	1	2
	R²	.31	.33

[a]The regression equations also include the following predictor variables: word length, word frequency, word repetition, word imagery, and passage cohesiveness.

Significance of the semipartial correlation for a predictor variable:

***$p < .05$, two-tailed test.

**$p < .10$, two-tailed test.

*$p < .20$, two-tailed test.

clause. There was an average regression coefficient of −7 milliseconds. Therefore, each new inference yielded a 7 millisecond decrease in end-of-clause reading time. We performed additional regression analyses in order to isolate those inferences that account for the negative correlation between reading time and number of inferences.

The second set of regression analyses compared bridging inferences and elaborative inferences. According to several comprehension models (Clark, 1977; Graesser & Clark, 1985; Keenan et al., 1984; Singer & Fernanda, 1983), readers tend to construct bridging inferences during comprehension, but not elaborative inferences. If this assumption is correct, then the reading times should be predicted by the bridging inferences but not the elaborative inferences. This prediction was indeed supported by the second set of regression analyses. The third set of regressions included only the bridging inferences (not the elaborative inferences). The amount of reading-time variance explained in the third set of regressions is nearly the same as the variance explained in the first set of regressions (which included both bridging inferences and elaborative inferences). These results indicate that the elaborative inferences do not significantly predict reading time. These results also support the hypothesis that the elaborative inferences tend not to be generated during comprehension.

The fourth set of regressions compares the bridging inferences that are goals/actions versus events versus states. There were substantial differences between these three categories of bridging inferences. Reading times significantly decreased as a function of the number of goals/actions and perhaps the number of events. However, the reading times were not significantly predicted by the number of state inferences. If anything, the state inferences had a positive correlation with reading times. These outcomes support the hypothesis that static inferences have a lower likelihood of being generated during comprehension than do goals, actions, and events (Graesser & Clark, 1985; Robertson, Black, & Lehnert, 1985).

In summary, the regression analyses supported three major conclusions. First, the data on the nonreferential bridging inferences were consistent with the scanty knowledge-base hypothesis, which predicts a negative correlation between reading time and number of inferences. Second, the bridging inferences had a higher likelihood of being generated during comprehension than did the elaborative inferences. Third, those bridging inferences that are goals, actions, and events tend to be comprehension generated, whereas the states tend not to be comprehension generated.

Differences Among Readers and Readers' Goals

The question arises as to whether the reported predictors of end-of-clause reading times were consistent across comprehension conditions and among readers. In order to answer this question, we compared the regression coefficients of those subjects assigned to the comprehension condition versus the recall condition. Within these two conditions, we segregated fast readers from slow readers; we inspected each subject's mean end-of-clause reading times and adopted a median split criterion for segregating fast readers from slow readers. A separate regression analysis was performed on each subject's end-of-clause reading times, and regression coefficients were observed for each of the predictor variables. Table 9.6 presents mean regression coefficients for the four groups of subjects: fast readers in the comprehension condition, slow readers in the compre-

TABLE 9.6
Regression Coefficients for Predictor Variables,
Segregated by Different Groups of Subjects

Predictor Variable	Comprehension Condition		Recall Condition	
	Fast Readers	Slow Readers	Fast Readers	Slow Readers
Number of bridging inferences	−4	−22	−8	−33
Number of GKSs in clause	−12	−56	−14	−183
Clause expectation	−43	−151	−5	−285
Passage cohesiveness	−27	−144	−78	−190
Mean reading time (milliseconds)	400	925	615	924
Number of subjects	8	7	8	7

hension condition, fast readers in the recall condition, and slow readers in the recall condition. Table 9.6 shows mean coefficients for the number of bridging inferences, the number of GKSs in the clause, clause expectation, and passage cohesiveness.

When we compared regression coefficients among different groups of subjects, the pattern of results was virtually identical for each of the four predictor variables. First, the regression coefficients were much higher in magnitude for slow readers than for fast readers. When we performed t-tests comparing the regression coefficients of fast and slow readers, there were significant differences for all four predictor variables. Second, the regression coefficients were slightly, but consistently, more extreme in the recall condition than in the comprehension condition. Although this trend was consistent, only one of the t-tests was significant when we compared subjects in the recall versus comprehension conditions; the coefficient of the passage cohesiveness variable was significantly higher in the recall condition than in the comprehension condition. It appears, therefore, that the reported effects of number of new inferences (and the other predictors in Tables 9.5 and 9.6) on reading time were more robust in the slower readers, but they did not vary appreciably as a function of comprehension goals.

We were impressed with the consistency of the regression coefficients among individual readers. Although the four groups of subjects in Table 9.6 showed variations in the *magnitude* of the regression coefficients, the *sign* of the coefficients stayed the same. We inspected the signs of the coefficients in the individual regressions of the 30 subjects. Again, there was a great deal of consistency. Number of bridging inferences had negative regression coefficients in 90% of the subjects' analyses. The coefficients were negative in 80% of the regressions for the number of

GKSs in a clause, 77% for clause expectation, and 93% for passage cohesiveness.

In summary, the reported effects of the predictors on end-of-clause reading times were very consistent across subjects and did not substantially vary when readers read text for different purposes. For the most part, the effects were strategy free. However, the magnitude of the coefficients directly increased as a function of overall reading time. The slower readers had steeper coefficients.

CONCLUSIONS ABOUT INFERENCE PROCESSES DURING COMPREHENSION

We have arrived at a number of conclusions about inference processing during text comprehension. These conclusions are based on the research presented in this chapter and in some previous studies. This section presents our conclusions in the context of three general questions. First, what inferences are normally generated during comprehension? Second, how is reading time related to inference generation? Third, to what extent is inference processing influenced by the goals of the comprehender?

What Inferences Are Normally Generated During Comprehension?

Two categories of inferences are generated during the comprehension of narrative plot. Inferences in both categories are needed to establish conceptual connectivity between the clauses in the text. The first category consists of referential inferences. When a pronoun is read, for example, the reader computes referent of the pronoun. Pronouns are not the only word category that requires referential bridging inferences. The nouns in definite noun-phrases normally require referential bridging inferences. For example, *the maidens* was a definite noun phrase in the C & D passage; the "maidens" referred to the daughters and therefore required a bridging inference (i.e., maidens refers to daughters). A more complete discussion of reference resolution and referential bridging inferences is presented elsewhere (Clark, 1977; Clark, Schreuder, & Buttrick, 1983; Sanford & Garrod, 1981).

The second category of comprehension-generated inferences consists of nonreferential bridging inferences that are goals, actions, or events. According to Graesser and Clark (1985), these inferences would be exposed when individuals are asked why-questions about the explicit actions and events in the plot. In contrast, answers to other question categories (how, when, where, what enabled X, what are the consequences of X, what is the significance of X) do not uncover a high density of bridging inferences. These other question categories expose many elaborative inferences that are not comprehension generated. The conclusion that bridging inferences, but not elaborative inferences, tend to be comprehension generated is consistent with conclusions of other researchers (Clark, 1977; Reder, 1982; Singer & Fernanda, 1983; Trabasso, Secco, & Van den Broek, 1984; Van Dijk & Kintsch, 1983), although these researchers have not precisely segregated bridging inferences from elaborative inferences. The conclusion that state inferences tend not to be comprehension generated is consistent with Robertson et al. (1985).

How is Reading Time Related to Inference Generation?

The research in this chapter indicates that there is not a simple, unidimensional relationship between reading time and the number of inferences generated by a clause. The relationship depends on the class of inferences under consideration. For referential bridging inferences, there is a positive correlation between number of inferences and reading time. Recall that the regression coefficient was significantly longer for pronouns than for other categories of words. There is an extensive body of psychological research which has firmly established that referent resolution takes a measurable amount of processing time (Clark, 1977; Sanford & Garrod, 1981). The reading time is particularly long if there is some uncertainty in constructing referential bridging inferences. For example, the reading time for a pronoun is longer if there are several potential referents than if there is only one referent. In summary, the strenuous inference generation hypothesis is supported when the referential bridging inferences are considered.

The relationship between reading time and number of inferences is altogether different when the other categories of bridging inferences are considered. There was a negative relationship between end-of-clause reading times and the number of nonreferential bridging inferences that are goals, actions, and events. Clauses that generate many inferences are supported by a rich knowledge base. There is a large node space in the GKSs that furnish the inferences; the reader has a larger data base for sampling conceptual chains which provide conceptual connectivity in the text. In contrast, a clause generates few inferences whenever there are very few nodes in the supporting knowledge base. Reading times are longer when the reader is trying to extract information out of an impoverished data base. The scanty knowledge-base hypothesis is supported when the nonreferential bridging inferences are considered.

According to Graesser and Clark (1985), it is useful to view comprehension from the standpoint of a *convergence* between and among knowledge structures. There are at least three classes of knowledge structure to consider in these convergence mechanisms. First, there are knowledge structures corresponding to the explicit information in the text. Second, there are GKSs which get activated by the explicit text. Third, there are knowledge structures associated with the reader's goals and other pragmatic aspects of the discourse. Comprehension is comparatively quick when there is a convergence among these knowledge structures. Successful comprehension is analogous to a large puzzle that falls into place.

Graesser and Clark reported that most inferences come from GKSs that are associated with the explicit content words in the passages. For example, the GKSs associated with *the dragon kidnapped the daughters* would be DRAGON, KIDNAP, and DAUGHTERS. Graesser and Clark used the Q/A methodology for mapping out the inferences during text comprehension and mapping out the GKSs that were associated with the passages. They found that 72% of the passage inferences associated with a clause matched a node in at least one GKS associated with the clause. They also found that *intersecting nodes* had a very special status in the inference generation mechanisms. An intersecting node is a node that overlaps between more than one GKS associated with the clause. For example, both DRAGON and KIDNAP had the node *X threatens Y*. The intersecting nodes (and GKS nodes that were proximate to the intersecting nodes) had a high likelihood of being passed to the passages structures in the form of knowledge-based inferences. According to Graesser and Clark's comprehension model, when there is a high degree of convergence among the GKSs associated with the passage, there will be many intersecting nodes and therefore many bridging inferences. It follows that there should be a positive correlation between the number of inferences and convergence. Moreover, if convergence facilitates reading time, then there should be a negative relationship between reading time and the number of new inferences generated by a clause. Graesser and Clark's model therefore predicted the negative relationship between end-of-clause reading times and number of bridging inferences.

Consider the following three sentences in the context of the model of comprehension that we are proposing here.

1. When the animal did something to the girl, she cried.
2. When the goat slapped the princess, she cried.
3. When the dragon kidnapped the princess, she cried.

According to the model, sentence 3 should generate more knowledge-based inferences and should be read faster than sentences 1 and 2.

Sentence 1 generates comparatively few inferences because the GKSs in the first clause (ANIMAL, DOING, GIRL) are not as semantically rich as the GKSs in sentence 3 (DRAGON, KIDNAPPING, PRINCESS). It is a struggle to construct bridging inferences from a meager knowledge base so the reading time for sentence 1 should be comparatively long. Sentence 2 would also generate comparatively few bridging inferences because there is a lack of convergence among the node structures associated with the GKSs. Specifically, there are few intersecting nodes among the GKSs for GOAT, SLAPPING, and PRINCESS. These three GKSs are richer than the GKSs associated with sentence 1, but the GKSs do not converge on sensible bridging inferences. It is a struggle to construct bridging inferences when the background knowledge structures are difficult to relate. Sentence 3 would produce the most bridging inferences and would be read the fastest. The GKSs in sentence 3 supply a rich knowledge base and there are many intersecting nodes.

Additional support for the scanty knowledge-base hypothesis lies in some comparisons between narrative and expository prose. Narrative text generates many more knowledge-based inferences than does expository text (Graesser, 1981; Graesser & Goodman, 1985), yet narrative text is read much faster than expository text (Graesser, Hoffman, & Clark, 1980; Graesser & Riha, 1984; Haberlandt & Graesser, 1985). The fact that narrative text produces more inferences also explains some reaction time data reported by Britton, Graesser, Glynn, Hamilton, and Penland (1983). Britton et al. used a secondary task technique to measure the amount of cognitive capacity used in a reading task. The primary task was reading narrative and expository passages. A click was occasionally presented during the reading session and subjects were instructed to release a response key whenever they heard a click. Responding to the click was the secondary task. The reaction time latencies in the secondary task were significantly longer when the narrative text was read than when the expository text was read. The latencies may be longer in the narrative reading conditions because more knowledge-based inferences are being generated as the GKSs converge on the bridging inferences. These convergence mechanisms and the large density of inferences make it difficult for subjects to disengage from the primary task and respond to the secondary task.

In summary, the construction of referential bridging inferences increases reading time. In contrast, there is a negative relationship between reading time and the number of nonreferential bridging inferences. The outcome for the nonreferential bridging inferences suggests a new metaphor for construing inference mechanisms during comprehension. The amount of time it takes to build a bridge does not appreciably increase with the number of girders, the pounds of cement and cable, and the length of the bridge. Instead, the amount of time increases when the materials are not readily available and when they are difficult to put together.

To What Extent Is Inference Generation Influenced by the Readers' Goals?

There is ample evidence that text comprehension is influenced by the goals of the comprehender (Frederikson, 1975; Graesser, 1981; Masson, 1982; Streitz, 1982). However, the available research has not unravelled the mystery of how inference mechanisms are influenced by readers' goals.

The results of the present study suggest that the construction of bridging inferences is not substantially affected by variations in readers' goals. The readers in the recall condition did have longer reading times than did the readers in the comprehension condition. However, the increase in reading times in the recall condition cannot be attributed to different *patterns* of inference processing or to a special allocation of cognitive resources to inference processing. Of course, a larger and more diverse sample of readers might be needed before statistically significant effects emerge. Alternatively, perhaps the differences between recall and comprehension instructions were not robust enough to have an impact on inference generation.

Graesser, Hoffman, and Clark (1980) proposed that variations in readers' goals should influence components at deep levels of analysis to a greater extent than components at shallow levels. Components at the deeper levels include semantic interpretation, inference generation, and the integration of information from different sentences. Number of inferences, clause expectation, and passage cohesiveness are predictor variables that tap the deep levels of analysis. In contrast, components at shallow levels of analysis include language codes and meaning codes that are highly automatized. Word length, word frequency, and word imagery would clearly be at a shallow level of analysis. The results in the present study did not show overwhelming support for Graesser et al.'s hypothesis. The hypothesis was confirmed when the most shallow component (word length) was compared to the deepest component (passage cohesiveness). The regression coefficients of the passage cohesiveness predictor were significantly steeper in the recall condition than in the comprehension condition (-134 vs. -90 milliseconds); the corresponding coefficients for word length were not significantly different (18 vs. 26 milliseconds). However, the hypothesis was not confirmed when the intermediate predictor variables were analyzed. All the other predictors showed steeper regression coefficients in the recall condition than in the comprehension condition (although the differences were rarely significant). More research is clearly needed before we can establish a satisfactory explanation of the impact of readers' goals on inference generation, and on comprehension in general.

If the results of this study are valid and general, then the construction of bridging inferences is not substantially influenced by the goals of the comprehender. We might extend our bridge construction metaphor a bit further. Bridge construction is a complex multifaceted industry that employs hundreds of interactive workers. Bridge construction is a sophisticated system that cannot easily be modified by outside forces or by a boss with an iron will. The boss might be able to speed up bridge construction or slow it down a bit, but the boss has a negligible impact on the guts of the system.

ACKNOWLEDGMENTS

This research was supported, to various extents and at various times, by National Institute of Mental Health grants MH-31083 and MH-33491 and by National Science Foundation grant BNS-8104958. Requests for reprints should be sent to Arthur C. Graesser, Department of Psychology, Memphis State University, Memphis, Tennessee 38152.

REFERENCES

Aaronson, D., & Scarborough, H. S. (1977). Performance theories for sentence coding: Some quantitative models. *Journal of Verbal Learning and Verbal Behavior, 16,* 277–304.

Abelson, R. P. (1981). Psychological status of the script concept. *American Psychologist, 7,* 715–730.

Black, J. B., & Bern, H. (1981). Causal coherence and memory for events in narratives. *Journal of Verbal Learning and Verbal Behavior, 20,* 267–276.

Bower, G. H., Black, J. B., & Turner, T. J. (1979). Scripts in memory for text. *Cognitive Psychology, 11,* 177–220.

Britton, B. K., Glynn, S. M., & Smith, J. W. (1985). Cognitive demands of processing expository text: A cognitive workbench model. In B. K. Britton & J. B. Black. (Eds.), *Understanding expository text.* Hillsdale, NJ: Lawrence Erlbaum Associates.

Britton, B. K., Graesser, A. C., Glynn, S. M., Hamilton, T., & Penland, M. (1983). Use of cognitive capacity in reading: Effects of some content factors of text. *Discourse Processes, 6,* 39–58.

Brown, G., & Yule, G. (1983). *Discourse analysis.* London: Cambridge University Press.

Clark, H. H. (1977). Bridging. In P. N. Johnson-Laird & P. C. Wason (Eds.), *Thinking: Readings in cognitive science.* London: Cambridge University Press.

Clark, H. H., & Clark, E. V. (1977). *Psychology and language.* New York: Harcourt Brace & Jovanovich.

Clark, H. H., Schreuder, R., & Buttrick, S. (1983). Common ground and the understanding of demonstrative reference. *Journal of Verbal Learning and Verbal Behavior, 22,* 245–258.

Collins, A. M., Brown, J. S., & Larkin, K. M. (1980). Inferences in text understanding. In R. J. Spiro, B. C. Bruce, & W. F. Brewer (Eds.), *Theoretical issues in reading comprehension.* Hillsdale, NJ: Lawrence Erlbaum Associates.

Crothers, E. (1979). *Paragraph structure inference.* Hillsdale, NJ: Lawrence Erlbaum Associates.

Frederikson, C. H. (1975). Effects of context-induced processing operations on semantic information acquired from discourse. *Cognitive Psychology, 7,* 139–166.

Graesser, A. C. (1981). *Prose comprehension beyond the word.* New York: Springer–Verlag.

Graesser, A. C., & Clark, L. F. (1985). *Structures and procedures of implicit knowledge.* Norwood, NJ: Ablex.

Graesser, A. C., Hoffman, N. L., & Clark, L. F. (1980). Structural components of reading time. *Journal of Verbal Learning and Verbal Behavior, 19,* 131–151.

Graesser, A. C., & Nakamura, G. V. (1982). The impact of a schema on comprehension and memory. In G. H. Bower (Ed.), *The psychology of learning and motivation: Advances in research and theory.* New York: Academic Press.

Graesser, A. C. & Goodman, S. M. (1985). Implicit Knowledge, question answering, and the representation of expository text. In B. Britton & J. B. Black (Eds.), *Understanding expository text.* Hillsdale, NJ: Lawrence Erlbaum Associates.

Graesser, A. C., & Riha, J. R. (1984). An application of multiple regression techniques to sentence reading times. In D. Kieras & M. Just (Eds.), *New methods in comprehension research.* Hillsdale, NJ: Lawrence Erlbaum Associates.

Haberlandt, K. (1984). Components of sentence and word reading times. In D. E. Kieras & M. A. Just (Eds.), *New methods in reading comprehension research.* Hillsdale, NJ: Lawrence Erlbaum Associates.

Haberlandt, K., & Bingham, G. (1978). Verbs contribute to the coherence of brief narratives: Reading related and unrelated sentence triplets. *Journal of Verbal Learning and Verbal Behavior, 17,* 419–425.

Haberlandt, K., & Graesser, A. C. (1985). Component processes in text comprehension and some of their interactions. *Journal of Experimental Psychology: General, 114,* 357–374.

Halliday, M.A.K., & Hasan, R. (1976). *Cohesion in English.* London: Longman.

Just, M. A., & Carpenter, P. A. (1980). A theory of reading: From eye fixations to comprehension. *Psychological Review, 87,* 329–354.

Just, M. A., & Carpenter, P. A., & Woolley, J. D. (1982). Paradigms and processes in reading comprehension. *Journal of Experimental Psychology: General, 111,* 228–238.

Keenan, J. M., Baillet, S. D., & Brown, P. (1984). The effects of causal cohesion on comprehension and memory. *Journal of Verbal Learning and Verbal Behavior, 23,* 115–126.

Kempson, R. M. (1977). *Semantic theory.* London: Cambridge University Press.

Kintsch, W. (1977). On comprehending stories. In M. A. Just & P. A. Carpenter (Eds.), *Cognitive processes in comprehension.* Hillsdale, NJ: Lawrence Erlbaum Associates.

Kintsch, W., & van Dijk, T. A. (1978). Toward a model of text comprehension and production. *Psychological Review, 85,* 363–394.

LaBerge, D., & Samuels, S. J. (1974). Toward a theory of automatic information processing in reading. *Cognitive Psychology, 6,* 293–323.

Mandler, J. M., & Johnson, N. S. (1977). Remembrance of things parsed: Story structure and recall. *Cognitive Psychology, 9,* 111–151.

Masson, M.E.J. (1982). Cognitive processes in skimming stories. *Journal of Experimental Psychology: Learning, Memory, and Cognition, 8,* 400–417.

McKoon, G., & Ratcliff, R. (1981). The comprehension for processes and memory structures involved in instrumental inferences. *Journal of Verbal Learning and Verbal Behavior, 20,* 671–682.

Meehan, J. R. (1977). TALESPIN, an interactive program that writes stories. *Proceedings from the Fifth International Joint Conference of Artificial Intelligence,* 91–98.

Meyer, B.J.F. (1985). Prose analysis: Purposes, procedures, and problems. In B. K. Britton & J. B. Black (Eds.), *Understanding expository text.* Hillsdale, NJ: Lawrence Erlbaum Associates.

Mitchell, D. C., & Green, D. W. (1978). The effects of content on immediate processing in reading. *Quarterly Journal of Experimental Psychology, 30,* 609–636.

Olson, G. M., Duffy, S. A., & Mack, R. L. (1984). Thinking-out-loud as a method for studying real-time comprehension processes. In D. E. Kieras & M. Just (Eds.), *New methods in reading comprehension research.* Hillsdale, NJ: Lawrence Erlbaum Associates.

Olson, G. M., Duffy, S. A., & Mack, R. L. (1985). Question asking as a component of text comprehension. In A. C. Graesser & J. B. Black (Eds.), *The psychology of questions.* Hillsdale, NJ: Lawrence Erlbaum Associates.

Reder, L. M. (1982). Elaborations: When do they help and when do they hurt? *Text, 2,* 211–224.

Robertson, S. P., Black, J. B., & Lehnert, W. G. (1985). Misleading question effects as evidence for integrated question understanding and memory search. In A. C. Graesser & J. B. Black (Eds.), *The psychology of questions.* Hillsdale, NJ: Lawrence Erlbaum Associates.

Rumelhart, D. E. (1977). Understanding and summarizing brief stories. In D. LaBerge & S. J. Sammuels (Eds.), *Basic processes in reading: Perception and comprehension.* Hillsdale, NJ: Lawrence Erlbaum Associates.

Sanford, A. J., & Garrod, S. C. (1981). *Understanding written language: Explorations in comprehension beyond the sentence.* New York: Wiley.

Schank, R. C. (1982). Reminding and memory organization: An introduction to MOPs. In W. G. Lehnert & M. H. Ringle (Eds.), *Strategies of natural language comprehension.* Hillsdale, NJ: Lawrence Erlbaum Associates.

Schank, R. C., & Abelson, R. P. (1977). *Scripts, plans, goals, and understanding.* Hillsdale NJ: Lawrence Erlbaum Associates.

Singer, M., & Fernanda, F. (1983). Inferring consequences in story comprehension. *Journal of Verbal Learning and Verbal Behavior, 22,* 437–448.

Streitz, N. A. (1982). The role of problem orientations and goals in text comprehension and recall. In A. Flammer & W. Kintsch (Eds.), *Discourse processing* (Vol. 8). Amsterdam: North-Holland.

Trabasso, T., Secco, T., & Van Den Broek, P. (1984). Causal cohesion and story coherence. In H. Mandl, N. L. Stein, & T. Trabasso (Eds.), *Learning and comprehension of text.* Hillsdale, NJ: Lawrence Erlbaum Associates.

Van Dijk, T., & Kintsch, W. (1983). *Strategies of discourse comprehension.* New York: Academic Press.

Walker, C. H., & Yekovich, F. R. (1984). Script-based inferences: Effects of text and knowledge variables on recognition memory. *Journal of Verbal Learning and Verbal Behavior, 23,* 357–370.

REMEMBERING READING OPERATIONS WITH AND WITHOUT AWARENESS. 10

Michael E. J. Masson
University of Victoria

OVERVIEW

The perceptual and cognitive operations performed during fluent reading cannot conceivably be under direct executive control throughout the entire course of their functioning. A much more reasonable assumption is that a number of these operations carry on outside the bounds of awareness and produce results or outputs that eventually are used by centrally controlled processes. In this article I consider the implications of this assumption for (a) the memory representation of specific reading episodes, and (b) the role played by such memory representations when material is read on multiple occasions. Special consideration will be given to a form of memory for reading episodes that appears to operate outside the domain of executive control processes.

In the first part of the article, some empirical demonstrations of automatic visual processing and associated consequences for memory representations are reviewed. I argue that although memory for automatically processed visual events appears to be poor, methods of testing memory that do not require introspection concerning specific prior episodes may produce a very different set of conclusions. Examples of such demonstrations are considered, including compelling neuropsychological evidence. Next I develop a characterization of automated and attention-demanding aspects of reading that is based on the concept of interacting memory systems. In support of this framework, recent experiments involving memory for reading operations are reviewed and their implications for the possible role of executive control processes in reading are discussed.

253

MEMORY AND AUTOMATIC PROCESSING

One view of how information is encoded into long-term memory is that encoding requires conscious, controlled processing. In the case of language comprehension, it generally is assumed that attention primarily is devoted to comprehension of the meaning of a message, not to its surface characteristics (e.g., specific lexical items and syntactic structure). A strong faith in this view has produced a number of celebrated demonstrations concerning the remarkable inability of readers or listeners to remember the nonsemantic aspects of sentences. Support for an attentional explanation of surface memory effects can be drawn from classic work by Schneider and Shiffrin (1977; Shiffrin & Schneider, 1977) on the distinction between automatic and attention-demanding processes.

Automatic and Controlled Processing

In their work with visual search tasks, Schneider and Shiffrin provided a theoretical and empirical distinction between two fundamentally different modes of processing. Controlled processing was conceptualized as under direct control of the subject, slow and attention demanding. A major purpose of controlled processing is to cope with novel events. Automatic processing was characterized as fast, not limited by attentional capacity, and not under direct attentional control. Well-developed skills that required extensive training were assumed to be based on automatic processes.

Schneider and Shiffrin's empirical demonstrations of these principles were based on a visual search task in which subjects were required to search through a series of briefly presented frames (displays containing a set of letters, digits, or both) in an attempt to detect the presence of a member of a target set. In the *consistent mapping* condition, the target was always a member of one category (e.g., letters) and the distractor items were always members of the other category (e.g., digits). After a modest amount of training, performance in this condition became highly accurate and was not affected by number of elements in each frame. The failure of frame size to affect detection accuracy was taken as evidence for fast parallel processing, characteristic of automatic detection. Performance was not so spectacular in the *varied mapping* condition. In this case, targets and distractors both came from the same category (e.g., letters) so that across a series of trials an individual item served both as a distractor and as a target. Accurate search performance required a much slower rate of frame presentation than the consistent mapping condition, and there was a large effect of frame size—higher accuracy with fewer elements per frame. The slow serial search apparent under these conditions was offered as an example of controlled search.

Shiffrin and Schneider (1977) speculated that although automatic processing of elements in the consistent mapping condition activated longterm memory nodes representing those elements, no controlled processing in short-term memory was involved. Furthermore, modification of long-term memory was assumed to depend on controlled processing, so that no appreciable long-term memory encoding would be expected in the case of automatic processing. Direct evidence for these claims has now been provided by Fisk and Schneider (1984). They had subjects carry out a visual search task involving a series of frames, similar to the task used by Schneider and Shiffrin (1977). This time, however, each frame contained two digits at diagonally opposite corners of each frame and a word in the center of the frame. One group of subjects was given the task of searching for a target digit among the frames while ignoring the words. In this case it was expected that any processing of the words would be automatic because the digit search task was attention demanding. Individual words appeared in the frames with varying frequency, and at the end of the experiment subjects were provided with a list of words and asked to make frequency of occurrence judgments for each. For these subjects the median frequency judgments were zero for words ranging in actual frequency of occurrence from 0 to 20. In addition, recognition memory scores based on the frequency judgments (zero indicated a miss) were at chance. Clearly, subjects had not encoded much reliable information concerning words when they did not attend to them.

In a second experiment Fisk and Schneider trained subjects to automatically detect members of a single semantic category in a search task. In this case the nonmember distractors were assumed to receive automatic processing without long-term memory encoding. To ensure that controlled processing would not be devoted to the distractors in this task, subjects were required to carry out a concurrent, attention-demanding digit search task. Again, frequency judgments for these words produced a median of zero, and corresponding recognition memory scores were very low and close to (but significantly above) chance. These results could be taken as rather powerful evidence for the claim that words can be automatically identified without producing a reliable long-term memory encoding.

Automatic Processes in Reading

Unfortunately, the study of automaticity in reading is much more difficult than is the case for visual search. Current evidence concerning automatic subskills in reading, however, has produced a pattern of effects similar to that obtained with visual search tasks. As a general example of the claim that automatization of processes leads to reduced long-term memory encoding of the targets of those processes, consider an experiment on the development of automatized word identification (Kolers, 1975a). Subjects were required to read typographically transformed (upside down) sentences, an initially slow and attention-demanding task because of the unfamiliar visual patterns. A rather powerful consequence of this procedure is an enduring and highly accurate recognition memory for sentences read in this manner (Kolers, 1975b).

Over the course of reading more than 160 pages of inverted sentences, skill improved to the point where subjects were able to read this material almost as fast as normally typed sentences. It was assumed that the pattern-analyzing skills responsible for word identification had become automatized. Kolers showed that once inverted reading skill had developed, memory for newly encountered inverted sentences was poor in comparison to the memory performance of less skilled readers. This result nicely fits the pattern that has emerged from visual search tasks— that automatic processing does not reliably produce long-term memory representations.

Clearly, not all components of reading are automatic, so we are faced with the task of determining which subskills most likely are automatized. A convenient and well-motivated approach has been to assume that controlled processing during reading is focused on the conceptual information conveyed by the text, and to characterize as automatic those skills that provide preliminary analysis of the surface features of a sentence. Automatization has been hypothesized to occur for such skills as letter and word identification (e.g., Baron, 1978; LaBerge & Samuels, 1974), and even syntactic parsing (Fodor, 1983).

Automatic word identification has been demonstrated by experiments involving the Stroop interference task. In this task subjects are required to name the color of the ink in which a color word (e.g., green) is printed. Among skilled readers difficulties (increased naming latency and errors) are encountered when the ink color and color word are not the same (e.g., the word green printed in blue ink). This is assumed to be a result of the conflict between word and color identification and naming processes. Even though word identification is not required and actually hinders color naming, subjects are unable to prevent these operations from being executed. As readers become more skilled, there is a tendency for this interference effect to increase, indicating the development of automatic word identification (Stanovich, Cunningham, & West, 1981).

With respect to syntactic parsing, automaticity has been implied by research that demonstrates rather poor memory for the surface structure of sentences (including syntactic and lexical information), even when semantic content is accurately represented (e.g., Bransford & Franks, 1971; Graesser & Mandler, 1975; Sachs, 1974). Converging evidence for the assumption that inferior surface memory is due to automatic processing consists of demonstrations of particularly accurate surface memory when attention is drawn to the syntactic and lexical features of a sentence, either by instruction or by use of unusual syntactic constructions (Graesser & Mandler, 1975; McDaniel, 1981).

DISSOCIATED MEMORY SYSTEMS

Theories of memory processes often include the fundamental assumption that memory consists of a number of separable or dissociable subsystems. For example, Atkinson and Shiffrin (1968) drew a distinction between short- and long-term memory and Tulving (1972) has built a case for the separation of episodic and semantic memory systems and recently has included a third system which he refers to as procedural memory (Tulving, 1983, 1985). The concept of dissociable memory systems also can be applied to the issue of executive control in reading. Here the question is which memory systems are involved in the attention-demanding aspects of reading comprehension.

Procedural and Declarative Knowledge

The difference between memory for the surface features of a sentence and its meaning can be accommodated by a theory of memory in which a distinction is drawn between procedural and declarative knowledge (e.g., Anderson, 1976; Tulving, 1983). One basis for this distinction rests on the notion that procedural knowledge consists of knowing how to do a task and often is characterized in terms of *skill*. Declarative knowledge consists of the representation of factual information. A second difference is that procedural knowledge typically is not accessible to consciousness and is difficult to describe verbally. In contrast, declarative knowledge can be accessed easily and verbally communicated to others in many instances. Third, procedural knowledge is believed to consist of skills that are independent of, or exist in, the absence of memory for the specific experiences that led to the development of those skills. Declarative memory consists of memory for the specific facts that have been acquired through experience.

The procedural/declarative distinction can be applied to the issue of remembering various aspects of a reading episode in the following way. Skilled readers are assumed to be able to carry out low-level reading procedures with little demand on attention and would be expected to retain virtually no information about the procedures applied in a specific instance. The results of applying these operations, however, provide the raw materials from which propositions or facts can be built for representation in declarative memory.

Although this characterization of reading seems reasonable and is compatible with the research on memory for surface structure of sentences mentioned earlier, there is ample evidence to suggest that it is not quite right. If procedures such as word recognition and syntactic analysis are based on highly developed skills that do not usually produce episodic memory representations, it should be difficult to find evidence for durable surface memory. But it is possible to show that subjects retain a form of memory for the surface structure of sentences if a memory test is constructed that does not require explicit judgments about surface features.

For example, when subjects are required to make recognition memory decisions about the meaning of target sentences that had or had not been encountered previously, they are able to verify verbatim sentences more quickly (Anderson, 1974; Anderson & Paulson, 1977; Hayes-Roth & Hayes-Roth, 1977) and more accurately (Begg & Wickelgren, 1974; Hayes-Roth & Hayes-Roth, 1977) than meaning preserving paraphrases. Moreover, Kolers (1976) has claimed that readers are capable of remembering the graphemic features of sentences over longer time periods than the semantic content, at least under some circumstances. A group of subjects read a number of pages of typographically transformed sentences and were retested about 1 year later. The subjects generally exhibited poor recognition memory when asked to reread the original pages and a set of new pages. Despite this deficit, they were able to read the old passages more quickly than the new ones. Kolers attributed this effect to memory for the operations (including graphemic pattern analyzing operations) that had been applied when the old pages originally were read. Of course, one could argue that analysis of surface features is not automatic when reading transformed typography. But the verbatim/paraphrase effects were based on normal typography in experiments in which it would be reasonable for automatic processing of surface characteristics to occur. I now turn to a consideration of memory processes that may be responsible for producing these effects.

Remembering With and Without Awareness

The demonstrations of a form of implicit memory for surface structure bear a striking similarity to recent experiments involving tasks that permit memory for an experience with an individual word to express itself, potentially without the subject's awareness or intention. One method of demonstrating memory for previously encountered words, without requiring conscious decisions about prior experiences with the words, involves what Jacoby and Dallas (1981) have called a *perceptual recognition* task. In this task subjects are required to identify a briefly presented word that is followed by a pattern mask. Memory for a recent encounter with a word shows up as an advantage on the perceptual recognition test for words that were included in a list of target items that was studied prior to taking the perceptual recognition test. Other methods produce similar results but are based on different tasks, such as identifying a word presented in a background of visual noise with the signal to noise ratio increasing over time (Feustel, Shiffrin, & Salasoo, 1983), or filling in the missing letters of a word fragment (e.g., H_Y __FT) to form a valid English word (HAYLOFT) (e.g., Tulving, Schacter, & Stark, 1982).

The kind of memory that is exhibited in these tasks possesses a number of characteristics that are markedly different from those associated with memory as it is expressed on more common memory tests such as recognition. First, perceptual recognition and fragment completion tasks can be performed without conscious recollection of the fact that a target word had occurred earlier in the experiment. In a recognition test this recollection is the fundamental issue. Second, performance on a perceptual recognition test does not appear to improve when the opportunity for elaborative encoding of a word's meaning is provided. Jacoby and Dallas (1981) had subjects encode a series of target items using semantic and nonsemantic processing tasks. They discovered that although recognition memory was highly sensitive to the kind of task performed at encoding (i.e., more accurate recognition of words that were semantically encoded), perceptual recognition was not affected by the use of different encoding tasks. Similar results were obtained with a word fragment completion task (Graf & Mandler, 1984). In fact, Feustel et al. (1983) found that with repeated presentation there were equal amounts of facilitation on the second and third occurrence of words and nonwords in an identification task involving visual noise.

Jacoby (1983a) has provided a third source of evidence for the idea that elaborative encoding of the meaning of a word is not an important factor in producing perceptual enhancement effects. He varied the context in which target words were initially processed in order to control the subjects' reliance on data and conceptually driven processing. For example, conceptually driven processing was induced by having subjects generate the antonym of a cue word. In this task subjects were able to anticipate the target word's identity and would be able to identify it with relatively little data-driven processing. On the other hand, when target words were out of context, subjects were highly dependent on data-driven processing. Recognition memory was enhanced when conceptually driven processing was invoked, but perceptual recognition was better when data-driven processing was emphasized.

Another major difference between recognition memory and the kind of memory expressed on these word identification tasks concerns durability over time. Whereas recognition memory typically shows significant loss over time, perceptual recognition (Jacoby, 1983b; Jacoby & Dallas, 1981) and word fragment completion (Tulving et al., 1982) have been shown to be resistant to decay over retention intervals of 1 day and 1 week, respectively. Finally, enhanced perceptual processing of a word often is independent of the ability to consciously recognize that word (Jacoby & Dallas, 1981; Jacoby & Witherspoon, 1982; Tulving et al., 1982).

Neuropsychological Evidence

The distinction between memory tasks that do or do not require conscious recollection of specific processing episodes has led some researchers to advocate the existence of independent memory systems (e.g., Tulving, 1983, 1985). One remarkable source of evidence in favor of this suggestion is based on work with anterograde amnesics. These neurological patients suffer from the inability to reliably remember new information once it is no longer available in short-term memory, although their memory for events occurring prior to the onset of amnesia has not been completely lost. This phenomenon is characteristic of the Korsakoff syndrome exhibited by some alcoholics and also is a temporary side effect of delivery of bilateral electroconvulsive therapy for depressive illness (Squire & Cohen, 1984). All the research involving amnesic patients described next is based on samples from one or both of these populations.

Amnesic patients who are given memory tests that require conscious reflection on the previous occurrence of events (e.g., recognition and recall tests for words on a study list) perform poorly relative to normal control subjects. But when given tests such as word fragment completion in which they simply are required to provide the first word that comes to mind and that fits the constraints of the fragment, the probability that they will produce a word from a recently presented study list is about the same as that for normal control subjects (Graf, Squire, & Mandler, 1984; Squire, Shimamura, & Graf, 1985; Warrington & Weiskrantz, 1970, 1974). Further evidence for the dichotomy between these two kinds of memory test comes from the finding that, for subjects who experienced temporary anterograde amnesia induced by bilateral electroconvulsive therapy, recognition memory was better for word lists presented later rather than earlier during the period of 45 min to 9 hr after administration of the treatment, whereas word fragment completion performance was normal throughout the interval (Squire et al., 1985).

The apparently normal level of performance of amnesics on these word completion tests has fostered the view that such tests tap a memory system that is fundamentally different from that involving recognition memory (Squire & Cohen, 1984; Squire et al., 1985; Tulving, 1985). More specifically, one view is that the two memory systems represent declarative (for recognition) and procedural (for fragment completion) memory (Squire & Cohen, 1984). This view is consistent with the finding that amnesics also show a preserved ability to learn new procedural skills such as rotary pursuit (e.g., Cermak, Lewis, Butters, & Goodglass, 1973).

In addition, Cohen and Squire (1980) have demonstrated that amnesics are capable of acquiring the skill of reading typographically transformed words at the same rate as normal control subjects. In their experiment subjects were given a series of words in mirror-image form and time taken to identify the words was recorded. Over a series of trials performance on novel words steadily increased. Particularly rapid improvement was apparent for repeated words, especially for normal control subjects. In this regard, Cohen and Squire made special note of an outstanding feature of the day-to-day learning curves for amnesics when reading repeated words. It was clear that significant ground was lost (forgetting had occurred) between the end of one session and the beginning of the next, as reading times were higher in the latter case. Cohen and Squire emphasized this finding as support for their claim that reading mirror-image words was based on a procedural skill that is independent of memory for the specific words encountered during training. They also have developed the more general claim that memory deficits in the kinds of amnesic syndromes discussed here involve the declarative memory system, and assume that the procedural memory system remains intact (Cohen & Squire, 1980; Squire & Cohen, 1984).

Reading Revisited

The proposed distinction between declarative and procedural memory, coupled with the respective characteristics of memory with and without awareness, provides the foundation for an account of memory for the surface structure of sentences. It is possible that readers retain a form of memory for aspects of a sentence that are automatically processed in service of obtaining a semantic interpretation. These aspects would include grammatical structure and the specific words used in the sentence. Although subjects usually do not exhibit an impressive ability to consciously remember a sentence's surface form, an expression of this memory might occur when the subject is required to reprocess the sentence. For example, a sentence can be read faster on its second presentation when a verbatim as opposed to a paraphrased form is used (Masson, 1984). One reason for this would be the establishment of a form of perceptual memory for the individual words in a sentence (cf. Jacoby & Dallas, 1981) and another would be the presence of a procedural memory for analyzing the syntactic structure of the sentence. Note, however, that this implies procedural memory for specific instances rather than a skill that is independent of individual experiences. This issue is given full treatment later.

The fluency advantage experienced when rereading verbatim test sentences may contribute to recognition decisions about sentence meaning (cf. Anderson & Paulson, 1977; Hayes-Roth & Hayes-Roth, 1977). When a sentence can be fluently read relative to other sentences in a recognition test, this fluency could be attributed to a previous reading of the sentence. By this logic, a fluently reread sentence is one that likely has been encountered before and so should be classified as an old sentence in the recognition test. Jacoby (1983a, b; Johnston, Dark, & Jacoby, 1985) has made a similar argument for recognition of individual words. Evidence that this heuristic operates during a sentence recognition task comes from a recent study in which it was found that for target and foil sentences alike, reading times were less for items that the reader classified as old (Masson, 1984).

A UNIFYING THEME

The dichotomy outlined in the preceding section implies that tests of memory that do or do not involve reflection about prior processing episodes are based on two fundamentally different memory systems. There is, however, another view. It is possible that different tests such as recognition memory and perceptual recognition involve the same memory system but simply inquire about different aspects of an episodic memory representation (Jacoby, 1983b). This would account for demonstrations of independence between different memory tests (e.g., Jacoby & Dallas, 1981), and for the fact that these tests share important characteristics as well. For example, like recognition memory, perceptual identification performance on previously studied words is sensitive to contextual manipulations such as proportion of old words in the test list (Jacoby, 1983b). Furthermore, recognition memory and perceptual identification are not independent when nonwords are used, indicating that in this case the two tests rely on similar aspects (most likely perceptual) of the original encoding episode (Jacoby & Witherspoon, 1982; Johnston et al., 1985).

A similar position has been taken by Johnson (1983), who proposed a multiple-entry memory system in which it is claimed that an event leads to a memory representation consisting of sensory, perceptual, and reflective (internally generated thought processes) components. Some memory tests, such as recognition and especially recall, involve aspects of attention-demanding reflective processes (e.g., semantic elaboration), whereas tests such as perceptual identification mainly depend on nonreflective aspects of an encoding episode. With respect to memory for reading episodes, the implication is that it may not be necessary to postulate completely dissociated memory systems to account for the results of experiments based on remembering with and without awareness.

I propose a framework that can account for the various methods of expressing memory for reading episodes and for the operations that give rise to memory in the first place. This view borrows from the multiple-entry memory model developed by Johnson (1983). The nature of the memory systems and the interactions proposed in this model carry a number of important implications both for reading operations as they initially occur and for the way in which memory for the operations may be demonstrated.

Multiple-Entry Memory System

A memory theory that is to be applied to the issue of memory for reading operations must include some means of developing memory representations of automatically encoded or nonattended events. A corollary result that must also be explained is the fact that such memory representations typically are not consciously accessible. The multiple-entry model of memory (Johnson, 1983) accomplishes this rather nicely. Johnson proposed the existence of three interacting memory subsystems: sensory, perceptual, and reflective. The sensory system is responsible for the initial "low-level" processing of sensory input, the perceptual system detects organized or familiar patterns, and the reflective system produces an internally generated record of thought (rather than sensory) processes. It often happens, of course, that reflective processes are triggered by sensory and perceptual experience (as when we compute and elaborate the meaning of words on a page). A heterarchical organization is assumed in which each of the memory systems is capable of making an entry that is part of the memory for an event, regardless of the contribution of attention.

Although this view of memory encoding is at odds with the claim that only information that is attended to can be encoded into long-term memory, it must be conceded that this claim is founded on results of experiments that used reflective memory tests such as recall or recognition (e.g., Fisk & Schneider, 1984). A nonreflective memory test (i.e., remembering without awareness) would be expected to produce evidence of a long-term memory record of unattended events. Eich (1984) has provided just such a result with a dichotic listening task. Subjects were required to shadow a word list presented to one ear while word pairs were simultaneously played in the nonattended ear. The word pairs consisted of a context word and homophone (e.g., taxi fare). On a later spelling test subjects more often produced the primed spelling of the critical homo-graphs than would have been expected by chance.

All three systems, then, are assumed to be capable of producing memory entries, which Johnson (1983) claims to consist of a record of the processes that created the entry (cf. Kolers, 1975b). In this sense all of memory is procedural in nature and is based on specific episodic experiences that consist of a mixture of sensory, perceptual, and reflective aspects of an event. This procedurally based memory system is consciously accessible only in those instances where significant reflective activity has accompanied an event. Reflective memory tests will fail to reveal evidence of memory for an episode that does not include a reflective component. Normal forgetting is assumed to be due to interference between entries or to confusion between perceived and imagined (reflective) entries. In this sense, all experiences receive a durable representation that is not subject to significant decay simply because of the passage of time. Finally, anterograde amnesia is characterized not as a declarative memory deficit, but as the result of dysfunction in reflective processes. This dysfunction is especially problematic when reflective memory tests are given. Nonreflective memory tests based on the encoding of sensory and perceptual aspects of an episode reveal normal functioning (e.g., the fragment completion task). According to this view, amnesics would be capable of remembering declarative information if the method of testing does not involve reflective processes (cf. Graf & Schacter, 1985).

Memory Representation of Reading Operations

The memory system proposed by Johnson (1983) can be used as a foundation on which to construct an account of the processes involved in reading and the associated memory representation. First, with respect to data-driven operations (sensory and perceptual processes responsible for analyzing graphemic features), Johnson's model implies that each encounter with a word produces an entry in memory. Later attempts to read that word will benefit from the initial encounters inasmuch as the reader is able to reapply the pattern analyzing operations carried out previously (cf. Kolers, 1975a). The development of word recognition skill, then, can be assumed to depend on memory entries representing the sensory-perceptual analysis of various words and their corresponding typographical features that a novice reader has experienced during training. According to this view of skill development, there is no place for a generalized procedural memory that eventually supplants memory entries representing the many specific word recognition episodes that a reader has had.

For the beginning reader, the acquisition of word recognition skills can be characterized as the development of memory entries that represent the sensory, perceptual, and reflective processing of specific word identification episodes. Repeated occurrences of the same word are more efficiently encoded because of the availability of relevant pattern analyzing operations in the form of previously developed memory entries. New words benefit from these pattern-analyzing skills inasmuch as the pattern-analyzing operations required to identify them are similar to the operations applied to previously experienced words. The notion of a lexicon as an amodal, conceptual representation of words (e.g., Collins & Loftus, 1975; Forster, 1976) is not required by this view. Instead, it is assumed that an encounter with a word in one modality may invoke the application of relevant pattern-analyzing operations represented in memory as a result of prior experience with the word in another modality.

It is assumed that reading a word creates a memory entry that includes sensory, perceptual, and conceptual processing operations. When the word is repeated later, all these kinds of operations may serve as sources for improved efficiency of identification. For example, in a lexical decision task involving visually presented words, prior visual presentation of a word has been shown to speed the lexical decision, and a smaller but significant improvement is found for words previously presented in the auditory mode (Kirsner, Milech, & Standen, 1983). A similar result has been obtained by Freedman (1985) involving identification of visually degraded words.

In the case of individual word recognition, the contribution of memory for conceptual processing operations may consist of providing a more efficient interpretation of the results of sensory and perceptual processes. It is also possible to support the interpretation of perceptual processing operations through constraints provided by a sentence context. The improvement may come about as a result of associative priming by semantically related words that occurred earlier in the sentence (Stanovich & West, 1983), or because the meaning of the sentence and its syntactic form constrain the possible words that may appear at a particular location in the sentence (Ehrlich & Rayner, 1981). This constraint could serve to reduce the threshold for appropriate words or to inhibit candidates that are partially consistent with the results of perceptual processing but inappropriate to the sentence context. (By terms such as *inhibit* and *priming*, I mean activity involving sets of memory entries that represent previous encoding experiences with the relevant words rather than abstract word concepts.) In addition, reflective processes responsible for interpreting the word's role in the sentence probably are more efficient when the word is highly constrained by context. These conceptu-

ally driven operations, like sensory and perceptual operations, are assumed to create memory entries but they more frequently involve reflective processing.

Even though they often involve reflective processing, memory for
conceptually driven operations appears to be revealed by nonreflective
memory tests. Evidence for this suggestion has been provided by Graf
and Schacter (1985). Normal and anterograde amnesic subjects were
presented pairs of unrelated words and were required to carry out an
encoding task that either did or did not involve semantic elaboration. A
word fragment completion test of memory was used in which the first
three letters of the response member of each critical pair was shown. The
fragment was presented in the context of the original stimulus word or
with the stimulus word from another pair. For both amnesics and normal
subjects, it was found that the probability of completing a fragment with
the target word was greater when presented with the appropriate stimulus
word, but only when a semantic encoding task was used. This result is
consistent with the view that nonreflective memory tests, commonly
associated with nondeclarative knowledge, are sensitive to reflective
encoding operations involving verbal material. A reasonable conclusion is
that memory for declarative information may be represented in terms of
the operations applied during comprehension of that information.

REMEMBERING READING OPERATIONS

In this section I review some recent evidence that supports the claims
made in the preceding section concerning the nature of memory entries
for data-driven (sensory and perceptual) and conceptually driven operations. The emphasis is on the use of nonreflective tests because these
allow subjects to demonstrate their memory for reading operations by
providing them the opportunity to re-enact those operations with a
second presentation of a word, sentence, or text.

Data-Driven Operations

Fluent readers appear to possess automated word recognition skill that
can be applied in many reading tasks. This skill is assumed to be based on
many individual episodes in which visually presented words have been
analyzed and identified. This view contrasts with the claim that well-
practiced skills such as word recognition are based on a form of procedural memory that is independent of memory for the specific experiences
that produced the skill (e.g., Cohen & Squire, 1980; Squire & Cohen,
1984). An important implication of this contrast concerns the kinds of

transfer effects that are predicted. If subjects learn a skill that is not directly tied to the specific experiences that contributed to its development, they should be able to effectively apply it to all new words. But if the skill depends on memory for specific instances, it should be difficult or impossible to demonstrate transfer of skill to new items that do not share features with training instances.

In a recent series of experiments, I set out to demonstrate that word identification skill was indeed founded on memory for specific training instances (Masson, in press). These experiments were patterned after a study by Cohen and Squire (1980) and required subjects to read typographically transformed word triads. The transformation consisted of rotating individual letters in a word to achieve a mirror image of each letter. This allowed subjects to read from left to right, as usual, but the visual features of individual letters were not very familiar. In the first study the goal was to demonstrate that transfer of newly developed skill at identifying typographically transformed words would be restricted to novel instances that shared features with training instances. A result like this would not be compatible with the view that readers acquire a skill that is independent of memory for specific instances.

In the first phase of the experiment subjects read a series of word triads, and time taken to identify the words in each triad was recorded. The words presented in this phase of the experiment came from a list of words that included only half the letters of the alphabet. The set of letters used in this phase was appropriately counterbalanced across subjects. In the test phase, subjects read three kinds of word triads: (a) items presented during the training phase, (b) new words formed from letters that comprised the words in the training phase, and (c) new words based on letters not presented during training. Consistent with the instance-based view of skill development, transfer of training was strongest with old triads, moderate with new words formed from familiar letters, and there was no evidence of transfer for new words based on unfamiliar letters. Had word identification skill been based on some kind of global skill (e.g., mental rotation), significant transfer should have been observed in all three cases.

In another experiment on reading words formed from mirror-image letters, all letters of the alphabet were used in the training phase, but half always appeared in upper case and half in lower case. Assignment of letters to these two conditions was counterbalanced across subjects. In the test phase novel words were presented with letters in their familiarized form (upper or lower case), as well as other novel words with letters based on the opposite, unfamiliar, pattern. Although significant transfer effects were observed in the first case, no transfer was found for novel words typed in the unfamiliar mixed case pattern. Despite experience with all letters of the alphabet during training, the fact that only one specific version (upper or lower case) was practiced placed a strong constraint on transfer of training.

These results contrast sharply with Cohen and Squire's (1980) claim that development of skill at reading mirror-image words proceeds independently of memory for specific training instances. In fact, their own data are consistent with the view that a form of nonreflective memory for specific instances is available. Although amnesics took longer to read repeated word triads at the beginning of a session than at the end of the previous session, their reading times on repeated triads presented later in a session consistently were lower than times for new triads.

The "forgetting" that Cohen and Squire chose to emphasize could be explained by noting similar phenomena obtained in studies with normal subjects. A similar pattern of reduced word identification efficiency at the beginning of a session was observed by Salasoo, Shiffrin, and Feutsel (1985), who required subjects to identify repeatedly presented words and nonwords under visually degraded conditions. Moreover, Jacoby (1983b) showed that when the percentage of repeated words was reduced in a perceptual recognition experiment, the advantage for all repeated words generally was reduced. In addition, Oliphant (1983) did not obtain any repetition effect for words presented in the task instructions that preceded a lexical decision test. These results imply that fluent identification of repeated items is dependent on reinstatement of an appropriate context. For amnesics it is possible that the test context is quite unfamiliar at the beginning of a session (e.g., they may have difficulty remembering that they have ever done the reading task before). Over the course of the first set of trials, however, the context may be reinstated and nonreflective memory for repeated triads may function effectively. Consequently, rather than being peculiar to the amnesic syndrome, the intersession forgetting effect is more likely due to the fact that a number of trials are required at the beginning of a session to reinstate the original context.

Even after word recognition skill has reached a high degree of fluency, readers appear to retain memory for specific encounters with a word, and to use this memory while reading. This was demonstrated in a proofreading study by Levy (1983). Subjects were asked to proofread a passage for typographical errors after having previously read an error-free version of the passage. In another condition, subjects read an error-free version of a text and then were required to proofread a scrambled version in which the words were arranged in a random order. Nonreflective memory for the first reading of the text was measured in terms of the percentage of errors detected during the proofreading task. The logic here was that familiarization with the text would make the presence of typographical errors more apparent. Familiarization with an error free duplicate of the critical text produced a significant improvement in error detection performance. The effect was equally strong in the normal and scrambled conditions, indicating that the advantage of familiarization was based on memory for specific words.

Conceptually Driven Operations

The effects reported by Levy (1983) and the repetition effects found by Jacoby (1983b) and others may be interpreted in terms of a perceptual effect (cf. the term *perceptual fluency* used by Jacoby, 1983b), implying an improvement in the perceptual analysis of a word. A large part of this effect may, however, be due not to improved efficiency of data driven processes such as feature extraction, but to a more efficient interpretation of the results of those processes. Support for this idea comes from the fact that cross-modal repetition effects have been reported in which the auditory presentation of a word facilitates processing of its later visual presentation (e.g., Freedman, 1985; Kirsner et al., 1983).

Furthermore, Freedman (1985) has obtained a result that suggests that the repetition effect may be completely due to the interpretation of perceptual output when normal typography is used. Homographs were presented twice each, separated by 15 intervening items, in a lexical decision task. Each trial consisted of a context word followed by a target item. In the case of the homographs, the context word was pertinent to only one of the possible interpretations. For some of the homographs a different context word was presented during its second appearance, in some cases preserving the original interpretation (e.g., CAVE bat, DRACULA bat) and in other cases implying a different interpretation (e.g., CAVE bat, BASEBALL bat). When the context word maintained the original interpretation of the homograph, a strong repetition effect was found. But when the first presentation of the homograph involved a context word that primed the dominant meaning (virtually ensuring that the subject would not carry out reflective processing of the subordinate meaning), and the second presentation primed the subordinate meaning, no repetition effect was found (i.e., response time for the second presentation of these homographs was just as long as for the first presentation of homographs accompanied by a context word that primed the subordinate meaning).

This result encourages the view that repetition effects may be characterized as a form of conceptually driven processing, in which nonreflective memory for prior processing of a word influences the interpretation of the results of data-driven processes. By this logic we should expect other forms of conceptually driven processing to be revealed through nonreflective memory tests.

An example of memory for conceptually driven processing in reading has been provided by a recent study of proofreading (Levy & Begin, 1984). Time required to proofread a text was significantly reduced when subjects had previously been exposed to an error-free version of the passage (cf. Levy, 1983). In addition, however, the amount of savings due to familiarization depended on repeating the original structure of the text. Four pairs of familiarization-test versions were used, representing a factorial combination of text structure during familiarization (normal or scrambled) and text structure during proofreading (normal or scrambled). Savings were optimal when text structure was repeated on both readings (i.e., normal–normal or scrambled–scrambled). Levy and Begin concluded that memory for text structure played a significant role in facilitating proofreading.

Because proofreading time savings were much greater when a scrambled test passage was familiarized using the scrambled form as opposed to its normal version, Levy and Begin suggested that memory for structure may not have to depend on standard semantic or syntactic organization. They speculated that subjects may have learned something about the scrambled word arrangement, and that this learning might operate like syntactic structure in normal reading. A problem with the suggestion that memory for text structure was involved in the case of scrambled texts is that the first reading of the scrambled version probably depended on data-driven processing to a greater degree than did the first reading of a normal passage. Jacoby (1983a) has shown that increased reliance on data-driven processes during word identification increases later perceptual fluency. Consequently, familiarization with a scrambled passage would place subjects at an advantage when tested on a scrambled version (where conceptually driven processes would not be of use).

This issue could be settled by demonstrating that when the text is scrambled, both during familiarization and test, the amount of savings depends on using exactly the same word order on both occasions. If savings are unchanged by using a new random ordering for proofreading, it would be clear that subjects do not retain memory for some kind of scrambled text structure. In accord with this line of reasoning, Levy (personal communication, July 25, 1985) reported that error detection in a time-limited proofreading task was unaffected by the use of different word orders in the familiarization and test versions of a scrambled passage.

In a recent series of experiments I attempted to provide additional evidence that readers form, and on later occasions use, memory for conceptually driven processes that were applied during the initial reading of a sentence (Masson, 1986). Memory was expressed in terms of fluent rereading of sentences so that the use of reflective memory processes was not required. To avoid problems with floor effects in reading times and to encourage the use of conceptually driven processing during reading, all sentences were typographically transformed by turning them upside down. The first experiment established that conceptually driven processes significantly reduced reading time. Four sentence types were constructed: (a) normal, (b) scrambled (normal sentences with words randomly reordered), (c) anomalous (grammatically correct sentences formed by making semantically inappropriate substitutions of words across sentences), and (d) anomalous sentences with words randomly reordered within each to produce an agrammatical word list. It was found that subjects read the normal sentences faster than any of the other three types which did not significantly differ. It was concluded that the conceptually driven operations applied when reading upside down sentences are based on comprehension of the propositions within a sentence. No independent contribution of syntactic structure was observed.

In another experiment subjects read a set of normal and scrambled sentences, then were asked to reread these sentences along with new normal and scrambled sentences, either immediately or after a delay of 1 week. Half the old sentences repeated their original word order (normal–normal, scrambled–scrambled), and half were changed to the alternative order (normal–scrambled, scrambled–normal). Reading times during the test phase were analyzed separately for sentences tested in normal form and for sentences tested in scrambled form. In the former case, both kinds of old sentence (normal–normal and scrambled–normal) were read more quickly than new sentences, but the advantage was significantly greater for sentences that were normal on their first reading. This indicates that subjects were able to reapply the conceptually driven operations used during the first reading. Moreover, the advantage of having read the normal rather than the scrambled version in the first phase of the experiment was the same in the immediate and in the delay test conditions. The apparent lack of forgetting is consistent with the idea that subjects were expressing their memory for conceptually driven operations in a nonreflective manner. Reflective memory tests such as recall and recognition typically show strong forgetting effects over a 1-week delay interval, whereas nonreflective tests are more robust (e.g., Jacoby & Dallas, 1981; Tulving et al., 1982).

Evidence for the claim that subjects were remembering conceptually driven processes based on the meaning of propositions rather than word order came from the results of the analysis of reading time for sentences tested in scrambled form. In this case both types of old sentences were read faster than new ones, but there was no advantage of repeating the original word order (i.e., originally scrambled and normal sentences were read with about equal speed). In contrast with Levy and Begin (1984), then, subjects did not show evidence of memory for the structure of scrambled sentences. The result reported by Levy and Begin was apparently due to greater reliance on data-driven processing during the initial reading of scrambled passages. The reason a similar effect was not obtained with upside down sentences might be that elaborate data-driven processes are used with both normal and scrambled items because of lack of familiarity with the typography.

The influence of memory for conceptually driven operations also provides an alternative interpretation of the demonstration that subjects remember for over 1 year pattern-analyzing operations that were applied to typographically transformed (upside down) passages (Kolers, 1976). Recall that subjects reread old passages faster than new ones, even though more than a year had elapsed since the initial reading and explicit recognition memory judgments were quite inaccurate. Rather than attributing this result to memory for graphemic pattern-analyzing operations (implying an emphasis on data-driven processes), it is reasonable to argue that a significant part of the effect may have been based on memory for conceptually driven processes.

CONCLUSIONS

The view of reading as a collection of skills, some of which are automatized whereas others demand attention, includes a number of important assumptions about the operation of executive control processes and resulting memory representations. Typically, concern has been devoted almost exclusively to the issue of memory for the meaning of what is read, probably because executive control processes primarily are directed at this aspect of text and reflective memory tests often yield little evidence of memory for other aspects of a text. I have argued that strong evidence exists for the claim that readers possess highly accurate memory both for conceptually and data-driven operations, including those that usually operate outside the scope of executive control processes. In fact, the development of reading skill, or at least its word recognition aspect, can be traced to memories of this kind. Rather than characterizing skill as a form of procedural memory that is independent of the individual episodes that nurtured development of that skill, it appears to be more useful to acknowledge the existence and influence of memory for the original episodes.

One important implication of this view is that the initial development and transfer of reading skill may be highly sensitive to the specific instances that the novice experiences in the early phases of training. As the experiments on reading typographically transformed word triads demonstrated, the ability to identify novel words was strongly influenced by their similarity to specific training exemplars. A second implication concerns the effects of skill development on memory for what is read. We should resist the temptation to conclude that because a skilled reader appears able to remember only selected aspects of what is read, just those aspects are given unique or privileged representations in memory (e.g., declarative memory representations), whereas processes responsible for producing comprehension are attributed to a collection of generalized procedures. There now is a growing body of evidence for the view that even automatic operations performed during comprehension are remembered, although perhaps not with awareness.

The discovery that memory for reading operations may be revealed through nonreflective memory tests raises a number of new issues associated with executive control processes. For example, memory for conceptually driven operations, many of which are believed to be under executive control, is expressed clearly on nonreflective memory tests. This could mean that reading operations that engage reflective processes create memory entries that can be expressed on nonreflective tests. The problem with this view is that it seems to violate the spirit of the multiple entry model proposed by Johnson (1983). In that model it is assumed that nonreflective processing creates memory entries that can be revealed only through nonreflective tests. Similarly, one might expect that memory for reflective processing would be evident only on reflective memory tests. An alternative and very intriguing possibility is that many of the conceptually driven operations with which executive control processes usually are credited may actually go on outside awareness. Nonreflective memory tests, then, might be influenced by memory for only these conceptually driven operations.

Another issue involving executive control processes pertains to the differences in reading operations that are applied on the first versus successive readings of a sentence or text. Successive readings are significantly faster presumably because the processing operations applied during the first reading are represented in memory and can be reapplied on later readings. What does this improvement in reading speed imply about possible changes in executive control processes? Levy (1985) has suggested that on second and successive readings of a text less demand is placed on executive control processes so that attention may be given to other tasks such as detecting errors in the text. An alternative suggestion is that operations that are not under executive control are reapplied more and more efficiently with each reading, and that improved ability to detect errors is a function of an increased sensitivity to deviations from the pattern on which those operations are based. On this view, the effect of familiarity on speed of reading and improved error detection is not due to changes in executive control processes.

Although it is possible that improved reading speed may be due to operations that are not under executive control, it appears that reading and word identification fluency makes an important contribution to explicit memory judgments (e.g., Johnston et al., 1985; Masson, 1984). The lack of executive control over certain perceptual and cognitive operations does not preclude the possibility that the impact of these operations on processing fluency will be noticed. One function of executive processes is to account for such changes in fluency. A reasonable explanation for the apparent ease of reading a sentence is to attribute the fluency to the beneficial effects of a previous encounter, and this attribution may contribute to a positive decision on a recognition memory test. It is likely that closer examination of this phenomenon will provide important insight into how we become aware of the existence of our memory for reading episodes and other kinds of events.

ACKNOWLEDGMENTS

Preparation of this chapter was supported in part by Grant A7910 from the Natural Sciences and Engineering Research Council of Canada. I am grateful to Betty Ann Levy and two anonymous reviewers for their helpful comments on an earlier version of this chapter.

REFERENCES

Anderson, J. R. (1974). Verbatim and propositional representation of sentences in immediate and long-term memory. *Journal of Verbal Learning and Verbal Behavior, 13,* 149–162.

Anderson, J. R. (1976). *Language, memory, and thought.* Hillsdale, NJ: Lawrence Erlbaum Associates.

Anderson, J. R., & Paulson, R. (1977). Representation and retention of verbatim information. *Journal of Verbal Learning and Verbal Behavior, 16,* 439–451.

Atkinson, R. C., & Shiffrin, R. M. (1968). Human memory: A proposed system and its control processes. In K. W. Spence & J. T. Spence (Eds.), *The psychology of learning and motivation* (Vol. 2, pp. 89–195). New York: Academic Press.

Baron, J. (1978). The word-superiority effect: Perceptual learning from reading. In W. K. Estes (Ed.), *Handbook of learning and cognitive processes: Vol. 6. Linguistic functions in cognitive theory* (pp. 131–166). Hillsdale, NJ: Lawrence Erlbaum Associates.

Begg, I., & Wickelgren, W. A. (1974). Retention functions for syntactic and lexical vs. semantic information in sentence recognition memory. *Memory & Cognition, 2,* 353–359.

Bransford, J. D., & Franks, J. J. (1971). The abstraction of linguistic ideas. *Cognitive Psychology, 2,* 331–350.

Cermak, L. S., Lewis, R., Butters, N., & Goodglass, H. (1973). Role of verbal mediation in performance of motor tasks by Korsakoff patients. *Perceptual and Motor Skills, 37,* 259–262.

Cohen, N. J., & Squire, L. R. (1960). Preserved learning and retention of pattern-analyzing skill in amnesia: Dissociation of "knowing how" and "knowing that." *Science, 210,* 207–209.

Collins, A. M., & Loftus, E. F. (1975). A spreading-activation theory of semantic processing. *Psychological Review, 82,* 407–428.

Ehrlich, S. F., & Rayner, K. (1981). Contextual effects on word perception and eye movements during reading. *Journal of Verbal Learning and Verbal Behavior, 20,* 641–655.

Eich, E. (1984). Memory for unattended events: Remembering with and without awareness. *Memory & Cognition, 12,* 105–111.

Feustel, T. C., Shiffrin, R. M., & Salasoo, A. (1983). Episodic and lexical contributions to the repetition effect in word identification. *Journal of Experimental Psychology: General, 112,* 309–346.

Fisk, A. D., & Schneider, W. (1984). Memory as a function of attention, level of processing, and automatization. *Journal of Experimental Psychology: Learning, Memory, and Cognition, 10,* 181–197.

Fodor, J. A. (1983). *The modularity of mind.* Cambridge, MA: MIT Press.

Forster, K. (1976). Accessing the mental lexicon. In R. J. Wales & E. Walker (Eds.), *New approaches to language mechanisms* (pp. 257–287). Amsterdam: North–Holland.

Freedman, L. (1985). *Multicomponent analysis of the repetition effect in word identification and lexical decision.* Unpublished doctoral dissertation, University of Victoria, Victoria.

Graesser, A., & Mandler, G. (1975). Recognition memory for the meaning and surface structure of sentences. *Journal of Experimental Psychology: Human Learning and Memory, 1,* 238–248.

Graf, P., & Mandler, G. (1984). Activation makes words more accessible, but not necessarily more retrievable. *Journal of Verbal Learning and Verbal Behavior, 23,* 553–568.

Graf, P., & Schacter, D. L. (1985). Implicit and explicit memory for new associations in normal and amnesic subjects. *Journal of Experimental Psychology: Learning, Memory, and Cognition, 11,* 501–518.

Graf, P., Squire, L. R., & Mandler, G. (1984). The information that amnesic subjects do not forget. *Journal of Experimental Psychology: Learning, Memory, and Cognition, 10,* 164–178.

Hayes-Roth, B., & Hayes-Roth, F. (1977). The prominence of lexical information in memory representations of meaning. *Journal of Verbal Learning and Verbal Behavior, 16,* 119–136.

Jacoby, L. L. (1983a). Remembering the data: Analyzing interactive processes in reading. *Journal of Verbal Learning and Verbal Behavior, 22,* 485–508.

Jacoby, L. L. (1983b). Perceptual enhancement: Persistent effects of an experience. *Journal of Experimental Psychology: Learning, Memory, and Cognition, 9,* 21–38.

Jacoby, L. L., & Dallas, M. (1981). On the relationship between autobiographical memory and perceptual learning. *Journal of Experimental Psychology: General, 110,* 306–340.

Jacoby, L. L., & Witherspoon, D. (1982). Remembering without awareness. *Canadian Journal of Psychology, 36,* 300–324.

Johnson, M. K. (1983). A multiple-entry, modular memory system. In G. H. Bower (Ed.), *The psychology of learning and motivation* (Vol. 17, pp. 81–123). New York: Academic Press.

Johnston, W. A., Dark, V. J., & Jacoby, L. L. (1985). Perceptual fluency and recognition judgments. *Journal of Experimental Psychology: Learning, Memory, and Cognition, 11,* 3–11.

Kirsner, K., Milech, D., & Standen, P. (1983). Common and modality-specific processes in the mental lexicon. *Memory & Cognition, 11,* 621–630.

Kolers, P. A. (1975a). Memorial consequences of automatized encoding. *Journal of Experimental Psychology: Human Learning and Memory, 1,* 689–701.

Kolers, P. A. (1975b). Specificity of operations in sentence recognition. *Cognitive Psychology, 7,* 289–306.

Kolers, P. A. (1976). Reading a year later. *Journal of Experimental Psychology: Human Learning and Memory, 2,* 554–565.

LaBerge, D., & Samuels, S. J. (1974). Toward a theory of automatic information processing in reading. *Cognitive Psychology, 6,* 293–323.

Levy, B. A. (1983). Proofreading familiar text: Constraints on visual processing. *Memory & Cognition, 11,* 1–12.

Levy, B. A. (1985, June). Familiarity effects during skilled reading. In M. Singer (Chair), *Language and text processes.* Symposium conducted at the meeting of the Canadian Psychological Association, Halifax, Canada.

Levy, B. A., & Begin, J. (1984). Proofreading familiar text: Allocating resources to perceptual and conceptual processes. *Memory & Cognition, 12,* 621–632.

Masson, M.E.J. (1984). Memory for the surface structure of sentences: Remembering with and without awareness. *Journal of Verbal Learning and Verbal Behavior, 23,* 579–592.

Masson, M.E.J. (1986). *Remembering conceptually driven and data driven reading operations.* Manuscript in preparation.

Masson, M.E.J. (in press). Identification of typographically transformed words: Instance-based skill acquisition. *Journal of Experimental Psychology: Learning, Memory, and Cognition, 12.*

McDaniel, M. A. (1981). Syntactic complexity and elaborative processing. *Memory & Cognition, 9,* 487–495.

Oliphant, G. W. (1983). Repetition and recency effects in word recognition. *Australian Journal of Psychology, 35,* 393–403.

Sachs, J. S. (1974). Memory in reading and listening to discourse. *Memory & Cognition, 2,* 95–100.

Salasoo, A., Shiffrin, R. M., & Feustel, T. C. (1985). Building permanent memory codes: Codification and repetition effects in word identification. *Journal of Experimental Psychology: General, 114,* 50–77.

Schneider, W., & Shiffrin, R. M. (1977). Controlled and automatic human information processing: I. Detection, search, and attention. *Psychological Review, 84,* 1–66.

Shiffrin, R. M., & Schneider, W. (1977). Controlled and automatic human information processing: II. Perceptual learning, automatic attending, and a general theory. *Psychological Review, 84,* 127–190.

Squire, L. R., & Cohen, N. J. (1984). Human memory and amnesia. In G. Lynch, J. McGaugh, & N. M. Weinberger (Eds.), *Neurobiology of learning and memory* (pp. 3–64). New York: Guilford Press.

Squire, L. R., Shimamura, A. P., & Graf, P. (1985). Independence of recognition memory and priming effects: A neuropsychological analysis. *Journal of Experimental Psychology: Learning, Memory, and Cognition, 11,* 37–44.

Stanovich, K. E., Cunningham, A. E., & West, R. F. (1981). A longitudinal study of the development of automatic recognition skills in first graders. *Journal of Reading Behavior, 13,* 57–74.

Stanovich, K. E., & West, R. F. (1983). On priming by a sentence context. *Journal of Experimental Psychology: General, 112,* 1–35.

Tulving, E. (1972). Episodic and semantic memory. In E. Tulving & W. Donaldson (Eds.), *Organization of memory,* New York: Academic Press.

Tulving, E. (1983). *Elements of episodic memory.* Oxford: Clarendon Press.

Tulving, E. (1985). Memory and consciousness. *Canadian Psychology. 26,* 1–12.

Tulving, E., Schacter, D. L., & Stark, H. A. (1982). Priming effects in word-fragment completion are independent of recognition memory. *Journal of Experimental Psychology: Learning, Memory, and Cognition, 8,* 336–342.

Warrington, E. K., & Weiskrantz, L. (1970). The amnesic syndrome: Consolidation or retrieval? *Nature, 228,* 628–630.

Warrington, E. K., & Weiskrantz, L. (1974). The effect of prior learning on subsequent retention in amnesic patients. *Neuropsychologia, 12,* 419–428.

CHARACTERIZING THE PROCESSING UNITS OF READING 11
Effects of Intra- and Interword Spaces in a Letter Detection Task

Alice F. Healy
University of Colorado

Gary L. Conboy
University of Colorado

Adam Drewnowski
University of Michigan

In a letter detection experiment in which asterisks or blank spaces were inserted between characters in continuous text, participants made significantly fewer errors when the test word subtended a larger visual angle. In a second experiment, the interword space before the test word *the* was found to be more critical for unit formation than the space after *the*. These results suggest that the size of the processing units used by readers depends on visual angle and that the reading units for frequent function words such as *the* extend beyond the word itself, include the interword space, and are influenced more by familiarity than by linguistic function. These findings are discussed in terms of the notions of cognitive module and input system proposed by Fodor (1983).

A fundamental question for any model of the reading process is what is the type and size of the units that are used for the processing of written text. In the present study we investigated this question by manipulating the spaces surrounding potential units. Following Corcoran (1966), we have developed a simple letter detection task in which participants are asked to read a passage of text and circle every instance of a target letter (e.g., the letter *t*). We have found that participants make more detection errors on very common words, such as *the,* than on rare words, such as *thy* (Healy, 1976, 1980). The pattern of errors is further determined by the structure of the search passage (Drewnowski & Healy, 1977) and by the participants' reading ability (Drewnowski, 1978, 1981). Results from these studies have been interpreted in terms of a "unitization" model (see Drewnowski & Healy, 1977; Healy, 1980; Healy & Drewnowski, 1983). The unitization model was proposed to account specifically for performance on the letter detection task. This model is comprised of five hypotheses about the reading process:

1. A hierarchy of text processing levels exists that is based on the sizes of the available processing units. These units include letters, syllables, words, and phrases.

2. All available units are processed in a parallel, simultaneous manner. This hypothesis differentiates this unitization model from many other models that also include a hierarchy of units, although this assumption is shared, for example, by McClelland and Rumelhart's (1981) interactive activation model.

3. Familiarity with a unit at a given level facilitates its processing. Familiarity is associated with word frequency in the language as well as the frequency and predictability of letter sequences within a word. Thus, for example, frequent words would be more easily processed at the word level than rare words, and the frequent and predictable suffix -ing would be processed more easily than less common word endings (see Drewnowski & Healy, 1980).

4. Completion of processing at a given level is tantamount to the identification of the unit at that level. Thus, completion of processing at the letter level results in the accurate identification of individual letters and hence accurate detection of target letters.

5. Once a unit has been identified at a given level within the hierarchy, subordinate levels are no longer processed and the reader proceeds to the next segment in the text. Thus, once a unit has been identified at the word level, the subordinate letter level is no longer processed. This terminated processing of the letter level will not interfere with text comprehension but should lead to letter detection errors. This hypothesis stands in contrast to the assumption made by the interactive activation model that there is excitatory facilitative feedback from words to their component letters.

According to this model, participants tend to miss letters in familiar words like *the* and *and* and in familiar word endings like -*ing* because they process such items automatically in units larger than single letters (such as syllables, words, or phrases) without completing processing at the letter level (see Johnson, 1981, for a review of alternative models that also postulate a hierarchy of reading units).

In the present experiments we therefore used the letter detection task to investigate how familiarity and other factors influence the size and the nature of the processing units used in reading text.

EXPERIMENT 1

A common finding in both tachistoscopic studies and studies involving running text is that, in addition to other factors, the ability to form reading units is dependent on the visual angle subtended by the stimuli (Patberg & Yonas, 1978; Purcell, Stanovich, & Spector, 1978). In tachistoscopic studies involving letter recognition, a word superiority effect has been found whereby letter identification is facilitated when target letters are presented within a word. However, this word superiority effect is no longer observed when the word stimuli subtend a larger visual angle. In contrast, paradigms involving running text (e.g., Healy, 1980; Healy & Drewnowski, 1983) commonly demonstrate a word inferiority effect, wherein letter detection is actually poorer for correctly spelled words than misspelled words, presumably due to the familiarity of correctly spelled words. In the letter detection paradigm with running text, the effects of visual angle have not yet been studied. In our first experiment, we therefore examined whether letter detection errors would be diminished when the words subtend a larger visual angle.

Earlier investigations with the letter detection paradigm used misspellings and alternating type case (e.g., Healy & Drewnowski, 1983) to manipulate the size of the available reading units. These manipulations influence the familiarity of the available reading units by changing features of the letters as well as supraletter characteristics. In Experiment 1, we manipulated only supraletter visual features and studied the effects of this manipulation on error rate in the letter detection task. We employed four passages differing in supraletter features. The first passage, which served as a control condition, consisted of standard text format. The second passage involved the addition of a single space between all characters, thus increasing the visual angle subtended by the text and decreasing the familiarity of multiletter sequences. This manipulation should facilitate letter identification both by disrupting the formation of reading units larger than single letters and by reducing lateral interference effects (Estes, Allmeyer, & Reder, 1976). The third passage involved replacing the single spaces in the second passage with double spaces. It is hypothesized that this manipulation will further facilitate letter detection by a greater interference with the formation of reading units larger than single letters. On the other hand, if the reading units are not sensitive to visual angle, then letter detection in the double-space passage should not significantly differ from that in the single-space passage. The fourth passage involved placing an asterisk between all letters and punctuation, which should greatly decrease the familiarity of multiletter sequences. The asterisk and single-space conditions have the same visual angle, but lateral interference should be greater and supraletter units should be harder to form in the asterisk condition than when spaces are present instead. Thus, by comparing performance in these two conditions, we should be able to determine whether letter detection errors are more sensitive to lateral interference effects or to the effects of disrupting supraletter reading units.

Method

Participants.   Ninety-six male and female University of Colorado undergraduates took part in this experiment for course credit.

Procedure.   Participants were instructed to read each of the four passages at their normal reading speed, in the order in which the passages were stapled together, and to circle all instances of the target letter *n*. They were instructed that if at any time they realized that a previous target had been missed, they should not retrace their steps to encircle it. Participants were also instructed not to slow their reading speed in order to be overcautious about detecting all targets. All 24 permutations of passage order were used, and the passages were stapled into booklets. The participants were assigned to one of the passage order conditions according to their time of arrival at the testing room. Four participants were used for each of the 24 orders of passage presentation.

Design and Materials.   Four versions of the 110-word prose passage used by Healy and Drewnowski (1983, Experiment 3) were employed. The passage was comprised of 24 test words, each containing a single instance of the target letter *n*, and 86 filler words, none of which contained *n*. The test words included 6 instances of the common function word *and*; 6 words containing the common suffix morpheme -*ing (having, sleeping, eating, sitting, playing, spreading)*; and 12 rare words (frequency 1–4 per 1,014,232 words of text; Kučera & Francis, 1967) with the letter *n* also in the penultimate position *(playground, flippant, abhorrent, virulent, valiant, vaccine, taint, surmount, abound, astound, amino, augment)*. This constraint on target letter position within a test word was imposed so that lateral interference properties associated with the target letters (Estes et al., 1976) would be controlled across all word types.

The four versions of the passage differed in the presence of extraneous characters and in intra- and interword spaces. The number of words per line was the same in all cases. Two of the 6 instances of the word *and*, 2 of the 6 words containing *-ing*, and 2 of the 12 rare words occurred at the beginning of a line, and only 1 test word (1 of the 12 rare words) occurred at the end of a line. Examples of text from each passage are presented in Table 11.1.

The "standard" passage had normal intra- and interword spaces and no extraneous characters. The "space" passage contained an additional space between all characters, including normal interword spaces. The "double space" passage was generated by placing two spaces between all characters and existing spaces. The "asterisk" passage involved placing an asterisk (*) in between all characters and normal interword spaces, as well as in the spaces at the beginning and end of a line.

Each passage version was typed with double spacing on the long axis of a standard sheet of paper, reduced by 4%, and reproduced by an offset press for distribution to the participants.

Results and Discussion

The results are summarized in Table 11.2 in terms of mean error percentages as a function of test word type (*and, -ing,* other) and passage version (standard, space, asterisk, double space). Only target misses are counted as errors here and in Experiment 2, because virtually no false alarms were

TABLE 11.1
Examples from Each Passage Version in Experiment 1

Passage Version	Example
Standard	That summer and
Space	T h a t s u m m e r a n d
Double Space	T h a t s u m m e r a n d
Asterisk	*T*h*a*t* *s*u*m*m*e*r* *a*n*d*

TABLE 11.2
Mean Error Percentages as a Function of Word Type and Passage
Version in Experiment 1

Word Type	Passage Version				
	Standard	Space	Asterisk	Double Space	Mean
and	61.3	41.9	22.1	27.5	38.2
-ing	41.3	31.1	24.8	23.3	30.1
other	13.1	7.8	8.6	5.3	8.7
Mean	38.6	26.9	18.5	18.7	

observed. An analysis of variance for repeated measures indicated that the standard error of the means in Table 11.2 was 1.7%.

As in previous studies (e.g., Healy & Drewnowski, 1983), the participants made most omission errors on *and,* fewer errors on *-ing,* and least on rare test words, $F(2,190) = 82.5, p < .001$. Most errors were made on the standard passage, fewer on the space passage, and least on the double space and asterisk passages, $F(3, 285) = 63.81, p < .001$. Further, the effect of passage version differed with word type; the interaction of passage version and test word type was significant, $F(6, 570) = 20.06, p < .001$.

Newman–Keuls tests ($p < .05$) showed that within the standard and space passages, participants made significantly more errors on *and* than on *-ing,* and least on other rare words. This finding supports the view that *and* and *-ing* are more likely than rare words to be read in units greater than single letters and that, more generally, the reader forms units of different sizes which depend on familiarity. The manipulations of double space and asterisk insertion resulted in no significant differences in letter detection for *and* and *-ing.* However, these word types still were significantly different from other rare words. For the word *and,* the greatest percentage of detection errors was in the standard condition, with fewer errors in the space condition, and the fewest errors in the double space and asterisk conditions, with no significant difference found between these latter two percentages. An identical pattern of results was observed for the common suffix morpheme *-ing.* For the other rare words, the only significant difference was that between errors made on the standard passage and the double-space passage.

The space passage differed from the double-space passage only in the increased visual angle and decreased lateral interference. This manipulation had a significant effect on letter detection performance for both *and* and *-ing* and a smaller effect for rare words. The substitution of an asterisk for a single space also resulted in a significant drop in detection errors for both *and* and *-ing.* Although these two conditions involve the same visual angle, the asterisk condition provides extraneous characters and thereby increased both lateral interference and disruption of supraletter units. These results suggest that the visual angle subtended by the stimuli is a crucial factor affecting reading units but that lateral interference is not crucial.

Overall, these findings suggest that reading units of varied size (or at various levels of the linguistic hierarchy) do exist and that, for frequent function words such as *and* or the common suffix morpheme *-ing,* these units are larger than single letters, whereas rare words are more likely to involve only letter-size units.

One issue raised in previous investigations using this paradigm was whether the units under study are perceptual units or merely response units (Drewnowski & Healy, 1977; Healy, 1976; Healy & Drewnowski, 1983). Response units are assumed to be formed by phonetic recoding of visual stimuli, whereas perceptual units are visual. Replacing single spaces by double spaces should, given phonetic response units, have no significant effect on the letter detection task. However, a significant effect of this manipulation was found for both *and* and *-ing*. This finding suggests that the units being characterized are in fact perceptual units.

EXPERIMENT 2

The results of Experiment 1 suggest that the units being tapped by the letter detection paradigm are influenced by purely visual factors. Experiment 2 was designed to confirm this finding and to characterize further these reading units. It has been suggested (Drewnowski & Healy, 1977) that for frequent words, such as *the* or *and*, the units that contain these words extend beyond the word itself and may include additional neighboring words. The interword space separating neighboring words would necessarily be embedded in such multiple-word units. To test this hypothesis a prose passage was created in which an extraneous character, an asterisk (*), was placed in one of three locations within the passage: either before, after, or in both the before and after interword spaces around a test word, with normal text, having no extraneous characters, serving as a control. If the units being characterized by the letter detection paradigm are syntactic units, defined in terms of word function, then the interword space after the test word *the* would be more likely to be embedded in the multiple-word unit than the interword space preceding *the*. This prediction follows from the fact that in a syntactic unit, such as a verb phrase or a prepositional phrase (e.g., "of the kind"), the word *the* is more closely associated with the following adjective or noun *(kind)* than the preceding verb or preposition *(of)*. In contrast, if the reading units in question depend more on word familiarity than on word function, then the interword space before the test word *the* should be more likely to be embedded in the multiple-word unit than the space following *the*. This prediction follows from observing a listing (Umeda & Kahn, 1982) of the most frequent two- and three-word sequences in the English language, which shows that 8 of the 10 most frequent two-word sequences contain the word *the* and in each instance *the* is the second word.

If the units being manifest by the detection task are primarily affected by word function, then the after condition should differ significantly from the control condition for the test word *the*, whereas a smaller effect should be found for the before condition. In contrast, if the reading units are primarily affected by word familiarity, then a significant difference should exist between the before and control conditions, whereas a smaller effect should occur for the after condition. For other test words, we predict no significant differences between the before and after conditions, because it is less likely that the other test words are contained in multiple-word units, and because we have no reason to expect, on the basis of either syntax or frequency, that the other test words would be more closely associated with the words preceding or following them.

Method

Participants. The same 96 participants were used in this experiment as in Experiment 1. They took part in Experiment 2 immediately before Experiment 1 began.

Procedure. The procedure was the same as in Experiment 1 except for two changes: Participants were instructed to circle the letter *h* instead of the letter *n*, and they each only viewed one passage version instead of four.

Design and Materials. Four versions of a 960-word prose passage were employed. Within the passage there were 28 instances of the word *the*, 84 instances of other test words containing the target letter *h* (with no restrictions concerning the length of the test word or the location of the target within the test word), and 848 filler words with no instances of the target letter. One of the 28 instances of the word *the* and 3 of the 84 other test words occurred at the beginning of a line, and 1 instance of *the* and 3 other test words occurred at the end of a line. Each test word was separated from the next test word by at least two filler words.

The four versions differed in the placement of an extraneous character, an asterisk (*). There were four conditions involving the interword spaces before and after the test words. The "none" condition had no asterisks either before or after the test word. The "before" condition involved placing an asterisk in the interword space before the test word. In the "after" condition an asterisk was placed in the interword space after the test word. The "both" condition involved placing an asterisk both before and after the test word. The spaces at the beginning and end of lines were also classified as interword spaces. See Table 11.3 for examples from each condition.

The four passage versions were constructed in such a way that every four successive instances of *the* and every four successive other test words included one word in each of the four conditions: none, before, after, and both. Across the four passage versions each test word occurred in each of the four different conditions. Additionally, throughout the

TABLE 11.3
Examples from Each Condition in Experiment 2

Condition	Example
None	of the kind
After	of the*kind
Before	of*the kind
Both	of*the*kind

entire passage, two asterisks were placed at random within each group of four successive interword spaces not immediately surrounding a test word (including spaces at the beginning or end of a line). These additional asterisks were in the same locations in all passage versions.

Each passage version was typed double spaced on four separate sheets of paper and reproduced by means of an offset press. Each version was shown to 24 participants.

Results and Discussion

The results are summarized in Table 11.4 in terms of mean error percentages as a function of test word type (*the,* other words) and extraneous character location (none, after, before, both). An analysis of variance for repeated measures indicated that the standard error of the entries in Table 11.4 was 1.3%.

Many more errors were made on *the* as compared to other test words, $F(1,95) = 124.9$, $p < .001$. Most detection errors were made when no asterisk was present; the fewest errors were made when an asterisk occupied both interword spaces next to a test word, and an intermediate number occurred when there was a single asterisk either before or after the test word, $F(3,285) = 15.2$, $p < .001$. Additionally, the effect of asterisk location was somewhat different for the two test word types, as the interaction of test word type and asterisk location was significant, $F(3,285) = 6.3, p < .001$.

TABLE 11.4
Mean Error Percentages as a Function of Word Type and Asterisk
Location in Experiment 2

Word Type	Asterisk Location				
	None	After	Before	Both	Mean
the	67.7	65.4	60.9	55.5	62.4
other	47.2	41.8	42.3	42.8	43.5
Mean	57.4	53.6	51.6	49.1	

Newman–Keuls tests ($p < .05$) confirmed that for the word *the*, the none and after conditions yielded the greatest percentages of detection errors. No significant difference was observed between these two percentages. Fewer errors were observed for the word *the* in the before condition than in the none and after conditions, and the smallest percentage of errors on *the* occurred in the both condition relative to the other three conditions. For the other test words, the greatest percentage of errors occurred in the none condition, with significantly fewer errors in the other three conditions (before, after, and both). No significant differences were observed between these latter three conditions.

On the basis of these data it is suggested that the word *the* is more likely to be included in a reading unit that also contains its preceding word than its following word. Because the preceding word and *the* are more likely to form a familiar two-word sequence (e.g., "of the"; see Umeda & Kahn, 1982) whereas *the* and the following word are more likely to form a syntactic unit (e.g., "the kind"), familiarity seems more important than linguistic function in the formation of reading units. Note that an alternative explanation is possible for the difference for the word *the* between the before and after conditions. This explanation refers to word predictability rather than familiarity. The word *the* is probably highly predictable from the preceding word, whereas it would probably be difficult to predict the following word given the word *the*. However, previous work has indicated that predictability does not play an important role in the letter detection task. For example, Healy (1976) showed that participants missed many target letters in the word *the* even in a passage of scrambled words where *the* was not predictable on the basis of the surrounding word context (see also Healy & Drewnowski, 1983, for a discussion of the effects of predictability or syntactic and semantic redundancy in the letter detection task).

The effects of asterisks on the detection of targets in other test words were generally smaller than for the word *the*. Further, for the other test words, there was no indication that the space before the word was more likely to be included in the multiple-word reading unit than was the space after the word. The results for the other test words suggest that these words are less likely than the word *the* to be part of multiple-word units, and that the differences among the before, after, and both conditions for *the* are not artifacts of the letter detection task.

GENERAL DISCUSSION

In Experiment 1 we manipulated the supraletter visual features of the text by adding spaces or extraneous characters. Participants made fewer detection errors for the standard relative to the space and the space relative to the double-space passages. We interpret these results as indicating that the units formed by readers are sensitive to the visual angle subtended by the text. Letter detection errors on *and* and *-ing* also decreased in the asterisk passage compared to the space passage, despite an increase in lateral interference. These results indicate that other factors, not just visual angle, influence the size of the reading units. In Experiment 2 we investigated the hypothesis (Drewnowski & Healy, 1977; Healy & Drewnowski, 1983) that the units for frequent function words, such as *the*, contain more than one word and are thus influenced by manipulations of the interword space separating any two words in the same multiple-word unit. In Experiment 2 it was found that, for the word *the*, participants made the greatest percentages of errors on the normal text and when an extraneous character was presented in the interword space after the test word, with significantly fewer errors when an extraneous character was present in the interword space before a test word. These results are interpreted not only as providing evidence for the existence of reading units that include more than one word, but also as supporting the hypothesis that the formation of these units depends more on familiarity than on linguistic function.

In our previous studies (see, e.g., Drewnowski & Healy, 1977), as in the present experiments, we found evidence that purely visual factors influence the pattern of letter detection errors. In the past we interpreted such evidence as indicating that the reading units elucidated by the letter detection task are perceptual, or visual units, rather than response units formed by phonetic recoding of visual stimuli. However, along with such evidence concerning visual factors, we also found that phonetic factors, such as syllable stress, affect letter detection errors (see Drewnowski & Healy, 1982), and that visual factors alone cannot account for the full pattern of errors in letter detection (see Healy & Drewnowski, 1983). These findings suggested that the letter detection task does reflect response units as well as, or instead of, visual units. However, when viewing the reading units in question as representations of the input system, in accord with Fodor's (1983) framework, we can remove the apparent contradictions and see why both visual and phonetic factors would be important. According to Fodor, the input system interprets sensory information (after it has been processed by the appropriate transducers) and forms a representation of it that is appropriate for central (or executive control) processes. Hence, the input representations can be seen as both perceptual units and response units.

More generally, Fodor (1983) provided a taxonomy of cognitive processes in which he distinguished between input systems, which are responsible for language and perception, and central systems, which are responsible for thought and the fixation of belief. Fodor also introduced the notion of "cognitive modules" and proposed that input systems are modules, whereas central systems are nonmodular. Fodor (1983) argued that "it is only the modular cognitive systems that we have any serious hope of understanding" (p. 38) and concluded his monograph by stating that "while some interesting things have been learned about the psychology of input analysis—primarily about language and vision—the psychology of thought has proved quite intractable" (p. 126). With this framework in mind, we can view our studies with the letter detection task as investigating the nature of the input system for visually presented text and exploring the modular properties of that system.

The Input System for Visually Presented Text

What is an input system and what are the defining characteristics of a cognitive module? According to Fodor (1983), the central task of input systems is to provide mental representations of stimulation or information about the environment in a format that is accessible to thought, i.e., appropriate for central (or executive control) processing. Input systems therefore include both perceptual and linguistic mechanisms. Although Fodor's discussion of input systems is focused on speech perception and visual object recognition, his arguments seem to extend naturally to the pattern recognition processes that encode visually presented text.

Fodor describes nine properties of input systems that constitute, or define, their modularity. We concentrate on the three of these properties that seem most germane to the present concerns:

1. "The operation of input systems is mandatory" (Fodor, 1983, p. 52). For the perception of spoken utterances, this property follows from the fact that the language-processing mechanisms are automatically triggered by speech stimuli. For example, participants who are asked to focus their attention on acoustic or phonetic aspects of speech seem unable to avoid word identification (Marslen-Wilson & Tyler, 1981).

2. "There is only limited central access to the mental representations that input systems compute" (Fodor, 1983, p. 55). According to this property, participants do not have conscious access to all the intermediate representations that they have formed prior to computing that representation which will constitute the final product of the input analyses. In fact, Fodor (1983) hypothesizes that "only such representations as constitute the *final* consequences of input processing are fully and freely available to the cognitive processes that eventuate in the voluntary determination of overt behavior" (p. 56). Fodor's discussion of this property is reminiscent of the discussion of phoneme monitoring studies

by investigators including Foss and Swinney (1973), Healy and Cutting (1976), and more recently Marcel (1983). Lower level linguistic units such as phonemes may not be detected in a monitoring task either because they were never identified or computed as such, or because they were identified before higher order units like syllables but were not accessible for the purposes of conscious report or detection on account of the limited central access to intermediate representations.

   3. "Input systems are informationally encapsulated" (Fodor, 1983, p. 64). This property of input systems is probably the most important with regards to modularity but also the most controversial. In this view, processing by input systems is not affected by feedback from higher level information such as semantic context. In other words, input systems operate largely with bottom-up, not top-down mechanisms. This notion runs counter to the "New Look" of perceptual theorizing initiated by Bruner (1957) and his colleagues and is inconsistent with more recent interactive theories such as that proposed by Rumelhart (1977). In order to account for the growing evidence that sentence context affects speech recognition, Fodor (1983) argues that the contextual effects observed in those studies are due to two factors: (a) "postperceptual" operations, or processes conducted *after* the input analyses have concluded and the input system has produced its representation for the central systems, or (b) associative relations among words within the mental lexicon, which is part of the language recognition input system.

The Letter Detection Task

Using the framework developed by Fodor (1983), we can view the reading units elucidated by the letter detection task as being the representations constructed by the input system for visually presented text, and these representations are those employed by the central system or the executive control processes of reading. According to this view, whenever representations formed by the input system are higher order units, participants are unable to detect letters in target words even if they have completed processing at the letter level, because of the limited conscious access individuals have to intermediate representations formed by the input system. The mandatory operation of this input system is illustrated in our earlier work with the letter detection task by the finding that the pattern of letter detection errors is not changed greatly when participants are given explicit instructions to comprehend the material they are reading (see, e.g., Proctor & Healy, 1985, and Schindler, 1978). It seems that word recognition is automatically achieved in the letter detection task, just as Stroop (1935) demonstrated that participants have difficulty disengaging their word identification responses when they are instructed to name the colors of ink in which different words are printed. The informational encapsulation of this input system is suggested by our earlier finding (e.g., Healy, 1976), that participants yield similar patterns of letter detection errors when they read normal prose or when they read passages of text that have been scrambled so that the words are no longer in predictable sequences. Because each of Fodor's (1983) three key properties of modular input systems is elucidated by the letter detection task, this task should provide a useful device for probing the representations formed by the input system for visually presented text. By viewing the outcomes of our letter detection experiments in terms of the broad framework developed by Fodor (1983), rather than merely in terms of the more narrowly defined unitization model we proposed earlier (see, e.g., Healy & Drewnowski, 1983), the more general implications of our findings should become evident. In particular, our findings concerning the input system for visually presented text should have implications for the operation of other modular input systems, such as those involved in speech perception and visual object recognition.

Although the letter detection task undoubtedly involves some processes not employed in normal reading for meaning, there are at least two lines of evidence that support the ecological validity of this procedure. First, as aforementioned, the pattern of errors in the letter detection task has been shown not to change substantially when participants are given explicit instructions to understand the text they are reading and are given a comprehension test on that material (e.g., Proctor & Healy, 1985; Schindler, 1978). In fact, comprehension instructions tend if anything to magnify the error rate on common words like *the* (see Proctor & Healy, 1985; Smith & Groat, 1979). Second, studies involving reading for meaning with no detection have shown effects of some of the same variables found to influence letter detection performance. For example, in an experiment in which participants read paragraphs for meaning and were given comprehension questions following each paragraph, both their comprehension scores and their reading speed were depressed when the paragraphs were presented with alternating upper- and lowercase letters (Fisher, 1975), and alternating typecase is a manipulation that has also been shown to influence letter detection performance (e.g., Healy & Drewnowski, 1983), as reviewed earlier.

The letter detection results on which we base our conclusions about the visual input system are in marked contrast to those from letter recognition studies involving tachistoscopic procedures. As we reviewed earlier, word superiority effects are found with the tachistoscopic procedures, but word inferiority effects are found with the letter detection task. We propose that the differences between these two procedures can be understood in terms of differences in postperceptual processes, or executive control processes occurring after the input system has formed its representation. We assume, following Fodor (1983), that when higher order representations are formed by the input system, participants have limited conscious access to single letters as intermediate representations of the input system, even if processing at the letter level has been completed. However, if we encourage postperceptual processes, such as inferences from spelling knowledge, (e.g., "I know I saw the word *the,* and *the* is spelled with a *t,* so I must have seen a *t*"), then participants may be able to report single letters that were hidden as intermediate representations of the input system. Participants may not normally engage in such postperceptual executive control processes when reading continuous text, because inferences about letters may interfere with other executive control processing employed by the individual to construct the meaning of the text. However, if participants view only one word at a time and are given as much time as they need for responding, as in the typical tachistoscopic procedures, then such postperceptual inferences about letters may be encouraged (see Estes, 1975, for a discussion of inferential and perceptual processes in this task). This hypothesis receives support from Estes' (1977) finding that the lower error rates on letters that occur in word contexts are associated with long rather than short response latencies in the tachistoscopic procedures.

According to this reasoning, one of the critical differences between the letter detection and tachistoscopic letter recognition tasks is the number of words shown to the participant at any given instant in time. In the tachistoscopic task words are shown singly, and although each word is shown for a short time, participants are not limited in their response time, so that postperceptual inferencing may be encouraged. In contrast, in the letter detection task participants are shown a continuous passage of text so that, in their attempts to construct the meaning of the text, they may be discouraged from postperceptual inferencing about letters. In an earlier study (Healy, Oliver, & McNamara, 1982), we employed a variant of the rapid serial visual presentation (RSVP) procedure (see, e.g., Forster, 1970; Juola, Ward, & McNamara, 1982) to compare the effects of showing one versus several words at a time. Participants were shown a passage of text on a display screen attached to a computer. Each display was shown for a fixed amount of time at the same location, and the participants were instructed to press a response button as soon as they detected a given target letter. In one experiment conducted with this procedure (Healy et al., 1982, Experiment 1), we measured both the proportion of correct responses and the latencies to respond correctly, and we varied the number of words that were shown on the display screen at any given instant in time. Either one or four words were shown simultaneously. The results were consistent with the hypothesis that postperceptual processes are encouraged to a greater extent when only one word is in view at a time than when multiple words are simultaneously available for processing: Both in terms of speed and accuracy, we found a substantial word inferiority effect when four words were shown on the screen, especially for the familiar test word *the*, but this effect was diminished and in some cases reversed when only one word was shown.

Because postperceptual processes are minimized in the letter detection task relative to other experimental procedures, this task seems to be ideally suited for investigating the representations that are formed by the input system for visually presented text and that are made available for subsequent processing by the central systems. In other words, to use the terminology employed in the current volume, the letter detection task seems ideally suited for characterizing the processing units of reading that will be available for subsequent use by the executive control processes.

ACKNOWLEDGMENTS

This research was supported in part by National Science Foundation Grant BNS80-25020 to the Institute of Cognitive Science at the University of Colorado.

We are indebted to R. Gregory and C. Wise for assistance with data tabulation and verification, and to W. Oliver for helpful discussions about this research and for computer formatting and data verification assistance.

REFERENCES

Bruner, J. S. (1957). On perceptual readiness. *Psychological Review, 64,* 123–152.

Corcoran, D.W.J. (1966). An acoustic factor in letter cancellation. *Nature, 210,* 658.

Drewnowski, A. (1978). Detection errors on the word *the*: Evidence for the acquisition of reading levels. *Memory & Cognition, 6,* 403–409.

Drewnowski, A. (1981). Missing *-ing* in reading: Developmental changes in reading units. *Journal of Experimental Child Psychology, 31,* 154–158.

Drewnowski, A., & Healy, A. F. (1977). Detection errors on *the* and *and*: Evidence for reading units larger than the word. *Memory & Cognition, 5,* 636–647.

Drewnowski, A., & Healy, A. F. (1980). Missing *-ing* in reading: Letter detection errors on word endings. *Journal of Verbal Learning and Verbal Behavior, 19,* 247–262.

Drewnowski, A., & Healy, A. F. (1982). Phonetic factors in letter detection: A reevaluation. *Memory & Cognition, 10,* 145–154.

Estes, W. K. (1975). The locus of inferential and perceptual processes in letter identification. *Journal of Experimental Psychology: General, 104,* 122–145.

Estes, W. K. (1977). On the interaction of perception and memory in reading. In D. LaBerge & S. J. Samuels (Eds.), *Basic processes in reading: Perception and comprehension (pp. 1–25).* Hillsdale, NJ: Lawrence Erlbaum Associates.

Estes, W. K., Allmeyer, D. H., & Reder, S. M. (1976). Serial position functions for letter identification at brief and extended exposure durations. *Perception & Psychophysics, 19,* 1–15.

Fisher, D. F. (1975). Reading and visual search. *Memory & Cognition, 3,* 188–196.

Fodor, J. A. (1983). *The modularity of mind.* Cambridge, MA: MIT Press.

Forster, K. I. (1970). Visual perception of rapidly presented word sequences of varying complexity. *Perception & Psychophysics, 8,* 215–221.

Foss, D. J., & Swinney, D. A. (1973). On the psychological reality of the phoneme: Perception, identification, and consciousness. *Journal of Verbal Learning and Verbal Behavior, 12,* 246–257.

Healy, A. F. (1976). Detection errors on the word *the*: Evidence for reading units larger than letters. *Journal of Experimental Psychology: Human Perception and Performance, 2,* 235–242.

Healy, A. F. (1980). Proofreading errors on the word *the*: New evidence on reading units. *Journal of Experimental Psychology: Human Perception and Performance, 6,* 403–409.

Healy, A. F., & Cutting, J. E. (1976). Units of speech perception: Phoneme and syllable. *Journal of Verbal Learning and Verbal Behavior, 15,* 73–83.

Healy, A. F., & Drewnowski, A. (1983). Investigating the boundaries of reading units: Letter detection in misspelled words. *Journal of Experimental Psychology: Human Perception and Performance, 9,* 413–426.

Healy, A. F., Oliver, W., & McNamara, T. P. (1982). *Detecting letters in continuous text: Effects of display size.* Paper presented at the 23rd Annual Meeting of the Psychonomic Society, Minneapolis, Minnesota.

Johnson, N. F. (1981). Integration processes in word recognition. In O.J.L. Tzeng & H. Singer (Eds.), *Perception of print: Reading research in experimental psychology (pp. 29–63).* Hillsdale, NJ: Lawrence Erlbaum Associates.

Juola, J. F., Ward, N. J., & McNamara, T. P. (1982). Visual search and reading of rapid serial presentations of letter strings, words, and text. *Journal of Experimental Psychology: General, 111,* 208–227.

Kučera, H., & Francis, W. N. (1967). *Computational analysis of present-day American English.* Providence, RI: Brown University.

Marcel, A. J. (1983). Conscious and unconscious perception: An approach to the relations between phenomenal experience and perceptual processes. *Cognitive Psychology, 15,* 238–300.

Marslen-Wilson, W., & Tyler, L. (1981). Central processes in speech understanding. *Philosophical Transactions of the Royal Society, B 295,* 317–322.

McClelland, J. L., & Rumelhart, D. E. (1981). An interactive activation model of context effects in letter perception: Part 1. An account of basic findings. *Psychological Review, 88,* 375–407.

Patberg, J. P., & Yonas, A. (1978). The effects of the reader's skill and the difficulty of the text on the perceptual span in reading. *Journal of Experimental Psychology: Human Perception and Performance, 4,* 545–552.

Proctor, J. D., & Healy, A. F. (1985). A secondary-task analysis of a word familiarity effect. *Journal of Experimental Psychology: Human Perception and Performance, 11,* 286–303.

Purcell, D. G., Stanovich, K. E., & Spector, A. (1978). Visual angle and the word superiority effect. *Memory & Cognition, 6,* 3–8.

Rumelhart, D. E. (1977). Toward an interactive activation model of reading. In S. Dornic (Ed.), *Attention and performance* (V). Hillsdale, NJ: Lawrence Erlbaum Associates.

Schindler, R. M. (1978). The effect of prose context on visual search for letters. *Memory & Cognition, 6,* 124–136.

Smith, P. T., & Groat, A. (1979). Spelling patterns, letter cancellation, and the processing of text. In P. A. Kolers, M. E. Wrolstad, & H. Bouma (Eds.), *Processing of visible language* (Vol. 1, pp. 309–324). New York: Plenum Press.

Stroop, J. R. (1935). Studies of interference in serial verbal reactions. *Journal of Experimental Psychology, 18,* 643–662.

Umeda, N., & Kahn, D. (1982). Frequency of occurrence of two- and three-word sequences in English. *Journal of the Acoustical Society of America, 72,* 2031–2033.

AUTHOR INDEX . . . .

SUBJECT INDEX . . . .